Yehudi Menuhin
Unfinished Journey

MACDONALD AND JANE'S · LONDON

First published in Great Britain in 1977 by
Macdonald and Jane's Publishers Limited,
Paulton House,
8 Shepherdess Walk,
London, N.1.

Printed in Great Britain by
REDWOOD BURN LIMITED
Trowbridge & Esher

Yehudi Menuhin

Unfinished Journey

To Diana

my heavenly host on this earthly way,
and to those unique and irreplaceable
predecessors and successors,
parents and children,
without whose dedicated upbringing
there would be no pages to fill,
this book is offered.

Contents

Illustrations

With Toscanini (*Photoworld*)

With Pierre Monteux, 1934 (*Alban, Paris*)

With Fritz Kreisler

With Dr. Wilhelm Brockhaus and
        Bruno Walter, 1932 (*Atelier E. Hoenisch, Leipzig*)

With Sir Edward Elgar and
        Sir Thomas Beecham, 1932 (*Central News, London*)

Enesco conducting Yehudi (*Eric Schaal*)

With Enesco (*Agence France-Presse*)

With Zoltán and Emma Kodály (*Harmath Istvan*)

Wilhelm Furtwängler conducting

Dressed as Paganini for a screen test, 1945

With Olivia de Havilland (*U.S. Army Air Force*)

With officers aboard the H.M.S. *Duke of York*, 1944

With Jacob Epstein, 1945 (*Central Press Photos*)

With Benjamin Britten, 1945 (*Planet News, London*)

Rehearsing with Oistrakh (*Agfa-Portriga*)

With Dmitri Shostakovich, 1945

With Mstislav Rostropovitch (*Agence France-Presse*)

With Nadia Boulanger, Bath Festival, 1964

With Pablo Casals (*Hélène Jeanbrau*)

(*following page 206*)

David Wynne's sculpture

With Margot Fonteyn, 1962

With Rudolf Nureyev, 1964 (*David Farrell*)

With Eugene Ormandy and the Philadelphia Orchestra
        (*Adrian Siegel*)

Practicing (*Clive Barda*)

Conducting (*Ramon Scavelli*)

With Ravi Shankar (*David Farrell*)

Acknowledgments

I wish to acknowledge my gratitude to the many characters, good and less good, who animate this account—all contributors to positive experience. In a book which attempts to relate the events of sixty years, it is, alas, impossible to do justice to all who have brought warmth, color and stimulus to the lives of my family and myself. I hope those not mentioned will forgive me, in the knowledge that they are cherished in my heart even if they do not yet appear in cold print. One day, I trust, there will be another book to repair the omissions of this one. I also want to thank Dr. Frederick Brown, who first prompted these archaeological self-investigations, and Maureen McConville, whose patience and perception lent coherence to my oral and written confessions.

Y.M.

Not a
Preface
But a Word of Thanks

Genius remains a mystery. There can be supreme technical skill, originality, intelligence, and yet an absence of genius. Initially, the word signified an attendant spirit, an animate power that gives to a very few human beings the secret of radiance. The ordinary man casts a shadow. In a way we do not quite understand, the man of genius casts light.

Instinctively, we flinch from this light. We assure ourselves that genius must pay a terrible price. Often history bears us out: the creator, the supreme artist, the master of politics carries the scars of his greatness. Either in some twist of personality or through private and public desolation and the dramas of rejection that seem to characterize famous lives. Racking illness pursued Paganini and tradition has it that his sole familiar was a dwarf.

To find genius and happiness united is nearly a scandal. Ordinarily those to whom the gods give their largesse are envied, even hated, by their peers and contemporaries. Yehudi Menuhin is probably the most widely loved personality in the history of the performing arts. It was so after his triumphant debut in 1927; it is so today.

This is far more than a question of pre-eminent artistry. There are other great violinists. Menuhin's radiance is tangible to anyone near him, but also to those who crowd the furthest row of a concert hall. The fineness of his features, the economy and elegance of gesture which xvi		*Not a Preface*

surround his performance are important, of course. But the force lies much deeper. Menuhin has made of the music he produces a total expression and embodiment of being. To hear him play the Bartók Solo Sonata (which he commissioned) or the Elgar Concerto, even at a distance or on a worn record, is to be asked, in a peculiarly intimate, directly focused way, into his complete presence. It is a presence that seems to encounter the world and oneself with a sovereign courtesy of heart.

Luck was there from the beginning: in a brilliantly gifted family, in a childhood guarded but also stretched to fulfillment, in a series of true teachers—Persinger, Enesco, Busch—in an accord between mind and sinew which enabled the very young virtuoso to pass almost unknowing from mechanical display to the inward meaning of a score. International acclaim followed as of itself, in an era, now lost, of transatlantic liners, firelit hotel suites, and a freemasonry of musical culture that admitted no frontiers. And behind Menuhin's individual gifts lay a three-fold heritage, stronger than any other: that of Jewish life in Russia, that of the open America in which the boy grew up, and that of a lineage of master musicians going back to the fusion of classical music with romantic intensity in the age of Liszt and Ysaÿe.

With a modesty so real that it is almost a kind of arrogance, Menuhin tells us that he finds language cumbersome. Yet he writes with a poignancy and cadence which recall his playing. Everyone who reads this memoir will have his favorite moments: Einstein surging across the Berlin concert stage and proclaiming to the boy wonder that there is indeed a God in heaven; Sir Edward Elgar off to the races; Enesco making Menuhin, then a world celebrity, repeat the last movement of the Brahms Concerto after the dispersal of the orchestra because it had not been flawless; the description of the piano as "inanimate and neutral"; or Menuhin hitting two bull's-eyes though he had never before handled a gun (a story of whose menacing connotations of exceeding luck the teller must be aware). And there are the proofs of humaneness that go much beyond art: the visit to Belsen shortly after that acre of hell was liberated, the vital involvment with Israel, the voyages to the Soviet Union and the part Menuhin has played in making it possible for Russian artists to be heard in the West.

But above all, this book is a love story. It records, unembarrassedly, Menuhin's love for music and for certain human beings. It is rare that a performing artist lets us enter the workshop of his craft. In a series of remarkable passages, Menuhin tells of the exact ways in which he has made the opening of the Beethoven Concerto or a Mozart sonata a part of his own self. "Music is given us with our existence." No doubt; but how many can return this gift? As to his family, it is nearly inseparable from Menuhin's sense of reality. Throughout this book, Menuhin's parents, his richly talented sisters, Hephzibah and Yaltah, and his own children occupy a central place, or almost. For if there is a center, a pivot of homecoming in so wide-ranging a career, it belongs to Menuhin's wife, Diana, herself an artist and summoner of art in others. Many illustrious figures cross the stage: Willa Cather, Toscanini, de Gaulle, Chaim Weizmann, Solzhenitsyn. Bartók towers. But it is Diana and the family who glow.

So much good fortune. Yes, but so much in return. Given to the many personal benefactions which Menuhin leaves out of the story, to the thorny cause of international understanding, to the dream of Israel-Arab reconciliation, to the conservation of an island on which puffins can nest in peace, and, of late, to the young musicians from a dozen lands who make up the Yehudi Menuhin School at Stoke d'Abernon in Surrey.

There are two proud mottos in this book: "I have never resigned myself," and "My life has been spent in creating utopias." They could be prouder still. From Yehudi Menuhin's refusals to resign so many have drawn courage; in his utopias so many have found welcome.

GEORGE STEINER

Unfinished Journey

1

Golden
Days

Looking back on the sixty years I have lived, I am struck most of all by the straightforwardness of the pattern. Everything that I am, or think, or do, almost everything that has happened to me, seems traceable to its origins with the simple clarity of geometrical proof. It is a curious, even a faintly disconcerting sensation to find oneself fulfilling what seems to have been a destiny. One wants to protest that initiative is not an illusion, that one could have influenced events quite otherwise; and such claims are surely reasonable. Take by way of analogy the composition of music. Laboriously the composer feels his way though the notes of his symphony to the last triumphant bar, only to discover that their choice and sequence were inevitable all along. The inevitability does not rob him of achievement, however, for only hindsight can preclude all other notes and only he could father these. So it is with my life. Once traveled, the route is clear, but prescience did not divine it and I am at least in part accountable for the turns it took.

I cannot of course claim sole responsibility for its direction. For one thing, a *leitmotiv* of my history has been the happy accident which demands from me no more energetic act of will than compliance (although compliance has generally exacted a handsome expenditure of energy). For another, I know myself to be the offspring of the past. Much of my life's design was laid before I was born, and I sometimes feel that I have brought to consummation not just my own yearnings but also those of my parents, and yet perhaps at their expense.

Fate could not have brought together for the benefit of their children two more different human beings than my father and mother. What they had in common can quickly be told. Both were born in Russia; both were Jews; both emigrated to Palestine in youth; both traveled from there to the United States. In appearance both were slight, blond and comely. Furthermore, both were, as they are today, methodical, romantic, ardent, high-principled, self-sacrificing and energetic.

But within every item in this litany my parents have found room to stake out an antithesis. My father's method made of him a mathematician, a keeper of orderly files, a prompt answerer of letters, a settler of accounts. My mother's method was long-term; it set itself a goal and progressed inexorably toward it, demolishing obstacles as they occurred and during the drab stretches of detail in between. She was and still is romantic in abandonment to action, he in dreams. His emotion is spontaneous and exuberant, a constant threat to the neatness of his files and categories. Hers is stringently controlled, shown only when she chooses, but intense enough to drive her into the fiery furnace should a principle or a friend require such immolation. Where my father is cautious, my mother is reckless. Where he needs outside impetus, whether approval or condemnation, a hero or a villain, to fuel his enthusiasm, she draws on resources within herself—or within her background, which to my mother is much the same thing. His principles involve him with humanity at large and with concern for its future. Hers ignore the nameless crowd to lavish love upon the individual and to honor the past. She identifies readily with nomads, captives, or with anyone whose lonely destiny leads him to martyrdom or greatness outside the comfortable norms of society. If, in youth, my father idolized, say, Eugene Debs, I doubt my mother would have been so prodigal of her admiration for anyone but a Tamerlane or Savonarola, a Judith or a Catherine of Russia. On the surface, *he* could not have been more gregarious and *she* less; they met at the extremes to which their natures transported them.

The circumstances of their early lives help to explain the differences between them, or at least to point them up.

The Mnuchins—for so my father transliterated the Russian МНУХИН on first arriving in New York—had settled in Gomel, a smallish city one thousand miles equidistant from the Baltic and Black seas, at the very center of the Pale. My mother's family, the Shers, on the other hand, lived on Russia's southern periphery, not far from the coastal town of Yalta on the Crimean peninsula. For Moshe Mnuchin to meet Marutha Sher in Russia, fate (or providence) would have had to intervene with bizarre single-mindedness, ferrying the young man down the Dnieper and urging him across the Prichepnomorsk Plain. It proved simpler to transport each separately to Palestine, where they met; then furnish each with separate reasons for going to New York, where they eventually met again and married. If such it was, the contrivance of providence was not solely benign, for behind these several journeys lay the pogroms. They gave me life in the same stroke that deprived so many fellow Jews of theirs.

My father is descended from Chasidic rabbis, holders of a hereditary office who kept a court of sorts at Lubavitch, near Gomel, a typical small Russian-Jewish community where the rabbi's spiritual standing gave him temporal authority as well, making him doubly the center of an ingrown society, rejected by the larger society it belonged to but finding sustenance in survival so far and in dreams of Jerusalem for the future. The Chasids, whose movement had its origin in the late eighteenth century, were once rebels among the People of the Book, glorifying ecstatic communion more than legal community, prizing mystics above scholars, and rejecting purely cerebral religion in favor of dancing and making music to the greater glory of God. Such a lively approach to piety would have suited my father's temperament admirably, had not Chasidic spontaneity become institutionalized by his day and he in consequence compelled to rebel anew. In 1904, one year before the anti-Semitic atrocities of 1905, when a pogrom broke out at Gomel, Moshe Mnuchin's widowed and remarried mother took the eleven-year-old boy to Odessa and put him aboard a steamer, the *Kornilov,* bound for Palestine and his paternal grandparents. He grew up in Zion, never went back to Russia, content to let its language and impressions fade. One memory remained poignant: he was a little boy when his father died, and he remembers trundling on his tricycle around the corpse laid out upon the ground. To this day he has not forgiven himself for the disrespect of his childish incomprehension.

One does not belong to orthodox tradition with impunity. In Jerusalem, under the aegis of his devout grandfather, he was constrained to read the Bible, to study, recite and rock in rhythm with his prayers all night, praying himself deaf and blind to the world about him. Dressed in the heavy black cloak designed for northern climes and worn to distress of mind and body in the temperatures of the Middle East, with his side hair in ringlets and his feet in clumsy shoes, he must have looked the archetypal poor Jewish student. But longings for freedom were constantly pulling him out of the frame his family willed him to inhabit, scandalizing his mentor and landing him in trouble. He flew a kite with Arab playmates and was reprimanded; he enrolled himself for a violin lesson or two and brought sorrow to his grandfather's heart: how could a Jew distract his mind with such frivolities while the Temple was not yet rebuilt? Of the several anecdotes my father tells, one in particular bears retelling because it illustrates his readiness to see the world in black and white, allowing shades of gray only to certain anonymous victims of society. It treats of those two privileged objects of Biblical concern, eyes and teeth. A front tooth in my father's mouth had grown up at a queer angle, jutting forward enough to make itself constantly felt and, more painful, constantly visible. What made this minor irritation major was his grandmother's warning that, the snaggletooth being an eyetooth, his eyes would "leak out" if he had it extracted. Preferring unsightliness to sightlessness, he lived for several years on the horns of this dilemma until, one day in Jaffa, a dentist's nameplate prompted a decision no doubt already made subconsciously. Within the hour he emerged the poorer by his offending tooth and happily able to see his way home. The dentist, as it chanced, was an Arab, who thereupon became a symbol of Arab virtue, and all unwittingly supplied a grain of substance to my father's growing disillusionment with Zionism. However, it was exasperation with narrow religious orthodoxy that led to his ultimate rejection of it, I believe.

He was fourteen when his grandfather's death and a bequest of a hundred dollars made emancipation possible. With less forethought than he was ever to show again, the young boy straightway set off for the United States, and got as far as Marseilles before the authorities there and his own sudden awareness of being totally unprepared brought him up short. Meekly he returned to Palestine—though not before making a detour to visit Paris—and set about grooming himself for a second flight to freedom. The apprenticeship lasted four years, during which mathematics replaced holy lore and the college in Jerusalem gave way to the Herzlia Gymnasium in Tel Aviv. At the age of eighteen he was awarded a mathematical scholarship by New York University and he left Palestine forever around 1912. Thus, before he reached his majority two homelands had been discarded; the third, the object of his own choice, which in his dreams stood at the opposing pole of all that was dark and oppressive, was never for a moment to be called in question.

Already the important encounter of my and my sisters' prehistory had occurred. While studying at Tel Aviv my father met Marutha Sher, then newly arrived from Russia with her mother, and fell in love with this proud, beautiful, adventurous girl. Either he didn't declare his love, or his declaration was drowned in the clamor of a crowd of like-minded aspirants, for when Marutha in her turn traveled to New York a year or so later, it was not with a view to reunion. For all its apparent inconsequence, the first meeting in Palestine was profoundly significant to us children, not only because it prefigured the storybook ending of their meeting and marrying in New York, but, the single point where my parents' early lives crossed, it gave us our one possibility of stereoscopic vision of the past. All the other tales we were told came separately from one parent or the other, without perspective, in the insubstantial colors of fable. Our family history did not subsist in anecdotes of aunts and cousins but in emblematic figures of faraway heroes, saints or martyrs firmly resisting closer acquaintance. Only upon my mother's mother did we have two views, the one account corroborating the other in love, respect and admiration. Usually my father's attitude to someone would swing from partisanship to repudiation, with no more chance of pausing at a compromise position than can a pendulum arrest itself in mid-oscillation; but his devotion to his mother-in-law never faltered. He adopted her as his revered ancestor too. These circumstances, and the fact that, of all our forebears, she alone played an active role in our lives, attracted me to her greatly. Sadly I never knew her. She died in Palestine when I was still a child.

What had led to her separation from her husband we children did not inquire. Suffice it to say that Grandfather Sher left his wife and daughter in the Crimea to emigrate to America and earn a livelihood as a minor functionary in a synagogue in the Midwest. My parents did their duty by him. It was a filial visit which brought my mother to the United States, although it was marriage which prevented her return. His old age was assisted by contributions from my father's modest salary. But he never figured in the family pantheon. My mother neither paid him further visits nor spoke of him. Her allegiance was exclusively reserved for her mother.

The only surviving child of seven, she lived in the Crimea until she was fifteen, when the thrust of anti-Semitism combined with the gravitational pull of the Promised Land brought mother and daughter to Jaffa. Like my father, she has never returned to Russia, but unlike him she cherishes its memories, speaks its language with native mastery, and honors its virtues in her own temper. If my father is more Jewish than Russian, my mother is indubitably more Russian than Jewish, having a Russian ruthlessness in serving a cause, a wild nature fiercely buckled down, and a heroic scorn for the imprisoning securities of the ghetto. Already when my father met her she wore her separateness like a badge. His memory lingers not so much on her blue eyes and honey-blond hair as on her "presence." Absolutely poised, she held herself aloof, not one Jewess among many but a lone descendant of the Tartaric khans. It is possible that the ups and downs of history had so confused Tartars and Khazars in family legend that the genealogical facts of the matter were beyond discovery. Some fusion of these different bloods ran in my mother's veins. She sprang from the Karaites, who, it appeared, lived at a tangent to Russians and Ashkenazim and spoke Tartar among themselves.

Her ideal, often held up to my admiration in childhood, was the Cherkessian (that is, Circassian) warrior, a perfect Galahad of honor, courage, accomplishment and chivalry, but sterner and more colorful than the devout Christian knight. Where the Jew survived by ruse, keeping his head low in the bad times and raising himself to distinction in the good, the Cherkess was careless of mere survival and demanded from life a more splendid assertion. We had just such a hero in the family: her grandfather had lost his life defending a poor Jew from a mob intent on lynching him. But the best substantiation of her heritage was herself. By the age of sixteen she had traveled, alone, at different times, to visit relatives in Kiev, Moscow, London, Manchester and the United States. Such unescorted journeys across half the world, no everyday occurrence in the life of a young girl before the First World War, gave the measure of her spirit, free, brave and self-sufficient to an extent that could be mistaken for arrogance. Wherever she went—and marriage and motherhood were to prolong the traveling—she was at home, not because she adapted but because she remained herself. She respects tradition, valuing other people who live up to theirs and magnificently living up to her own. As she conducted herself, so her mother had done before her. Every house we ever lived in reconstructed the harem, with a cushion-laden divan beneath the windows and Oriental rugs as soon as we could afford them. Receiving friends at home, she would dress in silken Turkish trousers clipped to her narrow waist with a silver belt. To a remarkable degree she contrived for herself and her daughters the privacy of the harem—rare indeed were press photographs of my mother, even at the most publicized moments of our lives. In the manner of her ancestors, she held the male of greater account than the female, but there was nothing dependent or submissive in her nature. Duty, purpose and self-discipline stiffened everything she did, as her perfectly unnecessary corsets stiffened her slender figure. Never once have I seen my mother other than dressed and girded for the day, or caught her giving way to fatigue or lassitude; and whenever I embraced her in childhood it was that unyielding corset that my arms enclosed.

Pursuing the pattern of their difference in similarity, I could say that both my parents are sensual—in their fashion. My father is capable of gluttony; indeed, as a boy in Jerusalem, he once brought on an attack of appendicitis by eating, so he told me, fourteen helpings of ice cream at one sitting! My mother has no such temptation to resist and in her entire adulthood has never gained an ounce of weight. But where his youth wore the austere coloring of texts, scholarship, intellectual ambition and piety, hers had vividness of a more barbarian culture which acknowledged the body and the five senses, respecting the prowess of horseman, musician or dancer, as well as the indolence of the pasha reclining in his tent at the end of the day. Her sensual pleasures are in rich fabrics, intricately tooled weapons, and above all in the shapes and colors of the Orient, its sounds and smells and artifacts. These things signify both her childhood and a fabulous land whose beauties no other country can match; her passionate attachment to them she has bequeathed to me.

As far back as I can remember, my mother represented at once a guarantee of family normality and an exotic elsewhere, bright with domes and temples of a design different from any I had seen, set in landscapes the more potent for their unfamiliarity. *The Arabian Nights* (expurgated version) was early a favorite book of mine; it bore testimony to her and fed my passion for the East. So did music. So, at length, did voyages, first to Rumania, then to Russia, ultimately to India, the primal source, the mother country in whose strangeness I felt at home. Thus, one of the straight lines of my life began in my mother's girlhood, if not many generations earlier, and my tracing of it proved a voyage into the past.

My being born an American established another important element in the pattern. A tidy mind looking for symmetry would expect this second line to lead to the future, but—and possibly not for the first time—insistence on symmetry, or on tidiness, would distort the facts. Of the many things America means to me, the excitements of the future are not the most important. Without a doubt, the first and most enduring is natural beauty. It was not a revelation granted by my native city.

Arriving in turn from Palestine, the two young people had not expected to meet in New York, but the arranging of this encounter put fate to no ingenious manipulation. New York, for all its size and variety, was pieced together from ethnic patches providing newcomers with an instant, if shallow, environment. It would have been harder to prevent their meeting than to promote it. I can well understand that their love for each other should have ripened swiftly thereafter and overturned Marutha's intention of sailing home to her mother. Apart from the appeal of their youth and attractiveness, each brought the other the reassurance of the known in an alien world. Without family to demand duty and absorb affection, without many friends as yet, they must have felt almost as alone as on a desert island—a circumstance which to the young and hopeful may suggest the Garden of Eden more persuasively than loneliness or isolation. In after years the family joke dismissed the romance of their youthful marriage as mere accountancy: two, after all, could live as cheaply as one.

For a year or so they lived as cheaply as was possible in a rooming house, and found the only diversion they could safely afford in themselves. Bronx Park in fact did duty as their Eden and they would walk through it singing Hebrew songs as though they were Adam and Eve and their language the names of every beast and fowl. My coming announced their fall from self-sufficiency. Obliged to find an apartment of their own, they searched the neighborhood and after several disappointments chose one within walking distance of the park. Showing them out after they had viewed it, the landlady observed, with every intention of pleasing her new tenants and clinching the bargain, "And you'll be glad to know I don't take Jews." History, in New York at any rate, has muffled that voice, but how bitterly in my parents' ears must have sounded the hostility which, having propelled them to the shores of the New World, had followed them there! Her mistake made clear to her, the anti-Semitic landlady was renounced and another apartment found where in due course they gathered friends about them, fellow students and other young people as poor and light-hearted as themselves, who created a cheerful haven against prejudice. But the landlady's blunder left its mark. Back on the street, my mother took a vow: her unborn child would wear a label proclaiming his race to the world. He would be called "the Jew."

In the circumstances, Yehudi might be thought a curious choice. Had avoidance of ambiguity been my mother's only motive, she might have done better to give me the name of any patriarch (except Moses, of course, since Jewish custom forbids a son to take his father's name), for how could an innocent gentile translate from the Hebrew? No Yehudi figures in the Old Testament to assist the understanding of outsiders. That she should make impulsive decisions and abide by them was deeply characteristic; that an insult to her race should prompt the proud assertion of it a reflex absolutely to be expected; but there may have been another factor in her apparently sudden resolve. Symbol was a language which came easily to my mother. An Abraham, an Isaac or a Jacob is a part of history, begotten and in turn begetting; "the Jew" is Everyman, evoking no model and continuing no line. As I hope to show, my mother was determined that no burden of the past, either claims of relations or Jewish tradition, should encumber her children. My name may have been the first entry on the clean page. What is certain, I was born on 22 April 1916.

My mother was twenty, my father twenty-three when they began, with my arrival, to subordinate their own interests to their children's, a regime which would end only in 1938 with the marriages of my sisters and myself. Twice my father was to abandon a career on my account—in 1917 when he forsook his university studies to earn his family's livelihood teaching Hebrew, and again ten years later when he gave up education to manage my concerts. Small wonder if I feel with much gratitude and no little guilt that my fulfillment has been gained at the cost of theirs, but such a reflection belongs to the weighing and measuring of adult hindsight. At the time I was not aware that their lives might be restricted by mine. Indeed I am one of those privileged people whose early years shine in retrospect as a time of unblemished happiness. The record of my memories begins securely only in San Francisco, where we arrived shortly before my second birthday, but the impression of my parents' total love was made long before, in the first months in New York and the succeeding ones in New Jersey.

In New York, before and after her marriage, my mother gave lessons in Hebrew. My arrival restricted, while it did not altogether stop, these lessons, but it did compel my father to take them up full-time, as a *melamed*, or tutor, preparing boys for Bar Mitzvah. His search for a job brought us to Elizabeth, New Jersey, a town whose charms escaped him so completely that he would ever after refer to it, with more passion than wit, as "Elizabethdump." The epithet bore witness to a clash of views between my parents and their employers which anyone in a position to give the question impartial consideration might have foreseen.

Neither of my parents was typical of Jewish immigrants in the United States. To begin with, they were *Chalutzim* (Palestinian pioneers), who did not speak Yiddish among themselves but treated Hebrew as an everyday vehicle for human communication, not a sacred language reserved for the Scriptures. Then, just as my mother was set apart by her Tartar inheritance, so was my father by his discipleship to Achad Ha'am, whose ethical Zionism he preached in class. Each viewed the world from an Asiatic fastness, ideal past on the one side, ideal future on the other, and in either case outside the historical continuum. The Jews of Elizabeth, in contrast, were still living, more or less, in Poland. Except for an industrial horizon of freight yards and oil refineries, an immigrant could have been translated from the Pale to South Court Street and remained none the wiser, so nearly intact was the old way of life in the new surroundings. The result was a certain ritual dustiness in the air. Though they might grumble, the children were sternly marshaled into the *Talmud Torah* to recite their chapters from the Prophets and the Pentateuch, but forbidden to take too lively an interest in the experience by teachers who upheld the view that the deader the language, the better. Into this cobwebby state of affairs my parents erupted with all the unsettling effect of new brooms.

I have it from a dear friend, Samuel Marantz, who was then twelve years old and serving the last months of his religious conviction, that their appearance astonished everyone. So young, fair, free and self-assured, my handsome father and lovely mother (her hair scandalously bobbed) might well have given their elders pause and made them wonder if such Jews did not render gentiles superfluous. If the adults looked for *gravitas* and didn't find it, the children rejoiced to find the impromptu, the messianism and the energy of youth. They would return from *Talmud Torah* not dolefully now but alight with enthusiasm. Children share with priests the need for an occult language, knowing that occultism enforces power; what they resent in elders they covet. The Hebrew guarded by a rabbinate (or, derivatively, by their parents) was now offered them, like fire stolen from the temple, and, indeed, represented as incendiary rather than sacerdotal, as a force of destruction or creation rather than a light from beyond the grave. If Sammy Marantz, fifty years later, still recalls Bialik's poem about the pogrom of Kichinev, "The City of Slaughter," in which he reproaches Jews for their meekness, such history as my father taught must have been martial and apocalyptic, calculated to recruit pioneers rather than parishioners. Like Nicholas of Cologne marshaling children for the Children's Crusade, he held forth an image of Jerusalem waiting to be captured by the young. That Nicholas was to become the legendary Pied Piper of Hamelin and Jerusalem Venusberg only underlines my parallel: my father prepared his pupils for a rite of passage very different in spirit from the official confirmation. Where the latter celebrates puberty and inducts a young man into the adult tribe, he urged them to join a tribe without elders, implying that on the far side of Bar Mitzvah lay not adjustment, but ecstatic renovation, not the humdrum world round about them, but a land of exquisite sentiments and valorous feats. When the text of the Balfour Declaration reached Elizabeth soon after our arrival, it made my father appear, in his pupils' eyes, its prophetic emissary. Sammy Marantz wrote a poem whose title, "At Last! At Last!", suggests that two months of Menuhin tutelage could generate as many millennia of longing in a twelve-year-old.

Never did my parents doubt that where they stood was anything other than a secure place to stand. Such assurance has immense power of attraction, but I doubt that it was only this which made them alluring to children. My mother in particular could not see a young person without wanting to weld him or her into the family, an urge she has never lost and which she has handed down to my sister Hephzibah. Sammy Marantz was, to my knowledge, the first to prompt it, and to such effect that he has remained an adopted member of the family ever since. On snowy winter evenings he would load a sled with firewood and pickled green tomatoes fished from his family's barrels like Jewish valentines, and haul it to our house on Julia Street. It was a symbolic exchange: he brought wood and sweetmeats; he sought warmth and the spiritual provender my parents alone were capable of feeding him. Some six years later Sammy was suddenly to appear at our door in San Francisco, having enrolled at Berkeley; hardly was he in the house before he sat down to read *Ivanhoe* with me. A couple of years later still, when he was back at home and we were marooned, temporarily fatherless, in New York, he would often come to lighten the gloom of banishment. By his youthful devotion I can estimate my parents' impact on the children of Elizabeth—by that, and by what happened when my parents suddenly left town.

The children's excitement had not escaped the rabbi's notice, nor his disapproval. Not that he was a cruel man, it's safe to guess, but guilt, exile and lamentation being his stock in trade, he could not stand by and see an enterprise so richly dour cheered into bankruptcy. He defended his closed universe against my parents' attempts to let in light and air. Their weapon was ardor, his red tape, but before battle could be truly joined, a newspaper item about California caught my father's eye and in the space of a morning grew to a vision and decided our future. The arrangements for leaving took scarcely longer.

Directly our flight became known, the *Talmud Torah* class staged a revolt and, with the same instinct that tells grown-up insurgents to occupy the National Archives and the Civil Registry, confiscated the school records. Naïvely the rabbi offered them bags of candy, then, as they were not to be bribed into submission, dismissed them from the school. My parents had bequeathed a sense of the messianic, but left no doctrine and arranged no apostolic succession among their twelve-year-old followers. Believers without tangible support for their faith, they drifted home and in time, one supposes, fell disconsolately into line.

We meanwhile had got as far as Grand Central Station and discovered that the cheapest journey, a patchwork of stops and starts on local trains, cost fifteen dollars more than we could muster. "Don't you worry," said a generous ticket clerk, taking pity on our dashed hopes. "I'll make the money up." Thus my first benefactor, whose memory and whose good American heart I salute: where would one find his like today? A week later we arrived in California.

I was four years old before Hephzibah was born and five and a half before Yaltah's birth completed the family. To have sisters, especially loving and admiring ones, is an experience I unreservedly recommend (a brother would perhaps have challenged my position). I believe, however, that just as I was eventually enriched by sisters, I was earlier enriched by four years of my parents' undivided love. It seems, looking back, that we were never separated, Aba ("father" in Hebrew), Imma ("mother") and myself. There is some truth in the recollection, for during the Elizabethan interlude my parents apparently carried me in a big basket-cot to the *Talmud Torah* to have me under their eye while they taught, but clearly there must have been many times when work took Aba away. So strong is my impression of security and happiness, however, it has submerged his absences entirely. One of several images sums up the early days in California: I am being toted on Aba's shoulders, Imma is walking beside us, we are all three together and have nothing left to wish for and above all nothing to fear.

A telegram to Aba's brother who owned a chicken farm near San Francisco had preceded us to California, bringing my uncle to meet us at

Oakland Pier, where the trains stopped. A few days or weeks on the chicken farm followed, but Imma's character not being shaped for dependence, we soon moved to Berkeley. After some further weeks or months there, Aba was appointed a teacher of Hebrew by the San Francisco Jewish community at a salary of $150 a month, and we moved across the bay to an apartment at 732 Hayes Street. Here we were to remain until I was six, when with two little sisters added to our number, one just walking, the other in her cradle, our modest apartment was coming undone at the seams and we bought a house of our own.

If my sensibility finds itself nowhere more at home than in a resonant wooden chamber whose walls curve round a sound post, it was organized to begin with in a tent. Imma's fancy ran to heights, coasts, unpeopled views. Halfway around the globe from the Black Sea to the shores of the Pacific she followed an itinerary of edges, until she found in vertiginous, sea-surrounded San Francisco sufficient reason to make a pause. But her longing for air and freedom could not be satisfied with mere views through windows, however noble, or mere excursions, however taxing, and so it came about that no sooner had we moved into Hayes Street than we moved out again, in a manner of speaking. Abutting the windows was a flat roof upon which an awning was pitched and there, if the weather was any way suitable, we slept. Four years later, when the house on Steiner Street was bought, the arrangements for escaping confinement were less provisional. A porch or small bungalow, separate from the house, was built in the garden, consisting of a wooden framework, floor, roof and walls to waist height, above which were netting screens. Inside, the structure was divided into two halves, one for my parents, the other further divided into a larger room for Hephzibah and Yaltah and a smaller one for me. There was common sense in the plan. Extra rooms were gained and a floor liberated for lodgers, but economy was not the prime impetus behind it. To bivouac on a roof or in a garden, as near as possible to the sky, was the way of the Cherkess. Undoubtedly we were the healthier for it. One of my most vivid childhood memories is the icy thrill of cold sheets on foggy nights, followed by the blissful sensation of drifting into sleep as the bed warmed up. We rose and retired with the sun.

Early among educators, the Jesuits were charged with believing that a child was formed or deformed by the age of eight. In my life certainly those years determined what was to follow, though I might argue that the Jesuits' allowance of time was too handsome by half. Adventuring from the cozy cocoon of infancy in a loving family, I

quickly discovered the enchantment of natural sounds. I can have been
no older than two or three when a first awareness of nature was given me
by the crowing of a rooster. A homely bird enough, to bear the weight of
interest in nonhuman creation, farming, conservation and ecology that my
life has since laid upon him; but his voice sounds yet with the exuberance
in being alive that I first responded to all those years ago. Although I
must in fact have heard roosters in the short time we spent with my
uncle, my memory fixes them not there, but on another farm, at Walnut
Creek, owned by another Russian-Jewish family, called Kavin. Mr.
Kavin, a tall man with red hair and beard, had a docile little wife and
two daughters, particular friends of mine named Ida and Zena, with
whom I built houses of wooden crates to hide in.

Another early memory is falling in love. From the earliest age I was
always fond of girls, always in love with someone about whom I wove
romances, up to whose image I lived, without saying anything about it.
The first of this procession of girls was a toddler called Lili, met when
we lived in Berkeley. Perhaps I was too young to conceal my passion, but
however that may be, my parents cynically exploited it to ensure my
good behavior. "Lili's asleep," they would reproach me, in the hope that I
would be chastened into following suit, and thoroughly taken in, I would
resign myself to the day's ending with lullabies about my love: *"Lili
alcha lichon"*—"Lili's gone to sleep." For in those days Hebrew was still
the language of the house. Overhearing one such cradle chant, a visiting
friend from San Francisco, Reuben Rinder, himself a cantor in the
temple, thought it evidence of musical talent and a couple of years later
encouraged Aba and Imma to take my ambitions seriously. I am sure the
word of a professional singer carried weight.

Both my parents were linguists, Imma notably so, and both spoke
English before coming to the United States. Until I was three, however,
they did not speak English to me; our family unity was expressed in a
family language. I am only sorry that English was introduced before I
had a chance to master reading and writing in Hebrew. Its sound is still
in my ears and I have, for instance, broadcast in Hebrew, but only with a
script written in phonetic letters and the proper emphases indicated. The
early fluency is lost, and the words I recall tend to cluster round the
physiological interests of a three-year-old, such words as *regel,* "leg," or
beten, "stomach," probably much used in connection with aches and
bruises as excuses for getting attention. After the transfer to English,
Hebrew remained a household code for instructions to do this or that or
be quiet and mind one's manners which outsiders were not meant to

understand. Neither of my sisters had my Hebrew opportunities, but thereafter in our pursuit of languages—of which there were to be several—we all three hunted together. Indeed, they went further than I.

Although neither of my parents spoke Yiddish to us children, both understood it and Aba spoke it fluently. Somewhat later in my boyhood, lying in bed on my side of the partition in the Steiner Street garden house, I would hear him read the works of Sholom Aleichem to my mother, and every so often a burst of laughter would reach me. Those were moments of happiness for all of us. To me, awake in the dark, they meant there was complete harmony in the household. Not that disharmony was otherwise the rule: on the contrary, so dependent were my parents on each other and so well-established their different functions— my father responsible for anything of a breadwinning or practical nature, my mother for keeping house and for the children's morals and education—there was no opportunity for dissension. But Sholom Aleichem provided occasion for a drop from high purpose into light-heartedness. So elevated was Imma's conception of existence, it was as if she were living an ideal script, handed down by her ancestors and pinned to some lofty level by her own self-discipline. I use an image from the stage deliberately, for someone who never capitulates to pain or sloth impresses us as heeding a greater power than his own, as the actor does; in the wings, however, the actor lets the illusion go, but Imma never did, for so far from illusion were her convictions, they penetrated every depth of her character.

She liked things to be seen in their global unity. An outing was not simply an outing, but had its moral and spiritual as well as its physical aspects; a holiday had its quota of related study; enjoyment was taken in awareness of other people who were not so privileged. She would relate with approval a little drama from her own childhood: given a new dress for a party, she was in a state of high excitement when her mother said, "Look, I know you love your new dress, but there are many children who don't have pretty clothes. Wouldn't you feel much better if you went to the party in your old dress and gave this one away?" From my own early years I recall an event less stern in its demands but equally rounded in its implications. This was my first excursion alone with her—memorable on that account, if for no other reason, for, three-year-old child though I was, she filled me with chivalrous self-importance by entrusting me with the responsibility of escorting her. Secondly, we went to Napa County, a beautiful agricultural part of California. Last but not least, our journey had moral justification because our purpose was to visit a patient in a mental hospital. I remember scarcely anything of the outing except an institution with great gates and a general notion of this poor man's pitiful case, but the lesson was implanted that pleasure had its debt to pay. As I have said, she identified with prisoners of every sort, but especially the "visionary" for whom the real world lay elsewhere. In Jaffa she had gone for a time to a school run by nuns, and retained a respect for those who renounce everything to serve others (in contrast, she was dubious about priests, rabbis, or anyone who made a profession of being godly). Her own life was one of renunciation, of course, requiring the sacrifice of assets more considerable than party dresses, such as freedom and fulfillment.

We were still at Hayes Street and I by now old enough to notice that my father went to work each day, when a Dutch windmill in a toyshop window caught my fancy. Our regular morning walk took us past the toyshop to a neighborhood park, but custom did not stale, but rather reinforced, the windmill's appeal. Here again Imma found occasion to link reward with purpose: when I could pronounce an r without lisping evasion of its difficulty, the toy would be mine. I knew exactly how an r should sound, but my wretched tongue was not nimble enough to deliver itself of this impossible consonant, clearly invented for another anatomy than mine. Valiantly, day and night, in corners, I practiced, and now became clear the usefulness of sleeping in a tent apart from the house. With my infant sisters abed and asleep before me, and my parents still up and about for a few hours yet, I was left at liberty to concentrate on rolling at my target. Then, one evening when Aba and Imma had just gone to bed, I knew I had it. What to do? If I wakened them in the middle of the night, they would hardly be pleased; if I waited until morning, my tongue might have forgotten its skill. With my head under the bedclothes, I tested myself surreptitiously at intervals through the night and when dawn was breaking, raised the household with a superb "rrrr!" And got my windmill. (I hesitate to find any deep significance in the episode, but it is nonetheless true that over half a century later, I have renewed my interest in windmills, and will preach them at anyone who cares to listen as the conservationist's electric generator.)

But I have still not done my mother justice. If, on the one hand, she gave shape to existence by her exalted idea of it, on the other she had the knack of the delightful surprise. She used the bonds of duty as much to fasten down her own temperament as to provide guidelines for her children's growing up, I am sure. That she had a wild spirit capable of devastating eruption was not in doubt, but so perfect was her control that one only ever glimpsed its reflection or caught its echo. Solely in the matter of pleasure, of picnics, holidays, interruptions of the agenda, would she unleash the unpredictable, spontaneous side of her nature; but then totally. She could not—still cannot—endure to have the savoring of existence blighted by prudence. It was Aba's inclination to foresee eventualities and prepare to meet them. In the ordinary course of events, this was accepted and acted upon, but if Aba's forethought trespassed on leisure, Imma would say, half warning, half ironical, "Moshe! P-p-p-plans!" and timetables would be cast to the winds in the cause of adventure.

Such holidays, overturning routine with delightful unexpectedness, were to be a feature of my childhood and youth. Naturally, when my sisters were still infants and the family still confined to public transport, enterprises of this daring character were beyond our scope, but I can't remember a time when pleasure outings didn't enliven our weeks like so many bursts of sunshine. There were Sunday picnics—a very San Franciscan diversion in those days. There were visits to the rural Kavins and to the Kayes, a prosperous tradesman's family in Berkeley. In return, my parents entertained at home. And from before my conscious memory records the fact, there was music.

In 1918, when I was two, my parents smuggled me into a matinee concert of the San Francisco Symphony Orchestra, and no misadventure occurring to dissuade them, regularly continued the contraband operation until I was old enough to have a ticket on my own account. In after years Imma let it be known that Aba and she had taken me with them because they couldn't afford a baby-sitter. No doubt baby-sitters were a luxury in their struggling young lives, but this granted, I have my reservations about the story. It was characteristic of her to puncture myth with a deft injection of matter of fact. It was no less characteristic to hold that the earlier an experience, the more valuable. When my sisters were expected, I remember her conviction that the life she led, the music she heard, the thoughts she had, were part and parcel of the environment of the coming baby, a subject now for theses by learned doctors, but to her simply a truth. So much the more forcibly must she have believed that as soon as I could be trusted not to disgrace myself, I should be allowed to share what she and Aba delighted in. In view of my future connection with concerts, it might justly be argued that it was rather I who took them; but my own interpretation of the facts concealed by the high cost of baby-sitters is based on the happiness of my early years. So sure is the memory of my being the apple of my parents' eyes, I can't believe they ever entertained the idea of going to a concert and leaving me behind. We went to concerts, as we did most things, together.

While I don't claim to remember the very first concert, a powerful recollection of the repeated experience remains with me. Seated on Imma's knee in the gallery, I am looking over a shadowy cliff, as through a telescope the wrong way round, at the bottom of which the musicians in a pool of light are miniature but distinct, their busy concentration down there producing sounds to ravish soul and sense.

This ravishment I owe to a ponderous edifice called the Curran Theatre, where the orchestra then played. As if that were not debt enough, the Curran put me under further obligation, providing additional sustenance for an imagination stimulated by music. Every year the Pantages Vaudeville Company would come to San Francisco, and every time it came, I was taken to marvel at the acrobats, clowns, conjurers and dancers, and to be enchanted anew by the first solo violinist ever to impress me, a swarthy fellow called Carichiarto, who had a regular slot in the program and played quite beautifully. Knowing somehow that my world did not begin and end in San Francisco, sensing in my mother the exotic East, feeling drawn to great distances myself, I was bound to confer reality on this magical world, and in time and in turn, to find my violin a theatre; for this box would prove spacious enough to hold jugglers, dancers, a Tartar horde, gypsies, souks, caravanseries, houris, in fact all of paradise. But no single experience of the theatre more lastingly marked me than a performance by Anna Pavlova. Twice, in fact, I saw her dance, the earliest occasions I remember of being absolutely carried away; hardly less transporting was the mere sight of her luggage. One morning in Geary Street, at the stage entrance to the Curran Theatre, we came across six or seven great wardrobe trunks, packed no doubt with her costumes and those of the *corps de ballet* and awaiting collection at the conclusion of her one-night stand. This image of the traveling artist affected me so deeply that I remember it yet with some flicker of my youthful excitement. On stage she would include in her program "The California Poppy," a dance which celebrated a favorite flower of mine, one I would long for in the years away from California, but vainly, for it flourished wild only in my home state, and there it grew everywhere in spring. Delicate, orange, sweet-smelling, the California poppy has a peculiarly touching manner of closing in upon itself as it droops; thus ended Pavlova's dance.

I lost my heart to her. Forsaking Lili and Lili's successors, I dreamed only of Pavlova for many many months, and though I did not see her dance a third time, nor ever meet her, the dream endured. Sown in a sensibility fashioned by my mother, the seed Pavlova planted, a conception of beauty and grace perfected by the discipline of the dance, was to come to flower in adult life in my wife, Diana.

2

A Chevrolet and
a Half-Size Violin

Perched high on the Curran Theatre cliff on concert afternoons, I let my gaze slide past the conductor, whose part in the delightful goings-on below rather defeated my comprehension, to focus on the concertmaster, Louis Persinger. Once in a while he would have a solo passage. I learned to wait for those moments when the sweet, lovely sound of the violin floated up to the gallery, thrilling, caressing, and more entrancing than any other. During one such performance I asked my parents if I might have a violin for my fourth birthday and Louis Persinger to teach me to play it.

If this narrative has taken its time to relate a detail which earlier accounts have furnished straightaway, it is to undo the impression that I was shapeless protoplasm one day and myself the next, that musical gift comes to light with the *éclat* of the transformation scene in a pantomime. The finger I pointed at Louis Persinger could base its choice on four years that had given me what as many years of college rarely give the graduate: a sense of vocation. Is this particular sense native to childhood itself? I wonder. Have the fortunate simply rescued from an otherwise lost age of innocence the conviction of unlimited possibility, the instinct for real worth, which make it easier for children to identify with great soloists or simple souls than with able middlemen? Certainly, looking at children from an adult perspective, I have long believed that the grown-up world consistently underrates the young, finding marvels in ambition and achievement where none exists. At the age of four I was too young to know that the violin would exact a price commensurate with the grace it conferred—the grace of flying, of occupying an absolute vantage point, of enjoying such dominion over nerve, bone and muscle as could render the body an ecstatic absentee. But I did know, instinctively, that to play was to be.

Quite simply I wanted to be Persinger, and with equal straightforwardness proposed the means of bringing this enviable situation about. I don't think my parents found my request far-fetched—Aba's childhood had set a precedent, after all—but they may have found it more whimsical than urgent, and hesitated to invest any of their small resources in what might prove to be a child's caprice. As events were to show, they retailed my plea to friends and relations, in the manner of fond parents everywhere, and as a consequence I acquired in turn a toy fiddle and a real one.

I shall never forget the disappointment of that imitation violin. Made of metal, with metal strings, cold to the touch, with a sound as horribly tinny as its construction, this travesty of my longings enraged me for, as far as I recall, the first time in my life. The setting of its presentation and my ungracious reception of it was a large, beautiful park on a hill at the top of Steiner Street, a park whose lawns and thickets were to become very familiar to my sisters and myself a couple of years later. Seated with Aba and Imma on a bench was a fellow teacher from Aba's school who there and then gave me his present. The poor man must have been taken aback when, getting no response from the toy, I burst into sobs, threw it on the ground and would have nothing more to do with it. I am sorry that my first patron in the matter of violins should have been so dustily rewarded for his kindness. I could not know that for myself gratification was only postponed.

Gratification was assured shortly thereafter by a check for eight hundred dollars sent by my Grandmother Sher in Palestine, who had been told of my musical inclinations and had sufficient vision, or generosity, or recklessness, to take them seriously. Wisely my parents decided that half of this very considerable sum was enough to spend on a beginner's violin, and diverted the rest toward the cost of our first car. I can't now determine which purchase added more to my happiness.

I might have met my grandmother but for Aba's anguish at the thought of being separated, however provisionally, from his wife. About the time of my grandmother's gift to us there was a plan that she should travel from Jaffa and Imma should travel from America, with the newly born Hephzibah and me in tow, to a reunion in Italy. It collapsed under the weight of Aba's distress, to remain ever after a sorrowful reminder to him of the sacrifice he had demanded of Imma rather than make himself. For Imma never saw her mother again. One morning, when I was six or seven and we were already living in Steiner Street, she woke up with a dreadful certainty that her mother had died. So heavy was her premonition that Aba sent a telegram to Jaffa, and when no answer, either good or bad, had come by the next day, rang the telegraph office. The dread news had in fact arrived, but the clerks couldn't bring themselves to pass it on. Thus solemnly and eerily was I made aware of the first irreversible event of my life.

With Grandmother Sher's death, our closest bond with Palestine had gone. Dutifully Aba still wrote to an older sister there, but as he was not fond of this particular sister, and indeed blamed her for his younger sister's unhappy love affair ending in suicide, Imma persuaded him, rather determinedly, that his dutifulness was mere hypocrisy, and the correspondence ceased. He was probably the easier to persuade in that Imma's arguments coincided with his own repudiation of his last Zionist loyalties, a decision which left him a confirmed anti-Zionist thereafter. But it was neither the one allegiance nor the other that motivated my mother. In her vision, her best gift to her children was a life emancipated from all restrictions, claims and inhibitions of the past, a world in which they belonged.

Our new car, a little open four-door Chevrolet, might have stood symbol for the freedom my mother desired for us. It had a personality and a name to go with it, which to my shame I no longer remember, and we all loved it extravagantly. Without roof or windows, it offered an airy journey unblemished by fumes. I actually liked the smell of gasoline in those days, before lead was put into it. In the morning, with the just risen sun warming the gas, the faint odor intoxicatingly conjured up the landscapes we would shortly be exploring, and affected Aba no less powerfully than myself. Our journeys always spurred him into song, the refuge for the emotional abandon he too often denied himself. He was a careful driver, never exceeding fifteen miles an hour in our first year of car ownership, then venturing as far as eighteen while holding those who overtook us at twenty to be reckless adventurers without thought for the lives of their families or of anyone else on the road. It took us four hours to cover the sixty miles to Santa Cruz, but they were relaxed hours, with the family together and adventure in front of us, which my father celebrated by singing the mostly very sad songs of Chasidic tradition. These haunting melodies, for the most part wordless (or if there were words, I didn't understand them), carried us up and down the verdant byways of California.

Private cars were still rare; for that matter, the population of California was still relatively small; and to own a car meant access to the countryside without today's pollution or crowds of fellow trippers to overcome. At a few hours' distance from Hayes Street lay the Santa Clara Valley, a bed of blossom in springtime, interrupted by few towns and those really no more than villages; and the Santa Cruz Mountains, not high but romantically wooded; and to the east the Sierra Nevadas, the coastal range whose trees have since been largely burned down or logged away; and the icy green depths of Lake Tahoe within its overgrown shores which seemed untouched by human foot—with reason, for the Indian feet which had trodden them for centuries had left no lasting mark. Our car gave us direct contact with nature and seemed itself to feel it. Up steep, narrow, winding, unsurfaced tracks it would labor to the top of some pass, there to boil dry from its exertions, obliging us to bring water to temper its heat and calm it down, rewarding our patience with vistas of a beauty to stop the breath. On such excursions California laid ideal landscapes in my mind which nothing later was to overlay; it sowed the seed of adult enthusiasms for a world embracing all creation, human, animal, vegetable, mineral; it prompted the first awed responses to my American heritage.

Once or twice we rented a cottage in this countryside, in a village calling itself Holy City, which concealed commercial enterprise under a veneer of utopian high-mindedness. It was run by a self-styled Father Ricker, whose pious acumen had screwed the life savings out of more than one Holy Citizen. We were not at risk, being only summer visitors, and my recollections of this fraudulent Garden of Eden are of the endearingly humble diversions it offered, typical of the early automobile age: a little zoo exhibiting the pumas and rattlesnakes which still roamed the surrounding woods, a hall of distorting mirrors, and an early jukebox or two. More impressive were the mountains and redwoods all around, where there was neither fraud nor commerce, but instead the infinite fascination of the natural world. The most memorable of these summer holidays was the first major one, in 1922, when we made the two-day, two-hundred-mile trip to Yosemite, finding at the end of it a valley so strange and majestic between its neighboring mountains, some wooded, some bare, we felt we must be its original discoverers (in fact, picnic tables at intervals suggested that someone had passed that way before). By 1922 I had some competence on the violin and on this particular holiday was practicing a de Bériot concerto. Afterward my father always called the slow movement "Yosemite," it being plaintive and nostalgic and summing up for him the magic of those days.

We had a tent to sleep in, and ate our meals at one of the long wooden tables considerately provided. Somewhere out of sight was another tent and other campers, two young men whom Imma would occasionally invite to eat with us. At one such meal I remember our visitors intriguing me with a first demonstration of the tossing of flapjacks. One of these young men further indebted me with the gift of a whistle cut from a rush, and it was wretched of me to repay him and his friend by subjecting them to an embarrassing family confrontation. They had been invited to breakfast, a very flapjack meal, at the end of which I left the table without ceremony, whereupon Imma summoned me back and instructed me to ask permission first. There is no accounting for human behavior. A moment before, my mood had been perfectly sunny; now stubborn pride surged up, leaving me no option but to sit, mumchance and miserable, over the remains of breakfast. The guests left in some confusion; after a time Aba also left; the world turned on its axis; still we sat there, Imma and I, locked into our contest of wills. I might have spared myself the discomfort, for who could outsit Imma? Finally I mumbled something, neither "Excuse me" nor "May I leave?" but sufficiently like human speech to bear interpretation and save both our faces. My first challenge to authority was over. There have been others since, none so unequal.

That is not the enduring souvenir of Yosemite, however. The impact of nature which preceded this episode outlasted it. Years later, when I was married for the first time and on a belated honeymoon, I saw there one of the most awesome sights of my life: a sunset and moonrise from the bald peak of Half-Dome, when the two orbs, facing each other, hung in space, identical in size, shape and hue.

But to get back to the spending of the other half of Grandmother Sher's gift: commitment being my mother's natural response to any situation, it was to be expected that once the violin had been welcomed into the house, my mastering it should become a serious business, and I given every opportunity to do my best, with no trifling countenanced. However, a couple of false starts had to be undone before I was launched in earnest. With my newly purchased instrument in hand, I was first trotted off to a neighborhood teacher whose reputation depended on a sign board, "Violin Lessons," hung over the entrance to his ramshackle house. Up the dark stairs we went, Imma and I, only to be driven down again by the dust and decay, the old man's winy breath and the tobacco fumes, at the top. If there was a lesson or two before we beat our retreat, they have left no trace in my memory. Our second approach was to Louis Persinger, possibly less in recognition of my original request than because, having seen the worst, Imma could be satisfied only with the best. Cantor Rinder duly sang my praises, but Persinger had heard that song sung in all its variations by doting friends and parents and had grown deaf to it. Four-year-old beginners offered no rewards to his full and busy life. Between worst and best the compromise, where I then came to rest, was the studio of the local Svengali, Sigmund Anker, who, with the techniques of a drill sergeant, transformed boys and girls into virtuosi by the batch.

Anker's business in life was to groom the young to brilliant performance of Sarasate and Tchaikovsky, and as far as I can gather from dim memories of those distant days, he had neither capacity nor ambition for anything more subtle. He knew nothing of style, the classics, chamber music; more fundamentally, he knew nothing of the process of violin playing, or if he did, lacked the skill to pass his knowledge on. Not that he was alone in his darkness, for violin teaching was altogether a hit-and-miss activity then, as indeed it still too largely is. Anker's method was to set up a target—correct intonation, full round tone, or whatever—and whip his pupils toward it by unexplained command. The result was that one taught or failed to teach oneself, as one had earlier learned to walk and talk mainly by self-instruction; but violin playing being more complex than such inbuilt human skills, an illumination beyond what one's own nerves and muscles could supply would have been gratefully received.

At the outset merely holding the violin, at arm's length, very tightly, lest it fall (or recoil), seemed problem enough; where did one find a second pair of arms to play it? I was invited to fly; I answered by hanging on for dear life. Where the left hand, in the "golden mean" position, should form spirals round the neck of the instrument (as the right hand does around the bow), mine pinioned it between thumb and the base of my first finger. Where the digits should arch softly over the fingerboard, each muscularly independent of the others, mine—all but the smallest, which drooped behind—cleaved to one another like three parade ponies, moving *en masse* from one positional rung to another up the chromatic ladder as if they found safety in numbers. Where the violin should lie on the collarbone, secured there by the head's natural but delicate weight, I clamped it tight. Where the right hand (and by extension the wrist, elbow, arm, scapula) and the bow function rather as the wheel and axis of a gyroscope, the former rotating in order to keep the latter on a true course, I sawed a straight line and, on every downstroke, swerved or "turned the corner" (to make matters worse, the bow was too long for me). At crucial points where sound should have vibrated freely, it was hopelessly grounded. These abominations were so many symptoms of my ignorance of the violin's nature, an ignorance which clearly was not going to be corrected by the explanations of a third party, but only by personal exploration. The gyres, the pendular swings, the waves required by an instrument that itself forms one continuous curve, I had to teach myself, and could do so the more easily perhaps for inhabiting my own absolute space, for lacking the linear perspective that relates people to one another, for feeling in circles.

After six months I had made remarkably little progress. Mr. Anker would bode the worst, having expected the best, Imma would report his diminishing hopes, Aba would fall silent, and I felt like a terminal case bandied by future pallbearers. Then, for no reason I could explain, the violin began to lose its foreignness, my grip relaxed, my body discovered the freedom to forget itself, and I could enjoy what I was doing. I was at last launched. At this distance what I recall most clearly is my conquest of vibrato. To teach vibrato, Anker would shout, "Vibrate! Vibrate!" with never a clue given as to how to do it. Indeed I would have obeyed him if I could. I longed to achieve vibrato, for what use was a violin to a little boy of Russian-Jewish background who could not bring a note to throbbing life? As with my struggle to roll an r, the problem was not to imagine the sound so much as to produce it; but vibrato proved a more elusive skill. I had already left Anker's tutelage and was perhaps six or seven years old when, lo and behold, one bright day my muscles had solved the puzzle. By such strokes of illumination, the solution proving as mysterious as the problem and leaving one almost as blind as before, most violinists learned their craft. (The quest to perfect vibrato was to last for many years yet. Even when I was regularly performing in public as a boy, my vibrato was never very fast, and it wasn't until, as an adult, I undertook to unpick the mechanics of the operation and put them together again that I really began to satisfy myself.)

Once a year at the Fairmont Hotel, Anker's budding virtuosi gave a concert, half display, half competition, to their friends and relations. My turn came in November 1921, when I played a little piece called "Remembrance" and was placed second, to my slight chagrin. I have not the world's best memory for names, but I recall my successful rival to this day, a girl of twelve called Sarah Kreindler, whose performance of Sarasate's "Gypsy Airs" justly merited first place. My early champion, Reuben Rinder, was in the audience and gave me a book, perhaps a prize for doing well, more probably a consolation prize for not having done better. This first public appearance was a milestone in more ways than one: it marked the end of the Sigmund Anker era. Either because Imma had concluded he had no more to offer me or, quite possibly, because I hadn't managed to play better than Sarah Kreindler, she contacted Louis Persinger again. What extra persuasions were used, I have no idea, but this time he agreed to take me on.

Of the many reasons I have to hold Persinger in loving remembrance, none is greater than his setting high my sights from the beginning. At our first lesson I was told to play some little thing and was advised on this and that, but these preliminaries speedily dispatched, Persinger invited Imma and me to sit down, took up his violin, and announced he would play for us. With admirable intuition, this man who made no profession of teaching little children chose not to stun us with pyrotechnics, but to exalt us with one of the noblest works ever written, the Adagio from Bach's Sonata in G Minor for Solo Violin. So passionate and moving is this improvised Adagio that many years later in my presence, Pablo Casals, abandoning himself at the keyboard, gave it a mock-Hungarian-cymbalom, broken-chord accompaniment, insisting that it proved Bach to have had gypsy blood! At the time, aged five, hearing the Adagio for the first time, such speculations were beyond me. I knew only that the music was very near to me and very moving. We sat spellbound, Imma and I, until the last note died away and stillness filled the room to overflowing: then went home, still transported to another plane of existence, drunk on Bach. I knew this sublimity was what I must strive for, and that she expected my striving no less than I did myself.

We had shared an experience that marked us both. Both my parents responded to music, but Imma had had the good fortune to learn something about it. At Hayes Street we had an upright piano which she played from time to time, and it was she who accompanied me in my second public offering, Paderewski's "Minuet," presented at some function at the YMCA club in the San Francisco Presidio early in 1922. Until the birth of my sisters, she took cello lessons, but thereafter she sacrificed her own formation to mine, putting all her heart, energy and imagination behind my efforts. She didn't oversee my practice; she overheard it. I recall the years at Hayes Street as crowded, not only literally, in that the family was outgrowing the accommodation, but also with activity. As well as running the household and bringing up the children—the task above all others which engaged Imma's commitment—Imma had a constant stream of Bar Mitzvah candidates to coach and friends to entertain. Busy with duties, she still had an ear to spare for me. If I happened to make particularly nice sounds, she would comment; if I scraped half-heartedly, she would tell me I was "no better than a shoemaker" and urge me toward a big tone. She bade me hold the violin at a Heifetzian tilt and made a game with me of solfeggio. My first lesson in reading music occurred on a park bench—in the park near the toyshop of happy memory—when I sang by name the notes she drew on a stave. As my mistakes seemed to amuse her, I occasionally played dumb, losing face sooner than lose the pleasure of seeing her laugh. It was she who tuned my violin. When Yaltah's birth in October 1921 removed Imma to the maternity hospital, emergency arrangements had therefore to be put into effect. Once a day Persinger came to tune the violin, which, if it didn't ensure the instrument's remaining in tune for the next twenty-four hours, was better than nothing; and I would practice very regularly, honestly and honorably, to be rewarded by a daily visit to the hospital to see Imma and my new little sister.

As soon as she was home again and routine re-established, Imma resumed the duty of escorting me to violin lessons, which now took place at Persinger's studio in Hyde Street. We traveled by streetcar, a solid vehicle able to negotiate San Francisco's more moderate hills, leaving only the steepest to the cable cars. One unforgettable day, at risk of arriving late for a lesson, we engaged a cab, and noticing my pleasure at this unaccustomed luxury, Imma observed that in the future, if I worked hard, I might be able to afford taxis quite often. Bach, and taxis, and Imma's expectations—I had much to live up to; but children are not blank pages for others to write on; the vaulting ambition, so to play that the world in turn would weep and rejoice was within myself.

Skepticism belongs to adults. Remembering childhood, most people will admit, I think, that then they had faith to move mountains. I too was convinced I could work miracles, but in my case no more than in other children's was this a judgment of my capacities; rather it was the conviction that a supreme effort of concentration, or of prayer, could release one from natural laws. Within a few months of my becoming

Persinger's pupil, our family left Hayes Street to buy on mortgage the big wooden two-story house, 1043 Steiner Street, which was to be our home for the next seven years. A flight of steps led to the front door above the basement, itself above ground level, and a back door opened into the sizable garden behind the house, where our sleeping porch was built. The disposition of these doors, in a house set in a garden all our own, occasioned a fantasy which regularly occupied me before I fell asleep. It was really quite simple. Starting at the back door, I would dig a tunnel and surface at the front door! The pleasure, the surprise this image afforded me could not have been more intense had my underground journey led to Outer Mongolia or the origins of Creation. I suppose tunnels must be an obsession with children, who, having lately tunneled their way into life, then industriously tunnel from infancy to freedom and responsibility. But what fascinated my imagination was the tremendous feat, which I felt I should be perfectly able to accomplish. Similarly, I believed myself capable of performing miracles in music. That only the passage of time accumulates skill and insight was a fact my faith easily ignored: if I really applied myself to learning a work today, I should know it by tomorrow, I was sure, and no doubt this confidence that all things were possible brought many things within reach.

Our new house cost eight thousand dollars, to be paid off at the rate of fifty dollars a month. By the time we moved into it, Aba's salary had improved from $150 a month to $200, or even $250, and his responsibilities had grown to match, from those of a simple teacher to the weightier ones of a headmaster with a school of his own. I remember its red-brick classrooms clearly, for I was present at the opening of this new school, when a tree was planted to mark its dedication. Before we left San Francisco in 1927 to spend a year in Europe, Aba's administrative and educational gifts had won him the job of superintending all seven Hebrew schools in the Bay area, at a monthly salary of $350. Once in a while the whole family would visit the schools in his charge. I have no doubt that had my father completed his university studies, he would have gone far in the world of education; had his ideal Jew been reconcilable with the Jewish nationalist, he could have occupied almost any position in Israel. Both these possibilities had been turned down by 1922, and in my interests he was to turn down the third, the career he was then succeeding in, five years later.

Meanwhile on his modest salary he contrived to give his family holidays, a car, music and our lovely house. The basement he converted into a garage for six or seven neighboring cars, whose parking in the exiguous space involved much delicate maneuver. The garage rents more or less met the mortgage payments, and further income—which paid for the construction of the sleeping porch—came from letting the two rooms on the upper floor. The larger room, overlooking the street, was rented by two old Russian ladies, whether friends or sisters I never discovered. We visited them once a year, on some Russian holiday, and were ceremonially invited to eat Russian pastry, an elaborate structure of plaited strands, beautifully crisp and sugary. In the smaller room, which overlooked the garden, lived a succession of lodgers, the last of whom, Ezra Shapeero, stayed for several years. Ezra was young, away from his family and struggling through law school, predicament enough to touch my mother's heart. She could not bear to leave him solitary upstairs, so he was brought downstairs and assured of warmth and welcome in the family. Ezra ceased to be a lodger when his studies finished, but he never left the family circle, and now that he is dead, his wife and two daughters still keep in touch with us.

Our family life was lived on the ground floor, where we had a kitchen, a living room and a dining room (we retired to the garden at night). Off the kitchen was an additional room, which served as sick bay when necessary and where, otherwise, I practiced, looking out on the garden and the porch, within earshot of Imma preparing meals next door.

The Steiner Street house gave scope to my mother's talent for entertaining and several times a year my parents would give a dinner party. Twenty or more people would sit down at the big table in the dining room, all its extra leaves put in, and the whole covered with splendid white linen. On such nights a wood fire was lit, and as far as I was concerned, the best part of the evening was the half hour or so I spent alone in front of it before the guests arrived. My sisters were in bed, my parents busy with last-minute preparations, and I in solitary possession of this mysterious, vital, dangerous beauty. Later the evening grew increasingly painful. Allowed to eat with the grownups, I was still too short in the leg to reach the floor, and my dangling feet became more uncomfortable as time and successive courses passed. I never said anything about it, but ever since, in memory of those evenings, I have supplied footrests for children, secretaries and anyone else who might benefit from them.

At one of the parties I disgraced myself. It must have been during our first year or so at Steiner Street, I think, because one of our guests was a nurse from the maternity ward at Mount Sinai Hospital who had looked after my mother when Yaltah was born. Perhaps the most Jewish characteristic Imma had was an urge to see young people marry each other, and valuing this nurse, she decided to promote a match between her and our then boarder, a man of about thirty who seemed grave and dignified to me. I was aware of Imma's hopes for him, and felt uncomfortably that he was the victim of a trick, coming happily to eat with us while plots thickened about his innocent head. The poor fellow would have to be warned; clearly it fell upon me to give the warning, and the fact that it would take courage only made it the more obligatory. Throughout the soup I several times approached my announcement and withdrew again, trembling, then finally blurted it out.

"Do you know why you were invited this evening?"

"Oh," said he politely, "such a charming evening! I'm delighted to be with your parents and their friends."

"You were invited to marry that lady."

As may be imagined, the evening never quite recovered from this brutal blow, but to my parents' credit, they neither punished nor scolded me for my awkward honesty, and only much later introduced the finesse of the white lie. When Yaltah was of an age to be up and about during preparations for a party, she once did something almost as bad: she emptied a bowl of salt into a dish that was cooking, and she too escaped unpunished. Really, for all the respect and obedience they demanded of us, my parents were remarkably forbearing of our misdemeanors, and remarkably unexacting in other ways. Sometimes Aba would say to us, "Your mother is very tired—she has worked so hard!" but this appeal apart, they never troubled us with their ailments, never asked for mercy, never asked us to do anything for them. They served us, carried things for us, worked for us. It is only as a father myself that I have come to know a different family organization, where doing things "for Daddy" has been a perfectly normal childhood reflex.

No more than Sigmund Anker did Persinger reveal to me the mysteries of the violin. He demonstrated and I imitated, winning achievement by ear without detour through the conscious mind. What he gave me as a musician was insight into music, and as a teacher, a degree of devoted attention which I only later discovered not all teachers were capable of. He took extraordinary pains with me. Our two lessons a week imperceptibly became three, then four and five (later, when he accompanied me on tour, we would study together every morning for three hours). To make practice tolerable, he improvised exercises for me, on one occasion drawing scales in thirds to resemble toy trains moving across hill and dale. I would not be surprised if this design had been inspired by a Bach autograph, but it bore witness to the unfortunate conviction I held that exercising was child's play and therefore inimical to my quest for reality. In Persinger I had found a teacher incapable of the autocratic method that rejoices in difficult scale work and *études* for their own sake. His virtue was common sense, a thing so unequally distributed it may have been mistaken for quirkiness by those whose faith lay in *idées fixes*. His belief that the ear should dictate the fingering, or that the hand should accustom itself to half positions, was scarcely axiomatic fifty years ago. Heaven knows how much I might have learned had I been a slower student! How many ingenious exercises he might have contrived had he taken umbrage at my ability to emulate him straightaway! No doubt even then he was arguing (and rightly so) for the usefulness of scales in thirds, but if so, the pragmatist in him let me run helter-skelter over his arguments. Did he feel that my strength was my intractability, or that in driving home fundamentals he risked distorting a gift simply to prove his point? It would be as foolish to regret his leniency as to imagine that one can benefit from a virtue without giving the devil one's hindpart. There is always the devil to pay. But the devil sometimes reimburses. Never having taught me a method, Persinger allowed me to beget my own, in my own time, so that even the omissions and loose threads formed part of a design. Where another teacher would have denied me the great works until I had attained whatever height and weight were deemed coefficient with depth, Persinger let his ears be his arbiter.

Born in Colorado, the son of a railway signalman, Persinger had studied under the great Belgian violinist Eugène Ysaÿe, and for a time occupied the first chair of the Berlin Philharmonic under Arthur Nikisch. His hope to make a concert career in the United States was never realized, ostensibly because there were no funds to finance its beginnings, perhaps because his ambition lacked a cutting edge. His violin was an exquisite Montagnana, with all the warmth characteristic of that instrument; from it Persinger fetched a sweet tone, but one without aggressive quality. He submitted to his wife's more forceful personality, scarcely ever lost his temper, and was altogether a gentle person. The milk of human kindness may not lubricate a soloist's career; it made Persinger an ideal teacher, at least for someone thirsty for instruction. Inspired teacher, concertmaster, leader of an excellent quartet bearing his name, first-rate accompanist, he was among the best all-round musicians I have known. Did I become a receptacle for his abandoned dreams? It may be so. Images, possibilities, never die. They transmigrate into the idols we create, the mates we take, the children we sire, the pupils we form, generating that energy we call attraction. Assuredly the world is not rich in mutual recognition. Love may be self-love, appearances to the contrary; but then who can say that appearances do not have a validity all their own? Love consists pre-eminently in the acts of love. If there was an element of wistfulness in Persinger's care of me, an echo of what might have been, I was not aware of it, however. As parents to children, so teachers were devoted to pupils, in my view, and if this seems a complacent assumption, it did imply an answering commitment on the pupil's part.

I knew very well that privilege carried with it an equal weight of obligation. I had a sense of responsibility as a child and believe I worked hard, but have no difficulty in imagining that other children similarly placed may have worked harder. Things were made easy for me by my practice hours being built into a family timetable, which became more complex as we children grew older and more activities had to be fitted in; but which from the first prevented slacking on the one hand and, on the other, obsessional overwork. Of course, no timetable, however rigorously observed, can ensure one's using one's time to best advantage. A violinist, whether eight years old or fifty-eight, leads a solitary, meditative, ruminative life, and only he is accountable for the direction of his meditations. At one period in Steiner Street I would find my mind wandering during practice, to engage in marvelous adventures and invent interesting conversations, while I played more or less automatically in a sort of happy trance. Naturally my parents couldn't know that an abstracted expression and glazed eye were symptoms of absent-mindedness rather than of concentration on the task in hand, but fortunately I myself realized what dangerous habits I was slipping into and was sufficiently worried to jerk myself out of them.

Perhaps a sense of responsibility, if keenly honed, can become anxiety, and perhaps it was anxiety to justify myself which led to my mismanagement of the Mendelssohn Concerto at the age of seven, in a contest which proved to be my last. Alternatively, I maybe just wanted to show off. Midway through the Andante, the adjudicator, Alfred Hertz, a bearded, brass-loving German of Bismarckian girth who conducted the San Francisco Symphony Orchestra, rose to challenge the fast tempo I had set myself. I explained that I wanted to get to the lovely third movement before my time ran out; as if I feared that only allegro fireworks could ingratiate me with my judges, that the prize would be laid in forfeit before I showed my stuff, that there wasn't a moment to waste. In spite of its faults, this performance gained me a bursary of twenty dollars a month for ten months. I could wish it had done me the greater service of teaching respect for every kind of music, but as was soon revealed, this was a lesson I had yet to learn.

We mortals at odds with our mortality always fancy a limit, an ultimate trial, a judgment to end all others. Mine was the Beethoven Concerto. It stood in relation to the rest of the violin repertoire as Men-delssohn's sparkling third movement to the Andante. Not yet eight years old, I had already learned various "student" concerti (de Bériot's, Lipin-ski's, Spohr's), the Bach Sonata in G Minor, which had sealed with glory Persinger's first lesson, the Mendelssohn Concerto, Lalo's *Symphonie Espagnole,* the first movement of Paganini's Concerto in D Major, the Tchaikovsky—wolfing down this huge corpus, hair, nails and all, like a glutton starved by the conviction that what he is eating isn't quite "real." The lengthening list served less to teach than to graduate me, creating an instant past, a biography-cum-repertoire which raised me aloft without giving me a sense of stature. I felt like a baby on stilts.

It was on a Wednesday afternoon that Persinger agreed to unleash me upon the Beethoven, provided I master the Mozart A Major. I am as unlikely ever to forget the day as a primitive to forget his first dance in the hide or plumage of a totem. Here at last was a promise of authen-ticity! Playing Beethoven would lend substance to my empty bulk and legs to my unjustified altitude. He would make me massive, tall, real. Mozart was the last trial before initiation. In eight hours of concentrated practice between my twice-weekly lessons I memorized the A Major and played it for Persinger. A crueler man than he would have thrown me a coin, complimented the monkey and suggested tunes more appropriate to the hurdy-gurdy, but Persinger mercifully lost his temper for once—in the middle of the Andante. "Go home!" he said angrily. "Use your good mathematical head and figure out for yourself the exact rhythms. I don't want to see you again until you have given thought to every note in each movement!"

His rebuke brought down upon my good mathematical head Imma's wrath for good measure. Failing was a relatively venial sin. To fail craving success marked me a common *arriviste.* To skimp one's duty, to hope that a slipshod second best would pass muster, was to betray the endurance, the self-discipline, the standards of the Cherkess. And to have thus disgraced myself publicly was double indictment. The harshest penalty Imma could impose was the very penalty by which ancient Athens tamed citizens whose ambition might disrupt the body politic—ostracism. I was confined to my room and fed a solitary meal. My sisters safely abed, Aba, under Imma's supervision, laid a strap to me, ruefully whipping the air, and convinced by his own show of violence, fled in terror. Strange justice, you may think; but I, who, being myself whatever my age, considered it natural for an eight-year-old to play the Mozart A Major well, found the punishment condign. Hubris is hubris, whether one reaches for Beethoven or the cookie jar. Even if guilt and gorge did not rise in me together, I may well have felt relieved rather than resentful; relieved to slow down, to find constraints placed against the tyrant who drove from behind and beckoned from afar; relieved to play Mozart, with whom I felt comfortably my age.

You may be sure I approached him warily the next day. The Adagio in movement one offered poor grounds for friendship. How insolent of him to invite a broad smile! Movement two recalled Persinger's score slamming on the table. The third movement . . . Well, we were about to exhaust his topics of conversation when I found myself utterly seduced by the passage in A minor that gives Mozart's concerto its nickname, "Turkish." How could my sense of humor have been so blunt as to miss this delightful episode which wandered over from *Die Entführung aus dem Serail,* startling the classical minuet with Turkish military buffoonery? or the ascending phrase that concludes the work on an inconclusive note, as if to pull a well-upholstered formula from under somnolent lords and ladies? or the gypsy elements that normally made my ears prick? At any rate, Mozart having won his way into my heart with Oriental tricks and enchanting burlesque, I became enthralled by his least grace note. It was love at second sight.

Only one thing marred the awakening. After a lesson that easily made amends for its predecessor, Imma drew Persinger aside. I knew her well, it seems, for my worst fears were borne out several minutes later on a tramcar carrying the three of us downtown to an audition with Ossip Gabrilowitsch. I had played badly; my teacher scolded me; I had played well; he congratulated me. I was a boy; he was a man. What could have been safer, tidier? Certain gestures excited certain responses, mistakes did not bring a fall from grace, one lesson followed another, I could expect to remain myself from one week to the next so long as he was he, administering these custodial sequences. What would I not have given to see the curtain fall before the denouement of Imma's script, to have been able to silence the apology Persinger made me at her behest! It came out, despite my entreaties, instantly transforming revered mentor into humili-ator humiliated, me into the instrument of humiliation. It was Imma's proud conviction that her children should not be castigated by outsiders; Persinger's reproof had to be erased from an otherwise clean record.

These years of my becoming acquainted with the violin were of course punctuated—as earlier years had been—with frequent attendance at concerts to hear the great musicians of the day. No visiting virtuoso, certainly no violinist, could pass through San Francisco unmarked by my adoring observation, and as far as possible, what I heard in the concert hall was rerun on our wind-up Gramophone at home to serve as ideal models for my own attempts. The swarthy Carichiarto apart, the first visiting soloist to impress me, almost as much by his swaying stance as by his wonderfully voluptuous sound, was Mischa Elman. A pupil of Leo-pold Auer in Moscow, Elman was the Russian-Jewish violinist *par excel-lence,* whose music came from the heart and the gut and rose to every opportunity for rich vibrato and affecting portamenti and slides, even to those opportunities which the "best" taste might not allow. I admired him greatly. Elman was soon joined in my gallery of heroes by Jascha Heifetz and Fritz Kreisler, and until the *coup de foudre* delivered by Georges Enesco at the Curran Theatre, this trio who had, it seemed to me, only the violin in common shared my awe and the flattery of my imitation among them.

I must have been seven or eight and Elman visiting San Francisco for the third or fourth time in my concert-attending experience when Persinger decided to produce me for the great man's inspection. An audience was arranged at the St. Francis Hotel, and I recall being hardly less keen to satisfy my curiosity about hotels than to play for my idol. Not that hotels were totally unexplored territory: shortly before the en-counter with Elman I had returned to the Fairmont to play to the Pacific Ladies' Musical Society, a group of kindly matrons who felt it their duty to encourage young talent, and as there was quite a crop of San Francisco talent, tidily gathered it into an annual event. (As a beneficiary of their interest, I should have responded with simple gratitude, but what sticks in my memory is my gloom at being called "cute." Had the dear ladies exclaimed "Isn't he strong!" I would have been highly pleased; had they observed "Too fat!" I would have accepted it philosophically. Instead they found me cute and cut me to the quick. I had my revenge, on that occasion or a later one, when one lady gushingly told me I was "just like Paganini." The example of Imma's balloon-bursting tactics served me well. "Have you heard Paganini?" I countered.) The displays of young talent arranged by the Pacific Ladies took place in some public place, ballroom or drawing room, furnished with gold chairs and chandeliers and with a stage in one corner. Before the interview with Elman I had never seen an individual hotel bedroom, and foreseeing they might feature in my life, was anxious for a first glimpse. It proved discouraging, the room dim and dismal, facing a noisy street, not at all like home. Aba and I sat meekly until called upon, observing the visiting personage and his impersonal surroundings, and leaving the burden of conversation to Persinger. For something to say, Persinger, who held Pablo Casals to be among the greatest of living musicians, as well he might, asked Elman if he had lately heard him play. With perfect naturalness and spontaneity, Elman dismissed the suggestion: "Casals? Oh, but he's just a cellist!"

It was Picasso, I believe, who declared that great art should cure toothache. I became aware of its therapeutic property when my playing of the Adagio from Bach's E Major Concerto made my mother smile. It was the afternoon practice hour, Imma was preparing dinner, and I was alone, playing away beneath a framed picture of my grandmother. These everyday circumstances suddenly brought forth the truth. In some mysterious way my heart and mind met Bach's, and at least four times in succession, the Adagio delivered its undiminished message to the empty room. My elation conjured an approving wink from the picture on the wall and where the door usually opened on a frown, on this afternoon Imma opened it jubilantly and might have gathered me in her arms if affection had not, at the last moment, saved face by embracing a proxy. Returning from work just then, Aba was met with such laughter and effusiveness as would sustain him for months to come. The ministering fantasies this scene inspired were incalculably more grandiose than Picasso's: I beheld myself as a peace-maker destined to cut Gordian knots, to adjudicate instantly the neurotic quarrels we pursue with one another, to make people evacuate their fortresses and stage a global embrace. Perhaps the knots left uncut, the briefs unresolved and the ramparts still standing should teach an artist to modify the scope of his aspirations. I have never resigned myself.

3

Family
Life

Aba was never at a loss to channel his energies and passions. Apart from the full-time task of earning a livelihood, he had ever the causes of justice and progress to engage his sympathies and give meaning to existence. His involvement in the world had not always been so sure of its objectives, however. He told me that during his boyhood in Jerusalem he was often perplexed by the striving which kept creation, human and animal, so constantly busy from birth to death, and would ask his grandfather what was the point of it all. Could it be that fanatically held convictions are sometimes only a filling for that void which the human being alone among animals creates by his insistent questioning of God and ultimate purpose? I suppose that such puzzling must be common to childhood, for several times I experienced something like it myself. One moment from my ninth or tenth year sums up many others. I was sitting alone in our car on a street which runs from Golden Gate Park to Temple Emmanuel while Hephzibah took her piano lesson. Suddenly everything round about me appeared preposterous. Watching people walk straight ahead in such earnestness, I could no more assign pith and weight to their motives than understand the feelings of ants in an ant hill. It was not snobbery, mind you, for my own life seemed as absurd as everyone else's, and indeed my own absurdity was the crux of the matter.

It was curious both to exist and to look upon oneself existing.

Certain conditions were necessary: I had to be alone, there had to be a lapse in routine, time had to stand still. Then it was as if a switch had been flipped, putting me into another gear from the rest of mankind, subtracting me from the human species upon whose cavortings I gazed with uncomprehending eyes. When the world resumed its normal rhythm, the problem of fitting words to this extraordinary sensation defeated me, but the momentary detachment remained in the undercurrents of my mind until, the conditions fulfilled again, again it took me by surprise.

Visionaries all seem to agree that our apprehension of reality is misleading, and science, demonstrating that what is solid is full of holes, that what is inert is alive with motion, gives substance to the visionaries' claim. It may be that meditation is nothing more than the cultivation of awareness beyond the observable, a retreat into a general or metaphysical state preceding the particular and physical; and that if we could evolve techniques which enabled us to submit the particular to the general, we might return enriched for having translated the one into the other and bridged a gulf in comprehension. Children, I think, approach such an awareness more readily than their elders. Still close to his point of departure yet awake enough to wonder, a child can withdraw from the circumstances of every day into that reality before birth, whether it be race memory or collective unconscious, which holds his essential self; and from this earthly analogue of the viewpoint of eternity, must necessarily find the world out of focus.

I wonder if there is not a tremendous shift in a child's life, either before birth or after it, from object to subject, from being pushed into existence to becoming the pusher, surviving of his own volition. If there is such a shift, one takes time to adjust to it. Had I been hungry or shelterless, I imagine the basic motives of existence would have been absorbed very rapidly, but with every want supplied in childhood, motives had to survive by proxy, sublimated into playing Bach and forming views on right and wrong; and in this suspense between fact and fantasy, it was only too easy to miss the point. It may be thought that early dedication to music was purpose enough for one lifetime. True, I earnestly desired to play the violin and in my playing to express joy and longing; no less true, I was capable of intense feeling, interest, concern or outrage according to circumstance. But again and again it would occur to me that my life was as selfish as it was senseless. How could one reconcile a strictly personal determination to achieve with the long-range aim of the deity or the unfolding destiny of the universe? What could it possibly matter if one did well or badly, played this music or that, or lived or died? For many years I wondered whether I would be able to work up any kind of enthusiasm for survival or for great activity to fill the time thus won, and even today, when the importance of detail no longer escapes me, when the ants scurrying about their own small concerns are seen to balance ecology on their backs, I still sometimes catch myself being involved with something—the length of a note, the teaching of string instruments, the desirability of electric cars—and draw back in momentary confusion to take a longer view.

As far as I remember, I never voiced the nihilistic doubts that seemed to challenge my family's whole way of life, indeed our lives. This may seem strange, since my need for moral rectitude reflected my parents' own high ideals. But what child is so articulate, or so unguarded, as to bare the dim and muddled depths of his soul? Very few, I think. The part of life we put into speech is the respectable part which is fit for public view; suggestions that would sabotage everything, including our own security, are left submerged. Furthermore, trusting myself more readily to music than to words, I had a means of expression which took care of most needs and in the violinist's daily solitude found the more reason for confiding myself to it. Finally, our life was so ordered that it was itself an argument against the delusions of anarchy.

To raise a gifted child is not unlike raising a cretin, I imagine. The exorbitant demands it makes can neither be ignored nor be reduced to normal measure, and the special concentration it attracts necessarily overturns ordinary priorities. There is no doubt that I shaped my parents' lives as much as they shaped mine, sending them traveling back the way they had come, drawing them into my career, leaving them without employment when in the end I left home. But for all that, I believe my sisters and I would have been the objects of no less care and organization had we never played a note. What I supplied was the framework, and perhaps the excuse, for their acting according to principle. Both Aba and Imma had very definite views on the upbringing of children and neither under any circumstances would have been greatly tempted to entrust the task to others. Fortunately in the 1920s the laws of California did not oblige them to do so.

I went to school for precisely one day, at the age of six, by which time I could read quite well and write and calculate a little. Tremendous discussions preceded the experiment, whose brevity suggests that my parents thankfully accepted the first token of its unwisdom to return to their basic convictions. My one day was not unhappy but bewildered.

Very quietly I sat in the class, the teacher stood at the front and said incomprehensible things for a long time, and my attention eventually wandered to the window, through which I could see a tree. The tree was the only detail I remembered clearly enough to report at home that afternoon, and that was the end of my schooling. Some time afterward Hephzibah attended this same school for a whole five days, at the end of which the superintendent asked for a private interview with my parents to tell them their daughter was backward; whereupon Hephzibah too was whisked home and within the year fluently read and wrote. After two failures, a third experiment for Yaltah was never even thought of.

So we were educated at home. What did we lose thereby? Most obviously we lost acquaintance with other children. By the time I was ten I was used to adults taking me seriously but was only on tentative speaking terms with boys and girls of my own age. The academic gains and losses of the system are harder to weigh. If we didn't take mathematics beyond the beginnings of algebra and geometry, nor even study physics or chemistry, nor learn Latin and Greek, I believe that the languages and literature we did concentrate on were taken beyond the levels offered by most schools. I was thirteen and my sisters nine and seven when a holiday at Ospedaletti was celebrated by daily readings from *The Divine Comedy* in the original.

For the refinements of foreign languages tutors were to be engaged, but in the early days in San Francisco my parents divided educational responsibility between them, Aba taking care of the sums, of course, and Imma, who had no mathematical skills whatever, looking after the other fundamentals. Later, geography, of a more three-dimensional than statistical kind, was to be a by-product of our lives, and what may loosely be called the social sciences were a constant accompaniment.

Aba's turn of mind was in the tradition of the real Russian socialist. He worried about what to do *for* people in general rather than *with* them individually, not so much taking them into his confidence or spending time with them singly, as constantly anxious to see action taken which would improve the lot of the masses. Any social injustice enraged him, but optimism survived repeated disappointment. Between his evocations of a great future and Imma's of a great past, the present could seem a dwarf begotten too early or too late. She couldn't have cared less what direction it took, but he followed it closely. She scorned newspapers while he devoured them: *The New York Times*, the *Jewish Newsletter*, especially *The Nation*, a liberal publication whose editor, Oswald Garrison Villard, was Aba's idol. He talked politics at table. Almost as soon as I could read he would daily clip items from his newspapers for my perusal, the newspapers themselves being forbidden me on the grounds that vice and violence were unsuitable fodder for a child's imagination. Sometimes the clippings would include the political topics which interested Aba, but he also studied my taste and chose stories about new inventions, adventures in jungles, attempts to fly by the sole power of human limbs, and suchlike boyish preoccupations. Like most American boys of my generation, I was fascinated by gadgets and machines, and now judge that as a conversationalist I must have been rather dull. (I still receive packets of clippings from my father. The subjects have changed and they come by mail nowadays at well-spaced intervals, but the practice, partly practical imparting of information, partly ritual expression of a relationship, continues.)

Protected as we children were from casual infection by other ways of life, we nevertheless knew, if at several removes from the actual, that strife, trouble and injustice were features of the world outside. Indeed I owe to both my parents, because of the utterly different loading of their moral compasses, the uncomfortable ability to see three sides to a question and the corresponding inability to identify with the group. Jews though we unequivocally were—the fact proclaimed by most of our acquaintance, my own defiant name, and the source of our income—we yet did not observe Jewish customs. On the other hand, a point was made of not spurning them ostentatiously. While my father continued his employment in San Francisco's Hebrew schools, we would never be seen driving the car on a Saturday, and it was only a blunder on my foolish part that led me once to remark to the rabbi, Aba's nominal employer, that at our house the corned beef was pinker and had fat around the edges. Our Jewishness denied virtue to no one. Particularly for Imma, a person's quality was in his or her authenticity, not in the reflection of race or class or public acclaim. Thus she valued Mrs. Wessels, an old Catholic lady engaged to watch over us children on those rare occasions when my parents went out without us; and thus she later had her reservations about Toscanini. Estimating so highly the free-standing individual, having a sense of style which ignored surface manifestation to find justification at the core, she would flinch from certain Jewish manners which she ascribed to the confined circumstances of the ghetto; but equally, and in family tradition, she would fight for Jews and Jewry under attack. Today I find myself in exactly that position.

The great virtues of home education were undoubtedly the amount of personal attention accorded by teacher to pupil, the swift progress thereby made, and the correspondingly short time devoted to lessons in the course of the day. We got up at seven o'clock, no hardship in San Francisco's invigorating mornings, and after breakfast and bath I practiced my violin until eleven o'clock. Then followed an hour in the open air when the sun was at its height; then luncheon, usually at home, sometimes a picnic on the beach; then a rest. The afternoon began at three o'clock with lessons which ended soon enough to permit a few minutes' running about before I rounded out the workday with an extra hour of practice from five-thirty. By seven I was in bed, and though bedtime moved later to eight and later still to nine, it never got beyond that hour, no matter how old I was, except of course on concert nights. The schedule was to lengthen, to fill out and grow more various in detail, but essentially it remained the same, acquiring by its continuity in change an outline firm enough to last until we grew up. The result was a coherence in family life which allowed all manner of speculations on the purpose of the universe without threatening the fabric of existence.

Almost from the first breath I drew, I was aware that the day had so many hours, each with its appropriate activity, but such regulation left no sense of harassment; on the contrary. Time was precious, but it moved slowly. The night before a holiday it moved so slowly that I developed a defense against the anguish of waiting for it to pass. I would divide the hours that stood between the present and the moment of departure in the morning into minutes, the minutes into seconds, and then begin to count off this astronomical total. It proved a useful device, for I never got beyond a thousand or so before falling asleep. Holidays, leisure, were as vital as work, and considered to contribute equally to our physical, moral and spiritual make-up. Thus the hour of outdoor exercise was never trespassed on by other duties. Hephzibah, Yaltah and I were to become familiar with parks the world over, being at different times released at the appointed hour to purge our high spirits in Central Park, the Bois de Boulogne, the Tuileries, the Tiergarten, Hyde Park, Sydney Botanical Gardens, and numerous counterparts elsewhere. But none of these celebrated pleasure grounds can efface from my memory Steiner Street Park, which, typically for San Francisco, was on a hill. No more than a couple of blocks from our house, it daily offered expanses to run on, vegetation to hide in, views to look at, fresh air to breathe, scope for imaginative games and, when we were older, courts to play tennis on. Earlier we had our own particular version of tag, whose arcane rules, invented by myself, made the simple business of flight, pursuit and capture a perfect logarithm table of points lost and won and led to much shouting and expenditure of energy.

We lived by daylight. Perhaps as a consequence I hated working after the sun went down. On those rare occasions when some act of God or man had put our schedule out of joint, the idea of unpacking my violin and playing away alone by the light of a single bulb filled me with desolation. Like many children, I was afraid of the dark. Sometimes I got out of bed in the small hours to stand by the window with my eye on the gas lamps in Steiner Street until the good man's coming to put them out told me that dawn was breaking; then I would return to bed without a qualm and sleep blissfully. If I wakened to the silence of the sleeping house, I would strain for the least sound that might tell me I was not alone, that everybody hadn't died in the night—hence, too, the reassurance of my parents' muffled laughter over the books of Sholom Aleichem. Even morning couldn't entirely banish anxiety. Uninstructed by familiarity with grandparents, I imagined Aba and Imma perilously old as they reached the end of their twenties, and did not altogether put this fear behind me until each in turn had safely embarked on the next decade. Were Aba half an hour late returning from work, I was straightaway convinced something terrible had happened to him.

Goodness knows why I should have been haunted by disaster. Perhaps the very tranquillity of our days seemed to invite expiation; or the closeness of the family conjured a dreadful alternative in my imagination. I think mine was a worrying nature in both senses of the word. I wanted everything to be supported by reason, and that reason to be clearly visible. Some question would make me uneasy—why green was green, for instance, or where the weight of gasoline went when it was burned up, or the point or pointlessness of existence—and I would tease the problem for hours on end. Not all my troubles were kept to myself, but faced with elucidating the mystery of green, the adult world proved so unhelpful that I deduced the existence of a policy to withhold fundamental explanations from children. It didn't occur to me that a puzzle which surely countless generations had contemplated might not have an answer; nor that my parents might not be omniscient.

Fortunately there were my sisters. They were always ready to receive what speculations I chose to let fall, accepting everything—views on music, the rules of the game, the possibility of traveling to the moon in a spaceship made of diamonds, this being the only material I conceived proof against the journey—with the respectful trust of acolytes.

The Menuhin family in San Francisco, 1924

Yehudi, age nine, 1925

Hephzibah and Yaltah, Paris

Yehudi with Louis Persinger

Sidney Ehrman, age 102, 1975

Yehudi on his first voyage to Europe, 1926

Fritz Busch and Yehudi in Dresden

With Adolf Busch in Basel, 1929

1931

The family in the garden at Ville d'Avray

At Carnegie Hall, 1933

Hephzibah and Yehudi
at Ville d'Avray

Yehudi and Hephzibah

With Hephzibah and Yaltah
in the Botanical Gardens,
Sydney, 1935

With Nola
in England, 1938

My place in the family was a very happy one, because I was the only boy, the first-born, but also because I had above me two elder beings and below me two younger, a symmetry of love to frame me, the one side matching the other in devotion.

Common sense concludes that Hephzibah must have been two or three, I six or seven, before extended communication was possible between us, but in my memory there is no gap between my delight and wonder at the newborn infant and her being my constant playmate, my other self, so close to me her hand did not feel foreign to my touch. Hephzibah (whose name means "the desired one") had always a strong perception of other people. In childhood it made her a most rewarding daughter and sister, quick to catch hints, to follow clues, to guess intentions; in adult life it has found expression in her involvement in social work and, less formally, in the presence of a warmth and serenity that put at ease everyone who meets her. As for Yaltah, fragile and wayward where Hephzibah was dependable and dutiful, she started life under two handicaps: Imma's disappointment that she wasn't a boy, the shadow of which somehow survived my mother's scrupulously impartial treatment of her daughters; and the inevitable exclusion from Hephzibah's and my already established and self-sufficient pair. I would rather not admit that we often made her our butt. We did. We loved her and were cruel to her, and Yaltah would take refuge before the mirror, dressing and redressing her long blond hair. The only unruly one of the three of us, the most spontaneous, she was repeatedly jerked back into a restraining reality from her dreams.

I can't pretend that the Oriental emphasis on the male left our household unmarked, but it never, curiously enough, made a difference to what we children were expected or allowed to do. In this respect, my mother's principles seemed more attuned to women's liberation than to ancestral ways. My sisters learned no womanly arts, whether of kitchen or drawing room, and were as helpless about the house as I was (it seemed not to be a disability when, eventually, they became wives, mothers and hostesses). Their lessons were my lessons, with the piano substituted for the violin and a shorter daily practice exacted. Outings were organized for all of us, to concerts, to Pantages' annual variety show, occasionally to a cinema on Fillmore Street, where a pianist still accompanied the silent drama flickering on the screen. We played and worked and studied at the same hours, and until I started touring, we were always together, myself the undisputed leader.

No doubt we supplied for each other the friends we would have made had we gone to school, but for all our dependence on one another, our lives were not wholly without other children. Having children of her own had not quenched Imma's interest in young people, only restricted the scope of its operation. When one of us acquired a teacher or a benefactor, we all got to know his or her family and would, for instance, visit Persinger's home on Sundays to play with his children or go on joint picnics with them. Such diversions were not allowed to overturn our timetable, but were provided with suitable slots in it, and no slot existed for the casual stranger. The discipline affected parents as much as children. Only very, very rarely did Aba and Imma indulge what must have been a natural desire to go out for an evening with other adults. They were always there, at our beck and call. As a result, life was private, compact, regular, ordered, its surface so much of a piece that any break in it had tremendous power to thrill. Just such an exciting dislocation of the pattern was my first meeting with the composer Ernest Bloch.

Even in a life crowded with incident Bloch would have been a memorable figure. He was the musician as Old Testament prophet, whose speech was thunder and whose glance lightning, whose very presence proclaimed the divine fire by which, on occasion, a bystander might feel himself scorched. I was to see him often in afteryears, so that my picture of him now is a palimpsest of many meetings and I can't recapture the innocent eye which first viewed him. I recall, however, that then in his forties, he seemed to me the incarnation of the patriarch. The overture to our encounter was an invitation to the home of Mr. Lichtenstein, a member of the San Francisco Orchestra and a friend of Bloch. It is the outing at bedtime which remains in my mind more clearly than what the composer said or what, if anything, I played for him. Subsequently Bloch visited us at Steiner Street once or twice and, with typical lavishness of heart, composed "Avodah," a short piece for violin with piano accompaniment, and gave it to me (avodah is a Hebrew word meaning "work," but with an added significance of religious dedication). All the music I had so far played was by composers dead and gone, or at least distant and unknown; to have a composition by a living master and written especially for me was a matter of great pride and excitement. I was to play it many times in many countries.

Music has never been abstract for me, and at that time it was peculiarly the expression of realities beyond my young horizon, suggesting experiences of living and traveling outside the confines of childhood and San Francisco. So with Bloch's music: close to me by reason of its Jewishness, it nevertheless hinted at vast distances and spaces. I don't think my impressions falsified it on either account. The difference between what someone appears to be and what he imagines himself to be is sometimes wide. Both judgments may be off center—as possibly his own and others' were of Ernest Bloch. His public image was that of a great Jewish composer, his private hope to be recognized as a composer with more claim to the title "American" than most. That he was indeed a very great Jewish composer was a truth he could not escape: he wrote a complete Jewish service, a noble and deeply moving work; he wrote many other pieces on Hebrew themes; his very appearance fitted the part; but to pigeonhole him as "Jewish" was to do him less than justice, for he was a great composer without any narrowing qualification whatever, and a forerunner of the world of music which has superseded dodecaphony and returned to counterpoint and modal juxtaposition. Bloch had spent much time with the Indians of New Mexico and studied their music very deeply. This knowledge, and the inspiration he drew from it, entitled him, he felt, to be considered more genuinely American than many a fellow composer who ignored the modes of native folk music to rely solely on European musical traditions. Before the United States had officially sanctioned a national anthem and was still hesitating between "My Country, 'Tis of Thee" and "The Star-Spangled Banner," Bloch hoped that the hymn ending his Fourth Symphony might be preferred to either. This happiness was denied him: as all the world knows, "The Star-Spangled Banner" was finally adopted. During the Second World War, I was to play it untold times and appreciated its martial virtues, although the unaggressive nobility of the chorale "My Country, 'Tis of Thee," better known to the British as "God Save the Queen," appealed to me more.

Apart from an extra-long siesta, and when Ezra Shapeero came to board with us, his company at table, life on concert days was even more usual than usual. As always, practice and outdoor exercise occupied the morning, a rest and lessons the afternoon. I would not remove my cotton knee pants for a velvet pair and my worn sweater for my best shirt until the very last minute. Ezra's presence in a routine otherwise unchanged was a happy inspiration: it put the coming concert in its rightful place as one event among others in a world where many people lived their different lives. Similarly, the reviews in the next morning's papers were never shown me: the concert was over and forgotten; what mattered was the agenda for today.

Between the ages of seven, when I made my first professional appearance, and twelve, when touring began, Aba and Imma allowed me to give no more than one or two concerts a year. As their very infrequency risked elevating them to special occasions, it was all the more necessary to behave as if nothing out of the ordinary was happening, and in my perception of it, nothing really was. True, the concert had the importance of a key event, the test, the proof and the promise of a career, but by the same token it was the whole point of the exercise. It was not playing for myself that had spurred my three-year-old ambition, but playing what others might want to hear and thus forging contacts between human beings; to find myself giving a concert was, for me, the most natural thing in the world. I never had to count the seconds the night before.

The various "firsts" that launched my career have left small mark on my memory. My formal debut on 29 February 1924, when I was seven, consisted of a performance, accompanied by Louis Persinger at the piano, of de Bériot's "Scène de Ballet," inserted into a program given at the Oakland Auditorium by the San Francisco Symphony Orchestra; which, if I am not mistaken, was repeated in San Francisco itself a few days afterward. Apart from the excitement of these appearances, I remember little about them, but recall far more clearly a pre-debut, non-professional performance at a children's Christmas concert a few weeks earlier. Every year a huge Christmas tree from the Sierras was put up in the civic auditorium and decorated with tinsel, and thus festively caparisoned, the great hall was delivered over one afternoon to the children of the city, several thousand of whom filled the seats while some dozen others provided the program. It was apt that my first real public appearance should have been before so vast an audience, even if my contribution to the afternoon's excitements lasted no more than five minutes, if that. The next year saw my first appearance with orchestra, in a performance of Lalo's *Symphonie Espagnole*, at the end of which the conductor, Alfred Hertz, lifted me off my feet with his embrace, pressing my face into his beard, which felt like a moist whisk broom. Then, on 25 March 1925, a month before my ninth birthday, the Scottish Rite Hall in San Francisco was engaged for a first full-length recital.

Thus gradually I became known in my home town, met my first audiences, received their acclaim, and absorbed the experience into a life scarcely altered by it. Approaching the question in their different ways, my parents met in a united refusal to exploit their children. First of all, the family was sacrosanct. Secondly, we had our routine, which was different from other people's. Thirdly, children were not objects, nor possessions, but their own flesh and blood, welded with them into a unit, no part of which could be exhibited without the whole suffering from the publicity. Aba had further motive in his disgust at the thought of exploiting a child's earning power. Concerts were necessary, at first as a test of achievement, later as a means of support, but at no time in my youth were they allowed to challenge the emphasis on family life and on the children's primary duty to study and to learn. As hitherto, time remained too valuable to be wasted on the idle curiosity of the outside world. Hence there were no interviews with newspapers; hence requests to play privately for some society's special occasion or in some rich lady's salon were equally refused; and hence we grew up naturally, shielded from the world of inquiry which would have turned us into self-regarding freaks if it could. I can't thank my parents enough for having had the common sense to regard us as normal children and the strength to resist contrary pressures.

In the autumn of 1925 the family faced the first breakup it had ever known. Persinger's plans to base his quartet in New York that winter left us with the alternatives of going with him or going without his teaching until he returned to California. It was a major decision. If we chose New York, it meant separation, for of course Aba could not leave his work for so long a period. The sacrifice he had not been able to make when Imma wished to see her mother he now steeled himself to make on my account. It was the first time we children had been parted from him, but we were young, taking part in an adventure and secure in Imma's custody; for Aba, the most desolate of us all, it meant his first parting from her.

He came to see us off on the *Overland Limited* at Oakland Pier. As once before I had been entrusted with escorting my mother on an expedition in which Aba did not share, so now, with the train on the point of leaving, he made me aware of my importance as the only man in the party. Solemnly and secretly, almost as if it were a rite of initiation, he confided to my keeping a little bottle of smelling salts, which I was to hold in readiness should Imma ever feel faint. I didn't keep my grave responsibility very long. Perhaps my solicitude betrayed me, perhaps the smelling salts were discovered when I turned out my pockets one night, but in whatever fashion Aba's precaution came prematurely to light, to Imma's amusement. She took the bottle in charge, assuring me that it would not be needed. I know now that even if she *had* felt weakness she would never have betrayed it to children dependent on her, but in the drama of our first separation this occurred to me no more than it had to Aba, and I was very proud of the trust he had placed in me.

The *Overland Limited* joined Oakland to Chicago, taking sixty hours about it. From Chicago to New York took another twenty hours on the *Twentieth Century Limited,* so that to cross the continent was a considerable undertaking. If equally long, this first eastward journey was more comfortable than the westward trek my parents and I had made seven years earlier. We engaged a room of our own, drawing room by day, sleeping compartment by night, which had its own water supply and lavatory. I was to become very familiar with such rooms in my touring days, when Aba and I shared them first with Persinger, later with different professional accompanists. Each drawing room had an upper and a lower berth, as well as a narrow divan. My place was always the upper berth. I became adept at scrambling up to it, to read in cozy contentment as the train swayed and sped across the United States, but on this first trip, when the experience was new, I sat at the window to see the scenery fly past and follow our progress on a map thoughtfully supplied by a friend of the family, Dr. Samuel Langer. Little did I guess how well I would come to know the different stops—Reno, Greenville, Omaha and the rest.

Several days after waving goodbye to Aba at Oakland Pier, we arrived, dizzy with movement and distance, in New York. It was like arriving in prison or in hell.

For all San Francisco's dramatic setting, the tilted streets giving a thousand vantage points upon the tumbling Pacific or the flat waters of the bay fringed by rising land, it was a human city where people lived in human-sized houses on human terms with their neighbors. The beauty of land and water, the relative cleanliness and quietness, the relaxed intercourse between people, added up to something I recognized as happiness when confronted by New York's terrifying canyon streets with the darkness of November closing in upon them; with the noise, dirt and stench of the subway; with haunted, tormented New Yorkers fighting for their lives (it seemed to me) against winter and wages and the pressure of constant scurrying crowds. My jaundiced nine-year-old judgment of my native city has, with the intervening years, only come to seem apter, although the countless visits I have since made to New York have revealed to my reluctant appreciation some of its excitements. If one climbs out of all that happens at street level to some great height dominating the sprawling metropolis, one is rewarded with a tremendous sense of animal exhilaration which perhaps no other city gives; but one must come down again to live. I have never quite banished my early prejudice against New York, and I suppose I never shall, in spite of friends, memories and a lively appreciation of the city's cultural excitement. Perhaps my reservations come from the conviction that New York should be the leading city of the world; but it seems to have missed its chance or to have thrown it away.

My father's absence no doubt aggravated homesickness, but as the future was to show, my preference for San Francisco was too deeply rooted to be effaced by family reunion. When Aba and I later toured the United States, my spirits and his would rise accordingly the farther we traveled west. With four months to endure before the trip home could begin, that first New York winter announced itself as depressing, something to be suffered with Cherkessian stoicism and forgotten as soon as possible (for months after that winter I crossed out the words "New York" whenever I saw them written), but even at the time there were compensations.

First of all Imma found us an apartment on a height, somewhere around 115th Street in the Columbia University area, from which we could look out over a modest segment of the earth's surface. Then there was the first really cold winter of my experience, bringing with it snowmen (built on the windowsill), a sled, and our being decked out in suitable clothes at Stern's department store on Forty-second Street. I was rather pleased with my new coat, a sort of teddy-bear garment described as chinchilla and in fact made of wool with a very thick, almost curly, nap. Within easy distance of our apartment there was Morningside Park, not as pleasing as the park on Steiner Street but a tolerable substitute, where the sled could be put to use. Above all there were frequent visits from Sammy Marantz, who came up from New Jersey to keep us company, and one evening—probably New Year's Eve—prevailed on Imma to accept an invitation to a party, leaving him in charge of us children for three or four hours.

An important experience was my first close encounter with medicine, hitherto observed only from the viewpoint of the patient under the stethoscope. On her return to New York, my mother got in touch with some of the friends made ten years earlier, among them Dr. and Mrs. Garbat, who had played a part in her life and Aba's and were to do so most generously in mine. Rachel Garbat was the only daughter of a well-to-do tea merchant, Abraham Lubarsky, whose liberalities in the Zionist cause had included a Sabbath meal on Friday evenings offered to Palestinian scholarship students such as my father had been. Rachel herself, as open-handed as her father with time and energy, was a patron and friend of musicians, and she and her husband—an excellent musician though a doctor of medicine by profession—lived at the center of New York's rich musical life. In a more literal sense they lived in two adjoining houses on East 81st Street, between Park and Lexington Avenues, using one as their home and the other as Dr. Garbat's offices. I date a lifelong interest in health, sickness and treatment, whether fringe or traditional, to the chance I had then to visit his consulting room, examination room, medical laboratory and library, and be impressed with such a quantity of books, files, machines and all manner of surgical paraphernalia. As will be seen later, I owe the Garbats a still greater debt, but in the winter of 1925–1926 their importance to me lay in the fascination of Dr. Garbat's profession and the occasional company of his son and daughter, Julian and Fifi. Another of my parents' friends whom I then met for the first time was Rabbi de Sola Pool, for whom Imma had worked as a teacher of Hebrew on her arrival in New York. In Palestine the rabbi had witnessed the influx of Jews from Russia, almost every other one of whom, he would tell me, disembarked with a violin case in his hand: to such a degree was music their symbol of liberation.

Music, having brought us to New York, was not neglected when we got there. Apart from practice and lessons, a new venture was tried. For some six or seven Thursdays, with Imma beside me, I attended sight-reading classes at the Institute of Musical Art (later rebaptized Juilliard). One faculty member, Dorothy Crowthers, was apt to describe me in later years as having stood foremost among my older classmates, but I think she had an indulgent memory, for my ear, which did very likely distinguish itself in solfeggio, proved stone-deaf to the nomenclature of harmony. Then, as now, I trusted music and viewed language askance, and a siege force could not have driven home those terms. I felt uncomfortably self-conscious in the anonymity of the classroom—too great a contrast, no doubt, to home, where the very clarity of our identities made it unnecessary to think about them. There had been an earlier experiment, even more short-lived, of exposing me to something resembling a class: in San Francisco I had briefly joined a children's orchestra, to gain a little experience of orchestral music rather than of children. Perhaps if one or another of these sorties into group life had been sustained, I might have grown up relating more easily to my fellowmen. On the other hand, and perhaps because they were not persevered with, my childhood was remarkably free of the deforming effects of competition. The standards against which I measured my achievements were the highest, and the attempt was made in reverent awe, not in a desire to be acknowledged superior.

About the time the sight-reading classes were renounced I was given my first Italian violin, a seven-eighths Grancino. My benefactors, a Mr. and Mrs. Rosenberg of Chicago and an unmarried gentleman who taught Hebrew at one of the schools Aba superintended and who was, by a curious coincidence, called Mr. Rosenthal, among them donated the eight hundred dollars for its purchase. Here was a "bed of Roses" to brighten exile and give rise to a recurrent dream which made New York nights warmer than days. I recall this much: Fritz Kreisler walks onto the stage of Carnegie Hall. The ovation swells, then dies abruptly when people, among them myself, seated in the first row, notice something peculiar. He is carrying two identical violins. From the edge of the platform he extends one to me and says in a solemn voice that easily carries through the hall, as if this constituted his recital, "Take it, my child. It is yours to keep."

I found Kreisler immensely attractive: Where musicians are often nondescript offstage, or else a mass of professional stigmata implying the absent instrument as a horse's swayback implies an absent rider, he, like Georges Enesco, had the self-sufficient demeanor of an aristocrat. The name Kreisler meant a certain sound before the sound became incarnate. Dazzling as Heifetz was, I felt confident that my "Perpetuum Mobile" and "Dance of the Goblins" held their own next to his. Kreisler mystified me or rather defeated me. The Heifetz sound lay on the surface of the records I played, wed to grooves, arm and spindle like a beautiful ribbon spooled at seventy-eight revolutions per minute. The Kreisler sound was all subtle emphasis, innuendo, dropped hints which those primitive recordings and I caught as best we could. How I longed to play "Schön Rosmarin" or the "Caprice Viennois" with such chivalry! Child though I was, I knew the missing factor in my imitations was experience of life. Only much living could hoist me to that level where tenderness and sophistication cohabited.

The Persinger quartet rehearsed in a duplex on Lexington Avenue belonging to Mrs. Cecilia Casserly, a distinguished patron of music and a charming *grande dame* who, from the time she generously allowed Persinger to give me lessons in her house, remained my friend until she died. From our apartment on the West Side to hers down in the Seventies was a longish journey, always made on foot, but to reward effort there was splendor at the end of it. I had never seen a place so elegant. A minstrel's gallery overhead particularly caught my fancy. Here indeed was a house built with music in mind! Unhappily these agreeable surroundings witnessed one of the few rebuffs of my life.

Although the praise or blame of newspaper critics and the flattering comments of the public at large were kept away from me, enough reaction leaked through the protective barriers to establish a pattern: criticism came from within the family, especially from Imma; adulation from outside it. Imma's praise, being rare, was not only highly prized, but also served to devalue other praise, no matter how fulsome. However, just as her encouragement was the more important for its rarity, so, and for the same reason, someone else's discouragement was rather shattering. Among the beneficiaries of Mrs. Casserly's musical concern was Nikolai Sokoloff, by then making his name as conductor in Cleveland. On a visit to New York he heard me play, and although he was very pleasant at the time, somehow the word got back to me that in his view any of the first chairs of his orchestra could play as well. This may not seem a very condemning verdict on a nine-year-old, but so unused was I to disparagement, it seemed a terrible wound. The wound healed, of course. Sokoloff was one of the first conductors I played with outside San Francisco, and I played with him many times, to our mutual satisfaction. But I never discovered if the report of his dismissive remark was true.

Three weeks before we were to go home, Aba persuaded the San Francisco Jewish community to send him to inspect Hebrew schools elsewhere, including New York. Before he came, there was a long correspondence between him and Imma—conducted by telegram and letter: no doubt coast-to-coast telephoning was possible, but not yet an everyday means of communication to us—to decide whether I should give a concert in New York or not. The decision was in favor, after consultation with Persinger, who was to accompany me. The Manhattan Opera House was engaged and the arrangements entrusted to a gentleman called Loudon Charlton, but perhaps Aba didn't find Mr. Charlton active enough, because as soon as he reached New York himself, he began mailing programs, distributing tickets, marshaling friends, contacting newspapers and alerting musical patrons. Our last three weeks were as lively and high-spirited as our first three months had been sober and withdrawn. On 17 January 1926 Persinger and I played Handel's Sonata in E Major, Lalo's *Symphonie Espagnole* and the first movement of Paganini's Concerto in D Major to an audience which included no musicians of note except Walter Damrosch. It did, however, include three elderly gentlemen sitting side by side in the front row: Papa Heifetz, Papa Elman and Papa Max Rosen. The reporter who said he espied them may have invented their presence to imply that the recital was not only a musical event but a rite of entry into a highly exclusive musical club, a super Bar Mitzvah as it were, in which the celebrant achieves divinity and his father joins the front rank of angels. Aba's efforts to convoke the powers that be had rounded up a *minyan,* the quorum of Jewish males needed for public religious service.

Then we left New York. My father's commission took us south, via New Orleans, and west, via Los Angeles. Imma found it peculiar that, on a guided tour of Los Angeles, our guide bothered drawing our attention to the home of Douglas Fairbanks and Mary Pickford. Who in the world were they?

Like seeds walled up in an Egyptian pyramid for millennia, which will sprout if only given air and water, certain impressions, ideas, enthusiasms may lie dormant within a life for many years before some impulse from events brings them to blossom and to fruit. I have spoken of influences upon me originating further back than consciousness or even independent life; and of shaping experiences—natural sounds, Anna Pavlova's beauty, the fascination of medicine—whose impact I can trace to a particular time and circumstance. Some of the seeds thus planted had to await my own maturity to mature, some grew as I grew, and some needed only a short measure of patience to be fulfilled. Of these last, the most important was the idea that one day I would work with Georges Enesco.

He came to San Francisco when I was seven or eight, to conduct his own symphony and play the Brahms Concerto, and before a note was sounded he had me in thrall. His countenance, his stance, his wonderful mane of black hair—everything about him proclaimed the free man, the man who is strong with the freedom of gypsies, of spontaneity, of creative genius, of fire. And the music he then began to play had an incandescence surpassing anything in my experience. In afteryears when I knew him intimately, saw him at times almost daily, watched him age, I never had the least cause to qualify this first judgment—if judgment isn't too cold a word for my wholehearted response. At eight years old, however, I had no reason to suppose I should ever see and hear him again, unless he undertook another American tour and again stopped a night in San Francisco. It might be thought that thus uncertain of a second encounter, I would feel deprived or frustrated. Not so; the seed was put away to incubate quietly and when we traveled to Europe three years later, I knew who lay at our journey's end. That my boundless reverence for him should win me his care and protection had the inevitability of something totally right.

To get us to Europe, however, involved a sequence of events so blessedly improbable, in the manner of a fairy story, that I daresay a writer of novels would blush to invent them.

The first actor in this truth stranger than fiction was Dr. Samuel Langer, he who had given me a map of the United States for the New York adventure. Dr. Langer was the superintendent of a Jewish orphanage, consisting of his own house and several other houses, each lodging twenty children or so, and the whole complex set in pleasant green grounds. He was a good friend of my family. Quite often we would visit him, his wife and his daughter, Ruth, at the orphanage, to be shown around the buildings, see what the orphans were up to, play with them, take part in raffles to raise money for them, and so on. In return Dr. Langer took a friendly interest in me. Shortly after my debut he drew my name to the attention of one of the best-known Jewish philanthropists in the city, Sidney Ehrman, a lawyer of great wealth and established family who had founded an educational trust for gifted orphans. By way of Dr. Langer, Mr. Ehrman offered my parents a sum of money, but as in all good fairy stories, a reverse or two had to be undergone before the happy ending. Aba and Imma turned the offer down on the grounds that they didn't need other people's money to bring up their children. Undaunted, Ehrman persevered and the question surfaced again in March 1925.

As already recounted, in that month I gave an orchestral concert and my first recital in Scottish Rite Hall. Still warm from the excitements of the recital, I was in the artists' room when Aba ushered in a tall, handsome gentleman wearing a dinner jacket. His demeanor was so elegant, the brief comment he delivered himself of so flattering, my father so manifestly proud, I could not account for Imma's reserve—neither then or later when we encountered him together with his family at the main exit. A Rolls-Royce drew up. Imma refused the suggestion of a ride home, explaining we had made other arrangements. Her other arrangements got us good and wet, as it took some few minutes to find a cab in the pelting rain.

Mr. Ehrman—for the urbane figure in the artists' room was indeed he—had earned Imma's second snub by proposing to sponsor my education abroad. He was not a man easily thwarted, however. Whether making money or giving it away, he rose to adverse situations, and several days after Imma's verdict appealed it in person. Like two attorneys prosecuting one another in defense of the same client, each set forth his brief. Imma declared she would sooner see her son a shoemaker than a

violinist if the life was to spoil him; furthermore, no good justified breaking up her family. Mr. Ehrman foresaw no inescapable degradation in
his scheme and dispelled her fears of separation by explaining that he
proposed to finance the family as a whole. However reasonably he
pleaded (and he was not a lawyer for nothing), I wonder if his plea
would have won him his suit in Imma's rational mind at any other time;
or if the fact of her having already decided it would soon be time to
discover our European heritage was not the clinching argument (in fact,
another whole year was to pass before we went abroad, and Mr. Ehrman's first gifts to us eased the interlude in New York). What is certain,
once she accepted his arguments, she accepted him, the only benefactor
about whom she had no reservations whatsoever. His modesty and authority, the splendor which rejected *éclat* and the patronage which made
no claim upon the protégé, merged into her prototypical image of a
Caucasian nobleman. Indeed he had qualities which drew devotion from
everyone who knew him.

He adopted us, not simply for a subsidized year or so, but into his
heart for life, and we children promptly recognized the bond of kinship
by calling him Uncle Sidney. My own father apart, no man has had a
greater title to my filial affection, not even my revered masters, Enesco
and Persinger. From the moment he won Imma over, family life took on
a new and larger dimension. As well as the generosity which realized our
dreams, he brought us a sense of human standards, the wisdom and
scope of an exceptional personality which comforted, strengthened and
inspired. Strong yet humble, wise yet simple, humorous yet serious,
benevolent yet selective, with the charm of intelligence and cultivation
allied to true sympathy, he was a shining example of what a man can be.
Thus he remained to me for fifty years until his death in 1975 at the age
of 102.

Like many another in my life, Uncle Sidney had been a violinist as
a young man. Apparently when he was courting his wife ("Aunt Florence"), he would become terribly impatient with the shortcomings of her
piano accompaniment, but this cause for dissension disappeared when he
gave up the violin for better things. His violin, a Guadagnini, he did not
give up until, having had it repaired and restored, he gave it to me. I still
have it. Both Uncle Sidney and Aunt Florence belonged to old San
Franciscan families, "old" in this context implying at least two or three
generations of wealth and influence and at any rate long enough for
wealth no longer to be valued in itself but for what it could achieve.

Their family was as close and loving as my own. As well as themselves, it consisted of young Sidney, then a university student, and Esther, with whom I fell in love.

As I have said, I was usually in love with someone. Once seen, Esther Ehrman outshone all previous incarnations of the beloved, and so remained the Dulcinea to my Don Quixote until I grew up. I doubt whether it was necessary that I should have seen her at all to be smitten, for the Ehrman daughter, beautiful, glamorous, elegant, mysterious, would by hearsay alone have occupied a very special altar in my childish imagination. Having met her, I needed few further encounters to feed my devotion. As it luckily happened, there were recurrent meetings across the years, each meaning a great deal to me. One incident affected me as powerfully as ever medieval knight was affected by the gift of his lady's glove at the jousting: after the first movement of the Tchaikovsky Concerto one evening in San Francisco's Civic Auditorium, I was groping in my pocket for a handkerchief when Esther, seated next to Imma in the first row, stood up and gave me hers.

Esther was almost ten years older than I, her brother a year or two older than she. Enrolled at Berkeley, he once invited Imma and me to luncheon in his rooms, showed us around the campus, then brought us back to hear his favorite records—a song by Lotte Lehmann and Heifetz playing Debussy's "Maiden with the Flaxen Hair." Young Sidney adored Debussy, an unusual enthusiasm in San Francisco at the time and another sign of the Ehrman family's wide cultivation. The desk at which he worked in that room on the Berkeley campus he gave to me when, having graduated, he went to England to pursue his studies at Cambridge. I was immensely proud to own anything of his, for Sidney, like his parents and sister, was haloed by my admiration. He deserved no less. He had inherited his father's human qualities and his distinction of mind. But all this youthful promise and brilliance were tragically cut short in 1929 by a fall on the hunting field. Terrible months followed, as operation succeeded operation to repair the injury to his skull; to no avail. Nothing more impressed me about Uncle Sidney than his extraordinary resignation during the months of suspense and after the death of his only son. Never embittered, as tender and solicitous of others as before, as ready to be interested in their concerns, unchanging in goodness, sweetness, humor, he left me an image of high human valor rarely equaled. Esther lived to marry and to mother a family; she too died before her father, but she left her children and her children's children to honor his old age.

Uncle Sidney's impact on my youth was to open up windows on the outside world. He took me to my first opera and to my first show in New York; he gave me my first book on Greek mythology; he played chess with me, and when I won a game one evening, celebrated my triumph with the gift of the works of James Fenimore Cooper. He introduced me to sports more taxing than games of tag, providing at different times swimming lessons, horses to ride at his country house at Lake Tahoe, speedboats for expeditions on the lake itself, and a bicycle. The bicycle arrived at Steiner Street very soon after the crucial interview with Imma, but as ill luck would have it, Alfred Hertz happened to be lunching with us that day. Brought up to believe that musicians should cherish their hands against the bumps and bruises of normal living, he held up his own hands in alarm and dissuaded my parents from accepting the infernal machine. Taking their refusal in good part, Uncle Sidney replaced it with less fatal playthings, but he had planted an idea which would germinate in my mind. If I felt no rancor when the bicycle disappeared, I was nonetheless confident that one day I would ride one. Several years passed before I did, and then it was in the gentle countryside of Ville d'Avray, near Paris, a more kindly setting for one's first bicycling falls than the steep streets of San Francisco. Perverse though it may seem, the ban on bicycles did not extend to automobiles, and as soon as I could legally hold a license, at the age of twelve, Uncle Sidney had me taught to drive. My instructor was his chauffeur, Barney, who had been sent from England in attendance on the Rolls-Royce. It was not in this noble vehicle, however, that I changed my first gears, but in the Ehrmans' second car, a Packard. Barney was the first Englishman I knew, as quiet, competent and thoroughly British as the motorcar he served and an excellent teacher. By the time I took and passed my test, I was at least as good a driver as a violinist.

But antedating most of these benefactions and revelations and more important than any other was, of course, the journey to Europe and Enesco.

As soon as a year in Europe became a practical possibility, Persinger saw the chance of my profiting from what he accounted most valuable in his own life: the guidance and example of the great violinist Eugène Ysaÿe. Persinger had first heard Ysaÿe during his young prime, twenty-five years before, in the Leipzig Gewandhaus, and immediately fell under his spell. One can easily imagine why. There stood a Jovian figure, a man so immense that a viola in his arms would have seemed no bigger than a violin and his Guarnerius three-quarters size, drawing with across-the-string sweeps and his incomparable vibrato sounds as warm, as rich as the instrument has probably ever produced. To him Chausson had dedicated his "Poème" and César Franck the A Major Sonata; to him Debussy had entrusted the first performance of his Quartet. Like Bernhardt in the theatre, Ysaÿe was a representative of the grand manner—perhaps, like her, the greatest such representative and certainly the last. After auditioning some four years later in Denver during his future master's American tour, Persinger began lessons with him that summer, the summer of 1905, in his country house on the Meuse in Belgium. He recalled, among other delightful anecdotes, that Ysaÿe would improvise accompaniment and play so beautifully his pupil felt compelled to listen. Indeed the sap had never stopped flowing through Persinger's memory of those days. I am convinced that in 1926 the summer of 1905 was still green for him and, so he thought, waiting for me. Letters were sent to Brussels, winning Ysaÿe's agreement to an audition, and thereafter it was accepted by everyone that Brussels was our destination. But not by me. It was time for another dormant seed to sprout. I was quite sure we were going to Enesco.

Whether Brussels and Ysaÿe, or Paris and Enesco, our new language would be French. Some time before Uncle Sidney's philanthropy made a knowledge of French a matter of some urgency, Imma had introduced me to it. Herself a linguist and well-read in the half-dozen tongues she spoke, she wanted her children to have what best she could give them. Accordingly, when I was nine she engaged a tutor named Rebecca Godchaux, one of four sisters, none married, who with one brother lived together in a remarkably closed, compact group uncomplicated by anyone of a younger or older generation. Although they differed in appearance and character, their ideas and language were so uniform that they seemed one person duplicated several times. A conversation begun with one sister could be continued with another without any sense of transfer, and when for some reason Mlle Rebecca was unavailable, her place in my life was smoothly assumed by Mlle Joséphine.

The first lesson, or rather its aftermath, I shall not easily forget. After teaching some idiomatic phrases, Mlle Godchaux read a brief poem about colors and flowers, to impress upon my ear the euphony of French. Imma quizzed me all the way home. When it became apparent that I had not forgotten any words, she rhetorically asked if I would care to memorize the poem. Would I indeed! The supper table cleared, we began. It was amusing enough at first, until a longing for sleep crept over me, whereupon syllables that had flowed stuck fast to one another like hardened treacle; every new line memorized dislodged several others. Bedtime had come and gone. Still Imma would not release me, barring the exit with that indomitable Cherkess who "never left anything unfinished." I didn't know whether to pity that poor Cherkess, who must have died an early death, or to wish he had died more definitively. Anyway, here was Yosemite revisited, Imma awaiting the proper sounds with ruthless tenacity, I feeling drowsier and drowsier, Aba trying in vain to intercede. When I staggered out to the porch—it was midnight, I believe—nothing made sense; yet the next afternoon I found myself reciting the poem without a slip. Mlle Godchaux, unaware of the flesh sacrificed to every line of her poem, would for decades thereafter advertise my remarkable linguistic gift.

At his house in the orphanage, Dr. Langer gave us a farewell luncheon on the day of our departure. Esther Ehrman was there to see us off and, quite aware of my infatuation, presented me with a Chinese puzzle ring. How I prized that ring! My violin case became its shrine, not only for this one year's absence from Esther and San Francisco but for many, many years. We left in a torrential downpour. On the train at Oakland other gifts awaited us, including a photograph of Persinger. It bore the following inscription: "To dear Yehudi, hoping he will one day develop into a great artist—one who will prove to be not only the *master* but also the worthy *servant* of the Beautiful. With the love and admiration of his friend and teacher, Louis Persinger." Persinger always kept my response, as I his photograph:

Sweet Master,

As the train is going eastward, within me are growing sentiments. For as soon as we parted last night I felt that lonely sensation, that one which I had a year ago for my father. Indeed, Mr. Persinger, you are my father of music. I have never felt you so near to me as I do now. Wherever life brings me, whether east, west, north or south, I will always hear your sweet voice. That voice which oft-times corrected me, and if I would be without it, only God would know the kind of life I would lead.

Your loving pupil
Yehudi Menuhin

The excitement of adventure carried its measure of sorrow. In a life of partings and leave-takings I have learned that it always does.

4

Eastward
to Home

Normally Imma made a boat or a train home away from home·so that
our routine was never completely disrupted. Crossing the United States
for days at a time, we children were made to run up and down the
corridor to ensure our limbs their regular exercise, and I had to practice
as best I could over the click of wheels on rails. I have since worked
untold hours on trains, gradually learning how to be comfortable about
it: sitting cross-legged, propped on pillows, enjoying both the view and a
pleasant timelessness induced by motion and isolation which proves propitious to experiment and to work.

Our first Atlantic crossing, in late 1926, was an outright holiday,
however, and we made the most of it. What mind-boggling sights,
sounds and smells the world offered! I may have lived by the side of the
ocean all my life and many a time boarded the ferryboats which linked
San Francisco with neighboring towns, but this was the first actual ship
of my experience, and had I grown fins and gills in celebration of the
novelty, it could scarcely have seemed more marvelous. Aboard the
French Line steamer the *De Grasse*, after an initial moment of queasi-
ness—my first and last subjection to seasickness—my sisters and I lived
in a condition of feverish discovery for the width of the Atlantic.

And if the ship had granted novelty enough for half a lifetime, Le
Havre—it was clear when we landed—had no intention of restoring us

to the familiar. Through the confusion of my first impressions, people moved and talked so briskly it seemed we had not traveled from hemisphere to hemisphere but from earth to some other planet, which revolved about the sun every twelve hours or exerted barely enough gravity to keep its inhabitants surface-bound. A little gnome of a porter approached us. Measured against our thirteen valises, his shortness and thinness suggested a comic turn or an impossible challenge, but technique is all and those were hard-working days. He slipped a leather strap through the thirteen handles, bent down, heaved ho, and instantly disappeared beneath the mass, moving toward the boat train like those haystacks on wee human legs one sees moving across Swiss meadows, in his free hand an extra case or two. Only eight years after the First World War, there were everywhere still signs of depletion of manpower and women doing what in America was man's work. Aboard the train in the wake of our luggage, I marveled at the grim, black-frocked lady who punched our tickets and (by way of gracious contrast, perhaps?) at the old-fashioned lace antimacassars on the seats, with the railroad company's insignia woven into the design. Late in the evening we got to Paris and the Hôtel des Saints-Pères and were sent to bed. The boulevard was still noisy with taxis, their klaxons fitted with rubber bulbs which, when squeezed, emitted an almost animal sound and filled the night with croaks and gasps of varying pitch and intensity as if a friendly garrulous zoo had been let loose beneath my window. Klaxoning was allowed then, even at night; it was only when organic croaks gave way to the electric horn's insistent, aggressive blare that the Paris city fathers revolted and put a stop to it. I lay awake listening to the jolly hubbub, thinking how different this night was from others, and anxiously wondering if, after a whole fortnight without practice, I could still play the violin.

Busy days followed. An apartment was found, the thirteen valises unpacked, the family settled in, practice resumed, arrangements concluded with Eugène Ysaÿe for the planned audition, and then one afternoon, Imma and I took leave of Aba and the girls and set off for Belgium on the last lap of the pilgrimage whose outcome would or would not justify all our long journey. Our appointment with Ysaÿe being fixed for a morning, we spent the night before it in Brussels.

My having recognized the supreme master in Enesco did not, however, reduce this visit to Brussels to a perfunctory duty. I had been brought up to regard Ysaÿe as superhuman, a colossus striding the world, and I believed what I was told. Unfortunately neither Persinger nor I had any of his recordings (it was only some fifteen years ago that I first heard any, and found them indeed overwhelming); but awe of his grandeur, power, verve and spirit had been implanted in me by report. True, Ysaÿe's greatness, which I knew only by hearsay, was a less potent attraction than Enesco's greatness, which I had seen and heard for myself, but nonetheless it was in a state of reverent suspense that I sat with Imma in the taxi carrying us to our rendezvous. Alas! In place of the giant of my childish vision, I found a too human man in too human surroundings.

Ysaÿe's house stood on a tree-lined boulevard in the Upper Town. We rang; time passed; finally a young lady, Ysaÿe's second wife, appeared wearing a dressing gown. Although her apparel was, goodness knows, perfectly appropriate at nine or ten in the morning, it struck me as dissolute, for I had never opened my eyes upon a woman who wasn't already dressed and working. She led us up two flights to a large room where, amid scores strewn everywhere and overstuffed furniture, Ysaÿe greeted us from an armchair; still an imposing bulk, but old, ailing, decayed, chained to his chair by (as I afterward learned) a diabetically gangrenous foot. The Guarnerius lay on a table beside him. After Imma had removed my coat, I played at his request the first movement of the *Symphonie Espagnole* (this was the first piece Persinger had ever heard *him* play). He, in turn, pizzicatoed chords, and so deftly as to create the illusion of an orchestral accompaniment, pausing only to watch my hands more closely. "You have made me happy, little boy, very happy indeed," he said. If only he had then dismissed me! For me, the performance had been less an audition than homage offered to a venerable king, terrifying in his obesity, remote, laden with age and honor. I had executed a brilliant passage and received his benediction. I had been faithful to Persinger. Now I could go, scot-free. Imagine then my surprise to hear him request that I play an A major arpeggio in four octaves! I groped all over the fingerboard like a blind mouse. "You would do well, Yehudi," he said laconically, "to practice scales and arpeggios."

We left as we had left the old man with a violin signboard over his front door six years before: down the dark stairs, fleeing a certain dilapidation. This time I was also fleeing some prophetic advice, but there was nothing else to be done.

If I felt I couldn't accept Ysaÿe's advice, nor his offer to teach me, the fault lay in my stars perhaps, or at any rate in the temperament I was born with. He might have added method to my working day (among much else besides, no doubt) and thereby shortened the long search for understanding I ultimately had to make, but learning an imposed method seemed not in my nature. In dealing with people I was, as I am, very trusting; in dealing with ideas, opinions, traditions, techniques, I never took anything ready-made, but reserved judgment until I had personally tested the matter. Music was something very alive to me, an essential means of expression, and I suspect that unending hours of work on dull material might well have blunted rather than polished my interpretation of it. Nor am I alone in this, I think. I have since seen how very rigid teaching of music, such as has been systematized in Russia, can steam-roller individual expressiveness into anonymous brilliance, so that only the most irrepressible survive the course with personality and musicality intact. Of course I don't wish to imply that Ysaÿe would have ridden roughshod over my finer feelings; only that what he might have given, I was not able to take. If it was unorthodox, my development as a violinist was nonetheless valid. Mine was an inspired way, shown me by inspired teachers, not mastery of scales and arpeggios; it was recognition of greatness and response to it.

We came back to Paris. Shortly afterward Enesco was to give a concert, which we would attend, of course, and which furthermore was my long-awaited chance of making myself known to him. This time, Imma told me, I must take my future in my own hands. Unsupported by parents or sisters, a very scared child indeed, I stationed myself in the artists' room after the concert until the serried mob overhead thinned into a half-dozen grownups. Poor Enesco! If he thought that seven more autographs would settle the evening's account, he had not reckoned correctly; only six people disappeared with a flourish of his pen hand—the seventh held fast. After all, it wasn't a memento, it was his soul I had come for. "I want to study with you," I said without further ado. Our conversation ran somewhat as follows:

"There must be some mistake. I don't give private lessons."

"But I *must* study with you—*please* let me play for you!"

"That's impossible, my dear child. I leave Paris in the morning," he explained, looking at Gerard Hekking, the cellist, who kept autograph seekers in line, as if to enlist his support.

Between the two sentences a policy had become a plea of inconvenience, and a plea of inconvenience invites inconvenience. So my proposal to play while he packed his valises left him no alternative but to reinvoke the policy or abdicate it altogether. Something must have disarmed him, my defenselessness or my urgency or his failure to think of a better reason why I shouldn't come. As soon as he capitulated, I felt perfectly certain he accepted me from then on as his charge, and when

Aba and I arrived at his apartment on the rue de Clichy at six the next morning it was, as far as I was concerned, for my first lesson. And so it proved.

Enesco wasn't just a teacher; indeed he never so described himself. He was the sustaining hand of providence, the inspiration that bore me aloft and that Ysaÿe, for all his massiveness, could not have given me. To be sure, I knew Enesco hardly at all—of his inner life I knew only what the violin could tell me, and of his face what I had discerned from afar; but the earthy vital tone, the shaggy crown of black hair, the Turkish cast, the aristocratic bearing, his penetrating blue eyes, the Rumanian Rhapsodies, perhaps even the romance with the Princess Cantacuzène, were fragments enough for me to assemble a Byzantine mosaic of Imma's folk hero. The fact that playing the violin represented time stolen from his "real" work—composing—made him triumphantly Cherkessian in my eyes.

He may indeed have had some Tartar blood, or Turkish, Greek, Magyar, or Ukrainian, for he came from Moldavia, a region so chronically invaded that the native Vlachs could not always distinguish their Latin stock from its multiple graftings. One ancestor on his father's side, a precentor named Enea Galin, had his son Gheorge baptized Enesco or "Son of Aeneas," as if to make short shrift of dubious genes with a consummately pure patronymic. Classical reminiscences (for example, the celebration of Roman festivals like Rosalia and Kalendrae), the Orthodox rite, and local pagan beliefs which neither imperial Rome nor the Church had ever quite extirpated mingled in the everyday life of Carpathian villages like his birthplace, whose many-layered culture was further enriched by the gypsies roaming freely about. His two grandfathers were priests and his parents deeply religious. Having lost seven children in succession, they made pilgrimages to various monasteries beseeching God to spare them their eighth, as yet unborn.

> Our house was almost hidden in a copse of acacias and hazel bushes. It was one-storied, with an old shingled roof and whitewashed walls. Along the front ran a veranda, painted blue; ropes of onions hung there to dry. I am a son of the soil, born in a land of legends. My whole life has been spent under the eyes of my childhood deities.

So wrote Enesco. His childhood deities sent him traveling far from his soil, but he never lost contact with it. At five, his musical gift had come to the attention of Caudella, a pupil of Vieuxtemps who gave lessons in Jassy, the Moldavian capital. "Fate," wrote Enesco, "in the person of my father decreed me a violinist." Two years later he was packed off to Vienna, where Hellmesberger at the Konservatorium taught him scoring and chamber music as well as violin. Having won the highest award at the age of twelve, he was relayed in 1893 to the Paris Conservatoire, where Marsick in instrumental technique, Gédalge in fugue and counterpoint, Massenet and Fauré in composition, further groomed his gifts. By 1899, when he took first violin prize, he was already celebrated as the composer of the Rumanian Rhapsodies. With the turn of the century Enesco embarked upon a virtuoso career that swept him hither and thither three seasons of the year; summers he invariably spent in the Rumanian countryside. Just as his musical life was a binary organism, so his physical life came to revolve about two nuclei: 36 rue de Clichy, his apartment in Paris, and a country house called Villa Luminisch, Villa of Light, in Sinaia, Rumania. To say that they housed, the one a supremely urbane man and the other a child of nature, could be to oversimplify matters, however, for, a Rumanian in Paris, in Rumania Enesco was a Moldavian.

The violin, far from being spared his conflicts, became their chief focal point. An ear tuned to polyphony, he complained, could not slake its thirst with monodic expression. Apart from de Bériot's exercises for two violins with double-stopping, which offered him four voices, he preferred to play the piano (and indeed played it masterfully) or, better still, to compose.

> When I gave my first solo performance, as ill luck would have it, I was a success. As the waves of applause rose up at me with the sound of shingle swept by the incoming tide, I heard three times the accursed words: Thou shalt be a virtuoso, a virtuoso, a virtuoso. . . . 'Tinker, tailor, soldier, by all means! But virtuoso? I could see neither profit nor pleasure in wearing motley. That same evening I made a wonderful plan; I would play the violin, play it as often and as well as I could; make money, if not a fortune, buy a piece of land in Rumania, retire there while I was still young and compose to my dying day. . . . Mad about composing, I grudged every minute I had to give to my violin and although I had no delusions about what I was writing, I very much preferred my own humble attempts to the persistent study of an instrument that gave me so little satisfaction in return for all my efforts. I have so often looked at my fiddle in its case and said to myself: You are too small, my friend, much too small.

It wasn't the violin he found too small; it was *his* violin (a Guarnerius).
"Far from despising the violin, I loved its tone—when someone else was
playing! What spells Thibaud's fingers could weave! My own, for all my
zealous efforts, only gave back the mocking jingle: You can do better,
can do better, can do better. . . ." Taken with his other thrice-repeated
phrase, "Thou shalt be a virtuoso, a virtuoso, a virtuoso," it sounds like
command and reprimand delivered by a stern patriarch, or Fate, as
Enesco called him. Composing, conducting, mastering piano and cello
were the profusion of a colossally rich man who always felt a bit impov-
erished by the limits of time and space imposed upon our small lives.

    If a great man entertains doubts, his disciple gives him the benefit
of every one. Enesco will always remain the Absolute by which I judge
others, finding them, but especially myself, wanting. Apart from those
ineffable qualities we gloss over with words like "presence" and the
mystic mantle my veneration threw around him, his musical prowess was
simply phenomenal. He knew by heart the Bach Ur-text edition, fifty-
eight of the sixty volumes having been given to him by Queen Marie in
his conservatory days (of the two missing volumes, one was the Index). I
recall the day he sat at an old upright piano and hammering, crooning,
whistling the various parts, evoked *Tristan and Isolde* more dramatically
than an operatic company—without score, for Wagner too had been
wholly committed to memory. No single feat, however, made a greater
impression on me than one performed during a lesson. Maurice Ravel
suddenly burst into our midst, the ink still drying on a piano-and-violin
sonata which he had brought along. It seemed his publishers, Durand,
wished to hear it immediately (in those days publishers did not accept
anybody's work unheard, not even Ravel's; what would they have done, I
wonder, with dodecaphonic scores?). Enesco, chivalrous man that he
was, craved Aba's and my indulgence—as though I might draw myself
up to my full four feet six inches and thunder, "What a nuisance!"—
then, with Ravel at the piano, sight-read the complex work, pausing now
and again for elucidation. Ravel would have let matters rest there, but
Enesco suggested they have one more run-through, whereupon he laid
the manuscript to one side and played the entire work from memory.
Such mnemonic *tours de force* bore out my conviction that this tree of a
man, as he seemed to me, drew musical intelligence straight from the
source.

    Enesco gave me lessons whenever his concert schedule allowed,
perhaps five in five successive days, then none for a fortnight, but each
one lasting an entire afternoon as if to make amends for their irregu-

larity. A lesson was an inspiration, not a stage reached in a course of instruction. It was the making of music, much as if I were his orchestra, playing under his direction, or his apprentice-soloist and he both conductor and orchestra, for while he accompanied me at the piano he also sang the different voices of the score. There were few interruptions. Sometimes he took up his own violin to illustrate a point of, say, vibrato or glissando; very, very rarely would he give me a dissertation on violin theory, for the circumstances of both our lives short-circuited the clumsy locutions of speech. Having started at the age of five, within no time Enesco played the violin expertly. The superb quality of his trills, vibrato, bowing, he must have had from the beginning, discovering them in himself with no more recourse to theory than the gypsies had, or than, for that matter, Rumania itself required to be the most naturally and effortlessly musical country in Europe. If his innate powers were cultivated in the rigorous classical schools of Vienna and Paris, the schooling in no way dampened their force, nor fastened them down to any man's technical directives. He remained himself. When I came to study with him, I too played more or less as a bird sings, instinctively, uncalculatingly, unthinkingly, and thus neither he nor I gave much thought to theory.

What I received from him—by compelling example, not by word—was the note transformed into vital message, the phrase given shape and meaning, the structure of music made vivid. I was ready to receive it. Music was hardly dead for me; it was a fierce passion, but I had never known it to have such clear and vital form before. When, occasionally, he did use words to make a point, they were not cut-and-dried injunctions, nor ready-made solutions, but suggestions, images, which by-passed reason to infuse the imagination with a completer understanding. He did not impose his views. Unlike most pupils, who do as their teacher or the printed music tells them, I would experiment with different fingerings in search of the "right" one, with the result that every time I played a given piece, it was with a new fingering. All Enesco permitted himself was the gentle observation that it might be as well to settle on one in preparing a public performance. He had the most expressively varied vibrato and the most wonderful trills of any violinist I have ever known. Depending on the speed and lightness of a trill, his trilling finger struck the string higher than the actual note, thus keeping in tune although the light, fast motion of the finger did not push the string to its full depth on the fingerboard. (I still have a copy of Paganini's Sixth Caprice, the trill caprice, with accompaniment by Enesco, which he and I recorded in the

mid-thirties to fill in the last side of a recording of the Dvořák Concerto.
It is a beautiful accompaniment.) Not surprisingly, it was the expressive
side of his temperament which most fired me, to the neglect of his
discipline, and once in a while he would call my too passionate playing to
account. It may have been this fault in me which led him ultimately to
advise that I should study with a different master, Adolf Busch, the
greatest exponent in his day of the pure German classical tradition. His
advice was another example of the selflessness which marked both my
teachers: as Persinger had wished to give me Ysaÿe, so Enesco wished to
give me Busch, wishes as disinterested as they were wise. Neither man
was for a moment capable of wanting to keep the formation, or the
credit, of a pupil to himself.

Above all, Enesco carried me on the wave of his conception of the
music. For years and years afterward I could hear his voice, sometimes in
words, mostly in music, telling me about what I was playing, and as my
experience grew these remembered counsels gained validity. Nothing he
said was wrong, nothing he pointed to misleading. Even insignificant
indications took on ever more weight and value, underlining over and
over again the profundity, the sensitivity, the richness of his musicianship, reminding me repeatedly how right I had been to trust him, how
fortunate to win his guardianship. Today his direct influence is submerged in a conception of the work itself, a conception which is unified,
its elements no longer traceable to distinct sources. I must make an effort
now to recall any specific thing he said, but I know that everything I do
carries his imprint yet.

Paris was the third city of my experience, the second great one. San
Francisco had grandeur but owed it to nature's setting, and wisely its
human architects had not tried to compete. New York's powerful personality derived from the abstractions of money and commerce, which
downgraded its inhabitants to mobs, the city to a corral in which to herd
them. Paris, in contrast, I found a city built for individuals. There was
space for human beings here, boulevards, avenues and streets threaded
the community like the arteries and veins of a living organism, and the
buildings themselves seemed loved. The spaciousness of Paris struck me
from the start, although I could not then explain my admiration in terms
of harmony and proportion, or comprehend the skill which constantly led
the eye down tree-lined vistas to some handsome palace, making Paris a
place of a thousand views, a picture in three dimensions composed with
all the care and cunning that ever two-dimensional picture had. Still

today I marvel at the scope given Baron Haussmann over a century ago to build a city for no more than a few hundred thousand people, and at Paris's now contriving, if not adequately, to accommodate a population inflated many times.

Loyal San Franciscan that I was, I kept bright the thought of my home town throughout the year in Europe, but homesickness was not nearly so troublesome as it had been in New York. For one thing, my father was with us, the family was complete; for another, I felt I was making progress. Early in 1927 I had the good fortune to give a couple of concerts in Paris which were well received. They came about through the intervention of Gerard Hekking, who insisted that Paul Paray, conductor of the Lamoureux Orchestra, should hear me play. The audition and concerts actually occurred in the interval between my bearding Enesco in the artists' room and his subsequent return to Paris, putting me in the odd position of winning an audience before I took my lessons —a back-to-front pattern which was to be maintained in a future. Today it is hard to imagine that an unknown soloist of whatever age or talent might arrive in a town, win a hearing and be inserted into the performing schedule. Such things could happen in 1927. In a funny little old hall before dim rows of empty seats I played for Paray and Hekking and was straightaway invited to perform Lalo's *Symphonie Espagnole* the next week and the Tchaikovsky Concerto the week after. It was a very exciting prospect: these would be not only my first concerts in Europe, but my first orchestral concerts anywhere outside San Francisco.

For the moment these two concerts were my only appearances, but their message, insofar as it was encouraging, had alarming implications for family life. There would be more concerts in the future; concerts involved traveling; San Francisco could not for much longer serve as a base; my father had to face a very grievous dilemma. Should he keep his job and lose his family for many months of the year, or renounce job and salary and put his faith in his eleven-year-old son's ability to earn a living? Granted the Paris concerts were successful, granted Enesco had confidence in my staying powers, but these facts, such as they were, could not help Aba to a decision which must depend upon faith. Nor could Imma help him, long and earnestly though they discussed the matter; nor could anyone else; he had to decide for himself.

Aba had been given leave of absence from the San Francisco schools for our year in Europe. His employers were generous to him: they valued him highly and had he gone back, he would have received a salary of four hundred dollars a month, no negligible income in those days though not enough to support two households, one in Europe, one in the United States. But however crucial, the financial aspect did not begin and end the question. To ask a man to give up his pride of place in the family, to cease to support it, to contrive for himself some other role made up of little duties, was much. To his great credit, Aba handled the problem beautifully apart from one or two moments of great tribulation. The enthusiasm of his nature supported him. He took his new task seriously, organizing trips, coming to lessons with me, taking notes of what occurred there, going over his notes with me when we stopped at a café on the way home, and generally throwing himself heart and soul into the small domestic scope allowed him. Fortunately the touring years were soon to begin, bringing responsibilities in which his gifts could expand. The most difficult time without a doubt was in Paris in 1927, when he put his faith in me and gave up his own work for mine.

With this commitment made and my increasing years, I moved at this point from the feminine to the masculine department of the family. Until 1927 the violin had been in my mother's stewardship, but between Ysaÿe and Enesco it was transferred to Aba's. Not only did he take me to lessons, he would also sit with me reading newspapers while I practiced. Hephzibah and Yaltah, however, remained in Imma's care, and once I had been safely settled with Enesco, it was she who took the initiative to arrange piano lessons for them. From everyone we met who knew the musical world of Paris—not to mention the evidence of a concert we attended ourselves at which he played with Enesco—we were left in no doubt that Marcel Ciampi was *the* man to have if one could get him. Ciampi taught in a studio at the Salle Gaveau, which at that time shared the burden of Paris concerts with the lovely opera-house-type hall at the Conservatoire, now no longer used for the public. So having made an appointment, to the Salle Gaveau we went, and while Aba and I remained downstairs, Imma took my sisters up to play for Ciampi. As Ciampi was to tell the story afterward, he was reluctant to take on these two youngsters aged seven and five, but undaunted by his reticence, they played and won not only his capitulation but a *bon mot* which was to go down in family legend: *"Mais le ventre de Madame Menuhin est un véritable conservatoire!"*—"Mrs. Menuhin's womb is truly a music school!" When Imma had accomplished her task, Aba and I were introduced, and so began an association with Marcel Ciampi which, to my great good fortune, endures to this day. On our return to France in 1930 Ciampi resumed his teaching of my sisters and even gave me a few piano lessons, but for lack of time or talent they were not persisted with. Having failed to make a pianist of me, he has done me greater service by teaching at my school.

Gradually the immense disorientation of moving from America to Europe was smoothed into a routine. In our apartment at 96 rue de Sèvres the pattern of our day was re-created: music and outing in the morning, rest, lessons and music in the afternoon, and early to bed; a pattern disrupted only by occasional excursions outside Paris and rather more frequent attendance at concerts in the evening. In our afternoon schoolwork, French of course assumed primary importance, and a tutor was engaged to give us daily classes at home. Many years after the events recorded here, I received a touching letter from a lady who as a young girl had applied for the job. Arrived at the rue de Sèvres, she took one look at my sisters and myself, all industriously working away at our books, got cold feet and left. She was charming enough to say she had regretted it since. The most modest of our daily outings took us up the rue de Sèvres to the Hôtel Lutetia and back, a more considerable one deposited us in the Bois de Boulogne, where in the first weeks we filled our pockets with shiny chestnuts. We walked almost everywhere, even to Enesco's apartment way north of the Seine, and thus painfully discovered that the sidewalks of Paris were made of harder stone than that quarried for other cities, a material so unsympathetic to the human anatomy that prolonged contact with it induced an ache which worked its way gradually through one's feet and legs up to one's back. If we didn't walk, we ran: my sisters and I had hoops with which we turned Paris into our playground, bowling deftly along the crowded *trottoirs,* dodging housewives at their shopping and strolling old gentlemen, and no doubt being altogether a nuisance to the sober adult world. I can't think why the hoop should have disappeared from toyshops, for there is no more exciting companion on a walk. I became an adept, able to send the hoop racing ahead, to brake it with a touch, or delicately to alter its direction without loss of momentum.

To go outside Paris was a delightful and uncommon experience. We paid our tourists' homage to Versailles, Rambouillet and Fontainebleau, and there was one unforgettable excursion to Barbizon when I saw a summer storm such as never occurs in California: above our heads the sky was serenely blue while advancing from the horizon were black sheets of cloud, ripped by lightning and ominous with thunder, like a stage effect displayed for our applause. In the summer I had the great pleasure of regular sorties into the countryside for lessons at Enesco's little house at Bellevue, near Meudon. This entailed traveling on one of the curious suburban trains composed only of compartments, without corridors, which shuttled between Paris and Versailles very noisily and leisurely, as if pursuing an animated conversation with the Seine, the woods and every whistle stop along the way. Aba and I would so arrange things as to arrive early at the little station with time for a walk up the avenue, through the trees, to the observatory at the top. Although there were plenty of trees in Paris, and the Bois de Boulogne was indeed a tongue of wilderness licking the city, Meudon offered great refreshment to the spirit: the smell of damp earth, the rich vegetation of the Île de France, the bird calls ringing through the woods. One piece studied there, the César Franck Sonata, became so imbued with the place that I only have to play it to see again the room on the upper floor, Enesco at the upright piano, and beyond the open window, the smiling French countryside.

As might be supposed, Parisian concerts widened and deepened my knowledge of music. Several times we went to the Opéra Comique, once or twice to the Opéra itself, sitting way up in the gallery and finding the experience tremendously exciting. Apart from opera, there were many concerts, of course, but the detail of all of them is obliterated now by the glory of the *Eroica* Symphony, first heard in the Salle Gaveau under Paul Paray's direction. I must have heard more than one Beethoven symphony in San Francisco; I had never heard the *Eroica,* and its meaning, its power, its capacity to move were a revelation. Not being tall enough to sit clear of the velvet-covered balustrade in front of the seats, I lodged my chin on the velvet, and so remained, literally transfixed, from start to finish. It was a landmark in my life, balanced a year or so ago by the exultation of conducting the *Eroica* myself.

To concerts we went as a family, as we did almost everything else. Determined not to spend an unnecessary penny of Uncle Sidney's money, Imma renounced entertaining during our European interlude, a renunciation the easier to make since our apartment was too small for parties on the San Franciscan scale, and anyway we knew few people. Hence the months in Paris reinforced family unity, if that were possible, teaching us to express it in a family acronym composed of the initial letters of our five names, MoMaYeHeYa, and thus permitting all to sign a telegram for the price of a signature. An autocratic family sends its telegrams in the father's name, a traditional English family in the names of the parents, but ours was a democratic, sharing family and no one was left out. (I enjoy a symbol which so neatly expresses reality, and am the more happy that my wife and I can now similarly represent ourselves on letters as "Yehudiana.")

Such people as we did come to know had great importance, for their rarity, of course, but more for the novel aspects of the world each represented. There was, for instance, Madame Simon, a patron of music and a friend of the Godchaux in San Francisco, whose beautiful apartment on the avenue du Bois de Boulogne (now avenue Foch, for military men must be honored) was a fascinating object lesson in how wealthy old French ladies furnished their homes, crowding them with a lifetime's collection of *bibelots* and producing an effect of rich personal consciousness unlike anything in my experience. Another acquaintance was Étienne Gaveau, owner of the piano manufacturing firm, who gave us an example of his workmanship for Hephzibah and Yaltah to share between them. I don't know which intrigued me more, Monsieur Gaveau or his piano. The piano was a small grand of blond wood whose ornate craftsmanship seemed marvelous to me after the functional surfaces of pianos in the United States. What most forcibly struck me about Étienne Gaveau himself was his beard. The beards of my experience till then had been rabbinical—long, loose, flowing, constantly pulled and twisted by rabbinical fingers and perhaps, upon close scrutiny, harboring a pea or two from the rabbi's last meal. In startling contrast to such venerable shagginess, Monsieur Gaveau's beard was a short, thick white tuft, neatly tailored to a point. He was altogether a very tailored man, and his apartment bespoke the same elegant grooming as his beautiful beard and pianos. The earliest and dearest of our new friends, however, were the Jan Hambourgs.

Jan was another Russian-Jewish violinist, but of English background. Although he had studied with Ysaÿe and achieved excellence, he neither performed nor taught; he did not need to; his American wife, Isabelle, daughter of Judge McClung of Pittsburgh, was as rich as she was beautiful and distinguished. Their apartment, in a luxurious modern block not far from the rue de Sèvres, faced onto a *cour* planted with trees, and just as their home looked inward, isolated from the bustle of the public street, so did their lives; and the one and the other were new to me. In the United States everything faces out, the way of life no less than the buildings, and the courtyard, which has traveled from the east as far as Britain, has never taken root there. The Hambourgs loved their life and found in Paris its ideal setting; amid good music, good books and good food, they dwelt in perfect contentment, seeing nothing to strive for and feeling no need to strive. We often visited them, and thus on more

than one occasion I witnessed Uncle Jan's constant ritual: every week-
day he attired himself in a wine-red velvet jacket, chose his Amati or his
Peter Guarnerius, and played one of Bach's six works for solo violin,
beginning the cycle on Monday, completing it on Saturday. Like God,
he rested on the seventh day. Some decades ago his edition of the solo
sonatas was published. He knew a great deal about wine and food—indeed he had been elected a member of the Société Gastronomique—and
often Isabelle and he took us to some noted restaurant, where our knowledge of French cuisine advanced by leaps and bounds. Perhaps because
they had no children of their own, Jan and Isabelle Hambourg took a
warmer interest in us three than might be expected of adults of their
sophistication; with the result that windows were opened onto their so
different lives, revealing to us new worlds in the most natural way possible without anyone's troubling to underline the novelty. The greatest
debt I owed them was the friendship of Willa Cather, who had lived
with Isabelle in the McClung family home in Pittsburgh twenty years
before and had never lost contact; but that encounter belongs to a later
chapter of my story.

One visitor met in Paris delightfully bridged the gulf in our own
history. This was Mrs. Cora Koshland, the epitome of an elegant San
Franciscan old lady, of whom the city could boast quite a few, but none
as grand as she. She lived there in a replica of the Petit Trianon, had an
organ built into her house, and when she took her annual vacation
traveled as a matter of course to Europe, ignoring the United States's
eastern seaboard entirely. To have a touch of San Francisco suddenly in
our Parisian midst was an extraordinary sensation. Mrs. Koshland was a
patron of the arts. In fact, she had once organized a formal tea on my
behalf at which it was planned I would receive five thousand dollars in
return for some musical courtesies. The tea was never poured, however,
for my parents would have none of the plan. Taking their refusal be-
nignly, Mrs. Koshland remained a friend until she died, and her daughter Margaret still is one. Two young artists whom she did contrive to
help became our friends in her wake and later our neighbors. They were
George Dennison and Frank Ingerson, who lived together up in the Los
Gatos Mountains, where they turned their hands to any number of
medieval arts and crafts—ceramics, inlay, tapestry, jewelry and so forth.
While we were in Paris, they were in London, studying at Mrs. Koshland's expense. Visiting their benefactor in Paris, they told us of a family
they had met in London, the Goulds, a boy and two girls just like us,
whose mother was a famous musician. Thus from the age of eleven I

knew of Diana's existence. It was to take me another seventeen years to
meet her.

Although Uncle Sidney had set no limit on the time we might spend in
Europe at his charge, we ourselves saw this as an adventure with an
ending which, after a round twelve months, would bring us back to our
starting point in San Francisco. Such being the plan, every minute's full
worth had to be wrung from the experience, and when Enesco left Paris
for Rumania in late summer 1927, there were no second thoughts about
our joining him. So began my lifetime's journey to the East and to the
past, for this was to prove less a lateral voyage than a vertical one, less a
voyage in space than in time.

Its first stages were accomplished appropriately enough by the romantic means of the *Orient Express,* a train which, in an epoch of
railroad travel, had a conviction of its own special glamour as the link
connecting Paris and Istanbul by way of such magical cities as Munich,
Salzburg, Vienna, Budapest, and which further expressed it in exquisite
polished paneling and pretty little red-shaded lights on the tables. It was
also very comfortable: we had two compartments and between them a
washroom to ourselves. When I wasn't practicing, reading, sleeping, talking, learning history from Aba, conjugating verbs for Imma, or jogging
up and down the platform with my sisters at the lengthier stops, I kept
my nose pressed against the window and watched Central Europe unfold
with the uncanny sensation of *déjà vu,* as if the landscape were not so
much out there as in my head, a familiar dream being recapitulated.
Sun, earth, vegetation, apparel—the color of everything grew brighter
the farther we traveled east, the nearer we drew to the regions which had
formed my mother and Georges Enesco, the more profoundly I entered
myself.

The multiple sense that this was indeed a "land of legends," as
Enesco called it, in suspense from ordinary life, and yet one to which I
thoroughly belonged, accompanied me throughout our stay in Rumania.
I felt it in Imma's fitting so naturally into the Oriental setting, with its
gypsies and its marketplace. How well the embroidered Rumanian shirts
became her! Aba bought her several and we loved to see her wear them,
happy and vivid in a country which was almost home. I felt it too in my
father's insouciance. For him no less than for me, Rumania was an
interval in which to cast aside consideration of past and future and live
for the moment. Above all, I felt it in the countryside.

Rumania represented the second impact of nature, but unlike the first at Yosemite when I was six, this was nature and civilization as one. In the United States one leaves the town to find the country. Superb though it is, the countryside produces no way of life, no music or literature, but is distinct from human activity and indeed damaged by it. Here the people and nature were part of each other. The shepherd knew the landscape, every sound, smell and sight of it, and belonged to it as effortlessly as his sheep or his dog, or a mountain or a tree. Equally, the gypsies grew out of the earth and possessed it in their music, and even the upper classes, who came and went from Bucharest and elsewhere, had their place in a feudal harmony which included the land. It was a greater unity than I had ever known, allowing me to move about in it and be one with it, appealing to me for reasons I could not yet recognize or formulate. Imma decreed that we should eat only chicken that summer, for she feared the meat (perhaps a first step toward vegetarianism), but small precautions, or any, struck me as pertaining to another world. In this land what harm could befall one when every step one took was a step on the sure ground of legend, when every face was accounted for and waiting, every instant self-fulfilling? If I felt blissful, what two-dimensional creature would not, suddenly falling into a third where his archetypes became flesh? I had entered imaginations of which I was a figment. I mingled with figures of whom I was a shadow. Time was a great buoyant sea where nothing died, nothing sank irretrievably to the bottom, and I swam in it feeling gloriously real. One night we heard gypsies entertaining the diners at an open-air tavern. It astonished me that they could fetch such extraordinary sounds from primitive instruments, using bows that were saplings strung with unbleached horsehair. At my urging, Aba made arrangements to have them visit our *pension,* where we matched nature against nature, they playing a repertoire as raw as bird calls, I playing the polished equivalent, Tartini's *Devil's Trill* Sonata. Their leader gave me baskets of wild strawberries; I gave him one of my three new gold-mounted Sartory bows.

Sinaia, the small, elegant town where we lived, drew its importance from the monarch's summer palace some three miles away and the consequent annual influx of courtiers. But social distinction, while it dignified, did not rob Sinaia of simplicity. There was a railroad station and not far from it a solid, elaborate hotel of late-nineteenth-century vintage, such as one finds all over Europe; scattered about the surrounding hills were the summer houses of the nobility and rich bourgeoisie of Bucharest; but only a short ramble away the plaintive line of shepherd flutes was to be heard, and peasants brought produce, embroidery and crudely made tools to market as peasants had done for centuries, forgathering at their Oriental bazaar while society forgathered at the thermal establishment. The bearded monks from Sinaia's monastery, founded by an ancestor of Enesco's princess, did not look anachronistic.

For the six weeks or two months that we were there, we took lodgings separate from the *pension* they belonged to, where we lived, worked, practiced, cooked and ate without disturbing anyone or being disturbed. Enesco's house, the realization of his dream and the fruit of years of toil, was some little distance away. He would usually send transport for us, a horse-drawn buggy on which the coachman was perched high above Aba and me. On fine days we sat in the open, but when it rained a sort of hood could be pulled up over our heads from the back, as though we were babies in a perambulator. Amateur of motorcars though I was, I adored our cloppety-clop progress over the unpaved roads and across the swift-flowing Prahova to the Villa Luminisch. Undoubtedly Enesco had bought his estate and built his house for Princess Cantacuzène. His own room on the top floor was approached by a staircase built in a turret at the side of the house, so that his visitors would not trouble the princess in her apartments below. As I was to have occasion to note, her rooms were opulently luxurious in the Oriental manner, but Enesco's studio, if austere, was no less impressive. It had great windows looking out over a valley and beyond to a range of mountains rising up clifflike. Autumn arrived while we were in Sinaia, setting the trees ablaze with color, and the mountains thus glowing, with a lonely fir tree or two in somber contrast to the yellows, ochers, golds and reds of the woods, were an awe-inspiring backdrop to my lessons.

Sinaia invited a relaxation of routine; we accepted gladly. We visited the palace, called Pelesh for the hill on which it stood, and I found it a castle to my taste, medieval as only nineteenth-century castles could be, its countless wooden gables suspended above the forest like a Platonic idea of the Gothic Age. Itself elevated above Sinaia, it stood in an immense open space backed by higher mountains. One day when we were walking in the grounds, a miniature coach drawn by two white ponies overtook us. From his photographs, not to mention the fairy-tale daintiness of his equipage, we recognized the coachman to be Michael, the six-year-old heir to the throne. Feeling envious, I picked up a stone and threw it, rather ineffectually, in his tracks—a piece of childish petulance I have been ashamed of ever since. Later, during a tour of the palace, I contrived to duck beneath a cordon and ascend the throne, to our guide's horror; as might be expected, I found the seat of state too large for comfort.

My crime had no consequences. Indeed the only reprisal was ours. When Queen Marie, Michael's grandmother and herself Queen Victoria's granddaughter, invited me to perform at court, Imma declined the invitation as she declined every other social exploitation of my playing. To reconcile us, Enesco proposed that the queen sit in Princess Cantacuzène's chamber while I had my lesson on the floor above, the studio door left ajar. This was accepted. When the lesson was over Aba and I were taken downstairs to be presented to Her Majesty. I remember the elegance of the room, a great bed, much rich drapery, carved furniture, velvet and gold, and the embarrassing prospect of being expected to kiss the queen's hand. I had never kissed a hand and did not feel like starting (now I can do it almost naturally), so offered my own hand to be shaken. Far from taking offense, the queen was sufficiently self-possessed to conquer by stooping. So we had an amiable chat, eye to eye, whereupon she gave me a copy of her book, *Queen Marie's Fairy Tales*, with the inscription "To Yehudi from Marie."

Another great lady left her mark upon our Sinaian holiday: Cora Koshland interrupted her European tour to descend upon us and give us three fantastic days. She hired three Chrysler cars, solid, open four-door vehicles capable of standing up to the rough roads of the district, and in them we explored the nearer reaches of Rumania. Mrs. Koshland was the magnificent American tourist before her time. Our excursions with her were recorded on a movie camera, including one to some spectacular caves and another to a castle—a genuine medieval castle this time, built as a fortification against invaders, but which, lacking recent invasion, had been transformed into a livable dwelling and thereby lost its grimness. My last view of Mrs. Koshland on this occasion was from the station platform: she aboard the *Orient Express* on its way to Paris, and filming our farewells until she was out of sight. Before very much longer we would be back with her in San Francisco.

Autumn had dwindled to nothing when a telegram arrived from New York, asking my parents if I would perform in Carnegie Hall with the New York Symphony Orchestra under the direction of the great German conductor Fritz Busch, and specifying the Mozart A Major Concerto. What more splendid seal could be placed upon our year in Europe! What greater justification could I desire for Uncle Sidney's generosity and my parents' commitment! I was very grateful, very honored, but secretly, or at any rate in the bosom of the family, I had a reservation: why Mozart, why not Beethoven? To play in Carnegie Hall was to play Beethoven, to arrive was to arrive. Moreover, I felt I would play the Beethoven better, and my parents knew that too. However, as with many another cherished hope—Enesco's tutelage, ownership of a bicycle—I held back my feelings until they could usefully be revealed. I was confident that I would try for the Beethoven and there the matter rested. Carnegie Hall's offer was accepted, the question of what should be performed left in abeyance. I was then eleven years old.

And so we came to my last lesson with Enesco—the last forever so far as I then knew. The storm, threatening as Aba and I left the *pension* that afternoon and climbed into the buggy, held off long enough to allow us to reach the Villa Luminisch. Then, when we were safely in the studio and I playing, lightning split the sky from end to end of the valley, illuminating woods and mountains again and again with fierce and sudden brilliance while the thunder crashed and the rain fell in torrents. Against the magnificent clamor of nature I played the Chaconne from Bach's D Minor Partita three times in succession.

I suppose Enesco wished to test my endurance. To practice is one thing, to perform another, and there is yet a third, requiring more stamina than either, which is to rehearse with one's colleagues, perhaps repeatedly, for a performance or a recording. One must be able to play for three or four hours without wilting, without any loss of attention or freshness; and it may be that Enesco planned an ultimate service to me by insisting on this sustained expenditure of effort and concentration. Bach's mighty Chaconne lasts thirteen or so uninterrupted minutes, in itself no mean test of a boy's powers, and the more so when it follows the other three movements of the Partita, which, however, I then did not know. I played three times and triumphantly survived. At this point Aba remarked to Enesco that I couldn't be described as obsessively hard-working; I did my hours of practice honestly and regularly but never demanded to push them beyond their allotted span, as many a colleague did and does (in my own view, my calmness in this respect was attributable to my possessing good low blood pressure, a blessing which has persisted and probably saved me any number of crises). Enesco was undisturbed. "It's God's gift to him," he said. "It will see him through life." Aba never forgot his words.

The worst of the storm was over, though rain still streamed down the muffled coachman and his stamping horse when we came out of the little turreted porch onto the gravel. My heart was very heavy. Whatever

I had learned, or failed to learn, from Enesco, nothing could change it now. I was on my own, and a few weeks and many miles away, my great engagement awaited me.

After a day or two in Paris we caught the boat train at the Gare Saint Lazare.

The return voyage had an important difference from the outward trip; not that we were seasoned travelers now and above taking pleasure in things no longer novel, but that we came back to a modest fanfare. While still in Sinaia, Aba had made various arrangements to secure a safe launching for my financial affairs, so having left the United States a private boy, I returned with the public dignities of an agent of my own and the services of a lawyer. Uncle Sidney had been appealed to for the name of a New York lawyer—I remember how remarkably the telegraph service functioned then: in the course of a single day three exchanges, that is six cables, between Sinaia and San Francisco and New York were completed and the business settled. The lawyer he recommended was one of New York's foremost music lovers, Edgar Leventritt, in whose memory the Leventritt Award was founded, a noted amateur pianist whose great delight was to fill his house with visiting musicians and play chamber music with them. Mr. Leventritt advised Aba to entrust my American affairs to the agents Laurence Evans and Jack Salter, and drew up a contract with them, but as was consistently the pattern with people who came into our lives for practical reasons, Mr. Leventritt and his wife and children remained as dear friends. So, for that matter, did Evans and Salter. These two young men from Atlanta, Georgia, began their climb to fortune when Galli-Curci chose them as her managers. Thereafter they went from strength to strength, taking on Lawrence Tibbett, Elisabeth Rethberg, and one or two other clients equally well known. I was in illustrious company when my name was added to the bottom of the little list of artists still headed by Galli-Curci.

As our ship reached the mouth of the Hudson, she was met by the pilot tug, aboard which were three or four newspaper photographers, who grouped Hephzibah, Yaltah and myself with violin on the boat deck for an improbable picture which appeared in next morning's press. At the pier a little later, the two young agents made our acquaintance, presenting me with a heavy black-and-white silk scarf to mark the occasion. Never having possessed anything as grand as this, I was terribly pleased and impressed (indeed, nearly fifty years later, it is still in pristine condition, still prized as my "best" scarf).

The flurry of arrival over, the issue had to be faced: Mozart or

Beethoven. Informed by someone, possibly Edgar Leventritt, that I had set my heart on the Beethoven Concerto, Fritz Busch had been dismissive. *"Man lasst ja auch Jackie Coogan nicht den Hamlet spielen,"* he was reported to have said—"One doesn't hire Jackie Coogan to play Hamlet." Inviting me had been Walter Damrosch's idea, not his, and one can sympathize with his gloom at discovering that in this land of philistine entertainments it was not enough to be an outstanding conductor, one had to be Barnum as well. He set himself up as a wall of reserve between me and the nineteenth-century German treasury, hoping that his blankness would induce me to forget my designs upon Beethoven. Walls, however, do not take special notice of other walls; I had as much mortar in my composition as he. Busch finally consented to let me audition for him at his hotel suite. Several days later Persinger (for he too was in New York), Aba and I assembled at the Gotham.

As I was taking off my coat Busch intercepted Persinger on his way to the piano. There was to be no collusion between teacher and pupil, no solace for me in the form of a compliant accompanist, no familiar ground. Busch would accompany me himself. If I could follow *his* tempi without tripping over my rotund little self, why then he might reconsider, but I suspect he didn't quite believe I'd negotiate the first broken octaves. By the second tutti, German endearments came raining down on me. *"Mein lieber Knabe,"* he explained, "you can play anything with me, anytime, anywhere!" "Let's do the Brahms as well," I said, seizing the opportunity. There is a passage in the Brahms Concerto in tenths, almost the widest interval demanded of a violinist. Rapidly and more or less in tune, I played these bars to prove to Busch that my hand was big enough for Brahms, but when my suggestion wasn't followed up, I didn't insist. He kept his open-ended promise to me: in later years we played it together in Germany and in England.

Then followed the rehearsal and the concerts, two of them, on successive days. I don't remember much of either concert, except that they were successful beyond our wildest dreams, vindicating so much that had gone before, promising so much for the future. At the first, on 27 November 1927, feeling too small an object for all the noise that broke from the audience, I tried to deflect attention to Busch, to the orchestra, to Persinger, whom I dragged onstage and pointed to, but I had to appear in overcoat, cap in hand, before they would let me go. Exposure to the public wasn't the real test, however: that had been passed in two parts, at the Gotham and at the rehearsal, and these successfully negotiated, the concerts followed automatically. When I walked onstage for the rehearsal, many musicians in the orchestra remained unconvinced by Busch's conversion to my cause, and my request to have my violin tuned by Mischakov, the concertmaster—for I had not the strength to turn the pegs myself—did nothing to reassure them. By the end of the first movement, however, I knew they were on my side. It was a very joyful experience—not so much the triumph over skepticism as the conviction that one was accepted among musicians who knew what they were about.

5

Building
from Above

On the afternoon before the second concert in New York, Hephzibah, Yaltah and I were sent to take our regular after-luncheon rest in the room we shared at the Colonial Hotel on Eighty-first Street. Usually we were very good about observing the silence of the siesta, but on this particular day I was too excited to keep the rules and my sisters' solidarity too complete to tempt them to protest. I wasn't worried about the coming concert: I knew I had made my success the night before and would probably play as well a second time; but these circumstances not conducing to slumber, I spent the rest hour holding forth on a number of topics to my receptive audience. What then first struck me—it is curious that I can date it so exactly—was that I couldn't feel the weight of my limbs. Perhaps this is what people call growing pains: the body, heretofore taken for granted, seems to escape one's control so that muscles stiffen involuntarily and lose the knack of relaxing. I forced my legs and arms flat on the bed, but achieved no sense of inertia thereby, which, considering how I set about it, was hardly surprising. More than twenty years were to pass before I began to understand the functioning of joints and muscles, or its importance to violin playing, since when progress has been steady to the point where I can now feel the weight of a single finger and appreciate in the shoulder muscles the smallest movement of an arm. But if it has taken a lifetime to solve the puzzle, from that November afternoon I knew there was a puzzle to be solved.

Similarly I knew, and from much earlier, that my life was in a manner full of holes. It is a feature of a violinist's career to burst abruptly into view. From his own standpoint, of course, there is nothing abrupt about an appearance which crowns years of work, but whereas most writers and painters, architects and composers, come to notice gradually, in accordance with human laws of growth, the stage personality is suddenly in the public gaze, like Aphrodite washed ashore on Cyprus, beautifully complete, and often younger than she. The completeness is in the eye of the beholder, however.

Music is given us with our existence. An infant cries or crows or talks with his own voice and goes one step beyond to sing. Above other arts, music can be possessed without knowledge; being an expression largely of the subconscious, it has its direct routes from whatever is in our guts, minds and spirits, without need of a detour through the classroom. That direct route I knew, thank God. I learned to love music before I learned to say so; I was given the raw material when I could scarcely read or write; I early felt the wonder of taking up a violin and making it speak, communicate with others, express the thoughts and feelings of great composers. No doubt I had great aptitude which enabled me to excel my teachers in specific performances, but this phenomenon is generally accounted more mysterious than it is. Violin in hand, a talented youngster with music in his heart, an inspiring master, and the capacity to play by "feel" and imitation can hurdle obstacles apparently insuperable to the adult mind, which would erect barriers of qualification to be surmounted before one wins the right to self-expression. Without qualifications, background or experience, without knowing adolescent yearning, excitement and disappointment, I could at the age of seven or eight play the *Symphonie Espagnole* almost as well as anyone and better than most. Where I was supremely blessed was in having great musicians to inspire me. Too many young people are ruined by bad teaching. It was not my fate to have bad teaching, or any teaching at all, in the literal sense of the word. Had I been put to study under a first-class "teacher," a Carl Flesch or a Dounis, the experience might well have proved mutually discouraging—to him for my playing adequately without his training, and to me for his system's depriving me of music. My teachers, however, were first and foremost superb violinists, so that I knew from the beginning the sound and feel of a phrase or a performance, drinking in example by intuition, by recognition, without troubling to analyze meaning and mechanics. The impact of the Beethoven on New York I owed to Enesco's insight.

Enesco's insight, however, was the fruit of time, and time was precisely what I did not have on my own account. It is one thing to play one's small repertoire beautifully, another to have lived long enough to understand Mozart or play through all Beethoven's quartets or simply begin to know something of the world. My devoted, careful parents saw to it that I wasn't confined to what I could easily do; they saved me from musical idiocy, if the expression may be allowed, giving me books, languages, the countryside, family life, and much besides; but there is no such thing as an instant biography. Maturity, in music and in life, has to be earned by living. Having started at the top, after a fashion and in one respect only, I had to construct my maturity from an unusual angle.

It was as if one were suspended from a balloon at the fiftieth floor without any scaffolding of patience to shore up against the balloon's deflation. Projected up to Beethoven, I knew that a vision had been in some way grasped, or at least perceived, before the intervening spaces had been filled—spaces to be filled by contact with life as much as, or more than, by contact with music. The difficulty was to let down threads from my balloon and surreptitiously build from the bottom up without ever living down there. Lessons had to be learned in later life which in the ordinary course of events children learn at school, at play, in the streets and among the crowds: that competition exists, for power, for leadership, for the satisfaction of greed, for an object, a person, a woman. There was no competition in my youth, nor any suggestion that one might willfully harm one's neighbor in the cause of self-advancement. For one thing, my gift spared me: as soon as I could play professionally, support, engagements, fees, fell to me without my striving. For another, the people I knew—by great good fortune, I believe, as well as by my parents' scrupulous selection—were all of a remarkable goodness. And thirdly, family principles built an ideal world about my sisters and me. True, it would prove hard and painful to reconcile the fluidity of actual life with the crystallized perfection of the standards which governed childhood; true, too, I probably lost something of resilience, alertness, color and fascination in the static security of my upbringing. Much, much later, Sasha Schneider told me that in spring 1929, when I was making my debut in Berlin, he—a boy and a violinist like me—was playing for his living in brothels in a little Polish town. He was, he said, very jealous. Well, had we met then, I'm sure he would have shown himself the more brilliant personality, I the more tongue-tied. But I am not sorry to have missed the rough and tumble of unprotected childhood. Even if I was unprepared to find life less than perfect, it was wonderful to have had so early a conception of the ideal.

After many years of building to meet my balloon, I think there are now few dangerous crevices left in the construction, although, as there is much I have not experienced, my completeness is perhaps not for me to judge.

Enthusiastic though New York's reception had been, I couldn't wait to get home. San Francisco remained the polestar of my compass and a year seemed a terribly long time to have been away. Also I was longing to see Esther, though this I mentioned to no one, of course. It would be wrong to say I found nothing changed, for there were several remarkable alterations to absorb: a lovely new Buick, the gift of Uncle Sidney, parked at our door when we arrived; my taking over the room once rented by the Russian ladies, which overlooked the street and was embellished with a turret; my father's return to San Francisco as a man of leisure, with no obligations except to his family. Nonetheless, in spite of changes, past and to come, for a little while life resumed its comfortable shape. Hephzibah and Yaltah went back to their first piano teacher, Lev Shorr (a dear good man and an accomplished teacher who gave them an excellent grounding and remained a friend of the family; become blind, he still attended concerts, guided by his good wife, until his death in 1975); but now my sisters shared the French lessons with Mlle Godchaux. In addition, I studied harmony with John Paterson, a violinist in the San Francisco orchestra, and was, of course, reunited with Persinger.

For most of 1928 Persinger was teaching at Santa Barbara, four hundred miles to the south, where his quartet was based. Once a week he drove overnight to San Francisco, gave me a lesson, stayed a good part of the day, then drove all the way back again. It was a curious period of music-making. In a way I had been indulged by Enesco, who let me concentrate upon one work indefinitely, and Persinger wisely decided that it was time I got to know a great many others. Each week he brought me a beautifully marked copy of a new work, each week I'd prepare it as best I could, but well or ill done, there was no turning back. So my repertoire expanded at a great rate to include, among other compositions, Brahms's Sonata in D Minor, Beethoven's *Kreutzer,* and numerous concerti by Vivaldi, Mozart, Vieuxtemps, Wieniawski, Bruch and Glazunov. My constant adulatory references to Enesco were ill-judged, to say the least. "I don't want to hear that name any more!"

Persinger finally shouted, but his devotion passed the test of my tactless-ness, and it was with him that I made my first records early in 1928, and with him that Aba and I set out on our first tour in the autumn.

Electrical recording had been the rule for no more than a year or two when I was engaged to make a ten-inch of Fiocco's "Allegro" and Franz Ries's "La Capricciosa," and a twelve-inch of the "Sierra Morena" by de Monasterio and the "Romanesca" arranged by Joseph Akhron. As if this were not novelty enough, the experience brought me in addition the rewards of being taken to the first sound film, Al Jolson's *Jazz Singer,* then showing in San Francisco, and a volume of *Robinson Crusoe* (renamed "Robinson Caruso" in our house). For nearly fifty years I have enjoyed making recordings, but no later occasion has blurred the thrill of the first one, which, and not only for myself, had about it a spirit of adventure. A church in Oakland was hired. While Persinger, Aba and I converged upon it from San Francisco, two engineers drove across the continent from RCA's headquarters in Camden, New Jersey, acquiring on their way through Texas a bullet hole in the windshield of their car, evidence of pioneering which was displayed with pride. Later in the year the tour took us to Camden itself, where further records were made. Here the bonus was a first invitation to a directors' luncheon—and my first oysters, Chesapeake Bay monsters too large to swallow whole, yet defying one to dissect them. I recall that the records made that morning were printed and processed overnight and in our hands on the morrow, so simple was life and even technology in those far-off days.

The first tour was an experiment. I remember the anxious delibera-tions preceding acceptance of the plan, and my parents' finally overcom-ing their concern to decide that traveling and playing regularly were after all parts of the career to be faced. By now the family was dependent on what concerts earned, but this was the least of their worries: in the 1920s it didn't take many concerts to live comfortably, nor would they ever have exploited me. Ultimately it was decided that on this first tour I should play once a week, for fifteen weeks or so, starting in San Fran-cisco and moving east to finish in New York. Although I have since covered the same ground many times, I recall the towns visited then with some clarity: Los Angeles and the immense Shriners' Auditorium; Chi-cago, whose auditorium declined later into a sports arena, then served as a United Nations center, before being rehabilitated for music some few years ago; Pittsburgh, where I first performed the Brahms Concerto; Minneapolis, where the conductor, Henri Verbrughen, invited me home after the concert to play chamber music (fortunately I could sight-read well and did not disgrace myself); Cleveland, where the conductor was Nikolai Sokoloff, whom I had met at Mrs. Casserly's house, and where, moreover, I made the acquaintance of Alan Geismer, a boy my own age who had a splendid electric train set covering the floor of the family attic. In Cleveland a new railroad station was being built, imposing hours of delay on passengers then and later. Waiting to go through Cleveland, Persinger and I would play chess. It takes a special teacher to have three or four months to spare from his commitments and to choose to spend them on a pupil. But Persinger enjoyed the tour, I think. He, my father and I were a very cheerful trio. Persinger accompanied me at recitals, was present at the concerts with orchestra, worked with me every morning, and in between times played chess and went sightseeing with us. And I took it all for granted, living in my balloon.

In New York Aba and I stayed with Dr. and Mrs. Garbat and their children, only moving to the Colonial Hotel when my mother and sisters joined us in the new year on our way to Europe. Partly the move was due to our number, five being rather overwhelming for a private house; partly it was due to Imma's love of freedom and the family's independence. Before the family reunion, however, the weeks spent with the Garbats brought about the most generous happening of my life.

By this time I owned two excellent violins and had the use of a superb one. As well as giving me his own Guadagnini, Uncle Sidney had enabled my parents to buy a charming Grancino in Paris which we had seen in Tournier's, the violin-maker's on the rue de Rome, in 1927, and with which I had made my New York debut. On the tour I was using neither of these, however, but a Guarnerius lent by Lyon & Healy of Chicago, and now that I was professionally launched it was generally held desirable that I should have an instrument of that caliber of my own. Among Dr. Garbat's patients was Mr. Henry Goldman, a very wealthy man who loved music and was known for his generosity. He came to a concert at Carnegie Hall in January 1929 at which I performed the Tchaikovsky Concerto, but long before then he had known of my existence from Dr. Garbat and in fact had heard me play, I think. Dr. Garbat now made known to him that I was playing on a borrowed violin, and shortly thereafter brought Aba and me an invitation to meet Mr. Goldman and his wife, Babette.

The Goldmans lived in an apartment on Fifth Avenue, overlooking Central Park and the Metropolitan Museum, which was far more luxurious than any I had ever seen, its walls covered with Old Masters. Although he was by then blind, Mr. Goldman would take one round his collection and point to the most minute and wonderful details of each painting; so well did he know them. It was an education, and an experience of unforgettable poignancy, to be shown such riches by a man who saw their glories only with his mind's eye. There was too much to be taken in at a single visit, but I remember being impressed by a Cellini bronze inkstand, a Van Dyck portrait of a very Dutch-looking gentleman over the fireplace, and a set of Holbein miniatures. Naturally, neither Aba nor I mentioned violins, but it was understood what we had come for, and after about half an hour Mr. Goldman—or Uncle Henry, as I came to call him—said, "Now, you must choose any violin you want, no matter what the price. Choose it; it's yours."

As may be imagined, Aba and I walked down Fifth Avenue on air. Immediately let into the secret, Persinger contacted the violin dealer Emil Herrman. As it happened, Herrman had been in San Francisco the year before, when he had brought to Steiner Street a capacious case of beautiful violins, including the one I eventually chose. I had fallen in love with it then, but had contrived to forget what we could not remotely afford. It was another recognition, as of Enesco, and like that one, due to reach fulfillment. In New York, after taking counsel with Persinger and Efrem Zimbalist, I turned down several magnificent instruments, including the Betts Stradivarius, then priced at $110,000, now in the Library of Congress, in favor of my first love, the "Prince Khevenhüller." Ample and round, varnished a deep, glowing red, its grand proportions were matched by a sound at once powerful, mellow and sweet. It bore the name of its first owner, an Austro-Hungarian nobleman for whom Stradivari made it at the age of ninety in 1733.

Henry Goldman wrote Emil Herrman a check for sixty thousand dollars, the Wall Street crash having preceded his gift by about one week. Herrman, for his part, included in the purchase price the Tourte bow which I still use, itself now worth a third of what the Prince Khevenhüller was worth then.

Enesco's parting advice, given at Sinaia in 1927, that I should work with Adolf Busch was not forgotten, but for various reasons it could not be put into effect for almost another two years. I have suggested that Enesco saw his great German colleague as a corrective influence; if such was his belief, correction of imbalance was only one good among others that he knew to be in Busch's gift. Adolf, the brother of Fritz Busch, was a man and a musician of the highest value, whose reverence for his heritage fitted into the moral context of his whole life, who played the violin

cleanly and beautifully if with no Russian or gypsy touch, whose string
quartet was among the most respected of the day, who was like Enesco a
composer. Enesco in his wisdom saw that my formation required the
compensating influence of Germany: after all, the noblest music any
violinist played was German, and it could only be useful to know it from
within the heart of the tradition. As he had had Vienna, so should I have
Busch.

Therefore, when the family assembled in New York early in 1929
for our second voyage to Europe, Busch's studio in Basel was our destination. Before we reached Switzerland, however, several preliminaries had
to be dealt with, including a concert in Berlin which can be said to mark
the start of my adult career. It took place on 12 April 1929, a few days
short of my thirteenth birthday, was conducted by Bruno Walter and
consisted of three concerti, by Bach, Beethoven and Brahms.

The concert was crucial because Berlin was then the musical capital of the "civilized" world, its prestige founded on the music of the past
and flourishing still in great orchestras and conductors, not to mention
the most informed audiences to be found anywhere. Musically speaking,
Germany was an empire where a soloist might make a livelihood—as
Adolf Busch did—without ever going abroad, and Berlin was its center.
No other European country was so musically self-sufficient. In recognition of this primacy American careers had to bear the imprint "Made in
Germany" if they were to advance at all and reviews of concerts in Berlin
and Dresden were carried full-length in the American press. The Ameri-
can musical scene was itself still largely German; there were occasional
French outposts—for example, the Russian Serge Koussevitsky brought a
flair for French music to Boston when he replaced Karl Muck, and was
himself succeeded in course of time by the Frenchman Charles Munch;
Toscanini started an Italian mode; but the rank and file of conductors in
the United States tended to be German, and not in the Midwest alone.
The first conductor of my listening and performing life had been Alfred
Hertz in San Francisco. Hence, to perform in Berlin at all, and especially
with Bruno Walter, among the greatest of conductors in Germany or out
of it, was a sort of apotheosis to which my American tour served as
overture. It was a tremendous event for me.

As first planned, Fritz Busch was to conduct the Berlin debut, but
at the last moment he was summoned to Dresden by his father's death.
He left me in good hands. From the Great War until Hitler's blight
descended on it, Berlin's musical life was ruled over by Louisa Wolff, a
partner in the foremost concert agency, Wolff and Sachs, and it was she

who asked Bruno Walter to stand in for Busch. It is possible he could not find words to deny her, for the queen of German music was not easily denied, but in any event his agreement ushered in a relationship of generous understanding on his part and grateful admiration on mine which lasted until he died. I do not believe that anyone else of his eminence would have cancelled an engagement at the opera, as he did, to conduct for a twelve-year-old traveling fiddler known to him only by report. This mark of kindness was not the only reason why, of all the great conductors whom I met in my youth, he remained my favorite. Rehearsing these three concerti, I marveled to find such support, such adaptability; it seemed that whatever I did, he was always there, perfectly with me, an accompanist such as I had never known, who left me with no sense of pushing, no sense of pulling (at the time I had not yet performed with Enesco; he was another such, an extraordinary musician and an extraordinary accompanist).

Bruno Walter always talked in terms of the human voice. Today music is too often thought of as if it sprang originally from the keyboard —or the typewriter: as if the interval from A to Z were no more trouble to encompass than the interval from A to B. But the voice is not a mechanical keyboard, and Walter, whose remarkable sense of other people was compassion in the most basic meaning of the word, knew in advance what degree of flexibility of tempo was required. I remember his pointing this out to me: several years after our first encounter, and having played quite often together in the interim, we met at the author Emil Ludwig's house in Saint Moritz. If the melodic line jumped an octave or more, a singer needed time to achieve it, Walter said; and I found the comment not only a musical truth but one which summed him up. He wasn't a man to defend a position brutally, he wasn't an authoritarian; as with music, so with musicians (and I don't think he separated the one from the other): they were living, pulsing, feeling human beings upon whom the grid of dogma could not properly be dropped. His adaptability did not imply a lack of principle. I will be forever grateful to him, in that when I was attacked by many of my colleagues for defending Furtwängler from accusations of Nazism after the war, Bruno Walter—Jew though he was and Furtwängler's greatest competitor—refused to sign anything against Furtwängler or against me.

Our first appearance together in Berlin has become known in family parlance as the "Mayflower" concert, for the audience has grown impressively numerous with the passing years, in the manner of the descendants of Massachusetts' first English settlers; either the audience has grown beyond the Philharmonie's capacity, or I have since met everyone who was there. This latter interpretation may be the true one, as it is surely the kinder one, for the audience was more than half Jewish and afterward dispersed to all corners of the earth; moreover, it included many musicians: Ossip Gabrilowitsch, Fritz Kreisler, Bronislav Gimpel, Carl Flesch, Sam Franko, the great critic Stuckenschmidt, and many others. It is gratifying to reflect that my hearers had well-established critical standards, for that fact gave the more value to their enthusiastic response. The Philharmonie's management, fearing the enthusiasm was getting out of hand, went to the lengths of summoning the police to restore order; but what, from the haven of the artists' room, I most clearly remember of the concert's aftermath is Albert Einstein's coming in directly from the stage—he had not troubled to go round the back way—and hugging me, with an exclamation of astronomically disproportionate immensity: "Now I know there is a God in heaven!"

At all events, the "Mayflower" concert was but the central episode in a succession of excitements that bore out the uniqueness of Berlin. On the morning of the concert there was an *öffentliche Hauptprobe*, the public rehearsal to which students came, followed by a sumptuous German luncheon given by Louisa Wolff and lasting three hours, before and after which everyone saluted everyone else with formal cries of *Mahlzeit!* There were meetings with Louisa Wolff herself and a visit to her partner's, Emil Sachs's, suburban home, its walls hung with sabers, spears and suits of armor. (Having got me out of a difficulty when Fritz Busch could not conduct, Wolff and Sachs thereupon became my German agents, and organized the four tours I made in Germany before Hitler's rise to power; both of them were to disappear in the holocaust.) Apart from my own concert and recital, there were others given by glittering names which made these few days incredibly rich. I heard Mischa Elman perform the Mendelssohn Concerto—and wished I might somehow be able to jump in and play it in his stead: not that he didn't play it beautifully, but in my youthful eagerness—or ignorance—I was sure I could play it more beautifully yet. Fritz Kreisler also gave a concert. I remember his being called back for encore after encore, and the consultation with his wife, Harriet, backstage about when he should bring the evening to a halt. It was on that occasion that I met him for the first time; we were to come to know each other well in the future. I also at last met Adolf Busch.

With my family I attended a concert given by the Busch Quartet in the Singakademie, a hall corresponding in capacity and function to Paris's Conservatoire hall, but unlike it, rectangular in shape. Impressed as I was by the integrity of the quartet's playing, what most struck me was a first hearing of music by Max Reger, an unexportable composer such as every culture produces, who so concentrates the ethos of a country that his music is incomprehensible anywhere else. Contact with the periphery of the alien is stimulating; immersion in its core leaves one without any orientation whatsoever. Given the opportunity to become familiar with Reger's work, learning to appreciate his weight and density and his immense power of organization—for Reger had perhaps the greatest musical skills, in terms of fugal construction, since Bach—I have yet to do him justice. His music was easier to admire than to love; it was like being shown into a library heavy with the works of Kant and Hegel and realizing with failing heart that not until all these volumes had been read and a thesis written could one be considered truly civilized. Just as there are composers who do not travel well, there are also artists who belong to a particular corner of the world. One such, whom I was to hear for the first time soon after the German debut, was the violinist Bronislaw Hubermann. Beloved in Berlin, Vienna, Budapest and probably Prague, he never quite achieved the same acclaim in other cities. Such artists reflect a certain culture, temperament, mixture of races, and they thrive most happily in home soil.

After the program, which included Beethoven as well as the *déroutant* Reger, I went backstage for a first meeting with my new master, without any of the preconceived notions which I had brought to my first meeting with Enesco. I found an eminently sympathetic man, youthful, blond, boyish, good; a face of such open goodness as to have melted prejudice, supposing I'd had any to be melted; and a musician, as the just completed program made plain, of great stature, absolute honesty and no flashy virtuosity whatever. Enesco's instinct was right. Without Busch I would not have entered into that spirit which later took me to the depths of the great German composers. He presented me with German culture; in afteryears the people and the literature would improve my acquaintance with it; but to him I owe the entry through music, and music expressed in a sensibility which combined scholarship and passion and was never dry.

Upon leaving Berlin we joined Fritz Busch for a concert in Dresden—a jewel of a city whose pointless destruction in the war was a tragedy and a crime; then went to Paris to repeat the three concerti at the

Opéra, Philippe Gaubert conducting. Uncle Sidney and his family were in Europe that year. Having met us in Berlin, they reached Paris before us and celebrated reunion with dinner at a Russian restaurant. After these various excitements we left for two weeks' holiday with Mr. and Mrs. Henry Goldman at Baden-Baden.

Henry Goldman had certain pleasurable routines. One was Bénédictine after dinner, another summer visits to Baden-Baden. This was the first small German town of my experience and its calm and excessively coherent character struck me forcibly: the ordered life, the quantities of efficient cheerful maidservants, the eiderdowns in snowy linen covers on the beds, the ample, delicious, fattening foods, the walks through woods where every little hill was crowned with a lookout post and a restaurant at which one could stoke up again on pastry and beer, the band playing daily in the square, the evening concerts at the Kursaal and Elena Gerhardt singing Schubert songs . . . I found it all too charming to be quite real. Brought up in Aba's large view of the struggling world, I judged this society which turned its back so firmly on the outside to concentrate on itself a survival of an earlier age, its ecstatic pleasure in green woods and good music a trifle forced; and the fact that Baden-Baden attracted the retired and the elderly strengthened the impression.

I enjoyed myself mightily nonetheless. The Goldmans wanted to put us up in their hotel, but my parents wisely considered such surroundings too *mondain* for us and rented rooms at a *pension*. We took advantage of what Baden-Baden offered, in my case more particularly the optical shops, at one of which I bought a splendid pair of Zeiss binoculars, the longest in stock. Every time we left the *pension* I carried them proudly, looking a figure of fun, I'm sure, as I wasn't much longer than they were, and raking the horizon from every possible hillock to see what I could see.

Arrived at last in Basel, we spent three weeks or a month in the Drei Könige Hotel on the Rhine while Imma found and furnished a house. Number 12 Gartenstrasse, then on the edge of the town, now well engulfed by suburbs, was the middle one of three houses covered by one large roof which swept steeply down on either side. Like most of New York's row houses, ours was one room and a staircase wide, but made up for narrowness with many floors. The architectural feature I most enjoyed was a balcony, where tea was served, my tea consisting by preference of rice pudding. Each Thursday at teatime, as regular as ourselves, the Graf Zeppelin from Buenos Aires sailed into view overhead on its way to Friedrichshaven on the Bodensee, an almost silent, vast, silvery cigar shining in the sunlight.

The months in Basel were a happy time for all of us, I believe. There was a certain security: my career was fairly launched, no financial difficulty threatened, my father's decision had been vindicated. Moreover, after living in apartments and hotels, we had a house of our own again, a circumstance which awakened in us children much nostalgia for Steiner Street. It was appeased only when Aba had various beloved pieces of furniture sent from San Francisco to join the Oriental rugs and other beautiful things Imma had bought in a local antique shop. (On a visit to this shop I was greatly attracted to a carved rosewood figure of a Chinese lady, and was given it. I realize now that I was really quite spoiled: most of what I wanted I got.) With our own house and our own car, a secondhand open Packard which took us all over Switzerland and Italy in the following years, sometimes stalling on a grade crossing but never when a train was upon us, we enjoyed the freedom of being independent once more.

As always, no matter where she might be, my mother established home and routine in the shortest possible time. Our ordered schedule of work, rest and play slipped easily into its new surroundings, but varied now by a mild dissipation suited to our advancing years: on Saturdays we would go to the casino to sit at outside tables, hear the band play and watch the dancers. For daily exercise there were Gartenstrasse's gardens, where we jumped rope, the fields only a block away, the zoo; for gala evenings there were concerts, and for lessons a new language, German. While I read the plays of Schiller with Herr Gehrig, an elderly man with a young wife and a very nice small son, my sisters confronted the harder task of mastering two languages at once, Italian as well as German, taking daily lessons in the former from Signorina Anna, a dear, good Milanese schoolmistress who was in every way voluminous, in size of heart as in girth.

As my mother shepherded us from language to language, her name changed. For the first eleven or twelve years of my life I called her mother in Hebrew, Imma. When we first studied French she became Petite Mère, and German, Mütterchen, her final metamorphosis being the Italian Mammina. Why Mammina stuck, to be used thereafter in all languages, I cannot say for certain, but it is sure that she felt a special kinship with Latin peoples and adored Italy particularly. My mother always sought to communicate with her children in the best way she could—through lessons. Thus, at meals we spoke whatever language was currently under scrutiny, Mammina having trod that path ahead of us, in her own girlhood. But through all our linguistic mutations Aba remained Aba.

My mother wrote the most elegant and fluent German Gothic script imaginable. A traditionalist at least for the traditions she valued, she insisted we learn German writing in our turn, and when we reached Russian classes a couple of years later, had us taught the hard and soft word endings which have been abandoned in modern Russian orthography. In all these matters, as well as in more basic linguistic skills—declensions, irregular verbs, and so on—I was allowed to get away with less well prepared lessons than my sisters. Hephzibah shone. So thoroughly did she learn her lessons that she knew every rule, and every exception to every rule, in every language. In recognition of her infallibility we called her Madame Larousse-Lablonde—a pun on the standard French dictionary, Larousse, which means "redhead," Hephzibah herself being very blond.

Our life in Basel was peopled in a modest way. Adolf Busch being a family man, there was more contact between our family and his than there had been with Enesco, the bachelor. Our language teachers were in and out of the house, and occasionally we had visitors from abroad. Of these the most splendid was young Sidney Ehrman, on vacation from Cambridge, who stayed at our house for a few nights with his valet. I was tremendously impressed by the valet—by a discretion so perfect that even in our busy house he was never in the way, and by the superb shine he achieved when polishing shoes. Knowing well Mammina's love of Oriental symbols of manly strength, Sidney brought her a Turkish dagger with damascene blade, in a scabbard encrusted with red corals, which he had found in an antique shop in Vienna. He and Hephzibah were very fond of each other. We went on excursions with him up and down the Rhine, and one evening when we came back late from such an outing, he made scrambled eggs, very succulent and rich, for all the family. He was proud of his scrambled eggs. It is immensely saddening to think that shortly after this visit Sidney had his fatal accident. In November 1929, when I made my first visit to England, he was lying between life and death, and died soon afterward when Aba and I were already touring in the United States. We saw his parents and Esther the next summer at Evian. It was then that I was so impressed by the generous interest of people who had lost their only son. I remember coming in one day and boring the company stiff with my admiration of a red Mercedes sports car I had seen, and my parents reproaching me for bringing up such a trivial matter at such a time, and Aunt Florence's defense. "Why shouldn't Yehudi dream of having a red sports car?" she said. "One day he will." After Sidney's death, his father and mother re-created his Cambridge study in their house in San Francisco, transporting paneling, furniture, paintings and books from England. It became their second-floor living room.

Adolf Busch's vision of the bond between teacher and pupil was almost religious; like a disciple with his guru, or a medieval apprentice with his master, a student should live with his teacher, making music morning, noon and night, sharing his life and thought as he shared his roof and his dinner. There was one such student in residence when we came to Basel—Rudolf Serkin, who studied piano under the watchful maternal eye of Mrs. Busch and gave Hephzibah and Yaltah piano lessons in what spare time he had. Busch was sorry that I too could not join his household. Undoubtedly I lost something in missing the evenings spent on chamber music and in singing Bach chorales, but I had my own family a few blocks down the road, and annual touring commitments to take me away from Switzerland. If there was loss in these arrangements, there was also gain—in the rounded experience of family existence, the big repertory required for touring, the adventure of touring itself.

The closeness between Busch and Serkin was to be demonstrated very markedly: when in 1934 the Nazis forbade Busch to give concerts with Serkin, a Jew, he vowed he would not visit the Third Reich again, and Serkin for his part married his master's daughter, Irène. Eventually he took her off to the United States, where the contribution he has since made to American musical life is impossible to measure. Not only is he one of the great pianists of our day, whose superlative performances set standards for young aspirants; not only does he head the Curtis Institute in Philadelphia and run the Marlboro Festival, where the best musicians of the country congregate yearly; but he keeps alive and flourishing that noble tradition of German music to which, as I have suggested, America owes so much and which is all the more precious now that native excellence challenges its primacy and threatens to submerge it. As befits a great pedagogue, Rudi is one of the kindest and gentlest of people. To this day I see Irène and him whenever I can, and whenever I meet them, the encounter evokes for me those adolescent years in Basel.

The Busch family lived in a comfortable old-fashioned house with high-ceilinged rooms and a large garden, presided over by Mrs. Busch, a small, wiry, vigorous woman of high and earnest principle. As well as keeping her husband's household in good order, she was his secretariat, and a very overworked organization it must have been. Mrs. Busch coped with all the correspondence for his engagements, kept an eye on his pupils' practice, and had energy to spare for me when I was in trouble or at fault. Once, on a holiday at Fionnay (a Swiss holiday resort for the Swiss—that is to say, a much more earnest place of pleasure than a Swiss resort for foreigners), I suffered the indignity of splitting my shorts; she promptly mended them. Another time, she reprimanded me quite severely for rolling pieces of bread between my fingers: bread was a serious food and not to be played with in a world where some were without it. She was quite right. Her daughter Irène, having no responsibility for my upbringing, could afford to cultivate a more relaxed relationship with me. As a leave-taking present she once gave me the first Swiss pocket knife I ever owned.

I have never known anyone to give as many concerts as Adolf Busch did. He was the unchallenged great German violinist, and as soloist or with his quartet performed two hundred times a year, if not two hundred and fifty. Although he made money enough to live comfortably, he didn't earn large fees for individual concerts, and it was a mark of his genuine amiability that he accepted as pupil without second thought a young boy who was probably making per concert about five times as much as he did himself. One thing that greatly impressed me about Busch himself was his being a composer. I recall coming for my lessons and seeing on his desk vast sheets of music paper, perhaps newspaper size, which had been specially made for the work he was then writing. Where the average orchestral score may have space for a dozen instruments or so, this had space for at least twice that number. Without knowing what the work was, I recognized in Busch's activity that, not satisfied with being a great interpreter, he had the desire and the power to experiment and create. His teaching was, again, musical rather than violinistic. If he didn't have Enesco's flair or glamour, as a musician he was extremely serious and deep, a passionate fundamentalist who ate, breathed and slept Bach and Beethoven. I think that musicians, more particularly chamber musicians, are to this day, whether knowingly or not, in debt to his combined passion and profundity.

On account, no doubt, of his own touring commitments, Busch had to leave me to prepare the program for the winter season, 1929–1930, as best I could myself. Fortunately he returned to Basel before I left it, in time to hear me through the various pieces and give his approval unqualified by much comment or correction. The most important of these new compositions was Bach's C Major Solo Sonata, which I had first tackled during the interlude at the Drei Könige before lessons with Busch began.

I have lately recorded this biggest of all Bach's sonatas and fugues for the third time—for only the first time, however, to my satisfaction. At thirteen I was unprepared for the task of mastering it: I understood the technical problems and got around them, but I did not solve them. In the fugue Bach wrote the accompanying theme in half notes (or minims), but all violinists, including Busch, chose to play it in eighths (or quavers). Thus, the change of harmony on each quarter note (or crotchet) was simply not heard. I first played it as everyone else did, but to abandon the harmony bothered me from the beginning, and as a result the C Major Sonata has twice in my life undergone a rebirth, as it were. Two years after Basel, in time for my first recording of it, I decided to play the accompanying notes for the length of a quarter plus a sixteenth, so as to allow the sound to mix on the second and fourth quarter note of each bar. This solution demanded much complicated wiggling and jig-gling of the bow, but it sounded good, resolutions of dissonances could be heard, and for many years I was content with it until the superior elegance of Bach's own intentions set me to work again. Even if I could not hold all the chords for their full length, I would, I determined, hold the main accompanying voice, the chromatic line, to the value of every half note. Since then the fugue has taken on an entirely new sound, so much more pleasing than before that I wonder why, all those years ago, I did not put my trust in Bach immediately but chose rather the complex-ity of a quarter and a sixteenth. I suppose change must happen, and wisdom come, by degree.

By the end of two summers with Adolf Busch the pattern of life was established. In October the tour began in Europe, somewhere about the turn of the year it transferred to the United States, and late spring united the family again for a summer of lessons and privacy. Holidays were taken when possible, usually out of season, always without plan-ning in accordance with Mammina's conviction that pleasure should be unfettered by forethought. From late 1930 to 1935 the summer base, from which tours began with premeditation and holidays without it, was Ville d'Avray, between Paris and Versailles.

If I can't now reconstruct the discussions that brought us back to France, the overriding reason remains clear enough. Grateful as I was to Adolf Busch, much as I admired and loved him, well though I knew he could teach me a great deal yet, I was still in my heart of hearts bound to

Georges Enesco. Not only for me, however, was Paris an uncompleted experience, as well as a city of great excitement. As a family we were more at ease in French than in German, and there may have been, besides, a premonitory chill from coming German events. I recall Aba's insistence that the opening recital of my first German tour should include Bloch's "Avodah," and this choice of as traditionally Jewish a composition as one could wish for seems, in the light of what was soon to happen, a justified inspiration—more especially as the recital occurred in Munich, a city already known for its anti-Semitism. Not that I experienced hostility myself: all the concerts, including the first, were huge successes and Germany to me meant a nation of music-lovers and an orchestra in every little town. From Ville d'Avray I continued to tour Germany until Hitler's coming to power.

Our house at Ville d'Avray was a real home, spacious and elegant in its way, a suburban Petit Trianon slightly ravaged by the numerous brood who had lived there. Returning to France, we had contacted Jan and Isabelle Hambourg, and it was under Jan's escort that we found and rented 32 rue Pradier. Leaving us in the taxi, Mammina went into the real estate agency and with characteristic speed made up her mind: she never hesitated about important decisions—she knew what she wanted and recognized it when she found it. Behind us we had the Parc de Saint Cloud, separated from us only by a pathway. In front of the house, which stood at the back, or top, of the property, the garden sloped down to the garage and the gates, these last protected by sheets of metal to block the glances of passers-by: the French are a very private people. Stone steps led to the front door, which opened into a salon. To the right was the dining room, to the left the music room, furnished with a piano. I, however, worked in my bedroom on the second floor, which had a balcony covered with wisteria and beyond it a view of lawns and trees to inspire me. There was yet another floor above, where my mother had a sitting room and where lived Bigina and Ferruccio, our cook and handyman, whom we might have inherited from an Italian operetta but who were in fact supplied by the Hambourgs. Ferruccio was suave and small, Bigina was enormous; he had been a runner and was very lithe on his feet; she was a real cook, massive, good-natured, rooted to the kitchen. Sometimes they would make ice cream, a lengthy operation by hand churn, which Ferruccio would turn, singing the while; in those days we called ice cream "Tra-la-la." Bigina and Ferruccio stayed with us until we left France (and, in fact, they traveled to New York with us for one American tour), then moved half a block away to a restaurant on the rue Gambetta. I looked them up the first night I reached liberated Paris, before the end of the war, and was delighted, but not overly surprised, to find them safe, sound and as endearing as ever.

With space at her disposal and old friends to invite, Mammina started entertaining again. We bought a Delage motorcar, a beautifully roomy car with four doors and, oddly enough, a right-hand drive. At crack of dawn every Thursday morning Aba and Ferruccio would sally forth in it to Les Halles, the central market of Paris, bringing it back shortly after breakfast, a four-wheeled cornucopia filled to overflowing with fruit, vegetables, cheeses, lobsters, fish, flesh and fowl. To help us eat this splendid produce we had a much larger circle of acquaintance than during our first stay in France four years earlier, but none of them could be described as specifically cronies of my parents. Committed to their children, Aba and Mammina made their friends through and for us and sought no one besides.

First in geographical proximity were our landlord neighbors, the Vian family, mother, father, one daughter and four sons (including Boris, the writer-to-be, and Alain, the youngest, whose fancy for cowboy clothes won him the nickname *le bandit de Texas*). As soon as I saw the Vian children I knew my long-postponed bicycling opportunity had struck, for they all had bicycles. Sure enough, their machines were at our disposal. The early experimental days had to happen in secret, of course, for clearly it was poor strategy to announce that one had fallen off three times and grazed one's knee; but once proficient, I emerged from the shrubbery for a demonstration, and straightaway Hephzibah, Yaltah and I were accorded three glorious machines of our own—with great balloon tires, multiple speeds, a light, brakes fore and aft—which were for years our delight and joy. We carved out a bicycling empire in the surrounding woods, sending our mechanical steeds up mounds and across ditches, learning every crooked bridle path, sailing down broad tracks through the awesomely beautiful cathedrals of the trees. Thursday being the French children's day off school, it was also the day for joint outings in the two family cars. Once, at Rambouillet, God put a fallen tree in our way, and this being France, where barricade-building was a national instinct, the eight of us children sweated and heaved and pushed and pulled to get it into position across the forest avenue, then heaped earth and stones about it. The authorities tried to find out who was responsible for this piece of mischief, but without result; I am happy to be able to close their dossier now.

Most of our friends came through music, of course. Distinguished visitors stayed at Ville d'Avray, such as Ernest Bloch, Sir Edward Elgar and Alexander Fried, the San Francisco music critic, one of only two professional critics—Olin Downes in New York being the other—who crossed the barrier between the family and the journalistic world. (Already working when I made my debut, Al Fried is working yet, his long service for music recently recognized by a prestigious award from the San Francisco Opera Association. Across all these decades our friendship has survived in undiminished warmth and fidelity.) Established Parisians also visited us, the Marcel Ciampis, Jacques Thibaud, Alfred Cortot, Nadia Boulanger, Noel Gallon, the teacher of harmony and counterpoint, and Emile Français, the great *luthier* of Paris. A violin-maker in a tradition of violin-makers, Français had also a splendid collection of instruments. At a time when the Prince Khevenhüller required a small repair he lent me Ysaÿe's Guarnerius, which I used for a few movements of the Bach Solo Sonatas, recorded in Paris in 1932 (Isaac Stern has that violin now). He also lent me the most beautiful Bergonzi I have ever seen.

Either Bloch or Enesco, I don't now remember which, introduced us to the writer and poet Edmond Fleg and his family, representatives of French-Jewish cultivation at its most refined and high-principled. Edmond Fleg wrote the libretto for Bloch's opera *Macbeth* and was to collaborate with Enesco on his masterpiece *Oedipe*. He was one of the most admirable human beings I have ever known, gentle, idealistic, dedicated to service, always with a smile on his face—a smile which grew only the more philosophical and benign when tragedy doubly struck him and his wife, robbing them of both their sons. These blows were still in the future in the early 1930s, and the two boys, Maurice and Daniel, brilliant and hopeful. The Flegs had a lovely apartment at 1 quai aux Fleurs, Île de la Cité. We visited them quite often. Always a special occasion, it was sometimes celebrated with one of those wonderful natural champagnes which must be drunk young and don't leave one with a thick head. Another family we came to know and have never lost touch with was that of Jacqueline Salomons, a gifted young violinist who, like myself, had overcome Enesco's disinclination to teach and was then studying with him. The Salomons lived in one of Paris's busiest *quartiers,* but as Paris architecture permits, in an apartment overlooking the courtyard, as peaceful as it if were in the depths of the country. Jacqueline used to visit Ville d'Avray every week for chamber music evenings with Enesco, ourselves and others. She was sweet and a darling and I silently cherished sentimental feelings on her account.

And of course we had new teachers. With her extraordinary intuitive flair, Mammina found for us the best teachers anyone could hope to have in France, then or now: Félix Bertaux and his son Pierre, who lived just across the railway line in the adjoining township of Sèvres and came to instruct us in French language and literature. Félix Bertaux was France's most distinguished authority on Germany, then working on a German-French dictionary which his son completed. But for all his professorial standing, he had a wild, nomadic Bessarabian or Spanish brigand look and a personality as colorful and commanding as his appearance. Pierre was no less striking, in looks, character or erudition. He had sailed through his *grande école,* collecting the highest honors in his passage while becoming an expert mountain-climber in intervals from his books, and was then the youngest university professor in the country. Hephzibah, age eleven, fell in love with this exciting, cultivated, romantic, fiery, witty young man, and a few years later, when Pierre announced his intention to marry Denise Supervielle, the lovely daughter of the great French poet, I took him for a long walk to talk him out of his plans and into waiting for my sister!* Pierre came to tutor us when his father was too busy, and of course we found his lessons more fun. His concept of education was the reverse of narrow or academic. Being interested in so many things himself, politics, social affairs and sport as well as scholarship and culture, he believed in picking up learning where one found it: in books and classrooms, yes, but also in newspapers, in the field, or in life generally. He was well equipped to play a brave and useful part in the wartime resistance, and postwar to become, first, Préfet of Lyons, later Chef de la Sûreté. He made us work at Ville d'Avray, extending his brief beyond French to philosophy and German literature, among other branches of learning. He once set Hephzibah to translate certain of Hölderlin's poems into French and still considers what she wrote for him among the most exquisite of translations. He won me over to Hölderlin too. I recall a dismal sea passage from Bergen to Newcastle when a volume of Hölderlin banished the narrow cabin and the inclement weather above and carried me absolutely away.

To improve our Italian, Giuliana del Pelopardi, a charming girl of good Roman family, joined us at Ville d'Avray (her father was later to feed my interest in organic farming, leaving perhaps a more lasting impression on me than his daughter's grammatical explanations); and to break us in to Russian, dear Mr. Lozinsky was engaged, an émigré from the Bolsheviks who was so phenomenal a linguist that he routinely

* Needless to say, he married the lovely Denise.

learned a new language every summer as a holiday task. Occasionally he would combine this with a family expedition into the Alps. On one such occasion, in 1935, I first met two of his compatriots, Vladimir Horowitz and Gregor Piatigorsky.

Volodya Horowitz had not been long out of Russia. He had already made his impact on the music of the West, but was still basking in the novelty of emancipation. It was a time of infatuation—with Wanda Toscanini, whom he was then courting, with a two-door Rolls-Royce he had lately bought, with new-found freedom, with the beginning of a great career. Volodya and Grisha sometimes joined us for a picnic up the Fextal, and while Volodya chafed to get back to his piano (for he was an indefatigable practicer), Grisha would regale the company with endless stories. I have never known a storyteller to equal him in keeping his listeners on tenterhooks, an art he has only perfected in succeeding years. The story itself is buried under the telling of it, but the telling is so beautifully ornamented that one willingly forgives and forgets the embellishments. In the evening we would go down to Horowitz's house in Sils Maria, to hear him play and to play trios among ourselves.

Back at Ville d'Avray a constant pleasure was drives in the Delage. My father—and in time I too—loved to drive in prewar Paris. It was a superb game, especially at some great roundabout like the Arc de Triomphe, where streets of every width at every angle fed new players into the free-for-all, and the players, being French and light on their wheels, staked everything on getting away first from an intersection. Driving was one small indication that I was growing up; others were my first razor, breakfast in bed, having a wallet of my own, treating the family to sherbet at the Café de la Paix; but I was in no hurry for the time when I should take full responsibility for myself. That daunting prospect was bracketed in my mind with the pleasanter one of getting married, the crystallization of being grown up as I saw it, and both were safely relegated to the future. With more adventure over the winter months than most adolescents enjoy all the year round, I found summers at Ville d'Avray a time to take breath as well as to work. The highlight of the working week was of course the visits to Enesco.

Because it lasted longer, because I was by now in my teens and a more experienced violinist with standards of comparison, this second exposure to Enesco allowed me to measure more adequately the depth and range of his greatness. I saw him in new roles—vitalizing our chamber music sessions at home, conducting concerti for me onstage or in the recording studio. I have said already that he didn't talk much when making music, finding words a detour from the direct path of musical comprehension. For other purposes he was impeccably articulate in several languages, with a marvelous flair for words and a ready stream of jokes, puns and wisecracks to lighten a conversation. No doubt his wit, his unfailing courtesy and his power of encapsulating truth in an image were elements in his success as a conductor—other elements being profound knowledge of the score and musical conviction. But even with an orchestra before him, he talked little, sang rather than talked, and never expounded as, for instance, Willem Mengelberg did in Amsterdam. Mengelberg would start a rehearsal with a lecture on the composer whose music was to be played. His explanations might last an hour or more, during which the musicians grew more and more bored, and leave time at the end only for a straight run-through that benefited in no way from all those preliminary words. The orchestra would eventually push a chair forward so that I might at least hear the lecture in comfort, but out of deference to Mengelberg—and eager not to encourage him in any manner—I would stay on my feet. Enesco never subjected soloist or orchestra to such trials—indeed his respect for other people was one of his outstanding qualities—but he had his own method of projecting one into the style and sensibility of a composer.

Such a way was his sending me, in 1932, I think, to the Salzburg Festival. Mozart's music, he said, was essentially a music of syllable and gesture; when I saw it presented dramatically and could visualize the situation behind each phrase, I would understand that even his orchestral and chamber works were built on the human drama and would play (or mime) it very much better. Enesco's word having the force of law in our house, Aba and I set off for Salzburg, traveling by car, a circumstance which gave our mission the jolly gloss of an escapade. Once in Salzburg we had a marvelous time, with sung Masses in the morning, operas in the evening, and between times picnics in the mountains. As Enesco said, the festival proved immensely helpful. Mozart's music had never been a closed book to me, but onstage at Salzburg it became truly alive and now I have a fair understanding of it. That I owe to Enesco and my father.

It was Enesco too who urged that Hephzibah join me on the concert stage. Our weekly soirées of chamber music during the Ville d'Avray summers helped engrave those years on my memory as among the happiest I have known. Introduced then to communal music-making, I have never had enough of it since and visualize an ideal retirement as a member of a string quartet endlessly playing to, for and with each other. But in those days I was just a learner in this most cultivated of pastimes, and carefully worked up each week the part Enesco gave me. At our gatherings Hephzibah would play the piano; Jacques Thibaud, Jacqueline Salomons and I took turns at first violin; Enesco, in this plethora of fiddlers, chose the viola unless, once in a while, Pierre Monteux was there; Maurice Eisenberg was our cellist. Monteux, compassionately noting that these permutations left Yaltah out, would sometimes insist on her taking the piano part, and she would rise to the occasion and play beautifully. One evening Hephzibah and I contributed a Beethoven sonata to the informal program. To everyone's consternation, Enesco's prompt reaction was that we should play together in public.

His enthusiasm took us unawares, projecting onto a real stage flanked by a real audience a domestic activity whose virtue lay in its being merely a diversion. Yet we were wrong to be surprised. At Ville d'Avray the understanding, closeness, trust and ease of relationship which Hephzibah and I had had since we had known each other matured into music and revealed that we had a Siamese soul. The duet seemed an instinctive act: even back to back each could strangely divine the other's exact feelings and intentions. "Yehudi used to go over scores with me," Hephzibah wrote some years ago, "explaining musical associations, putting life into phrases, filling in wide outlines with pertinent detail, so that I was intellectually safe, within well-reasoned arguments." In fact, we never embraced so closely in our well-reasoned arguments as in our lapses, for the latter were a consummation of the former. Leaving the text and covering one another's mistakes deftly, instinctively, could make us feel like trapezists rescuing life from near-falls, embracing on the verge, exulting on the far side; or it could simply give us the pleasure of a private joke. "I remember one Mozart sonata at the Metropolitan Opera House in New York, 1938," wrote Hephzibah, "and it went so beautifully, of its own accord, that we were both quite thrilled with it. In fact, just at the coda I was listening so spellbound that I forgot to play, and only came in, a split second late, by a tremendously shocked effort of will. We both laughed at this, and then very much enjoyed the after-concert crowding of well-wishers, because we felt we had for once deserved their praise."

But before we could reach that point my parents' initial reluctance had to be overcome. They hesitated to send another child into the con-

With Enesco (at left) and
Thibaud at Ville d'Avray

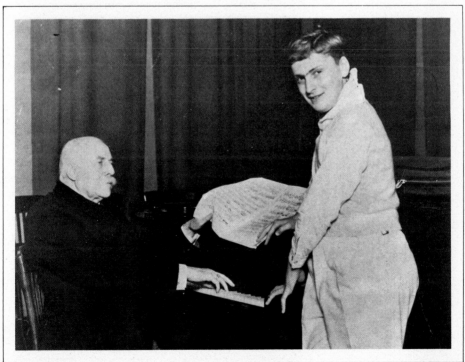

With Sir Edward Elgar

Toscanini and Yehudi on board the S.S. *Rex*

With Pierre Monteux, Paris, 1934

With Fritz Kreisler

Yehudi with Dr. Wilhelm Brockhaus, Director of the Leipzig Gewandhaus, and Bruno Walter, 1932

Sir Edward Elgar, Yehudi, and Sir Thomas Beecham in London, 1932

Enesco conducting Yehudi

Going over a score with Enesco shortly before his death

Zoltán and Emma Kodály with Yehudi

With Wilhelm Furtwängler as he conducts the Berlin Philharmonic

Dressed as Paganini for a screen test of *The Magic Bow,*
for which Yehudi recorded the sound track, 1945

With Olivia de Havilland
in the Aleutian Islands, 1942

With officers aboard the H.M.S.
Duke of York at Scapa Flow,
1944

With Jacob Epstein and his bust of Yehudi, 1945

With Benjamin Britten in 1945

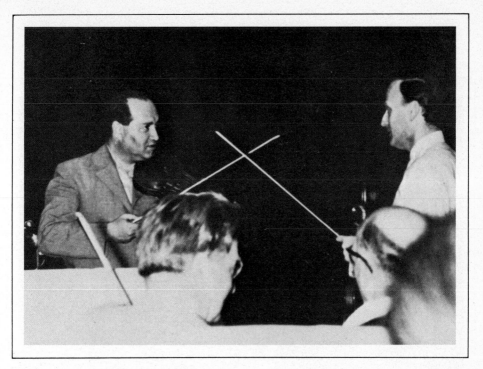

Oistrakh and Yehudi rehearsing the Bach Double Concerto

In Moscow with Dmitri Shostakovich, 1945

Mstislav Rostropovitch and Yehudi in Paris
at the UNESCO concert, 1974

With Nadia Boulanger, Bath Festival, 1964

Yehudi and Pablo Casals, Prades

cert arena, feeling it was no place for virtuous young ladies, however accomplished (Hephzibah was all of thirteen at the time). Doubts and disinclination dissolved, however, before the cogency of Enesco's opinion and the reassuring fact that Hephzibah was not to seek public acclaim in her own person, but with me. Our debut took place in that halfway house to the stage, a recording studio. We played Mozart's Sonata in A (K. 526) and received from our invisible audience a silent accolade called the Candide Prize, awarded to the best disk of the year. Ten months later, on 13 October 1934, we appeared before a live audience in the Salle Pleyel performing the Mozart Sonata in A, Schumann's Sonata in D Minor and Beethoven's *Kreutzer*.

When I play with Hephzibah today, it is almost as if nothing had changed. Despite womanhood, experience of life, work with the most deprived human beings, she still walks onstage with the simple, warm, trusting expression with which she walked onstage at the Salle Pleyel. The music has taken on depth and intensity, I believe; but it is still the embodiment, the sound, of a relationship which existed before we ever played together. Her trust—in herself, in the music, and in me—was so natural that it survived public appearance and indeed embraced the audience. It was the reverse of arrogance: although she was sure of herself and her performance, her assurance came from service to the music, so that she performed with simplicity, humility, almost naïveté, and certainly without exhibitionism or self-indulgence—virtues which were to make her particularly loved in England and France, two nations which, for all that separates them, share in rejecting emotion for emotion's sake, in valuing those who keep their feelings under control.

For Hephzibah music was a natural means of expression, a further bond between us, a happy duty. She never accompanied me in small brilliant pieces designed to show off the violinist's virtuosity. Together we played sonatas, equal voices in dialogue with one another; and being so close, needing to make no effort to bend and blend our personalities, we played them with a natural unity of conception and approach. It is true that from time to time I urged her to make more of some feature of the music—a bigger attack at such a point, a more assertive molding of a phrase here or there; and obedient sister that she was, she adopted my suggestions. But this compliance did no violence to her nature or her conscience. She never distorted a phrase from arbitrary conviction that it had to be made more "interesting." Certainly an audience could not deflect her from the path of righteousness. Such things can happen:

excitement or nervousness or a sense of occasion may enhance or damage one's performance; but I never knew Hephzibah to play any differently from what the music dictated to her.

Holding my hand, turned half to the audience, half to me, she bowed at the end of our first recital. I felt extraordinarily protective, very much the big brother, introducing her on stages where I was the old experienced hand.

6

Winter
Journeys

In the course of half a century I must have been through more heart-rending partings than almost any other human being. This aspect of the touring life is not, I think, sufficiently understood. For all I know, there do exist traveling artists who accept leave-taking with a light heart, who are restless when they must be still; but I am very much a family man, as I was a family boy, and I love being at home. I don't suggest that the constant traveling which characterizes my life has been nothing but a burden borne with inward grief and outward fortitude: no indeed; touring was a habit acquired early and offering great rewards, but in return it has always demanded the sharp pain of parting. During the first touring years Aba and I would leave my mother and sisters and Europe for the three months we spent in the United States. One farewell during that period was particularly anguished: it occurred at Naples on 7 January, Mammina's birthday, but in the flurry of departure the day's significance was entirely overlooked. My mother was too proud to remind Aba, too human for his forgetfulness to have no importance, and absolutely in the dark, my poor father attributed her mood to imminent separation until, only an hour or so before the ship left, light and memory broke dreadfully upon him. Even without such calamities to darken the occasion, the separations which broke up the family every year were always poignant, and yearning for reunion always underlay the pleasures of adventure.

Nonetheless I looked forward to the open road. The smell of autumn and of steam engines blended in my nostrils into the very breath of the nomadic life which, beginning in October, lasted six months of the year. I would sniff it like a colt scenting green fields. Over the many years since, touring has become almost as much a routine as going every day to the office is for another man, and new stations, hotels and concert halls have a remarkable similarity to all the other ones. But this may indicate the blunting of curiosity as much as its satisfaction. In my youth every voyage was a voyage of discovery, even if it had been made before.

I loved the excitement of travel from inland to a seaport. The boat train itself seemed not as other trains, trundling round their poor little domestic circuits, but already wore the glamour of the eventual sea. If the port was, say, Le Havre, from train to ship was an easy link, on foot along a covered pier, but many a time we crossed to the United States by a British liner, joining her at Cherbourg, where a tender connected shore to ship. Usually it was night and a gale blowing when the little craft loaded with passengers and packages bounced into the Channel to be thrown about by the waves, cut through by the wind, splashed by spray and rain; but when from these chilly tribulations one drew close to the great lighted palace lying at anchor, sighted the seamen waiting to attach the gangplank, came aboard into the wonderful release of light and warmth—what heady pleasures these were, and how much the world has lost in losing them!

On the other side of the Atlantic lay the United States waiting to be explored, a task so vast it required several years of tours to be accomplished even approximately. Crossing the prairies or the Great Salt Lake, Aba and I would sit in the observation car, with the smell of iron wheel on iron rail in our noses, the clickety-click in our ears, and get very dusty and gritty before coming in again. Thus we saw Texas for the first time, and the Southern states in their spring profusion of dogwood and azaleas, and the Everglades of Florida. We traveled to New Orleans by the *Crescent Limited,* a train so grand it consisted only of private rooms and all the service was white (it is hard to believe such snobbery was taken for granted only a relatively short time ago), and ate soft-shelled crab on arrival and marveled at the wrought-iron balconies on the houses. Tours were comparatively leisured; a few days were spent at each stopping place, allowing time to see sights and scenery and generally to appreciate the tremendous variety of my homeland. When I first went to Palm Beach, it was in the company of the whole family, and only after much persuasion was used on my parents. Jack Salter, my agent, had reported an offer of five thousand dollars for a concert at the Everglades Club, the elegant center of an elegant town, none of which facts, however, was calculated to evoke enthusiastic agreement from my father or mother. Very probably this was a club which excluded Jews, they suggested. On the contrary, Mr. Salter said, the contract had been drawn up by a Mr. Seligman. With this assurance, my parents made their first concession to society and we all went to Florida to discover that Mr. Seligman was about the only Jew on the premises. It was interesting to get an insight into the life of the upper crust, to see them play polo, which of all sports seems to me the most fun to watch, to bathe on the beautiful beaches and marvel at the strange vegetation of the Everglades. Moreover, at Palm Beach I heard grass-roots jazz for the first time in my life. On the wrong side of the tracks a group of Negro boys with washboards and other instruments were playing for their own amusement. I was deeply impressed.

After a year or two of splitting the family for the three American months, my parents decided it would be more satisfactory for all of us if Mammina and my sisters established a base in New York where the family could be reunited between concerts at Boston, New Orleans and elsewhere. Traveling remained the business of Aba and myself. A constant stream of letters, telegrams and, in course of time, telephone calls bridged the division, arteries that kept the family blood warm and flowing.

On our travels my father and I were more or less two chums. I never felt him as mentor or teacher, still less policeman, although he was naturally solicitous of my welfare. He was a solicitous man. If Mammina teased him with her "P-p-p-plans," his unrepentant slogan was ever "Check, double check." A foremost object of his double-checking was any sudden change of temperature, against which peril he would have his family sleep with socks and slippers near to hand, defenses against the cold morning floor's malignant design. He often had cause to chide my mother for taking her life into her feet, for she gave not a hoot for such dangers; but I found compliance no burden. Curiously enough, it had not been my practice to change my shirt after performing until, at the end of a concert in Leipzig, Bruno Walter taught me better, giving me a bottle of his own pine-scented liniment and advising a rubdown and a change of clothes every time. Aba, always rigorously faithful to a precept he has embraced, never neglected the task thereafter until I was out of his charge.

However careful he was, he could not altogether save me from the wear and tear of touring, however. At Boston once I had an experience which was, no doubt, inevitable—had it not happened then to forewarn and forearm me, it would have happened later: I fell asleep in midperformance. During the second tutti of the Beethoven Concerto, I simply lost track of what was going on and drifted into a pleasant relaxation which left me perfectly blank, like a horse slumbering upright in a field. About two bars before I was due to come in I realized I was on a stage, with an orchestra behind me, an audience in front, Serge Koussevitsky trying to catch my eye, and something expected of me within the next five seconds. So much for the usefulness of the conditioned reflex; but although I was glad to save the situation at the time, I have since regretted that my sleep was not deep enough to carry me beyond my entry, for that would have proved my story beyond doubt.

One of my father's responsibilities was to shield me from journalists, a duty he performed very effectively. He gave a few interviews over the years, my mother gave a single one, and I gave none at all before I grew up. Once in a while there would be photographs, when a few reporters would gather with the cumbersome cameras then in use, fill the little trays with powder, activate the flash and overcome everyone present with filthy smoke. But such brief encounters were all I saw of the journalistic world.

Without a doubt Aba was more protective of me than of himself. In the early touring years he suffered intermittent attacks of severe pain from gallstones, grew thin as a lath, and was finally operated on in New York. His operation coinciding with my American engagements, Mammina took his place on tour. I felt suddenly that I wasn't a child; very cleverly and sweetly she made me aware (as on previous occasions) that I was in charge of her, and all unsuspecting, I showed her around, advised on ordering breakfasts, pointed out features of interest, quite the expert patronizing the novice.

Whether my father or my mother came with me, a third person always shared our travels: my accompanist. Unlike the pianist, the violinist does not present himself without support, for only a limited number of works are conceived for his solo performance. On my first concert tour ever in 1928, Louis Persinger had accompanied me, but in Europe a professional had to be engaged. It was not a job every candidate could undertake: not only had he to play the piano adequately, he had also to fit our family circle. At one point the young Louis Kentner was briefly considered for this difficult position, but the size of his talent and personality rendered him too big for it; he would have sprung the tightness of the family. By a pleasant quirkishness, the future was to bring us together as equal partners onstage and brothers-in-law in private life. Several accompanists came and went over the years, some remaining friends for life. The first, who brought with him Adolf Busch's recommendation in time for the 1929–1930 season, was Hubert Giesen. He was a good musician, absolutely reliable and firmly within the German tradition, if somewhat inelastic. He respected my mother and her rule; I in turn trusted his playing and on the whole enjoyed his company. After two seasons with "Hoopsie," as we called him, the American violinist, teacher and composer Sam Franko, who had retired to Berlin, proposed Arthur Balsam.

Arthur Balsam was, and is, one of the best musicians I have known. A Polish Jew by origin, he needed music as he needed oxygen, and had come to Berlin to breathe, to study at the Hochschule, to miss not one concert, recital or public rehearsal. The very image of a kind, gentle, sensitive young scholar, instead of spending his days and nights with the Talmud, he passed his days in practice and listening and every spare minute with his head buried in a pocket score. As some women knit to soothe their nerves and concentrate their minds, he copied music, fashioning each note with careful love. He was a very dear person, shy away from the piano, full of vitality and authority in front of it. During the time that he was with us, Willa Cather gave me Heine's poems and Goethe's *Faust,* and Balsam, who spoke German well, would read the poetry with me. Later he was for years the New York Philharmonic's pianist and is now a celebrated soloist and teacher. When Balsam left us to pursue his own career we brought into the family an excellent Belgian pianist, Marcel Gazelle.

Like my sisters, Marcel studied piano with Ciampi, and it was on Ciampi's recommendation that he came to us in 1933, to stay until we left Europe, touring every winter, going around the world with us in 1935, and thereafter losing sight of us only temporarily. As I hope the following chapters will make plain, few men have played a greater part in my history than Marcel. It was with him that I rediscovered Europe as the Second World War drew to its end; it was with him that I began my school, and he spent his last years as its musical director; he was among the dearest and most valued of my friends and colleagues; and from the beginning he fitted so easily into my family it was as if I had suddenly been given an older brother.

Small, light, agile in mind and body, he was also the sweetest, kindest, best companion one could wish for, and eminently teasable, preserving his good humor unsullied even when, pinned queasily to his bunk by the rough Tasman Sea, he received at the malicious instance of Hephzibah, Yaltah and myself a choice collation of herrings and chocolate pudding. We all loved him. To be so completely of one mind about a person, without the least reservation, was more than proof of our acceptance of him; it was a further bond among us. For his part, Marcel understood us as well as we understood ourselves. He had been brought up in a horticultural region of Belgium, which gave him a permanent bias for the out of doors as well, perhaps, as a gardener's patience for the child developing at its natural rhythm. Self-reliant at a young age and blessed with an infinitely practical Belgian-French mind, he was a born solver of difficulties, painlessly dispatching in the early days the problems of travel, luggage, timetable, rendezvous, and afterward proving the organizing dynamo first of the piano department at Ghent conservatory, then at my Stoke d'Abernon school. But what was remarkable was his combining managerial genius with the most self-sacrificing readiness to serve. In the late 1930s Marcel married and carried off to Ghent my childhood friend and fellow violinist Jacqueline Salomons. Years later, when I persuaded him to work in England, she of course came too, to help teach the young violinists at Stoke d'Abernon. I love to see links with the past thus preserved, and to know that something of Enesco survives in Surrey, by way not only of myself but of Jacqueline.

If my travels over a lifetime have taught me anything, it is that music reflects society, scenery, even climate and geological substructure. Take Brahms: the products of the misty landscapes of north Germany, his works are full of groping, dreaminess and introspection. Mist gives a sense of infinity: it may be only two feet deep but equally it may cover the world, there is no knowing; and in this uncertain, unplumbable infinity of mist, one is turned in upon oneself to search one's soul. It is no accident that the people of Hamburg and Bremen understand Brahms as no other public does; nor that Toscanini, formed in the clear hard light of Italy, could not fill the quiet spaces in Brahms's music. It is still too soon to say whether modern music, having largely lost its roots and being at the mercy of every cultural wind that blows, will express our global society as satisfyingly as the music of the past expressed more stable societies; possibly a composer cannot survive without a local base. But for an interpreter, trying to do justice to many composers, it is rather an advantage than otherwise to have many lines of descent. I am not conscious of the different influences on my playing as separate entities—they have long fused themselves together. I picture, however, an overlay of French, German, Italian, English elements on the Russian-Jewish-American foundation, among them all supplying a compass with half a dozen polestars, each correcting the other's reading: ensuring that a performance is classical enough for the German, expressive enough for the Russian, polished enough for the American, elegant enough for the French, true enough for the English. . . . Of course, the compass isn't consciously operated: these national qualities have importance only insofar as they are part of me, rendering me musically, at any rate, a citizen of the world. The foundations of citizenship were laid in these journeys in my teens which took me not only throughout the United States but also the length and breadth of West and Central Europe and across the Channel to the British Isles.

On our first landing in Great Britain in November 1929, even the wharf, it seemed to me, exhaled an atmosphere different from the American and French wharves of my experience: an atmosphere of mature calm which convinced me that here was a people whom the centuries had taught the wisdom of restraint. Two images stand clear in my memory from the London of nearly forty years ago. One is the gentleman in Rotten Row who dismounted from his horse the day after my recital to introduce himself, show us some of London's monuments and then, at his home, his own collection of woods from every part of the globe. He was Mr. Alexander L. Howard, a wood merchant, whose knowledge of his subject went beyond the demands of commerce into delight in the thing itself. He was my first example of that amateurism, an elevated interest and pleasure in life, which I count among Britain's most admirable qualities.

My other image is of the starched, immaculate apron of the chambermaid coming to set or replenish the fire in our hotel room from a brass bucket. The traditional English open coal fire, reminiscent of Charles Dickens, seemed infinitely quaint and wonderful to me; combined with the quiet, cheerful, self-possessed chambermaid who tended it, it gave me a picture of England in which coziness held grimness at bay.

On this and subsequent visits to Britain, however, my overriding impression was that here my father relaxed. In general while we were touring, Aba was happy: he enjoyed the mixture of freedom and purpose as much as I did; but in England he breathed quietly and took the world on trust, never questioning the concert returns, for instance, as he might do elsewhere. Even when we came as a family we lived at a different rhythm, as if supported by a society which shared our views on the virtues of work, patience and discipline, and did not set us apart on their account or find it mannerly to acclaim us too extravagantly.

This land of decorum harbored, surprisingly enough, some of the first blood relations I ever got to know (there were to be others in after-years, in Russia and in Israel). Even someone whose days were thickly peopled with cousins and uncles would have valued the Miller family; for me they were a find indeed. Distant relatives of my mother, Uncle Jack and Aunt Edie Miller lived with their son and daughter, Jon and Sonia, in a big old handsome house near Richmond Park. Uncle Jack, who made his money from a chain of tobacco stores, was the sort of man whose generosity leaves one helpless: to admire his watch, for instance, was to risk his immediately making one a present of it, and although I learned to keep such dangerous admiration to myself, I still became over the years the recipient of innumerable objects of real value, simply because they happened to be there and Uncle Jack thought it would be nice if I had them.

Aunt Edie I loved at first sight. She was a fine, sensitive, distinguished person, a very good amateur pianist, well-known among English musicians. No less generous than her husband, she expressed generosity in the warmth of her welcome. On each trip to England we visited the Richmond Park house; in return, she came to the concerts and took us out. When, on my second English tour, I fell ill, it was she who took charge of the problem (the illness, proving to be appendicitis, was eventually remedied by an operation performed at Basel in 1930). Aunt Edie always had a special present for me—a basket of tropical fruits: custard apples, persimmons, lychees, passion fruit; things which in those days could be bought only in London among the capital cities of the developed world—not even Paris or New York supplied them.

I did not know it then, but contact with the Miller family represented a second neglected opportunity to meet Diana: Diana's mother and Aunt Edie, living in the same musical circle, knew each other well, and when Diana and I married, Aunt Edie was the dearest person we had in common. Aunt Edie Miller is dead now; I shall always miss her; I loved her very much. But Sonia and Jon still connect me with those happy, far-off days.

If London was lavish with exotic fruits, it treated fruits more familiar to me in a way any Californian would find extraordinary. Another encounter from my first sojourn, leading to another lasting friendship, was with Mr. Tattersall, a member of the horse-breeding and horse-racing dynasty which was already a feature of London in the days of the prince regent. It was Mr. Tattersall who first showed me the Tower of London, but hardly less intriguing than this historic pile was another novelty he introduced me to: grape scissors. Where I came from, one ate grapes by the handful; at this distance from any vineyard, however, a curious little implement was used to cut (or to wrench, for they functioned poorly) a modest allowance from the bunch for each person at table.

In preparation for the first London visit I acquired a British manager, Lionel Powell—whose office was arranged as a sort of terrestrial microcosm, each continent assigned a different room—and I established a recording connection which endures to this day. Much of the credit for the longevity and agreeableness of my relationshp with HMV (later EMI) must go to David Bicknell, who represented the company at the signing of that first contract in 1929 and continued so to represent it for many years thereafter. His warm, always smiling, rubicund English face brought a sense of friendliness to every kind of discussion. Both he and his wife, the adorable, warm-hearted, passionate Italian violinist Gia-conda da Vita, with whom I have played and recorded, have now retired to cultivate their garden near London in contentment. I see them far too rarely.

Of all the visits to England, one shines in my memory with particu-lar glory. It occurred in 1932.

One summer Friday in a departure from the normal touring pat-tern, Monsieur Vian, my father and myself set off from Ville d'Avray to drive to Calais on our way to London. Our outing was rather a lark: Monsieur Vian had never been to England before and his high spirits infected even us seasoned travelers with more than normal gaiety. For my part, I had ahead of me a great, even intimidating, privilege: the recording of a contemporary work under the composer's own direction, the composer being Sir Edward Elgar and the composition his Violin Concerto, upon which I had worked alone, submitting it, however, to Enesco before I left for London. I remember Enesco's commenting on how English the soloist's second theme was, a judgment which, in spite of my travels, I didn't then thoroughly understand, but which I have since come to agree with, seeing "Englishness" in this context as a kind of passionate innocence, very different from the passions—volcanic, aggressive, sophisticated, etc.—of other countries. If climate fashions music, Elgar's music—English to the point of being almost unexportable—expresses the flexibility within restraint of a weather which knows no exaggerations except in changeableness; and the response to it of a people able to distinguish infinite degrees of gray in the sky and of green in the landscape, never taking either to unseemly extremes. In England (I was later to learn) one can survive between do and don't; indeed to stand upon do or don't is to be a fanatic attracting general distrust, even in the best of causes.

On the English side of the Channel we were met by a handsome old Rolls-Royce belonging to Harold Holt, my English agent (the successor to Lionel Powell), and driven to Grosvenor House, where my knee pants and shirt were barred from the dining room (I rather enjoy formality and made no fuss). The next morning Ivor Newton arrived to run through the concerto with me in anticipation of Elgar's hearing it in the afternoon, as a preliminary to the recording. This was my first meeting with Ivor, with any English pianist, for that matter; it was to be some time before we met again, but in later years we gave concerts together and met often besides, and I learned to value him greatly. His qualities of urbanity, charm, consideration and wit served him well in accompanying certain lady singers (who must be cherished, their possibly erratic tempi taken account of, the accompaniment transposed if one day they don't feel up to a particular pitch) and made him a delightful companion to travel with. At two o'clock he and I were in place when Sir Edward arrived, a composer such as I was not prepared for: composers in my experience were Biblical prophets (Bloch) or heroes of chivalry (Enesco), not grandfatherly country gentlemen who should properly have had a couple of hounds gamboling at their heels and whose attitude to duty seemed, to say the least, relaxed. Ivor and I started to play at the soloist's entry and hadn't even reached the "English" second theme when Sir Edward stopped us: he was sure the recording would go beautifully and meanwhile, if we would excuse him, he was off to the races! It was comforting to know he thought me adequate, although I couldn't quite banish a suspicion that the attraction of the races thrust all question of my merits and demerits into second place. However, learning from Sir Edward what best to do with a fine Saturday afternoon, Aba and I took leave of Ivor and went out.

We were right to trust his judgment. At the recording studio Elgar was a figure of great dignity but without a shred of self-importance. I had never seen anyone conduct less, or show less determination to impose himself. All was ease and equanimity, almost as if his presence and movements were superfluous (of course they were not). This too taught me something about England: that authority must present itself unobtrusively, even humbly, the hard fist showing not in badges or manner of office, but in the leader's own comportment under fire; the cooler he is, the less assertive, the greater his authority. It is an exercise of authority developed through handling dogs, horses and regiments, through running an empire with a handful of civil servants, through centuries of reconciling opposition within a system. Not that Elgar had opposition to contend with: the orchestra surrendered itself to his invisible authority with joy, confidence and devotion. The recording was not only successful, but good. Some months after this first meeting we performed the concerto again, this time in the Royal Albert Hall. This was a concert to make a sixteen-year-old boy at once proud and humble. In the first half Sir Thomas Beecham conducted me in concerti by Bach and Mozart; after the intermission Elgar, propped on a red velvet stool, conducted his own concerto. To appear with England's most beloved composer as well as with her most distinguished conductor was like being given the freedom of the city or made a member of the family. Today these metaphors are not too exaggerated to express the friendliness I meet throughout Britain.

I was very anxious to present my newly discovered concerto in France. What should a musical cosmopolitan do but carry pollen from flower to flower, inseminate, disseminate, weave webs and build frail bridges? It has remained my mission. Enesco rehearsed the orchestra superbly, comprehending the work so well that when Elgar came over for the performance he took us through it without once stopping. The French audience received it politely, but it has never been performed in Paris since. Apart from England and England's former dominions, only the United States has welcomed Elgar's music, for it is a country so varied, so open-minded—to the new as to the old, to the exotic as to the overfamiliar—that every music finds its public there. It is a great American virtue to admit one doesn't know and give novelty a chance. I have often played the Elgar Concerto in the United States, the first time in New York with Sir Malcolm Sargent conducting, and I have seen its popularity grow. Usually I make a cut in the last movement, before the magical cadenza, where the recapitulation tends to sag and lose the audience's attention. Once I tried the cut version in England and was pounced upon—and rightly: one should not play fast and loose with a country's national heritage, however pure one's intentions.

Of all our displacements, the one which contributed most to musical development was the recurring winter in New York, and the man most largely responsible for this contribution was Toscanini. Only those who never knew the Maestro will find it hard to imagine how he dominated the city's musical life as no other conductor dominated any other city's. Berlin's pre-eminence was not in doubt, but in Berlin a half-dozen or so great conductors—Walter, Kleiber, Muck, Busch, Furtwängler—jostled for attention: in New York Toscanini was unassailable. Upon me his impact had the peculiar power of a first impression. Although I had played with (for instance) Bruno Walter, I had not lived in a musical atmosphere of his creation. To return to New York in the 1930s meant reimmersion in a superlative milieu fashioned by a superlative conductor. Even far from the city Toscanini was a potent force, for every Sunday morning he directed the New York Philharmonic in a broadcast program. In the mountains near Denver once I remember my father stopping the car we had hired or borrowed to listen to one of these Sunday concerts; and even through the inadequate medium of a car radio the incision and drive of a Toscanini performance were unmistakable.

Listening to his recordings now, I often argue with his interpretations. I own him to have been, unwittingly, a not altogether beneficent presence in New York, for he left behind him a generation of conductors who slavishly reproduced his outward characteristics—the speed, the unyielding tempi, the rhythmic strictness—but not the rhythmic spring, the flexibility, the slight unevenness which came from his profound understanding of music. Whereas he, in concerts and broadcasts, established standards of excellence new to the United States, his imitators multiplied dry, rapid, vapid, empty performances, ruining Beethoven for the American public in the process. These grumbles disposed of, I know I am greatly in Toscanini's debt. His own performances of Beethoven's symphonies still ring in my ears through countless versions heard since, and when I myself conduct one I can detect the echo.

Toscanini was not the perfect accompanist after the fashion of Bruno Walter. Indeed it would be hard to find conductors more antithetical—Walter the wayside stroller who admires every flower, Toscanini the purposeful traveler with his eye fixed on the goal. He, I am sure, separated music and musician, subordinating the second to the overriding importance of the first with an integrity that could seem ruthless in its refusal to tolerate the least self-indulgence of ornament or exaggeration. To me he couldn't have been more fatherly, nor I to him more filially respectful. One winter we did the Beethoven Concerto together, going through it carefully on the piano beforehand and reaching perfect unanimity. Whether he conceded anything from his ideal interpretation to my views I doubt, but equally I don't recall my views being affronted or displaced by his.

It was during the preparation for this performance that Toscanini showed me what it meant to be sure of oneself. In his apartment at the Hotel Astor on Times Square—which had an Italian proprietor and no doubt reliable pasta—we had reached the middle of the slow movement where, after the second tutti, the sound marked *perdendosi* hangs by a thread, when the telephone rang. Naturally I ignored it; so did my father in his unobtrusive corner; so, fumbling at the piano (for he was not a great pianist), did Toscanini. There was a second ring. We went on playing, I at least tensely aware that the pressure in the room was boiling up to a reaction. At the third ring Toscanini stopped, rose from the piano stool, and with light quick determined steps walked not to the telephone, but to the installation in the wall and jerked the whole thing bodily out, wooden fitting, plaster, dust, severed dangling wires; then, without a word uttered, he came back to take up where we had stopped, in total serenity. When the third movement ended there was a timid knock at the door. Relaxed, unembarrassed, amiable, Toscanini gently called, "*Avanti!*"—his first word since the incident—and the door opened on an abject trio, his wife, the hotel proprietor and an electrician, all promising to do better another time.

Toscanini's outburst, even more the completeness of its purging, which disturbed his pulse not one whit, left me half aghast, half envious, but in all our encounters I only received from him the benign protection that a person so utterly at one with himself can impart. Once when we crossed the Atlantic together, from Genoa to New York, I was stricken with a cold and every day he would spend several hours in the cabin where I was confined, hearing me play, advising me, discussing interpretation. He offered me a morsel of wisdom for use off the platform: whenever he felt miserable, he said, he thought of the thousands of people worse off than he and immediately cheered up. It was only later that it struck me his moral position wasn't exactly watertight, but no charge of smugness could be maintained against someone so unafflicted with self-analysis. At the end of that voyage I was to make my first broadcast, playing the *Symphonie Espagnole* with Walter Damrosch, an engagement threatened by my wretched cold. At first Mammina insisted that I shouldn't risk my health in the studio, then, softening before Aba's and my urgent pleas, she compromised: I could play—provided I wore a mustard plaster. To my father this seemed hardly less horrifying than canceling the broadcast, but feeling myself the equal of the Dutch boy who kept his thumb in the dike, I promised to abide by these unusual conditions. My promise was enough; I had passed the test. My mother, whose remedies were always 150 percent the strength of other people's, made the mildest mustard plaster imaginable, which I barely felt.

Toscanini did not win Mammina's unqualified approval. Partly this was my fault. She considered me overly humble in his presence, and when we played the Beethoven together a day or two after the destruction of the telephone, rather chided me for exaggerated subservience, perhaps fearing I would lose a sense of my own person in his powerful magnetic field. But partly she simply judged him as falling short of her standards of human greatness, and given the height of those standards, no doubt he did fall short. His failure to command his temper was calculated to win her contempt rather than her applause, and she attributed it not to his Mediterranean but to his peasant origin. Moreover, Toscanini was indeed capable of pettiness. Years later, in June 1946, I saw an example of this when various artists, among them myself, gave concerts in Milan to raise money for repairs to La Scala and afterward all went to a supper offered by Toscanini's daughter, the Contessa di Castelbarco. At the table where he, I and some others were sitting the conversation turned, inevitably, to conductors, and while Toscanini tore to shreds one colleague after another, the table sycophantically gobbled up his malice. When the fifteenth conductor had been laid to rest, albeit without blessing, I could contain myself no longer: "But surely, Maestro, you would find some quality in Bruno Walter?" "Bruno Walter?" retorted Toscanini. "A sentimental fool!" And so the sixteenth colleague tumbled in the dust.

Our New York base was an apartment in the Ansonia Hotel on upper Broadway, a hotel accustomed to musicians, which made no objection to their practicing. As well as bedrooms, we had a kitchen and a living room to ourselves, all at far less expense and more in keeping with our style of life than we could have found on Fifth or Park Avenue. We came and went as we pleased, engaged a buxom, warm-hearted Negro cook, and gave dinners to our friends and acquaintances, including the black singer Roland Hayes and Olin Downes, the music critic of *The New York Times*. The Ehrmans visited us whenever their New York sojourns coincided with ours, while the circle of local connections grew wider and deeper. Until we traveled to the United States *en famille,* Aba and I had continued to stay in New York with Dr. and Mrs. Garbat. I remember how motherly Rachel Garbat was, particularly on one occasion in 1931 when an indisposition threatened a recital at which I was due to play the Franck Sonata and Toscanini to be in the audience. Between Mrs. Garbat and my father, I was looked after hand and foot and delivered to the concert hall in tolerable shape.

Our friendship with the Edgar Leventritts became an increasingly important part of my life, principally on account of Mr. Leventritt's daughter Rosalie, of whom I was, and still am, very fond; and through the Leventritts we met Lionello Perera, an Italian banker blessed with three charming daughters, my particular friend being Lydia. Rosalie and Lydia were my New York girl friends, but our meetings were generally in a family context at either of their houses, where all the younger generation got together to play charades. Rosalie's brother Victor was then a student at Harvard. He played chess beautifully and always beat me—except once: after a matinee concert in Boston with Koussevitsky, I came back to the hotel for chess with Victor and chalked up my one triumph. Like too many of the brilliant young men I have known, Victor died young.

Sometimes we had the great pleasure of entertaining Enesco in New York. One visit of his I recall with particular clarity. My parents had often taken us to the Yiddish Theatre, a center not only of theatrical excellence and vitality but of Yiddish folk culture as a whole, one of the unique entertainments of New York. We were determined Enesco should not miss it, and so embarked on a most unusual exception to our otherwise well-regulated lives. After dinner at a restaurant we went on to the theatre, and from there to another restaurant to make merry until four o'clock in the morning, feeling thoroughly dissipated. It was the first time I had been up all night. In New York Enesco attended a rehearsal of the Brahms Concerto at which I played so badly that he made me go over the last movement again when the conductor and orchestra had dispersed. After the rehearsal I was due to have lunch with Esther, by then married to the dashing young Claude Lazard, and expecting their first child—yet nonetheless my Dulcinea—and distracted by this appointment, fearing I would be late for it, I took the last movement far too quickly, losing all its vigor and tension. There could be no question of leaving matters in this unsatisfactory state, Enesco admonished me; the movement must be put right for the evening. It was. I recall telling him that the lady I was to lunch with was pregnant; his chivalry per-

fectly comprehended my concern: "Ah! That is the most sacred condition of woman," he said. Nevertheless, my duty to Brahms came first.
At the age of ten or eleven Enesco had sat in the string section of the
Vienna Konservatorium orchestra, its youngest member, playing the First
Symphony under Brahms's own direction. Brahms was ever a favorite
composer of his, and I know that his rendering of the music has left an
indelible impression on mine.

The Ansonia Hotel apartment being too small for parties, my
mother's entertaining had to be select rather than lavish, but there were
some friends who came frequently. Of them all the most beloved was
Willa Cather, to whom Jan and Isabelle Hambourg had introduced us in
1930. From the outset there was between us a family closeness which we
children accommodated with the title "aunt" while Mammina, always
drawn to the utterly authentic, embraced her as a sister. I don't know
if each ever knew that the other had created scandals, half a world
apart, by wearing her hair shingled in adolescence, but it appears to have
predestined them for sisterhood (their confidences must have been fascinating; sadly I never overheard them). As if to enshrine that relationship
and make it immortal, perfect and inalienably hers, Mammina, when
Aunt Willa died, burned her letters.

Willa Cather was the embodiment of America—but an America
which has long ago disappeared. Her books, as everyone knows, describe
a country still overwhelmingly natural, a way of life still rural, lived by
settlers lately arrived from Europe whose traditions were all the more
precious for their transplantation to a strange land. Only recently has the
United States become a society of abstractions; no doubt the abstraction
of the pursuit of happiness existed then, but happiness itself had not
become an abstraction and was still rooted in the earth, as Aunt Willa
was herself. She had an eye and an ear for the aesthetic wonders of
nature, the fall of light on a landscape, the rustle of trees, and a realistic,
penetrating, compassionate understanding of the human animal in his
setting. The people she wrote about grew out of and belonged to their
environment, whether the Middle West, New Mexico, or Quebec, and
it is this which makes her work so American of its period. It is not too
much to say that she revealed a face of America to us youngsters who
were growing up among adults largely born abroad. Her mannish figure
and country tweediness, her let's-lay-it-on-the-table manners and uncon-
cealed blue eyes, her rosy skin and energetic demeanor bespoke a
phenomenon as strangely comforting to us all as it was foreign, some-

thing in the grain like Christian Temperance or the Girl Scout movement. In reminiscences a quarter of a century old she provided historical perspectives to my lament for New York, resurrecting a Manhattan where whole houses belonged to single families, the breadwinners of which walked or rode to Wall Street, tipping their hats to acquaintances met en route. Even by the 1930s the thought of knowing one's neighbors on Fifth Avenue was absurd.

She was a rock of strength and sweetness. Ever since coming east she had reserved time during the week for walking in Central Park, which was to her native Nebraska as a nosegay to an interminable prairie. Her favorite walk was around the reservoir in the park, where contact with the earth renewed her sense of belonging in a metropolis in which so much conspired to alienation. Park veterans ourselves, my sisters and I often joined her, taking turns at the honor of walking by her side. When I had the opportunity I saw her very frequently, not only in New York but in Los Angeles, where sometimes a tour delivered me when she was visiting relatives there. At one period I had particular cause to lean on her: in the unhappiness of my first marriage Aunt Willa was someone to be utterly trusted. One could tell her everything in one's heart: it would never be misused, never turned against one, never cause her to alter her regard. In those days she and I took many a walk around the reservoir. Her strength had a patience and evenness which did not preclude a certain severity. There were abuses and vulgarities she refused to tolerate, such as exposure in newspapers or on radio. She had a contempt for anything too much owned or determined by mobs, reserving admiration for high individual endeavor, withdrawing more and more from society even as she drew closer to us. The outside world became increasingly obscure for her, as on the fogbound island of Grand Manan in the Bay of Fundy, where she built a summer cottage. But indoors life burned bright, with parties and birthday luncheons, excursions to the Metropolitan Opera, baskets of flowers and orange trees arriving in snowstorms, and always books and walks in Central Park.

She adored what she felt had not been her birthright—the old, the European, the multilayered, and above all music. But her reverence did not cause her to stray into the self-doubt which some Americans used to show when confronting Europe. Early in 1936, on the point of returning to California, I must have expressed some uncertainties about the future, for in reply I received these words (words which, it must be said, have since been overtaken by time):

Yes, my dear boy, you *are* confronting a problem. But it is the problem which every American artist confronts. If we remain always in our own land we miss the companionship of seasoned and disciplined minds. Here there are no standards of taste, and no responses to art *except emotional* ones.

On the other hand, if we adopt Europe altogether, we lose that sense of *belonging* which is so important, and we lose part of our reality. I know a few very talented young writers who at the age of twenty-one or two decided that they would be French. They went abroad to live, and have never amounted to anything since. They can't be *really* French, you see, so they are just unconscious impostors. The things his own country makes him feel (the earth, the sky, the slang in the streets) are about the best capital a writer has to draw upon. A musician is much less restricted. The very nature of your work means "pack your kit." You, Yehudi, will simply have to do both things and live two lives. But I think you must spend your vacations in your own country when possible.

Her friend and biographer Elizabeth Shepley Sergeant wrote that she "made a story" of us Menuhins "as if she had at last, by proxy, a family exactly to her taste. Not at all like her beloved father's family with its pioneer tradition; in this brilliant Jewish milieu, erudition and art were primary, and everything else of secondary importance." When this passage is considered in the light of a remark uttered by Harsányi in *The Song of the Lark,* "Every artist makes himself born," it becomes apparent that creating fiction and merging with us celebrated a single impulse, that we who had found our American author gave our author her European novel.

If so, she returned our gift in kind and overmeasure, sharing her perception of European literature, making us presents of the German poets, taking us by the hand through Shakespeare's plays. In our apartment there was a little room, nobody's property in particular, small enough to be cozy, and furnished with a table around which Aunt Willa, Hephzibah, Yaltah, myself and often Aunt Willa's companion, Edith Lewis, gathered for Shakespearean readings, each taking several parts, and Aunt Willa commenting on the language and situations in such a way as to draw us into her own pleasure and excitement. She herself ferreted through secondhand bookshops to procure us copies of the plays. As originally chartered, the reading circle did not include me since I was often away on tour; but when present, I pressed for membership and was granted it. Her favorite author was Flaubert and her own style had his economy and elegance. She would polish her prose until it shone like a jewel.

Thus, representing America and presenting us with the values of Europe, Aunt Willa possessed the unity in diversity which underlay all my life. I had by now seen many other Americas than my own, but at a remove; the real discoveries were yet to come and in consequence were launched from a base as much European as American. Long before we saw Europe, we were conscious of it: it formed our parents, it gave us the books we read, it was the fount of music. Languages and travel confirmed the tendency, never excluding the United States but complementing it with a wide circle of attachments. The twice-yearly transatlantic crossings of adolescence did not split my life in half; rather they linked my double heritage into a seamless whole.

7

Interlude
in Eden

Whenever our American tour brought my father and me to the beginning of the West—Kansas City, let us say—I started to feel excited, and
the excitement mounted the farther we advanced across the prairies to
the coast and San Francisco. Although repeated visits had begun to give
other cities the charm of familiarity and build up friendships for us
throughout the United States, San Francisco never lost its primacy in my
heart and no other countryside had California's power to move.

All my feeling for my homeland is rooted in love of California. I
am tempted to commiserate with all those whose destiny condemned
them to grow up elsewhere and at another time; for how can they know,
these cheated millions, what beauty is? Certainly I haven't words to re-cre-
ate what they miss and can only hope they believe that the California of
the 1970s is but a poor plundered ruin of my childhood paradise. Even
then the process of spoliation was under way, as I have reason to remember. As already recounted, on our first family outing to Yosemite our car
had to struggle up a single rough track, stopping at the summit to cool off
and be watered like a beast of burden. I shall never forget the awesome
sensation that here, amid immense tracts of great trees and subtle sounds
and scents of alien lives, man met something stronger and older than
himself. Two or three years later nature was already seen to be in retreat.

The Ehrmans had invited us to their country house at Lake Tahoe, an ample, handsome wooden building in the much-gabled Central European style, inherited from a forebear and set in a vast estate which had a frontage on the lake of some three miles and measured another seven miles into the forest and mountains (so unconsidered was mere acreage in the nineteenth-century West that one could acquire whole principalities by federal grant—the property, of course, of the Indians). To reach this beautiful place one no longer had to cosset one's car springs over a primitive track, but coasted smoothly up a well-paved highway at sixty miles an hour. Allowed to dine with the grownups the night of our arrival, I regretted the journey hadn't been harder. "I wish they hadn't built that new road," I said, and was bewildered by the glacial silence which descended on the table. In fact, I deserved to be put up against a wall and shot, for I could have said nothing more un-American, more frankly treasonable. My lack of enthusiasm for the new road challenged the conviction which sustained our way of life: that two lanes were better than one, three better than two, and any paved road must lead to greater happiness.

I must have been eight or nine when I let slip this conversation-stopping remark. At that age I knew nothing of conservation or pollution or the pressure of population on resources; but between the regret I felt then and the causes I espouse now a line can be drawn. Indeed, as I have suggested, all the patterns of my life, of belief, emotion, action, are simple ones, emerging in childhood and developing thence without great interruption or divagation. An early puzzle, among the many that preoccupied my childhood years, was the harvest: so much taken from the earth and nothing, so far as I could see, put back; surely the whole risky operation was going to founder into bankruptcy one of these days (only less puzzling was the fact that no one, including my parents, seemed to share my concern). That this represented more than a city boy's ignorance of country matters needs no arguing today. Neither the United States nor any other country puts back what it takes from the earth, and in the last decades we have begun to measure the gap. We Americans have begun to appreciate how well the Indians preserved their inheritance before it was delivered to our rapacity.

I was not alone in cherishing special feelings for California. For all my family the Garden of Eden could be very exactly pinpointed in the Santa Cruz Mountains, and if anyone felt more strongly than I did, it was my father. Like every Jew, he longed to restore contact with the land, to plant a tree and see it grow to bear blossom and fruit. It was a Biblical urge become a Zionist urge in Palestine, but for Aba it took root in California one day in 1934.

Not for the first time, our tour that year allowed us to spend a day or two after the San Francisco concert at Cathedral Oaks, the estate of our friends the artists George Dennison and Frank Ingerson. "The boys," as we called them, had been among the earliest new settlers in the mountains, taking the place of farmers who abandoned their orchards for the city lights; but so recent were these movements of population that the untended trees still produced delicious apricots and cherries while one after another the farmhouses fell vacant and the hills grew emptier. On this occasion the boys told us that the property adjoining theirs was up for sale.

This news brought Aba's unspoken cherished vision to the verge of realization: to have somewhere on the earth's surface that was his; to cultivate his garden by the sweat of his brow, secure from everybody's interference; to own a piece of land precisely here, in the family's refuge, the family's holiday country, next door to valued friends who were artists besides and could advise on the building of a house; to build a house to my mother's design, of which she would be chatelaine, and to call it Villa Cherkess in her honor! It was a glad, glorious, romantic prospect, surely the most intoxicating one of Aba's life, a holy chalice holding all his dreams. He bought the land, approximately a hundred acres. Between the end of the American tour in 1935 and the beginning of the round-the-world tour which took us to Honolulu, New Zealand, Australia and South Africa, we all spent three weeks with the boys, talking, thinking, dreaming, eating and drinking house design and engaging and briefing an architect. When we finally returned from the other side of the world, it would be to take possession of our new home, the first we had owned since Steiner Street.

Alas, although the vision of the Villa Cherkess in the hills sustained us round the world, we never lived there.

The world tour was very wonderful, but what now stands clearest in my memory is less the passing sequence of countries, towns, halls and audiences, less the discovery of strange new continents under new skies, than the fact that midway through our travels I first analyzed a piece of music to my own satisfaction.

I have almost never taken anything from anybody for granted. Why this uncomfortable conviction that the truth must be seen to be believed should so mark me I am not sure, but I suspect it may be a consequence of my growing up in a climate of absolutes which tolerated no loose ends of preference or prejudice but demanded that opinion be anchored in a certainty beyond dispute. I have reacted against the dogma in various ways, now seeing reconciliation as the better part of dialectics and extravagantly admiring spontaneity; but the need to test instinct, my own or others', against some surer canon still flourishes undiminished.

For some time before the 1935 world tour the thought had been nagging me that I could no more explain *why* I played given passages as I did than *how*. Although my teachers had expounded on the repertoire, their commentary, like scaffolding against a blind wall, only created the illusion of windows. True, when it came time to perform this concerto or that sonata, I straightaway gained entrance and by sheer ardor carried my audience; but reason stood outside, urging that other people's explanations could be no more than working hypotheses, provisional until I was able to justify them to and for myself. The moment to attempt this occurred in a two-week lapse in the tour on the Indian Ocean crossing from Australia to South Africa.

We were passengers on the *Nestor,* a small, comfortable, old-fashioned ship of the Blue Funnel Line—one of the last coal-burning ships afloat, I imagine. Our cabins gave onto the promenade deck, so that one opened the porthole not on the restless movement of the waves, but on one's fellow passengers parading up and down. In the intervals of this interesting spectacle and of practicing, I sat myself down before a composition determined to understand it and, if possible, vindicate my interpretation of it. Significantly it was a sonata for violin and piano, a work, that is, which I shared with Hephzibah. I owed my introduction to it to the great French pianist Alfred Cortot, whom I once visited during the Ville d'Avray years. In his apartment on the avenue du Villiers, Cortot had assembled an impressive music library; one mounted a narrow iron staircase, in itself suggestive of the solitary, self-sufficient delights of scholarship, to discover riches ranged upon the shelves. Among them was this sonata, written by Guillaume Lekeu, a Belgian composer, one of those tragic figures which French civilization seems to produce, showing great promise and dying young, their gifts not protecting them from the ruthless hazard of illness and accident. His sonata, a romantic work, had been a favorite in Eugène Ysaÿe's repertoire; on Cortot's recommendation I added it to mine. Hephzibah and I made a recording of it.

We played it with instinctive feeling, no doubt. I remember a

moment of mutual congratulation earlier on the same tour, in Wellington, New Zealand, when my sister and I were practicing not the Lekeu
but another sonata and our playing had what I described to myself as an
"American" quality. By this I meant a confidence, a brilliance, a finish
that in my experience American audiences were particularly responsive
to. To have given a performance this finish, in ways I did not understand
and for reasons I could not give, was no longer enough. Nor could I now
be content with conclusions drawn from basic musical analysis, listing
exposition, development, recapitulation and coda, and noting a series of
modulations in this or that major or minor key. Such information remained in the end as unilluminating as the description which tells you a
man has the normal furnishing of limbs and features, weighs so much, is
dark-haired and has brown eyes; the man himself slips through the categories. Like a biochemist discovering that every human cell bears the
imprint of the body it belongs to, I had to establish why these notes and
no others belonged to this sonata; and it was important that I do it
myself, no more accepting ready-made explanations than I would consider myself acquainted with someone at second hand. I would track
Lekeu's inspiration from the first note of his sonata to the second, thence
to the third, and eventually to the last, explaining each in terms of what
preceded it; and thus (I hoped) basing the shape I gave his phrases, the
speed, the volume and the relation between these factors, on certainty.

The results of these efforts were sufficiently cheering to tempt me
further into my repertoire. Other much-played works followed Lekeu's
Sonata into the mill, delivering up to my understanding the inevitability
of the notes chosen to carry the impulse of the music from start to finish.
Analysis became a necessary habit which persists to this day; each new
work must go through the process; and thus I provide myself with arguments for following instinct. Which does not alter the fact that I am
most happy when the subtleties I've spent so many hours searching for
occur of themselves, spontaneously, without any reasoning at all.

To give a clearer idea of my approach to musical analysis, let me
take the first solo bars of the Beethoven Concerto, the work which,
following the Lekeu, I next tackled. It was a useful inspiration. Not only
had the Beethoven symbolized musical seriousness in my childhood, but
there was to be thereafter no other concerto that I played, or that anyone
perhaps has ever played, in as many different places with as many different orchestras. I doubt if I hold other world records, but fifty years of
performing the Beethoven Violin Concerto have, I would be willing to

wager, given me one: a circumstance not necessarily enviable, and perhaps exposing the record-holder to the danger of mechanical repetition. I believe that my efforts to comprehend the work as an organism have helped to avert this peril.

The solo part begins thus:

Pondering these notes, I realized for the first time that, as a group, they are the inversion of the two preceding bars, which are themselves preceded by units of one and two bars:

It became evident that the violin answers two groups of four descending notes with two groups of four ascending notes. Here one encounters the first ascending chord which covers these two octave ranges: it has been preceded by a broken chord descending, toward the very outset, before the first fortissimo in the opening tutti:

—again in groups of two bars, four notes plus four.

The following double forte represents a span of one octave, but is only one bar long:

The solo entry is the first example of that particular form ascending over two bars.

Already I understood that it is, more than an arpeggio, an integral part of the whole. Equally important is the rhythmic element. Unlike the four opening notes, the drumbeats which establish a basic pulse, the first solo bars come halfway to being a melodic figure—not *quite* melodic (since the notes bear no unique, independent, idiosyncratic relation to each other), nor purely rhythmic like the initial timpani bar, but more melodic than the latter. While retaining something of the punctilio of the opening bars, it *must* at the same time have wings and soar.

It occurred to me, furthermore, that the span of the violin entry has significance, extending as it does from the A to the G, for that constitutes the structure of the concerto's opening phrase, which is:

achieved by melodic contiguous motion rather than the disjoined motion of the broken chord; as if to stress its derivation, the solo violin continues with:

which gives us the opening melody, the sequel to the first four notes above:

These eight notes thus acquired more and more meaning as I thought about them in context. The further I pursued my inquiry, the clearer it became that these notes could not be any others. There exists, for instance, a very close relationship in Beethoven's music between scales and broken chords. In the slow movement of this concerto, he extrapolates the intervening notes, leaving a broken chord pure and simple:

which in the first movement is:

It is the same figure, but worked, latticelike, into an arpeggio.

Perceiving this relationship was one thing, knowing how to use it another. I had already discovered that the span is from A to G, necessarily rising as many octaves as it had previously descended. Beethoven adds a third octave in the form of a grace note:

The grace note provides the impulse, a surprising sort of spring, or the anticipation, the feint of a spring not yet taken. The octave also belongs organically to the piece, as it comes first:

then:

then, as I had already seen:

The violin therefore begins with the spanning of an octave, which, when it finally reaches the solo melody, becomes:

and states a rejoinder to the preceding octave scale on the dominant.

I concluded that there must be three stages in an interpretation: the exaggeration, reducing and assimilating of all justifiable deviations from a structural norm. Ideally one would play a passage so that it sounds even, yet retains enough of the original distortion for its vital element to be recognized, accommodating what one might call *la part de Dieu*, the nuance or twist that each performance unconsciously dictates. Any interpretative variation is valid that doesn't flout the inherent form, that doesn't justify itself outside the relationship of the notes.

Thus, knowing that the C sharp and the E in this opening solo bar do not enjoy as much prominence as the A and the G, I would try to elide the former, arching over these intervening notes. By holding the A, hurrying the C sharp and E, then accenting the G—in other words, playing the two middle notes less strongly, yet effecting a crescendo to the G—and by continually testing these distortions against the essential basic pulse, I could produce a dynamic image: a rise not so dignified as to lose its sense of expectancy, nor so precipitate as to lose the dignity enjoined upon it by that first timpani bar, a rise whose very "evenness" lives for being the resolution of opposite forces.

Obvious? Stating the obvious made me feel less contingent. Discerning a form glassed in its smallest constituent part, I saw myself through a mirror and thus made a first conscious step to adulthood, to analysis and synthesis, to consciousness and clarity of sight. Years ago many photographers on New York's Lower East Side, whose clientele was the immigrant Jewish community, kept handy a pair of spectacles with window glass for unmyopic boys having their confirmation portraits done. Where the gentile made an equation between physical strength, athleticism, gladiatorial prowess and virility, and tended to regard intellectuals as effete, the Jew equated insight with manhood. It therefore behooved every young initiate to wear his mind upon his face. My instinctive *tours de force,* the recognition accorded me, the fantasy of matrilineal descent from a martial figure, did not confirm me so emphatically as one small triumph of reason, one unaided perception of significant form. I had yet to discover its human coefficient, the shape of my individual history, the significance buried in events, those reasons of the heart that made my relationships with certain few people as fated, as necessary, as the relationships among notes. Still, having found internal significance in music, I found myself significant; having entered knowingly what had hitherto seemed opaque and given, I no longer beheld myself as nature's sport. Having grasped something, I would during the difficult years ahead, when life lost its miraculous coherence, when my violin itself became enigmatic, husband the assurance that I could solve riddles.

Before retiring to our Pacific fastness, we briefly returned to Paris in the spring of 1936 to take leave of Europe and Enesco (whose opera *Oedipe* was then in rehearsal for its Paris première), and to fulfill a final engagement or two. With Hephzibah and Eisenberg I recorded the Tchaikovsky Trio and, above all, I at last agreed to record some Kreisler pieces. In my romantic way, I had long wished to convey the most subtle and chivalrous sentiments to ladies, particularly to play "Schön Rosmarin" meltingly and irresistibly; but until now I had not dared to try, knowing how elusive was the degree of sophistication, worldliness and ease in elegant company which had formed Vienna and Kreisler. Fifteen years of attempts to capture Kreislerian nuance were at last to be rewarded. To prepare myself I bought a recording of Kreisler's own performance of "Schön Rosmarin," shut myself up in my room at the Majestic Hotel, listened to it, played in the intervals of listening to it, played with it, and after a solid week's work I knew I had it. Recently rehearing that 1936 record, I had no cause to judge my confidence misplaced: it was Kreisler, all right.

    With this ambition at last achieved, our days in Paris hung not too heavily on my hands, but beyond Paris, California beckoned, especially for my father. Since 1927 Aba had been in Europe on sufferance. If he had given up his job and our Steiner Street house on my account, the land now bought guaranteed the sacrifice as a provisional one, but at the same time it increased a hundredfold his impatience to be gone. An occa-

sional explosive "That tomb!" directed *sotto voce* at the Arc de Triomphe
relieved his feelings, but only partially. On the one hand, he yearned for
California; on the other, he sensed Europe's impending collapse and
wanted us all well out of it. And there was a third reason for his eagerness to get away: 1936 was to usher in a year without travels, hotels,
concerts, records, engagements or commitments of any kind, a year of
idleness and staying put and enjoying ourselves. Although we did not
know it then, this break in routine closed a chapter in our history. Before
we emerged into public life again, in late 1937, I would be twenty-one;
before a further twelve months had passed, Hephzibah, Yaltah and myself would be married, almost literally all together, and my parents suddenly bereft of the purpose which had shaped half their lives. The "year
off" in the family's favorite haunt was to prove a last celebration of the
family. Aba called it "Mother's year."

It began disastrously. Some months earlier, in midtour, we had
received the architect's plans of the Villa Cherkess and his final estimate,
and at the prospect, suddenly become real, of spending sixty thousand
dollars of family funds on something so personally precious to him, Aba
lost courage. The small allowance of abandon which he permitted himself leaked away before the enormity of his vision made flesh; he had
construction halted before the main work began. But although he gave
up the house, he didn't give up the dream, for dreams remain intact as
long as they are dreamt. So it was with beating heart that he brought us
home—and found home to be a little, hot, dusty, flimsy cottage, planned
as an overflow for guests, without charm or even space enough, standing
in bulldozed earth by the side of a road, with no expanse of garden, no
trees or flowers to soften its crude nudity, miles from any shop. It broke
his heart, of course: every day he would go there and, literally, cry.

Mammina saved the situation. Without waste of time or emotion
she marshaled us into a hotel in Los Gatos and scouted the countryside
for available properties. It took her three or four days at most to find one
to her taste, on a hill above the town, a lovely family house which
rambled in every direction, with flower beds and greensward framing an
ancient oak, and a guesthouse in whose main room we could perform
plays among ourselves, as the previous owner had built a stage there. Our
terrace commanded the Santa Clara Valley and the far-distant San Francisco Bay. Behind us, extending to the very top of the mountain, were
orchards tended by the fathers and brothers of the Sacred Heart Novitiate. No sooner had we become his neighbors than Father Dunn introduced himself, welcoming us to use the novitiate's trails and tennis

courts whenever we chose. It was almost implausibly appropriate that our deed should have given us a foothold in paradise, for Mammina's Caucasian dream had already made lifelong novices of us all.

After its inauspicious start, the "year off" recovered, to prove as happy and carefree as had been intended. For my part, I had my first car to help me make the most of it, and I don't think human being has ever enjoyed a car as I enjoyed that one. I bought it in New York on the way to California, a secondhand open Cadillac V-12, and had it sent freight to Oakland Pier. When I collected it there, three tires promptly blew, a result of its having stood too long in the warehouse, but this small set-back was turned to good account, giving me the opportunity to put on splendid white-walled tires (I had a sense of style in motorcars), and thus dashingly equipped, I drove in triumph to Los Gatos. My car fairly widened my scope. Those were the days to drive for pleasure, for the roads were not yet crowded and one could lose oneself for hours in the country without meeting another soul. I would make expeditions to the sea at Monterey, to the observatory on Mount Hamilton across the valley or just up into the hills, always choosing the least used, most romantic roads. Few motorists can have backed up more one-way tracks, or fought their way over more impassable trails, than I did in my Cadillac. I had one memorable escapade in it when I invited my mother to an opera in San Francisco. We did the thing in style—best tickets, hotel rooms for the night, formal dress—then had an adventurous return journey through a fog so solid one could just make out the line of the road.

Aba may have called this interlude "Mother's year," but in fact it was my sisters' year, and more particularly my year, just as everything my parents planned was on our behalf. It was our fling, our time of freedom, of unconcern, of letting duty slide, of summer excursions with young friends come to stay. One of these was Daniel Fleg. He came at my mother's invitation but in response to the wishes of all of us: we never liked to give anything up, and being in California, longed for a piece of the France we had loved. Daniel was a clever, melancholy boy, with the face of the scholar, the yearner, the dreamer whose ambitions are beyond his physical capacity. He came to be nursed and fattened up, and indeed returned from Mammina's ministrations to France several kilos heavier than he had left it; but his heart was in the Old World. When the Spanish Civil War broke out during his stay, it took all our persuasion to prevent him from enlisting in the Republican cause. Wild horses could not have held him back when his own country went to war in 1939: he was rejected as a pilot on grounds of health, and in despair

at what he saw as his uselessness, committed suicide. His brother
Maurice fell in the early days of the war.

Part of Daniel's cure at Los Gatos was hard labor. He helped build
our swimming pool, wheeling barrowloads of cement for the workmen,
who thus found themselves co-opted into the campaign to build Daniel
up; and when he was at work, my sisters and I often joined him. He was
a good companion, quick, articulate in English as well as in French and
prepared to fall in with any suggestion for an outing or a pastime. For
Yaltah's fifteenth birthday there was a surprise party, to which everyone
came masqueraded—Aba as a coolie, the pianist Beveridge Webster,
who was a special friend of Hephzibah's, as an American Indian, I as a
Bedouin, Daniel as a Rumanian gypsy. Other light-hearted activities
took place. On my parents' wedding anniversary we performed the third
act of *Cyrano de Bergerac,* I playing Cyrano, Hephzibah Roxane and
Yaltah de Guiche, then the Monk. An elegant gentleman from San
Francisco, Mr. Keath, taught us to dance the tango to the "Cumparsita."

My own special visitor was Rosalie Leventritt from New York, a
very vital, interesting, pretty girl with a wonderfully archaic Jewish face
—thin mobile features, deep lively eyes, her father's pronounced nose,
dark hair. Rosalie had one weakness—an ungovernable horror of cats;
which was a trifle awkward because, being in the one place for many
months, we acquired a whole menagerie of animals including a couple of
strays, Gemila and Pascha, a German shepherd, Alupka, and Feodosya,
the goat; not to mention a wild duck that mistook our pool for somewhere else but came to its senses and flew off before acquiring one of
those names that transformed Menuhin beasts and Menuhin children
alike into heraldic emblems (Alupka and Feodosya are Crimean cities,
the latter a center of Karaitic culture). In adult life Rosalie has done
remarkable work for music in the United States, helping organize tens of
thousands of concerts given by young people for young audiences in
schools, to whom the compositions and instruments are explained. At Los
Gatos, I had, of course, no idea that she would win her epaulets in this
way, but indeed I needed no proofs of zeal, musical or any other, to
nourish my affection for her.

When Rosalie had gone, I wrote to my favorite confidante, Aunt
Willa, to tell her of my loss. With a truly auntlike combination of
sympathy, moral stiffening and humor, she remarked in reply, "A little
heartache is a good companion for a young man on his holiday," then
took the opportunity to give me some serious advice on the choice of a
wife—advice which in retrospect might be thought prophetic:

You will need fundamental honesty in a wife more than anything else, I think. By honesty I mean the knowledge that two and two make four and can never be sighed or dreamed into making five. Also the knowledge that real love is not so much admiration as it is the drive to help and to make life easy for the other person. If the man is a man with a career before him, she must have good sense and stamina as well as charm. . . . But I doubt if you will marry an American at all. I rather think you will need a girl with a more disciplined nature than our girls are likely to have. . . .

Fortune has always been good to you, my boy, and I rather suspect her crowning favor will be a girl like that: slight, heroic, delicate, unconquerable (sounds as if I were describing Marutha, doesn't it!). Well, like enough you will marry someone much your mother's type.

We took advantage of the novitiate's open invitation and explored every corner of the mountainside, by day when it was too hot but the views were magnificent, and by night when the cool air was balmy with the scents of vegetation. Those rambles at night were the loveliest of all, sometimes lit by the moon or by the powerful starlight of the countryside, but without any light at all I could find my way surefooted, so well had I come to know the different fragrances of copse and trail: through clumps of bay and manzanita, faintly clammy from some hidden spring where, as often as not, a shrine to the Virgin Mary had been built; out into the dry air of the open vineyard to pick grapes forgotten in the harvest, slightly shriveled and raisiny, but sweeter than any other grapes and still juicy if one chose wisely; up to the top of the mountain crowned by four or five immense rustling eucalyptus trees, the folded landscape beneath us dimly sensed in the night's faint glow; and so home again in a state of exaltation to make ourselves omelets at dissolute hours. . . . I didn't touch the violin for three months, then picked it up with a refreshed love and joined friends like Nathan Firestone and John Paterson in sessions of chamber music.

It was a blithe, young, joyful, golden time, careless of tomorrow. A recital in San Francisco in October 1937 brought it to an end.

8

War
and Peace

There was more than a touch of California about Nola and Lindsay Nicholas: only a new young country in the sun could have given this handsome brother and sister the carefree exuberance, the physical vigor of people who live much out of doors. In fact, they were Australians and by virtue of the fact had an un-Californian orientation to the culture and traditions of Mother England. We were introduced backstage at the Royal Albert Hall, London, by the conductor of the Melbourne Symphony Orchestra, Sir Bernard Heinze, at the end of a recital one afternoon in March 1938—they being on the modern Australian version of the grand tour of Europe and I safely back in harness after the year off.

At first view it might seem little had changed in my life except that my fixed address, so far as I had one, was Los Gatos. The pattern of winter tour and summer break had already been re-established, and this visit to Europe—during which I would celebrate my twenty-second birthday—was more of a family enterprise than ever, involving my mother and sisters in addition to my father. Superficial appearances notwithstanding, I imagined that I had crossed the unmarked boundary that separates the men from the boys: I no longer had a teacher to spend summers with, I had progressed beyond regular tutelage, I was ready to fall in love. So I did.

We might have met Nola and Lindsay three years earlier in Melbourne, for they had attended my concerts there and Lindsay was an informed amateur of music who read scores for pleasure and had amassed a notable collection of records; but by chance our meeting was delayed until this bright London springtime when I was of an age to value it as an offer from fate to float me into independence and in a state of mind to have neither power nor inclination to resist. Nola, then nineteen, was an attractive, auburn-haired, enormously energetic girl who swam, played tennis and drove her white Jaguar motorcar with assurance and panache. Lindsay, as athletic as his sister, was a tall, handsome, open, agreeable young man, and if anything were needed to increase the power of their individual attractions, their fondness for each other supplied it. Hephzibah and I saw, admired and were bowled over. We all four went out together quite often until concert engagements took me off to Holland.

Our first night there, I locked myself into my room to put through a call to London, muffling my voice as best I could beneath pillows, and as soon as Nola answered, made her a proposal of marriage. Nola, interrupted in the middle of a late-night supper with her brother, was understandably startled; we scarcely knew one another, she protested. Yes, but had I "known" Persinger and Enesco before electing them? or learned the violin before playing it? Her prudent demur was utterly beside the point. I was perfectly serious in my proposal, desiring her with the urgency of youth and knowing no accommodation for my desire other than eternal vows. The strength of my conviction convinced her. By the time we came back to London I had pretty well made my point: Nola's agreement had been won, so had my parents' support; there remained nothing to do but await the arrival of George Nicholas, Nola's and Lindsay's father, who, although taken aback by this so sudden turn of events, was soon persuaded to add his approval to the general harmony. Hephzibah thereupon announced her engagement to Lindsay and Yaltah hers to William Stix, a young man from Saint Louis whom we had met several touring years before. Our parents gave us a mass benediction.

I had not supposed otherwise. Ever encouraging the young to marry, my mother couldn't be unsympathetic to an enterprise which she, like myself, saw as a natural goal of growing up, the happy end to the story. The idea of losing Hephzibah to the Australian outback and Yaltah to Saint Louis must have cost her sadness, but being herself, she did not show emotion or suggest she might have a claim upon our lives. Instead she welcomed Nola as a new daughter. Young, lovely, full of good will and the wish to please, Nola had many graces to recommend her, not least the pathos of having lost her own mother when she was a little girl. For her part, I imagine she found in our close family unity an intriguing warmth. When my commitments ended at the beginning of May we all, Nola and Lindsay included, spent two weeks with the Hambourgs at Sorrento, then came back to London and the wedding. Scarcely two months had passed since our first meeting.

Nola and I were married on the morning of 26 May 1938 at Caxton Hall, in the presence of our immediate families, by a British civil servant who read the service imperturbably while carpenters constructing an air-raid shelter in the basement hammered an obbligato. Originally the ceremony was to have taken place the next day; I advanced it twenty-four hours so that we might not miss a performance of Verdi's Requiem conducted by Toscanini. Carried westward on a conjugal progress to Yaltah's wedding in New York in June and Hephzibah's at Los Gatos in July, our family spent its last united week on the high seas; but my sisters' departure from home did not prompt me to hasten my own.

Only I was to blame for my failure to grasp independence more wholeheartedly; it was as if I had not completely shed my earlier clothes or earlier incarnation, and in this half-and-half condition I knew I wasn't making Nola happy. Her father knew it too. George Nicholas was a remarkable person, upright with Protestant principle, shrewd and successful in business, strong with the strength of the self-made man in an open society. He came to California for Hephzibah's and Lindsay's wedding (celebrated beneath the oak tree in our garden), and before returning with them to Australia took me aside and gave me a talking-to about Nola's unhappiness. There were many things in my personal life at this period which, were I faced with them again, I would tackle differently; or so I now think, but can one be sure he would not fail in precisely the same way again? Clearly my parents were not going to thrust me out of their house, but they managed to bring about my departure nonetheless. A month or two after Mr. Nicholas's scolding, Aba gave Nola and me the never-lived-in cottage built in 1935. It was large enough for two, and when our children came I had it extended—spending more in the process than the Villa Cherkess would have cost, had it ever been built—and called it Alma after the railroad station at the bottom of our land. I first took Nola to the cottage from a belated honeymoon in Yosemite, writing my parents that I wasn't coming back and waiting in some apprehension for their reaction. How little I understood them, after all! They accepted the development serenely, as though it were perfectly natural for a married son to leave his parents. From that moment I began to grow into independence.

Undoubtedly the birth of our children gave this growth a useful impetus. It was an extraordinary adventure to embark on fatherhood, an experience not the less miraculous for having happened God knew how many million billion times in the history of the world. Surely every new father or mother shares my awe, and rightly, for repetition doesn't rob natural wonders of their fascination and every life is unique. I followed Nola's pregnancy with both philosophical and medical attention, interrogating the gynecologist for information, but nothing he told me prepared me for the sound of a voice which had never been heard before, or for returning from San Francisco with an extra person.

Zamira, my only daughter, was born in 1939. In time for her arrival I ordered from England a tall, elegant baby carriage such as used to throng Kensington Gardens in a more gracious age. I still think these stately perambulators an excellent idea, much more healthy than the low-slung push-chairs of today which expose infants to the full blast of car exhausts; but in a way Zamira's English pram sublimated an urge of my own: suspecting I should never own a Rolls-Royce, I made sure of the baby-carriage equivalent. Among other advantages, it had space enough for Krov, once he was born, in addition to Zamira. If I catered adequately for Zamira's promenades, I did her a grave disservice, however, in allowing the inordinately fat nanny to feed her on Karo syrup (all people want to create life in their own image), thus burdening the child with a weight problem which only teen-age determination, stiffened by Diana's counsels, cast off; those were the days when I knew nothing of nutrition, but I rapidly learned better and none of Zamira's brothers was so unfortunately launched.

In 1940 the pattern of our life was varied with a visit to Australia, which took us from spring to autumn at a rhythm as leisurely as the voyages that framed it (how unimaginable now to have half a year without commitment!). We must have seemed more a migrant clan than a holiday party: Hephzibah and Lindsay on their sheep farm being our objective, Yaltah joined Nola, Zamira, Zamira's nanny, my accompanist and myself for the trip, and on our return Krov, born in August, was added to our number. This was my second experience of Australia, but the first time the country penetrated my flesh, as it were. Never before or since have I spent so long shoulder-to-shoulder with the four-legged as then, on my brother-in-law's 21,000-acre sheep station and at his father's racing stables. It was an open-air life whose components were sun and sea and the pungent, invigorating, eucalyptus-flavored breath of the out-back. Hephzibah and I made our musical reacquaintance at concerts in Sydney and Melbourne. There were many concerts: our sunlit, active days were a distant backdrop to events in Europe where the Luftwaffe was then losing the Battle of Britain, and I played for every cause that offered, British, Jewish, Free French. . . . It was a hiatus in my life which seems in retrospect a period of waiting for the inevitable storm.

Krov was born in Melbourne at a hospital run by the Sisters of Mercy, who gave me a room for the duration of Nola's confinement, brought me breakfast each morning, made no objection to my practice and altogether treated me with the greatest consideration. The hours before Krov's birth are curiously vivid in my memory. A wealthy Melbourne merchant had lent me his collection of violins, and I remember trying them out in the hospital, then walking to the Town Hall for a rehearsal of the Brahms Concerto, not knowing which would arrive sooner, the baby or Brahms. We called our son Krov Nicholas—Nicholas after Nola's family, of course, and Krov for reasons of my own. Like my mother, I avoided the Toms, Dicks and Harrys of generational conservatism in favor of something more exotically individual, and having wished "Zamira" on Zamira, only later discovered from my father that the word meant "songbird" in Hebrew. As Za mir also signified "for peace" in Russian, our daughter's name was doubly satisfactory. Our son's name demanded no less ingenuity. I wanted it to be short and to have an r in it. I respected the letter r, or rather its sound, thinking it suggested bravery, courage, power, aggressiveness, strength—all of which words, it will be noted, are endowed with an r—and found our family's names somewhat flabby in its absence. My mother, Marutha, had the only r-blessed name among the Menuhins until Zamira's naming, and Nola's family was equally underprivileged. No doubt my early struggle to master the English r, repeated some years later with the French and German ones, enhanced its value in my ears. Anyway, both my specifications were met in the made-up name Krov, which had a third attraction in its Russian provenance: with a hard ending it means "blood" and with a soft one—approximately "Krovyeh"—it means "roof" or "shelter." Saddled with this piece of fancy, the poor child must often have wished on his progress through youth that he had less to explain away, but in the extraordinary manner in which people and their names coalesce, Krov's name, for all the forethought that went into it, has come to mean Krov.

He was a delicate little boy, but he grew to be active and wiry, and in manhood is now a splendid example of physical prowess and hardiness. As a boy he was always extremely winsome, his character more direct and less complex than his sister's. When he behaved badly or simply unthinkingly, he would always be ready to admit his mistakes and to make up for them, never harboring ill feelings against anyone else or against himself: the negative occurrence was forgotten, the new phase happily begun. In his and Zamira's early years, constant touring prevented me from seeing much of them except in the summer, and my interventions in their upbringing may well have seemed sporadic and theoretical. I would give them raw brains to eat, milk from a neighboring cow to drink, and take them pickaback on long arduous walks in the hills.

There were many warm and happy moments, but they could not ease or conceal the growing strains upon our home. I would have taught Nola the innocence of Eden, she would have sponsored my assimilation in the world. Sometimes she came on tour with me. She would sit high up among the two-dollar ticket holders, hoping by that expedient to make me play to the gallery, or make reservations at supper clubs (for all my traveling, the restaurant remained a somewhat foreign institution) whose soft music and hard drink created a *goyishe* Lethe that filled me with existential alarm. Soon the war would increasingly separate us, taking me all over the free world, leaving her more and more with the children; and she, being very young, spontaneous and undomesticated, would grow weary of Penelope's role and seek other outlets for her affections.

The first two years of the Second World War, however, before the United States joined the combat, found me at home in summertime. These years wore for me a visage of mingled leisure and impatience: I was eager that we too should come to grips with Hitler, but until we did and in spite of extra South American tours, there seemed to be longer summers and more spare time than I was ever to know again. One personal worry was losing sight for a while of Marcel Gazelle—he was caught in Belgium by the German invasion of May 1940 but managed to smuggle himself out with the retreat from Dunkirk and surfaced in London to join the Free Belgian forces. Not that he could have continued working with me had there been no war, for he was by then at the Ghent conservatoire and married to Jacqueline. For two seasons after the Los Gatos break I worked with a Dutch pianist, Hendrick Endt, whose niceness as a person made up for a certain weakness in technique. He was a high-minded young man, a disciple of Rudolf Steiner, and he gave me a book of Lao-tsu's sayings which to this day is my constant companion. Devoted to him though I was, it was nonetheless a relief to be able to rely upon the musicianship of Adolph Baller—Usiu, as we affectionately called him—whom I met in New York in 1939.

A Jew originally from Poland (like Balsam before him), Baller was among the best musicians I have known, the genuine fruit of Viennese musical culture. He studied piano with a pupil of Leschetizky in Vienna, where he was caught by the Nazis after the Anschluss. As soon as they heard he was a pianist, they broke all his finger bones, then let him go to face an empty future. With the help of a clever doctor, he got his hands working again, then, with his wife, Edith, escaped to the United States. Husband and wife matched each other in gentleness of disposition. The horrors they had seen and suffered drove them not to vengeance but to cling together, protecting each other and their little daughter from the traps life might yet have in store. When it became possible to travel again to Europe, I would ask Usiu to come with me; he always found some excuse. But he made all the wartime tours, to South America, the Pacific islands, the Aleutian archipelago, and later visited Australia with his trio (the other members were Gabor Rejto, cello, and Roman Totenberg, violin), named the Alma Trio after our house, where it first saw the light of day. It was only the Old World which had worn out its appeal for him.

Usiu and Edith made their home in a cottage on our property and lived there for several years. They comforted me at a difficult time, Usiu joining the walks with the children up the mountain trails and, back at home, playing through libraries of new music with me.

Those quiet summers were marked for me by the experience, too rare in my life, of playing string quartets. Two's company, three's a crowd, they say, and one knows situations where the rule applies; but for string soloists, four seems the ultimate right number, providing range, contrast and maximum independence within a united group. No voice dominates, all are equally important, passing the subject from one to another or blending together in the restraint of intimacy, not attempting operatic climax or symphonic scope. This is music which refines emotion to its purest distillation, to be overheard, to be discovered rather than performed. It is musicians' music. The quartet which is not dedicated does not exist. From a purely technical point of view, quartet playing supplies a necessary discipline. Playing with a pianist, the violinist must always make some adjustment of intonation to the piano's tempered intervals, whereas, left to its own devices and obliged to master certain passages of harmonic modulation most difficult to keep in tune, the string quartet develops an intonation, and an ear, incomparably more exact. The infinite possibilities of delicate inflection and phrasing, of balance and reciprocity, of taking and yielding the lead nurture a sensibility to sound and to one's place within it not otherwise much fostered in Western music. Every string player should have opportunities to cultivate himself in this most demanding of schools. To me the pleasure and the benefit have come in time rescued from duty. Knowing the perfect suavity and balance of quartets who have long lived together, I would hesitate to attempt to match them without first serving a rigorous apprenticeship.

Our quartet playing brought to Alma once a week, for a day or longer, my old friend Nathan Firestone, along with the violinist Henry Temianka and the cellist Willy Van den Burg. I had known Nathan, for many years the only violist of my acquaintance, almost as long as I'd known Persinger. He played the viola in Persinger's own quartet and, as the oldest and most experienced of us, organized our sessions at Alma. He was a most gentle, touching man. When he died in 1944 his wife brought me his Testori viola, which Nathan had bequeathed to me. I played it at his funeral and it is now on loan to one of the young violists at my school. Temianka was an asset to any gathering, supplying fine musicianship for the serious side of the business and endless quips and stories to keep us laughing the rest of the time. In the thirty years and more that have passed, he has shown himself one of those well-rounded musicians with talents in many fields: he teaches, conducts a chamber orchestra, has established a first-rate quartet and in spare moments writes readably of the disasters that befall violinists.

On 7 December 1941 the shock wave of Pearl Harbor caught Adolph Baller and myself at El Paso, Texas, on our way to engagements in Mexico City, rendering our passports null and void from one day to the next until intervention at Washington reinstated them. Immensely relieved that we had at last joined the side of right, I could, however, make no more immediately useful contribution than leave the country. While America prepared for war, I trundled south with Baller, using the journey, which lasted a couple of days and nights, to put myself on a cure. Except for a few oranges and walnuts, I starved myself, and worked, rested and learned automassage, with gratifying results: I arrived in Mexico feeling absolutely free, loose, floating and light. We were in Mexico about ten days. Each day I telephoned California, to learn, among other things, my own position in the national draft then under way. Exempted at first as the father of two children, I was not called upon until the last week of hostilities in 1945, then to be told by the local draft board to delay presenting myself for another seven days: once in, it would take a year to get me out again. Another week ended the war and the doubt of my civilian status.

In the intervening years I did what I best could do. Between 1942 and 1945 I gave hundreds of recitals for Allied troops and relief organizations, first in the Americas, later in the Pacific theatre, ultimately in Europe. It was this experience which helped me break through the shell I had lived in. Before I played for the soldiers, music (whose purpose is communication, however) had fashioned round me a shell which I carried intact onto platforms and off again, in complicity with audiences who understood their part and mine in the operation. I had never played in cafés, cabarets or—as dear Sasha Schneider in Poland—in brothels, nor had I been obliged to woo my listeners to listen. Now I had to please men who had never attended a concert, who were not bred to its conventions, whose patience could not be relied upon, far less their informed appreciation. It was a useful, humbling and finally exhilarating experience. Normally the artist is impersonal to the extent that he is not expected to engage his audience by any means other than music, but in the barracks and hospitals of the war there was no escaping personal relationships, with the group and the individuals in it. Some remark had to preface the pieces, some conversation had to be made with the wounded in the wards. Thus my war cracked open many inhibitions and helped me to communicate with others, and thus my exclusive microcosm of music, violins and performance discovered its social dimension.

I first met the GIs at what seemed the world's edge or end, on the bleak outposts of the Aleutian Islands, bare rocks jutting out of the North Pacific like stepping stones between Russia and America, between the Western Hemisphere and the Eastern, but nowhere in themselves. It was an extraordinary sensation to inhabit a land having no past with which one could associate human life, no frame that could accommodate one's own experience, no cultural shape, no recognizable form, nothing; islands totally virgin, totally original, where men, lacking their customary diversions, fell further back upon themselves than ever before.

For the troops stationed there life was not tragic or even dangerous, natural hazards apart, for the Japanese had been expelled from the westernmost islands some months earlier; but it was miserable. Marooned on empty rocks, they found in the remoteness, dampness, boredom, new levels and subtleties of feeling, and music had space to spread itself in their minds; and particularly in hospital. The man in hospital who has strength to think and feel at all feels unaccustomed emotions waken in his heart. In this tender, passive, softened mood, the most unexpected people are sensitive to the most unexpected music. In one hospital on the Aleutians where half the piano keys were found to be frozen solid, the young conscripts responded wholeheartedly to a program of unaccompanied Bach: the Praeludium and Gavotte from the E Major Solo Partita, the entire G Minor Sonata, and finally the Chaconne. Probably most of them had never heard of Bach.

At the other end of the spectrum, the war gave me the most depressing audience I have ever played for. It was in Honolulu and my listeners were several thousand Marines who were to be flown the next day into the front line. In spirit and almost in body each young man there had already left this earth. For three days they had been in isolation, so that no revelry or drunkenness or sentimental entanglement might blunt the physical perfection to which they had been brought, and thus strung up for action, they moved like ghosts under a burden of unhappiness and dread. One thing omitted from their training was spiritual and psychological preparation for the last hours of waiting—the next day they would act heroically, but they did not wear the aspects of heroes then.

I may have encountered some of the same men before I left the Pacific, for there was on Honolulu a military hospital to which the wounded were brought within hours of their injury. From the docks and the airport endless lines of ambulances, moving bumper to bumper, ferried the wounded almost directly from the field of battle to the doctors' hands. I played for this returned audience too, spending twenty minutes or so in each ward, and though the men were bruised, bloodied and bandaged, their gaiety and high spirits were in wonderful contrast to the tension and misery of the Marines on the way to war.

Honolulu, being the tropical island of one's dreams and the travel posters, and then in pre-tourist innocence, offered the senses all the caresses refused by the stark Aleutians. Traveling from island to island, I often gave three "shows" a day, but however laborious the days, the nights restored me. I was quartered in a cottage on the beach, furnished within to American standards of civilization but lulled without by the ocean. However early the start, I would swim first; however late the return, I swam before going to bed. It was here one early morning that I saw Japanese women gathering seaweed: their husbands had been forbidden to fish, a prohibition which struck the Japanese diet at its most sensitive point; the seaweed was a wartime necessity. Curious to see what plants were chosen, I waded out with the women, and was given some souvenir bottles of seaweed to take back to Alma. This little adventure in a way put its stamp upon the Pacific interlude.

All this time Baller was with me, as unlikely an inhabitant of the Aleutians or the South Pacific, as unlikely a participant in any military venture, as can be imagined. Try as he might, he could not look comfortable in the clothes supplied by the army, and at Seattle, from where we first flew to Anchorage, he nearly gave up the project altogether rather than suffer the endless preparatory inoculations. No one could consider them a pleasure, but poor Usiu really hated them. On Adak, then feverishly being transformed into an air base, the only people to boast private lavatories were the commander and the chaplain. Quartered with the commander, I was fortunate: his lavatory was indoors; but Baller, farmed out to the chaplain, had only an outdoor accommodation, which, with Chaplinesque infelicity, was blown from over him by an Arctic gust. Another time, in Phoenix, Arizona, I suggested we hire a couple of horses, on the principle of doing in Rome as the Romans do. Two less convincing cowboys than Baller and myself would be hard to find, but wisely the stables produced for us the lamest and quietest ponies on their books. They also produced chaps, as I believe the leather protection for one's legs is called. "Now," said Usiu, "do these go *under* the trousers or on top of them?" Such innocence could not remain unexploited. "Oh," I said, "you have to take your trousers off!"

Such incidents, the rigors of traveling, the masculine free-and-easiness, were so many symbols of my relief to be at last at war and doing, however marginally, my part. If my days were rather too full for comfort, I had only myself to blame: wherever civilian engagements took me, I offered in addition a concert to the nearest army camp or other good cause, a schedule which on one-night stands left time only to travel, to unpack my violin and to play, without punctilio observed in the matter of practice. Suddenly as it seemed, flying became the normal means of moving from one point to another, at first uneasily enough on the metal-frame seats of army planes. As was only to be expected, these early flying experiences offered occasional excitements, such as the time when our pilot took us just above sea level under the fog blanket from one Aleutian island to another, then rose with stomach-heaving abruptness as our destination loomed ahead; or the time our aircraft, threatening to overshoot a sea-girt runway, came to such a jarring stop that it tilted on its nose; or the day when the pilot lost the island we were making for and flew on into enemy territory. . . . On this particular island, Shemya, a mere sandbar bearing a hut or two and a strip for front-line fighter aircraft, huge oil flares burning extravagantly round the clock marked the runway. Hastening back from the Japanese side of the ocean, we were relieved to see them glowing through the fog, but I was equally relieved to quit a station so isolated and so tense. The only plane crash I was ever in was a little affair *de rien du tout*. It happened in Puerto Rico; the aircraft, attempting takeoff, ended up in the sugar canes, but happily not afire. Once I was allowed to take over the controls of a four-engine bomber. In those days, before the automatic pilot was standardized, one steered by judgment and the joy stick; my judgment erring on the side of prudence, I steered the machine firmly skyward to clear a mountain safely hundreds of feet below. Such adventures could happen in war-time, when incidents were too many and powers of decision too widely spread to be contained within the proper channels. I was often subse-quently to beg favors of the U.S. Army and was never, so far as I recall, refused.

More effectively than marriage, war cut me adrift from the past, deposit-ing me in situations which the wildest prophetic skill could not have foreseen. Once I even fired a gun. After luncheon at a private house on Long Island one late summer day, the company repaired to the beach for target practice and I along with them, reflecting that I could not know how I might be called upon to serve. Never before having handled a rifle, or any weapon, I put the gun to my left shoulder, violin-fashion, until corrected; then, with the first and so far only shots of my life, hit the bull's-eye twice. Perhaps the world lost a sharpshooter in my prior commitment to music, perhaps my achievement was a fluke which I was wise not to attempt to duplicate; but to my own astonishment, and prob-ably to that of everyone present, I had shown there was life in the Cherkess yet, and I still possess a trophy to commemorate the occasion.

A contest of more considerable impact which also took place during the war was my long-running battle with the musical unions of the United States, a battle I ultimately lost. I readily recognize that labor unions are essential; that in their absence the powerless have no defense against exploitation. Human beings, however, always tend to overcorrect and go from one extreme to another: the defensive power becomes op-pressive in its turn.

As a solo artist, one of a category thought to be able to defend their own interests, I was not eligible for membership, even had I wanted it, in the American Federation of Musicians, which existed to protect the salaried worker. As this was the only musicians' union in the country, I could afford to be dispassionate about the subject until Jascha Heifetz founded the American Guild of Musical Artists and tried to recruit me into its ranks. For some reason, probably an oversight, the federation excluded ballet dancers and choristers (if it was indeed a slip, the omission seems a Freudian, and peculiarly American, one, indicative of a way of life in which every human activity requires a tool; as one doesn't dig with one's nails or journey on foot, so art too must have a device other than mere limbs or vocal cords); AGMA hoped to attract the neglected categories as well as accompanists and solo artists, particularly young ones who might need champions against their own managements, but names were also wanted to give the new organization weight.

By this time I had often encountered Heifetz, but our relationship remained curiously flimsy, in that the intensity of my young admiration, having failed for many years to generate a meeting, now failed to inspire intimacy. Apprehending most things, and especially music, animistically, I was used to feeling at one with colleagues without the long labor of becoming acquainted. Heifetz was a figure aloof—in his distinguished impassive appearance, in the incredible perfection of his playing, and in his generally uncommunicative manner. Those detractors for whom technical perfection is not enough inferred from these characteristics that he was cold. I think they mistook for coldness a degree of discipline and method which no other violinist of our time possessed. With a Heifetz performance, you could be sure that everything, down to the smallest inflection, was calculated, controlled and willed. The Walton Concerto, dedicated to Heifetz and edited by him, bears witness to the minuteness of his planning, indicating expressive marks in unusual detail, tiny crescendi and diminuendi on single notes. He strove for a control so complete that each performance would be identical—a valid, admirable approach, but not mine. Nor did I find the man himself easy of access beyond the wall of correctness and deliberation encasing him. However, on this occasion, it was not his musical but his tactical approach which I took exception to. As a further motive for joining AGMA, Heifetz pointed out that the war could not last forever, that when it was over European artists would flood the land of milk and honey, and that we Americans must stick together in self-defense. I refused to join.

Not noticeably hindered by my refusal, AGMA prospered until the day it started enrolling orchestral players and thereby attracted the ill will of the immensely more powerful federation. The AFM was then run by a trumpeter called Petrillo, with whom I was long linked by correspondence although we never actually met; I have no reason to consider him other than perfectly amiable, and no doubt an excellent trumpeter, in spite of his worrying preference for bulletproof cars. *A priori* Petrillo approved of me for resisting AGMA's blandishments and I had in addition fortuitous importance in his eyes in being one of the last, if not the last, musician not yet in any union fold. He determined to recruit me, partly to strike a blow against AGMA, partly in furtherance of his strategy against American recording companies: he planned a strike which would be jeopardized by even one stray violinist available for recording. Compared with Petrillo's, my cards were not powerful. I knew that if AFM boycotted me from appearing with orchestras under their command—and that meant all the principal orchestras—I would have to succumb; but I decided to delay submission as long as possible, and managed to spin out our passage of arms over two years or more.

The opening shot was friendly. I would be most welcome in the union: would I please consider joining it? In reply I was grateful for the kind invitation but didn't see that AFM quite met my needs. Each summer Petrillo organized open-air concerts at a stadium in Chicago. His next communication was a proposal that I should appear at one of these at a very high fee, with the extra inducement of an introduction to the "most important people" in Chicago, with which dubious figures the federation was apparently on the best of terms. All he asked in return, predictably enough, was that I should join the union first. My answering telegram was deeply appreciative of his proposal, but suggested that enrollment amid such signal marks of favor might imply either bribery or compulsion, and if I joined, I would prefer to do so of my own free uncorrupted will. Thus a few months were gained.

Then came a more peremptory letter: they were afraid there was no alternative to my joining and would I please find enclosed my membership card? Above the space for the holder's signature the card promised on his behalf to observe all the laws, bylaws and regulations of the American Federation of Musicians; seizing on this straw, I wrote back asking to see these regulations before committing myself to abide by them, and so added another year or so to my freedom. The little red book—so it turned out to be, less famous than some little red books which have left their mark upon the world, but scarcely less in need of interpretation—fueled many a wearisome exchange with the bureaucrats of the AFM, first about the lack of provision for my particular circumstances, then about the privileges given officers of the union. The first paragraph I kept for my last throw. It read: "The president has the right and duty . . . (a) to enforce all the laws and bylaws of the American Federation of Musicians; (b) to annul all the laws and bylaws of the American Federation of Musicians . . ." Once this *Alice in Wonderland* absurdity had been ritually aired, my delaying tactics were exhausted (in the event, my request for clarification of this clause was never answered). When the threat came that the Philadelphia Orchestra would not play with me, I gave in. My last act of independence was to select the local of my choice: I chose San Francisco. A few days later Petrillo called his strike to begin at midnight. Baller and I were recording until within minutes of the deadline in an old hall in New York City, so by a hair's-breadth, I avoided starting my trade-union career as a scab.

Perhaps I should have fought Petrillo longer, or made the issue public. The AFM's more disgraceful aspects—the bulletproof automobiles, the strong men in Chicago, the president's totalitarian powers—deserved more exposure than I gave them. True, these scandals were put right in the course of time, but even at its most honest and plain-dealing, the union's influence seems to me not altogether happy. Just as there is a tendency, and not only in trade unions, to treat a person as a replaceable item, so centralized organizations try to iron flat the differences between groups. It is ridiculous to demand the same rights and impose the same restrictions throughout a country the size of the United States upon a membership as heterogeneous as AFM's, ranging from nightclub performers to orchestral musicians of every caliber. But the ridiculous happens; I believe it was a factor in the decline of the American Symphony Orchestra. The nucleus of the American Symphony was the orchestra put together for Toscanini by NBC and dissolved when his prestige was accounted no longer equal to his expense and he was dismissed (an outrageous return for a man whose priceless service merited, in simple justice, that he fulfill his days in peace; television having seduced away the radio audience, Toscanini was condemned on the first pretext that offered). Leopold Stokowski kept some of the NBC players together and added new ones straight from Juilliard and other schools to form this new orchestra, the American Symphony. The old-timers contributed experience and authority, the youngsters enthusiasm, dedication and readiness to work. Adequate work was precisely what the union rules forbade, however. Rehearsals could not last more than the stipulated two and a half hours a day, a reasonable allowance for established orchestras of great virtuosity, especially when preparing works already in the repertoire, but a fatal handicap to a new enterprise. One might think the rules could be flexible enough to admit a training orchestra; but no; egalitarianism is blind to the needs and rights of the individual.

Some years later, with no reason any longer to deny solidarity to my fellow solo artists, I joined AGMA as well.

By 1944 it had become clear that Nola and I were hopelessly at odds. So often physically apart, we had grown ever further apart in emotion, but had the circumstances been different, the outcome would have been the same—a truth which she was ready to acknowledge sooner than I was: on an early holiday, before the wartime commitments began, she suggested we hadn't enough in common to build a marriage on. For my part, I could not imagine that a wife could be any less permanent than a parent or a sister, or any less ideal. Each of us had married an illusion, she as well as I, for the life a virtuoso leads can appear totally glamorous only in the eyes of the beholder. Our relationship was dislocated in time: had it been a more youthful or a more mature encounter, it would not have done the damage or caused the anguish that it did. It was half dream, half sadness. Like my father dreaming of the Villa Cherkess, I had built a fantasy on an insecure base and given what might have been a perfectly legitimate affair a weight of permanence which it could not carry. In retrospect my first marriage seems a stepping stone, which was hardly how I imagined it then. Perhaps it is a lesson in humility to find one can so misinterpret oneself; but equally the misinterpretation may offer a lesson in the need for maintaining illusions. Perhaps one should not spend one's life doubting the validity of impulse, but just live with intensity and conviction at whatever cost. Such consolation by hindsight could not help me then, as my marriage fell apart. Nola's eventual admission that she loved someone else took me by surprise, though it should not have done so. I knew it was over, but I was too immature to adjust my perspectives, too traditional not to flinch from rupture, too much at a loss to know what next to do. There was nothing in my past to teach me how to cope with failure, and between my indecisiveness and her long refusal to divorce me, there ensued three very painful years, the most troubled and mismanaged of my life.

Long after her own divorce Hephzibah wrote a letter voicing our twin sentiments:

> Perhaps the worst was that lack of contact with life as it is generally lived amongst those who are not absolutely sheltered from every day's troubles, as we were. It made awful fools of us when we faced

our first life situations. We were incapable of functioning as creatures of free will; we were mentally cognisant of every problem, but
only as a theoretical dilemma. We had *overcome* ourselves and
readjusted ourselves to inevitable problems many times before, but
we had never *solved* a problem. Other people had never entered our
lives before as definite factors to be contended with; there had been
a fluidity in a life built on the achieving of mastery in one well-
defined field. There had been work, holy, absolute work performed
in a spirit of extreme self-giving—and the rest was not important.
As soon as our structure became invaded by the utterly different
values of other people, we were helpless in coping with the conflict
it set up between what we had been taught, and what we were
being taught. . . .

    After all this time, I feel that the best is still ahead of us. We
have had much misery to shed, for in spite of nursing the world's
finest intentions, we have done more harm to people we loved than
we ever believed ourselves capable of doing to people we didn't
love.

Just as I had married without being prepared for marriage, so I
played the violin without being prepared for violin playing, and it was
inevitable that, the strain imposed by the breakdown in personal life
coinciding with the unprecedented pressures of wartime touring, my lack
of preparation would begin to tell. Considering that I played without
thinking, without analysis, without, as it were, taking the machine apart
for overhaul, just keeping it running at any cost, my performance stood
up remarkably well; but there were times when I knew I wouldn't be
able to go on until I understood technique and could recapture that ease
I had once possessed without thinking and which was now deserting me.
I also knew I had fallen into bad habits. This double warning drove me
to a search for first principles which was to last for years (indeed it has
not ended: every day brings new discoveries), the detail of which I shall
postpone to a later chapter. Suffice it for the moment to say that from the
outset I knew motion to be the essence of the problem and, with open
mind, gleaned from every potentially useful source—medical, athletic,
gymnastic as well as violinistic. I read the classics, Dounis's *Technique
of the Violin* and *The Independence of the Fingers*, Carl Flesch's *The
Art of Violin Playing*; I discussed the matter with colleagues and friends
such as Joseph Szigeti; in New York I made the acquaintance of two
violin teachers, Theodore and Alice Pashkus, who—apart from bringing

to mind the Italian intriguers in *Rosenkavalier*—had some useful ideas and some which were not useful at all; and thus brooding and groping, I inched my way toward enlightenment. Any meeting could be turned to account. Among my New York friends was Paul Draper, the tap-dancer, who would invite to his apartment the most unlikely and fruitful combinations of diverse people. Meeting the American runner Borrican there one evening, I questioned him on his training methods and was invited to participate in a session at Yankee Stadium the next day. I took a taxi for the long haul up Manhattan. Given the address, the driver looked around from his steering wheel and offered helpfully, "There's nothing happening at the stadium today." "Oh, yes, there is," said I. "Borrican is running, and what's more, I'm running with him!" Rarely has disbelief worn a more eloquent expression than that taxi driver's.

During this time of professional anxiety, personal trouble and over-work, life granted me a musical encounter of profound and lasting importance. Through his music first, then in person, I came to know Béla Bartók.

It was Antal Dorati who played the part of providence. At the time Bartók was just another refugee, swept by the tide of war onto American shores, living in a New York City tenement, ill, poor, and known outside Hungary only to a happy few. Among them was of course Dorati. He too was in New York in 1942, before his appointment at Dallas, and he and I struck up a close friendship. A tremendously gifted musician, Dorati had also enjoyed the priceless advantage of being trained in Budapest when Bartók, Kodály, Leo Weiner and others had established musical standards unmatched perhaps anywhere in the world. As one might expect, the professionals flourished on a broad base of public appreciation, which also fertilized a crop of literally hundreds of amateur string quartets. To take but one example, Dorati's own mother could sing from memory each part of each of Beethoven's quartets, and when the Nazis rounded her up with other Jews she kept her sanity by doggedly going through this repertoire in her head. Dorati is a true son of his mother and his city, a musician too complete to be labeled simply a conductor or a composer or a pianist, and a man too complete to be labeled simply a musician; he also draws beautifully. Like many great conductors—Ansermet and Monteux are others—he had, in the early days, conducted much ballet and won himself a fearsome reputation among dancers for his explosive temper. Fortunately I never saw the worst of it, but found a childlike freshness in his sensibilities: mischievous as a child when things went well, he pouted like a child when they didn't.

One day Dorati invited several friends, myself among them, to his home for an evening's chamber music which lasted long enough to provoke the reproaches of irate neighbors. Before the interruption he spoke of Bartók, pressed me to discover his music for myself, and played excerpts from various works at the piano. Like all important revelations, it seemed clear, obvious, even familiar, once it had been made. Deriving from the East, Bartók's music could not but appeal to me, but in his greatness a local heritage had been absorbed, interpreted and recast as a universal message, speaking to our age and culture and to every other. As he elevated folk music to universal validity, so he gave noble dimensions to human emotion. Strong with the earthy, primeval strength of its origins, his music has also the cultivated strength of a steely, ruthless discipline which refuses all indulgence. Here, in the twentieth century, was a composer to bear comparison with the giants of the past.

So, at Dorati's urging, I came to love above any other contemporary works the compositions of Bartók, and more particularly the Second Violin Concerto and the First Sonata for Piano and Violin (Bartók's own instrument was the piano, but like all Hungarians, he understood the violin). I decided to include both works in the 1943 season, playing the Concerto at Minneapolis with Mitropoulos—he conducted not only the performance but the rehearsals from memory, an unbelievable feat that he repeated each week with a new program—and the Sonata with Baller a few days later at Carnegie Hall. Between the two concerts, in November 1943, I met Bartók. Before my first performance of the Sonata I wanted Bartók's comments on my handling of it, and wrote to ask him if he would hear me. My old friend "Aunt Kitty" Perera—a violinist herself and a friend of Toscanini, a charming lady, full of warmth and good works and zest for living—readily agreed that Bartók, Baller and I should meet at her apartment on Park Avenue. When Baller and I arrived toward the end of a wintry afternoon, Bartók was already there, seated in an armchair placed uncompromisingly straight on to the piano, with score laid open before him and pencil in his hand: an attitude both chilling and, in my experience, characteristically Hungarian; Bartók, like Kodály, was pitilessly severe with his students. There were no civilities. Baller went to the piano, I found a low table, put my violin case on it, unpacked, tuned. We started to play. At the end of the first movement Bartók got up—the first slackening of his rigid concentration—and said, "I did not think music could be played like that until long after the composer was dead." If I were truly modest I would not record this tribute; I do so because it was an unforgettably glad experience to know one had penetrated to the very heart of a composer through his music, and that he, the living man, who had given his all, knew that it was understood. It broke the ice completely, of course. Without idle words we made each other's acquaintance. Baller and I played the remaining movements.

Knowing that I had just performed his great Concerto, Bartók probed to see how well I had grasped it, asking particularly my opinion of a passage in the first movement. "It's rather chromatic," I offered. "Yes, it's chromatic," he said, but then, nudging me toward the point he was making: "You see that it comes very often?"—which it does, some thirty-two times, never exactly the same. "Well, I wanted to show Schönberg that one can use all twelve tones and still remain tonal." Here was one of Bartók's barbs: any one of these repeated sequences would supply a dodecaphonist with material for a whole opera, but Bartók pours them out with a lavishness of invention which the twelve-toner, working away with his slide rule, will never know. His was that kind of profligate exuberance which throws away something, never to be used again.

Except for the extraordinary precision of his speech and manner, reduced to a diamondlike sharpness and brilliance which concentrated meaning and rejected superfluous expression, Bartók's presence in the last two years of his life, when I knew him, belied the fire of his character. The contained surface gave no evidence of the barbaric grandeur and mystic vision within. If I had known him in his youthful, exuberant mountain-climbing days, my impression might have been less awed, and his impatience with conversational exchange less total—although I doubt that he was ever socially loquacious. A creator's life being in a sense secondary to his creation, Bartók's genius was permitted to devour him, leaving him exposed. Words were no longer necessary, even life was hardly necessary alongside the expression his music gave to life, to his own life and his convictions. Thus, exile made of him unaccommodated man, solitary, intense, requiring for material support only a bed, a table to write at and—but this might be considered a luxury—absolute quiet in which his inner concentration might bear fruit. These wants provided, he poured out the riches of his spirit, needing apparently neither critical acclaim nor the affection of the public.

What he did need, and missed in the streets of New York, was contact with the natural. Among the gasoline fumes one day he stopped in his tracks, sniffed the air, and exclaimed, "I smell a horse!"—he had the keenest senses imaginable. Sure enough, following his nose, he came upon a little stable which hired out mounts for riders in Central Park, and filled his lungs with its nostalgic fragrance. Animals would come to him with extraordinary confidence in his sympathy, and this sympathy was one and the same as his feeling for human beings who were rooted in their land. The longing he felt for such natural societies is demonstrated, I believe, in the greater simplicity of his last works, written in his race with death in the unfriendly urban environment of New York. Despite what must have struck him as the inhumanity of the streets, Bartók closed his ears to the roar of traffic, but opened them with interest to the rhythms and tunes of that American-African-European synthesis which is jazz; moreover, he incorporated some of what he heard into his Concerto for Orchestra.

I knew he was in financial straits, that he was too proud to accept handouts, that he was the greatest of living composers. Unwilling to waste a moment, I asked him on the afternoon of our first meeting if I might commission him to compose a work for me. It didn't have to be anything large-scale, I urged; I was not hoping for a third concerto, just a work for violin alone. Little did I foresee that he would write me one of the masterpieces of all time. But when I saw it, in March 1944, I admit I was shaken. It seemed to me almost unplayable.

That first hasty impression was ill-judged: the Solo Sonata is eminently playable, beautifully composed for the violin, one of the most dramatic and fulfilling works that I know of, the most important composition for violin alone since Bach. It is a work of wild contrasts. The Tempo di Ciaconna, the first movement, translates the greatest of Bach's own works for solo violin, the last movement of the D Minor Partita, into Hungarian idiom, free but disciplined. It is a grandiose movement of daunting breadth of expression. Then comes the violence of the Fuga, perhaps the most aggressive, even brutal, music I play; followed by the complete serenity of the Melodia and the fast, elusive, dancelike rhythms of the Presto. That I should have evoked this magnificent music is a source of infinite satisfaction to me; that I should have played it to Bartók before he died remains one of the great milestones of my life.

In his original conception the recurring passage in semiquavers, or sixteenths, in the last movement was to be played in quarter tones—the notes between the semitones of the tempered chromatic scale, which since Bach have been pretty well outlawed in Western music, but which are still used in Oriental and gypsy music and in emotional, improvisational compositions under Oriental or gypsy influence (for instance, Enesco's). However, Bartók gave me the option of playing these passages in half tones, and given that I had only weeks to prepare the

Sonata, I found the demand of accurate quarter tones in fast tempo too intimidating and chose his alternative. I am still doubtful whether quarter tones would allow the music sufficient clarity, but I regret not having included the quarter-tone version in the published edition: other violinists should share my privilege of choosing the one or the other; I mean to include both in any future edition.

Bartók mailed me the score from Asheville, North Carolina, where he had been sent by his physicians, under sentence of death from leukemia. He had accepted an invitation to spend the summer of 1944 at my home, and was also interested in a proposal from the University of Washington at Seattle to continue his study of folk music with the Indians of the Northwest. Alas, both musicology and myself were robbed of the experience by his wasting disease. He could not travel so far. Instead he wrote to me:

> I am rather worried about the "playability" of some of the double-stops, etc. On the last page I give you some of the alternatives. In any case, I should like to have your advice. I sent you two copies. Would you be so kind as to introduce in one of them the necessary changes in bowing, and perhaps the absolutely necessary fingering and other suggestions, and return it to me? And also indicate the impracticable difficulties? I would try to change them.

I suggested very little, finding what he wrote possible if difficult, but for the technical suggestions I did make there were further thanks in further letters. We met again in November 1944, just before I gave the Sonata its first performance, to resolve some few problems. Briefly he commented upon the suggestions I had made, his softness never belying his finality. When I asked him if he would alter one chord, he said, fixing me with that mesmeric gaze for a few moments: "No." Again the audience's applause brought him to Carnegie Hall's stage. Again the critics refused to consecrate his genius. And again he was pleased to have heard himself live from beyond the grave. "It was a wonderful performance," he wrote to his friend Wilhelmine Creel. "The Sonata has four movements and lasts about twenty minutes. I was afraid it is too long; imagine: listen [sic] to a single violin during twenty minutes. But it was quite all right, at least for me." He was more pleased than I was: possibly he read my good intentions and understood that in another twenty years I would do the Solo Sonata justice.

Bartók died on 26 September 1945.

9

Liberation

From the time that the German occupation of Europe left Britain beleaguered, I sought ways and means of going there. In the summer of
1942 I almost brought the venture off—discussions between the Allies
had established that a concert artist might be flown over when conve-
nient, a truffle in the next cargo of Spam. At New York, however, I was
pre-empted by "a rush shipment of a secret nature" (aircraft engines, I
ultimately learned), which left me no option but to go home again with
my battlefield model of the Prince Khevenhüller. Nothing daunted, I
made further representations and at length, in the spring of 1943, found
myself crossing the Atlantic in an RAF bomber, delighted as much by
the prospect of falling from the sky into a besieged fortress as of touring
once again with Marcel Gazelle. We played all over the British Isles, in
factories, at military installations and in concert halls for wartime charities. London had all the mysterious beauty of apocalypse; I loved groping my way down blackout streets and mingling with the crowds who
took shelter for the night underground.

Two bastions linked by the sky, one on either side of the Atlantic,
London and New York were jointly capital cities of the war: New York
the refuge, the powerhouse, the war chest; London the battered front-
line headquarters where military strategists shaping Europe's present
elbowed governments in exile who had scrambled off Continental shores

in time to dream Europe's future, first among them all the Free French led by General de Gaulle. Marcel and I played for the Free French too, at the Royal Albert Hall, where de Gaulle decorated me with the Croix de Lorraine; but more interesting than such public celebrations were several luncheons with him and his "cabinet" at the Savoy Hotel. Given my comparative youth and inexperience of statesmen, I was in no position to indulge or invite confidences; nor would I, even with the benefit of subsequent encounters, claim to have known him well. But if the outsider can't appreciate all the subtleties of the game, he can at least catch glimpses hidden from the involved. As I did not figure in the conflicts, rivalries and vanities which spiced de Gaulle's relations with the rest of the Allied camp, as I represented no threat to French integrity, I was shown a side of his nature not displayed in more official company, or if shown, not recognized: a gentle, touching quality which reached beyond the urgency of the moment to human intercourse. When I met him later, both in the war's immediate aftermath and after his return to power in 1958, he always greeted me with more than diplomatic warmth, as if our acquaintance, having developed outside the framework of war and politics, still occupied a happy niche in his memory.

More than a year had passed when I next came to London, by which time General de Gaulle had ridden into just-liberated Paris, no longer the lonely standard-bearer of national freedom, but the acclaimed leader of his country. It was to take me four weeks to reach Paris in my turn. Meanwhile the whole course of my life changed: I met Diana Gould.

Looking back it seems as if I had suddenly decided to obstruct destiny no longer. I had known of Diana since 1927, I might have met her on any of the prewar visits to London, I had failed to make use of Dennison's and Ingerson's introduction when I arrived in 1943. Now, in September 1944, telephoning her mother, Lady Harcourt, at the number given me by "the boys," I may have had a premonition that this was no ordinary social overture. What is certain, my *savoir-faire* deserted me. "Hello, this is Yehudi Menuhin," I baldly announced. "Is it indeed?" a high English voice replied. "What do you want?" I? Want? I rather hoped she would tell me, but as there seemed little chance of this, I abruptly invited myself to luncheon the next day without even explaining how I came by her name and address.

Our meeting was not to be at Mulberry House, the family house in Chelsea, where the boys had known them; a bomb in 1941 had closed

Mulberry House for the duration and scattered the family—Lady Harcourt to Bath and her daughters Diana and Griselda to a shared apartment in Belgravia. But Lady Harcourt, deciding London was worth a wartime risk or two, had come home again, to a larger apartment in the same building as her daughters'. Here the guests gathered, the actor Michael Redgrave, the film director Anthony Asquith, and myself. Diana and Griselda supported our hostess. Introductions were made.

From the pouf where she was seated the most beautiful woman I had ever seen rose to greet us, a tall, dark, slender girl whose grace, intelligence, ardor, vitality and depth of feeling so completed one another that each was the other's aspect. To some people this and that characteristic may be attributed and a composite picture patiently built up; Diana defeated attempts at lists and analysis. Everything about her was totally right, every word, expression and gesture totally herself. To get to know her was not to adjust first impressions, only to give them depth. Lost in contemplation, I was, very likely, poor company that day, but any shortcomings in my social contribution must have gone unnoticed in the conversational volleys between this lovely girl and her lovely sister. Like two long bolted blades, one dark, the other light, they scissored language with incredible rapidity, throwing upon our heads a confetti of fanciful cut-outs and profiles in epigram. I watched and listened, delighted and bemused, and at the end of luncheon attempted to carry Diana off with me, with only partial success. She accepted my escort as far as the dentist. Already I knew she was my girl, that she was meant for me; whether I was meant for her never troubled my mind.

Thus, briefly our acquaintance began and for the moment ended. I had immediately to leave for the Continent, now partly liberated, and did not contrive to return to London for any length of time until the spring of 1945. But given the power and certainty of that first impression, it is right that I should anticipate here what was to give it substance and explanation.

Diana's was a beauty—of mind and soul as well as body—which was the result not only of gifts but of great cultivation, of human endowment worked and disciplined within a tradition to the most refined and durable expression. On stage Anna Pavlova had long ago shaped the model in my mind; now I found the living, breathing, feeling woman who matched that model and, in her rounded, various humanity, consigned it to oblivion. I have said Diana was formed in a discipline; it was an understatement; her upbringing was an interaction of disciplines, her most priceless heritage a strength of selfhood which survived them all and benefited from them. She had the discipline of the English family, whose decorum never slackens, no matter what bombs overhead, no matter what domestic upheavals within. She had the discipline of the ballet at a time when this was fierce indeed. She had had, moreover, the discipline of Christian Science, which ignored pain, subdued indulgence, discounted claims of self, found always a duty to be done and did it without counting the personal cost. Seeing the pure product, I knew it had been fashioned in the refiner's fire; the detail of the fashioning I was to learn piece by piece over many meetings.

The Goulds were originally Irish gentry. Ruined by the Penal Laws, which forced Catholic landowners to parcel out their estates among their sons, they expatriated themselves to France in the 1830s and preserved thereafter as much French coloring as Irish or British. Diana's father, Gerard Gould, spoke French more fluently than English, for all that he was educated at a British public school and took his Foreign Office examinations, and Diana herself has always been equally mistress of the language, whichever side of the Channel she was on. At the beginning of his career in the diplomatic corps, Gerard Gould died, aged thirty, leaving his wife three small children, eight servants, a beautiful house and a comfortable fortune upon which the government levied disastrous death duties. Only an observant eye would have noticed any alteration in the family's way of life, however, for Evelyn Gould made every sacrifice sooner than sacrifice her heritage, paring it to the bone yet sparing its essence. Thus, her children took public transportation, wore their collars turned, had no pocket money, learned to recognize a bargain sale when they saw one and survived winter in unheated splendor (though barely: Griselda in adult life contracted tuberculosis). But they were bred up in more than social airs and graces, their souls nourished with music, theatre, painting and the literature of two languages, their minds whetted on the intelligentsia who gravitated to Mulberry House, their personalities formed in an extraordinarily fruitful cross-fertilization of European culture at its highest and British tradition at its best. Mrs. Gould's second marriage was to Cecil Harcourt, a distinguished naval officer whose services were recognized when he was appointed, successively, an admiral, Second Sea Lord at the Admiralty, and Commander in Chief of the Nore. (Sir Cecil, as he ultimately became, was the first captain of the battleship *Duke of York*, in which vessel he carried Winston Churchill to the historic meeting with President Roosevelt in Chesapeake Bay.)

Music had been the background of Diana's life from birth. Her mother, as Evelyn Suart, had been one of the foremost pianists in England, a contemporary of Myra Hess. She had studied with Leschetizky as a girl, made her debut with the great conductors of those days, Hans Richter and Nikisch, was a friend of Ysaÿe, and introduced the music of Debussy to Britain. On marrying she had retired, but only from professional appearances: every Sunday afternoon she gave elegant parties to which native and visiting musicians were attracted as pilgrims to a shrine (as I myself was drawn, and Louis Kentner, who was to marry Griselda). But Diana's own first love was the dance. She acquired her first dance slippers at the age of eight, having already dreamed of them for years. In fact, what the Pantages Vaudeville Company was to me, the Diaghilev Ballet was to her; her sovereign childhood memory features her mother invading the night nursery on an impulse, rousing her from bed, to the fury of Nanny, and sweeping her off to the Coliseum as to another world, a world whose ethereal beauty would sustain her under the punishing regime she endured for years. I left the Curran Theatre, my ears ringing. Diana left the Coliseum, her nose flaring. "The ballet has its own peculiar smell," she reports, "a smell of tarlatan and sweat and rosin and benzine; of size and secotine and dust, layer upon layer of dust, stirred and blown about by the legs of countless dancers, and by the drafts of a hundred 'flies,' stamped into cloth and canvas and ironed in, painted over, sealed, forever imprisoned in costume and décor. Once I could have told you in pitch dark the *Carnaval* from the *Scheherazade* backdrop."

I could never imagine as a musician that any other part could in fact intensify and reveal more profoundly and clearly the message and sincerity of a musical score. Yet I must confess that when I saw Balanchine's choreography to Stravinsky's Capriccio for Piano and Orchestra there was not a quaver nor a rhythmic inflection nor an emotional, intellectual, or humorous communication which was not elucidated in the dances. The pace and tension of even the slowest pieces were conveyed in a remarkable sense of weight, of gravity, of continuity, of length of line and precision of timing. I *saw* a musical interpretation and was thrilled to admit that Balanchine is one of the greatest interpretative musicians of our era, as well as the most creative choreographer. It is an overwhelming revelation to be made so palpably aware of the transfigured expressiveness of the total body. The occasion had a particular and moving significance, for Diana and Balanchine, embracing each other, recalled their joint exploits on the same stage of the Théâtre des Champs-Elysées forty-three years ago when Diana and he danced in *Songes* by Milhaud,

with Balanchine's choreography and Dérain's décor. Diana still has in
our bedroom a wistfully beautiful pen-and-ink drawing Dérain made of
her on the spot.

The ballet required of Diana nothing short of total, votive dedication. Competition was keen, opportunities to perform restricted, and no
union existed to protect the dancers from the exigencies of the autocrats in
command. But Diana's training began peacefully enough when she and
other little sisters were enrolled in the Thursday afternoon dancing class
at Mr. Gibbs's school for boys in Sloane Street, attended by her brother
Gerard. When their teacher pronounced her gifted and urged she be put
in a proper ballet school, Lady Harcourt made inquiries. Although there
were several ballet masters and mistresses in London—Diaghilev's retired dancers showed a distinct predilection for the city whose balleto-
mania had kept the Ballets Russes alive from year to year—there was
only one Enrico Cecchetti, the same Cecchetti of whom Karsavina, his
greatest pupil, wrote that "he was the only absolute teacher of the academic dance in our time."

Age had only slightly mellowed the irascible nature for which he
had been famous in Saint Petersburg. Shivering next to her mother as
she waited for an audition, Diana could hear such Italian-Russian salvos
booming from behind the studio door (directed, incidentally, at Pavlova!)
as led her to envisage some ogre instead of the pleasant old man with
pepper-and-salt white hair who began to prod her bones directly he
appeared and introduced himself. "I will take her," Cecchetti said after
the briefest of auditions. "She must come here every morning from ten to
one." It was not to be, however, for Lady Harcourt declared that she
could not let Diana quit school and abandon her mind to her toes.
Cecchetti thereupon recommended his former assistant in Diaghilev's
company, Marie Rambert, who might accept a part-time student, as she
was not yet well established. Henceforward Diana led a double life,
coming top of her class in schooltime and cramming a day's ballet into
the leftover hours.

Madame Rambert was anything but a gentle teacher, dynamic in
the tradition of Russia and the dance but ruthless besides, her teaching
method employing insult and sarcasm. In the ten long years Diana
studied with her, she cannot recall one word of comfort or praise, nor any
attention paid to the physical well-being of the children, who in winter
practiced their *pliés* in freezing studios; but simply a relentless perfec-
tionism, as of a stern circus master training a team of ponies. Despite or
because of the pitiless treatment meted out, the Rambert school came to

be recognized as the best in London, before Sadler's Wells was started, and Marie Rambert's contribution is nowadays acknowledged to have been invaluable.

In spring 1929 Rambert telephoned Diana's mother one Monday morning with instructions to keep her daughter out of school and send her to the studio "with a clean tunic." Offering no explanation, she rang off. When Diana arrived the other dancers were already aflutter with the news that Diaghilev would attend the class, and indeed, midway through it, a smallish man, his face appearing the whiter for a Chinese-black mustache, entered the studio. The class over, Diana was asked to stay behind and perform the Carnation Fairy Variation from Tchaikovsky's *Sleeping Beauty* and, with Frederick Ashton, the Adagio from *Leda and the Swan,* which Ashton had created with her in mind. Still bemused from having seen her god, Diana was in the dressing room, one shoe off and one on, when God knocked at the door. "Mademoiselle Diana," he announced, *"vous allez venir dans mon ballet"*—"You are going to join my company." Turning to Rambert, who was behind him, he entreated her not to work Diana too hard in the intervening months. *"Je ne veux pas de muscles dans les femmes"*—"I don't want muscles in women." Rather he preferred Diana's tendrillar, *art nouveau* beauty, which prompted him to declare gallantly, *"C'est la seule jeune fille que je voudrais épouser"*—"She is the only girl I would have liked to marry." During the next two weeks he had her attend every ballet at His Majesty's Theatre, took her backstage, introduced her to his company and, above all, to Tchernicheva, who would be her surrogate mother come September, in Monte Carlo.

But the prince who would rescue her from obscurity died that summer. Two years later the pattern repeated itself. In turn Pavlova came to Rambert's class, in turn she chose Diana from among all the other dancers—this time as a soloist—and in turn she died before the invitation could be taken up, sealing Diana's belief that she would receive no calls but mocking ones. Singularity was built into her very frame, it seemed, for during adolescence she grew by leaps and bounds, every extra inch disqualifying her from the long-coveted conventional roles. Although Arnold Haskell, the dean of British ballet critics, pronounced her "the finest young artist the English dance has produced," her career continued to be fraught with difficulties. If the difficulties were persistent, so was she, however. After leaving Rambert's tutelage she joined Balanchine's company, dancing in *L'Après-midi d'un faune* with Serge Lifar and in other roles, while continuing to attend classes at

Matilde Kshessinskaya's studio in Paris. Later she danced with de Basil's ballet, with Nijinska, with Massine, with the Markova-Dolin company, always as soloist in a great variety of parts. When no dancing engagement was to be had, she acted in straight plays, finding the transition no problem, for dramatic interpretation had always been her strong point. In fact, when I first met her, she had just returned from dancing and acting the part of Frou-Frou in *The Merry Widow*, in a production by Cyril and Madge Ritchard; an engagement which had already taken her to entertain the troops in Egypt and Italy and which was later to take her to France, Belgium and Holland, shortly after I passed that way myself.

In 1943 I had found Marcel Gazelle living in military celibacy apart from Jacqueline, who had, however, escaped the Occupation and got as far as Lisbon on the roundabout route to reunion. By 1944 she too was in London, only to be left behind once again when Marcel joined me on a sortie into Europe in the wake of the Allied invasion.

When we landed in Brussels in September 1944, the Battle of Arnhem was being fought out to the north, Antwerp was under nightly bombardment, and the fate of all Belgium seemed still balanced on a nod from destiny. Physically and psychologically the country belonged for the moment to no one in particular, the conquerors having gone, the liberators only sporadically and unpredictably present. Between danger zones, mined roads and blown-up bridges, travel across the devastated landscape was an ingenious sequence of contrivances in borrowed cars and trucks, over army pontoon bridges and by private-enterprise ferry. Repeatedly stopped by one self-appointed authority or another, one never knew from whom the challenge would come, Americans, Canadians, returned Belgians or the local maquis, and to have a *laissez-passer* acceptable to all of them was quite the trickiest problem we faced. Liberation was too recent and uncertain for euphoria, but gleams of hope were growing brighter by the hour. It may be imagined that to Marcel our brief skirmish into his homeland meant even more than it did to me.

After our first concert, in Antwerp, we were invited to a dinner given by the municipality in a building next to the just vacated Gestapo headquarters. It was an unforgettable occasion, the most eerie festivity of my life. At the table opulent with the finest silver and crystal and furnished with a succession of excellent wines, all brought from hiding for this first official dinner of freedom, no one spoke above a whisper. Four years and more of keeping one's mouth shut formed a habit sooner caught than overcome, it seemed. My neighbors to either side whispered the horrors and hardships they had suffered, and I found myself whispering along with them, in sympathy in both senses of the word. When glasses were brought for a change of wine, the waiter announced the vintage in a whisper, and in a whisper toasts were drunk, like oaths taken by some desperate secret society. It was indeed curious to see pomp thus furtive. Because of Antwerp's continuing vulnerability, we were not permitted to stay there beyond sundown, but sent back on the circuitous, much interrupted journey to Brussels, where there was to be another performance. That done, we should have returned to England, but I was determined not to cross the Channel again until I had seen Paris; as much a Parisian as myself, Marcel was equally determined to come.

Transport being slow and unreliable where it existed at all, we hitchhiked a lift to Le Bourget in an American plane and arrived by jeep in Paris, unannounced and without prearrangement. To have got thus far was ample excuse for indulging an old whim: we booked into the Ritz. I managed to secure a rare taxi and kept it most of the night, descending—out of another age, it must have seemed—on one friend after another amid an unfailing popping of champagne corks: Jacques Thibaud, Marcel Ciampi, Pierre Bertaux, Bigina and Ferruccio at their Ville d'Avray restaurant, my manager Maurice Dandelot.

Thus passed a truly extraordinary Wednesday night. By Saturday evening I had to be in London, ready to drive the next morning to the BBC's wartime studios at Bedford to broadcast the first English performance of the Bartók Concerto with Sir Adrian Boult. I was left with less than three days in Paris, a shortish time in which to arrange, advertise and attract an audience to a concert; but I could not endure leaving without having celebrated France's freedom. I appealed to my regular guardian angels in the U.S. forces: Would they like me to give a concert? They would. The condition was that they arrange a flight to London on late Saturday afternoon. That was okay by them. It only remained for me to ask the devoted Maurice Dandelot to organize the concert. Miraculously he did it, overcoming shortage of time, confusion and red tape as if such obstacles simply did not exist. The Opéra, which had been closed for months, was opened and its cobwebs hastily dusted away; the tickets printed in time to be put on sale on the morning of the concert; the orchestra and the conductor Charles Munch engaged. On Saturday morning we rehearsed, there was a celebratory luncheon offered by the Ville de Paris, and at three o'clock that afternoon the concert began.

Three hours later it showed no promise of ending. The reopening of the Opéra, the first chance of playing the *Marseillaise* since mid-1940, raised the occasion to a national, to an almost mystic significance. I don't know who was the more thoroughly affected, the audience or myself and the other musicians onstage: it seemed our hearts would break together for gladness. In the wings a couple of Americans agitatedly waited to drive Marcel and me to the Villacoublay air base and see us on our way before nightfall. The applause went on, and the encores, and the further applause; the Americans took my violin from my hands; I desperately grabbed the concertmaster's for a last encore, said farewell, and within half an hour, after a dizzy career by jeep through the empty streets, was climbing, still in concert clothes, aboard our little two-engined plane. Over the Channel the aircraft's electrical system failed. The pilot nursed it to the English coast and, in the gathering dusk, landed for safety in a plowed field. Leaving him with his machine, Marcel and I walked to the nearest road and by and by a bus came, the blue lights stipulated by blackout regulations just perceptible in the darkness. It deposited us at a railway station, where we took a local train and arrived in London in the middle of the night. I sat up writing letters, made the broadcast as scheduled and the next day left for the United States.

Back in California, I received a telegram from Harold Holt, my English manager, offering a handsome fee for participation in a side of the entertainment industry so far unknown to me: I was asked to supply music for a film called *The Magic Bow*, supposedly a life of Paganini, which the Rank Organisation was to begin shooting in the summer of 1945. Holt, the successor to Lionel Powell, who managed my London debut, was one of the great impresarios, a warm, convivial, forthright human being who told a good story about the eccentric virtuosi of the past and was loved by everyone. I am glad to have known him. He didn't marry until late in life, he and his sisters being required to dance attendance on their mother beyond the normal line of duty. During the war I met old Mrs. Holt in her suite at Claridge's, where her daughters waited on her hand and foot, and kept the fruit bowl by her divan constantly supplied with oranges—something virtually unobtainable then.

I jumped at the Rank job, of course. Out of the blue it opened the prospect of a return to London and Diana, and had it been twice as suspect I would have embraced it gladly. However, foreseeing that the cinema industry's view of Paganini might not coincide with mine, I made one stipulation, namely that I should record the music first—I didn't want to be required to trim my performance to other people's timings. In addition, I voiced the pious hope that the script would stick to the letter and spirit of the Maestro's life—which was quite as colorful as any fantasy Hollywood might fabricate—and announced that I was bringing with me authentic material, including Paganini's letters, published by the city of Genoa. I might as well have left the extra baggage in California. Rank had bought the rights to a fictionalized "treatment" of the subject and had no intention of being distracted by the facts. On arrival in London I was sent the script, and anything more abysmally vulgar and nonsensical I have yet to read. One could laugh or one could weep, and having Diana to share the absurdities with, I laughed. I washed my hands of the film and just did my job, which was delightful, recording the music I had chosen in the way I wanted it.

Tongue in cheek, I suggested I might act the part of Paganini as well as play for him. In fact, my schedule precluded any such commitment, even had I possessed the necessary dramatic skills, but my suggestion was taken seriously enough for a screen test to be arranged and for Stewart Granger, already engaged for the role, to be a trifle put out. He was proud of his physique, as well he might be, and asked me, with supercilious intention perhaps, where I was to find clothes for my test. "Oh, I don't think you need worry, Stewart," I consoled him. "I'm sure yours can be stretched." Came the day. Diana had done her best to coach me but I proved uncoachable. A figure of fun in knee breeches and a wig, looking as unlike the mercurial Paganini as one might suppose, I found myself sharing a Paduan balcony with Phyllis Calvert, in mid-love scene. The lines were enough to make anyone blush, not from amorous sentiment but out of mere embarrassment, and my unconvincing delivery of them brought my acting career to a deserved halt. The episode had its rewards, however, for the stills taken then were preserved to enchant our children.

The war in Europe had been over some weeks, the war against Japan had still some weeks to run, when, in July 1945, I returned to Germany for the first time since the Weimar Republic fell to Hitler; not this time to the orchestral circuit of my youth, but to play for displaced people, survivors of the death camps, where, having nowhere else to go, they were still living. Like many in those days, Jew or gentile, I had to impress upon my mind an actuality beyond imagination and to offer the living victims the sorrow, the repentance, the solidarity of the unharmed. I asked the British authorities if I might visit the camps in their sector, the British gave me permission to go, Gerald Moore agreed to come with me. Then, about a week before our departure, at a party given in London by the music publishers Boosey and Hawkes, I met Benjamin

Britten. Returned to England after spending the war years largely in the United States, he too was casting about for some commitment to the human condition whose terrible depths had been so newly revealed, and was immediately enthusiastic about my initiative. He urged me to take him, and Gerald Moore very gracefully gave way.

Not every composer makes a good accompanist, but mine has been the happy fate to know composers like Britten and Enesco, who, even in the service of music unsympathetic to them (as Beethoven's music is unsympathetic to Britten), showed a grasp of intention too rapid and complete to be the result of effort, suggesting some deep-lying free-masonry among composers defying time and giving comprehension the speed of thought. As admirers of Ben's recitals with Peter Pears will divine, he was an exceptional pianist who inspires accompaniment with remarkable sensitivity, imagination and support. To play with him has always been for me a privilege and a joy.

Before leaving London, Ben and I made an attempt at rehearsing a repertoire, only, after five minutes, to abandon it: there was so much more than we could ever do, our understanding of each other's approach seemed so intuitively sure; we put our trust in luck and musical compati-bility and set off for Germany. We took with us more or less the whole standard violin literature—concerti, sonatas, little pieces—and played it, without rehearsal, two or three times a day for ten days in the saddest ruins of the Third Reich. At Belsen we played twice in one afternoon. I shall not forget that afternoon as long as I live. The inmates of the camp had been liberated some weeks earlier, the prison huts burned down, and the ex-prisoners transferred to the adjoining SS barracks, which had, among other comforts, a theatre. Men and women alike, our audience was dressed in army blankets fashioned by clever tailors among them into skirts and suits. No doubt the few weeks since their rescue had put a little flesh on their bones, but to our unaccustomed eyes they seemed desperately haggard, and many were still in hospital. Among these was a little gypsy boy whose sweetness and pathos so struck me that had my domestic life not been a shambles, I would have adopted him there and then. In the thirty years since that afternoon several members of the Belsen audiences have come backstage to make themselves known, re-stored to the living in Israel, Australia or elsewhere; but the gypsy boy I never saw again.

London was my base, Diana the lodestar drawing me back, and when I was with her sadness fell away. As long as we were together I put out of my mind the necessary absences, the problem I had not tackled, secretly hoping that I should find some way to wind up the old life and offer her a new one, a road with minimal burdens.

I never saw Diana dance (except on film: very fortunately a reel of sixteen-millimeter film has been preserved and is in my possession), but that summer I saw her act in Franz Werfel's *Jacobowsky and the Colonel* and found her the most vibrant and communicative personality on the stage. In return she came to my concerts and together we attended other people's, notably a recital given by Pablo Casals. One way and another I commandeered all the spare time she had, and in endless hours of *tête-à-tête* made the fascinating discovery that we shared a whole world. Although everything incidental in our backgrounds and histories was different, in essentials we met; no subject was touched upon which wasn't held in common. Diana, it seemed to me, was thoroughly mistress of rooms to which I held the keys but had never properly entered—rooms of poetry, literature, the use of language. She gave me a tongue to articulate myself, for such obstacles as I met belatedly had, early along, turned her eyes inward where she could perceive my darkness better than I. Conversely I saw in her the mirror image of my own experience, the inner life which we both had had as children—the longing to achieve the highest expression in beauty and in art, the sadness the artist cannot escape who can express only what is within himself and must search and suffer disappointment and search again. I loved her deep compassion, her understanding of pain, and no less the wit, courage and vitality which carried her buoyant above the worst that life could do.

Every encounter was precious, whether a dinner *à deux*, the inanities of *The Magic Bow,* a walk through war-weary London, or a meeting on other people's territory. Jacob Epstein asked me to sit for him. After a session or two, I invited Diana to animate subsequent ones. Her conversation put the light of intelligence on my face and the sculptor was making remarkable progress when I had to leave for Eastern Europe. On my return, with only a couple of sittings to complete the business, I was told that the cat had got into the studio one night and overturned Epstein's handiwork onto the floor, reducing my features to an unhappy pancake. . . . A second head was rapidly modeled and cast and is now in my London house. I have known artists—at least one sculptor, the late Sir Charles Wheeler, among them—whose studios were models of grooming, never to be caught in their slippers or with their hair down, as if every day were Sunday. Epstein's was not one of those: everywhere finished models were drying and half-finished works stood shrouded in wet cloths, while the floor was littered with fallen lumps and pellets of clay. Like his sculptures, he seemed as if God had formed him with a few grand strokes, not attending much to detail. Everything about him had size: his presence, his vision, his emotions, to say nothing of his conversational resources, whose copiousness flooded irresistibly over the sitter, battering him into submissive stillness.

Such treasured moments with Diana had to be fitted into the brief days between my restless comings and goings—movements which grew only more numerous and lengthier as Europe was liberated. Having inquired at the Soviet embassy in London about a trip to Moscow, and still uncertain of the outcome of my inquiry, I left yet again in October 1945, for Prague this time, to add my contribution to Czechoslovakia's rejoicing with a performance of the Dvořák Concerto.

It was a journey made in intriguing company, for I was an extra in a planeload of the returning government, all agog to have done with the years of exile. As luck would have it, fog prevented our landing at Prague, deflecting us instead to Carlsbad airport, then in Russian military hands, and no sooner had we disembarked than an altercation broke out between the Soviet airmen and our English crew. Seemingly the only passenger with two words of Russian to rub together, and those halting, I was called upon as go-between and smoother-down of both sides' ruffled plumes. Hospitably the Russians had offered to guard the aircraft while we dined and stayed the night, but the pilot had his orders, and no doubt diplomatic pouches aboard to give them point. Even the Russians' offended questions—"Don't you trust us? Aren't we your allies?"—could not tempt him from his post. The rest of us, however, were taken to the mess hall to eat with the troops. If the food was simple—a single course of meat and vegetables served in a bowl—the array of glasses confronting each diner, a glass for every conceivable beverage as it seemed to me, betokened that wholesome nourishment was not the purpose of this party. For about two hours we sat there being plied with beers, wines, schnapps, vodka—everything but champagne— until someone announced that cars had been found to take the Czechs and myself to Prague. We arrived, through the fog, in the early hours of the morning. The concert inspired all the glad national enthusiasm proper to the occasion: the first big musical event since liberation, the music of the country's hero, etc.; but I must confess my part in it did not exactly benefit from the alcoholic stopover at Carlsbad.

The next day, as I was on the point of leaving for London, my Russian proposal matured with disconcerting suddenness. Yes, the message said, I would be very welcome in Moscow; would I please go directly to Prague airport, where a plane was standing by to take me to the Soviet Union. Now it was my turn to stall. I was not prepared to disappoint either Diana or myself by failing to return as promised, so while expressing delight, gratitude, and so forth, I asked the Russians to transfer arrangements to London and postpone departure for a couple of days. Upset to have their plans collapse, they demurred, but did as I asked. (Curiously, what might have been an ironic counterpart of this incident, or perhaps repayment for my troublesomeness, occurred a few years later, in July 1948. Again I was in Prague, having just come from Budapest with Marcel Gazelle, and making a connection for London on my way to the Edinburgh Festival. This time, instead of laying on an aircraft for my use, some Russian and Czech military policemen came aboard the one on which I was already comfortably installed and took me off. The incident had neither dramatic sequel nor explanation: put up in a hotel for long enough to witness a people's democratic parade embellished with huge pictures of Stalin and other heroes, I was released the next day to continue my interrupted journey, still wondering what it all signified. Marcel was not arrested; on landing he telephoned Diana, by then my wife, who spent a nightmare twenty-four hours lurid with visions of Siberia. That was just a few days before our first son, Gerard, was born.)

En route to Moscow in November 1945, one changed planes, airports and social systems in Berlin, Tempelhof being in the American sector and serving the West, Adlershof in the Russian zone and serving the East: arrangements which have merely hardened into policies in thirty years, although one flies directly to Vnukovo nowadays and Aeroflot has offices throughout the world. Once landed, I found myself trapped, for the fog which some days previously had blanketed Prague now descended upon Berlin, cutting off the sky. The American authorities provided me with quarters and I spent a couple of idle days wandering through the ruins of the great city I had last seen almost fifteen years before. I had to keep in touch with the local Russians to know when my onward flight would eventually leave. At first I used the normal chain of command and communication, my request going up the American ladder, across to the Russian, down their ladder to the rung dealing with my affairs, and all the roundabout way back again. To make one successful contact by this method took a whole day, so in desperation I borrowed a car from the U.S. Army, drove to Adlershof and exchanged telephone numbers with the airport authorities. On the third morning I was told to report, ready for takeoff.

It was still so early that the Soviet troops were only just awake, each soldier wandering about with his little tin shaving basin and dressed to some indefinable halfway stage between uniform and individual whim. I was shown into the presence of the commandant, a terrifying woman such as only Russia produces, wearing all the signs of virility including a mustache, and clearly in effortless control of Adlershof airport. From behind her makeshift desk she surveyed me coolly and asked if I had heard of David Oistrakh. Not only had I heard of him, but I was looking forward to meeting him that very day. And did I know how great a musician he was? Yes, indeed, I admired him enormously, I said. But my knowledge of him, my admiration, my eagerness to meet him were not enough to soften her: the next question put me in my place. Had I ever won any medals? Shamefacedly I admitted I hadn't really won anything so far. Oistrakh, it appeared, had won dozens of decorations: he was a Hero of the Soviet Union, the darling of the people, the holder of this, that and the next award; she knew them all by heart. I said I was sure he deserved them and she let me go.

As far as I could see, every piece of equipment on the airfield was American, including the plane I boarded, a DC-3, but a DC-3 furnished to a Victorian Scheherazade's fancy, with velvet settees and pretty little tassels on the window blinds. Undoubtedly it was intended for people of distinction, though of the seven or eight of us, none was distinguished enough to merit accommodation on the divan. We took our seats and then, without any of the customary routines, the testing and revving of individual engines and so forth, we simply proceeded to the runway and took off. A few hours later we landed at Moscow airport and there, in the wind and wet of the November afternoon, at the foot of the mobile stairway, on the tarmac itself, stood Oistrakh, for almost thirty years to be a friend beyond price until his untimely death in Amsterdam in 1974.

For all that my mother spent vast reserves of energy and discipline in controlling her children's environment, put to the challenge she would declare heredity of greater account. I follow her at least part of the way into the cult, in that the bonds between present and past (and future) have crucial importance for me. Linking the human adventure into a whole, they make sense of it and are severed at our peril. My visit to Russia had, therefore, a significance not measurable by its brevity or its confinement to Moscow. It drew me further and deeper than even Rumania had done into my past, into the language, the rhythms, the landscape of my forefathers, into my mother's real and dream worlds. When, a few years later, I discovered India, I discovered yet profounder depths to that strangely familiar homeland called the East; but in 1945, with India seven years distant, Russia was the ultimate, immensely attractive legend made flesh, giving perspective to existence. Owing much of my temperament to Russia, I felt—still feel—I had a claim upon her. I longed to visit the Crimea, Georgia, the infinitely romantic countries of the south which had formed my mother. Time cut short such hopes, but even in northern Moscow I found reproduced my mother's ruthless idealism, a determination to shape life to ends of duty and excellence, rather than passively to be shaped by its hazards.

No doubt another sort of ruthlessness lay upon Stalin's capital, the monstrous, brutish ruthlessness of a regime which trampled over ideals and individuals to cringe before a tyrant; but the worst of this I was spared. For one thing, I met few officials, responsibility for my entertainment being entrusted wholly to musicians; for another, I was not an official myself, but as a civilian, unencumbered by military, political or diplomatic import, I was given a welcome which embraced in my person the symbol of alliance between East and West. Thirdly and of greatest consequence, my coming coincided with the euphoric interlude between war and cold war, when happiness in victory and hope for peace seemed, to me and to the simple citizens I met, perfectly reasonable responses. The result was a warmth of affection outstripping my fondest hopes. To give point to my sense of exploring my own history, I actually did meet some relations. Waiting for me at the airport with Oistrakh and some others was a hearty, jolly, broad man, a functionary of Gosconzert, the state agency responsible for musicians and performances, who introduced himself as Mr. Schneerson. "Oh!" said I, "but that's a name in my father's family! We must be related!" He accepted the suggestion placidly enough, but did not pursue it. Later two middle-aged aunts or cousins of my mother's made themselves known, two most charming, proper, self-contained ladies whom I promptly fell for and have seen on each subsequent stay in Moscow. They outlined their life for me: modest in material terms on their government pensions, but rich in art, their resources stretching to frequent evenings at the concert, the opera, the ballet.

Because of the delays since my first asking to come to Russia, a visit which might have lasted two weeks or more was cut to five or six days, for I had commitments elsewhere. Into those few days I had to squeeze my own three concerts, a couple of formal banquets, attendance at several spectacular productions, meetings with as many Soviet musicians as could be rounded up and enough first impressions to fill the twelve months I could with profit have stayed. From the airport I was taken to the Metropole Hotel, a relic of Czarist times, still retaining somewhat rubbed and battered traces of grandeur in its chandeliers and furniture and carpets. I was given a suite overlooking Red Square and the Kremlin, and was no sooner installed than in tumbled a joyous rabble of young musicians, bringing extravagant quantities of that wonderful unsalted caviar which no longer seems to exist.

Caviar apart, Moscow offered little to eat but black bread and sour cream, a diet for which my hosts apologized although personally I could think of few I would prefer. To many in the city it would, I am sure, have seemed Lucullan. Moscow wore a look of exhaustion; the war had not left such dramatic scars upon it as London's broken streets or Berlin's acres of craters and rubble, but there was an air of overcrowding, makeshifts, disrepair, struggle simply to live; and everywhere patient citizens standing in line. One day, avoiding the guide assigned to me, I went alone into the streets to feel the people's hardships somewhat nearer at hand, and joined a queue waiting for some scant reward, two shrunken apples perhaps, or a bag of oats. Between the food lines and the state banquets the gulf seemed as pitiless as that in France before 1789. On that same outing, hunting for a memento for Diana, I entered a bookshop which at first sight appeared to stock only five-year plans; interesting in their way, no doubt, but no good to Diana or to me. Concealed in its dim depths, however, I found a treasure: an illustrated history of the Russian dance called *Nash Ballet*—"Our Ballet." Having no rubles, I offered dollars. Panic-stricken, the shopkeeper hustled me off his premises, and I had to return to the hotel, find my guide—by this time as frantic as the bookseller—and turn the problem of my purchase over to him. The book was added to the many gifts I carried away.

Moscow's grimness and its strength were embodied in the view from the hotel: the great square, without elegance or warmth, lay bare, impressive, forbidding beneath the Kremlin's fortress walls. As my Russian colleagues and I were looking at this somber prospect one morning, someone said, "That's how Moscow is now, but you wait: in a few years we will have skyscrapers, we will have white bread, and we will give you the welcome you deserve!" I tried to tell them I'd just as soon they never had skyscrapers or white bread. It was no use. Such were the insignia of progress; to question their desirability was absurd.

Congratulating my friends on their country's achievements since

the Revolution and on the promise of its future, I said there was, however, one thing it would give me great pleasure and reassurance to see:
someone who had done the same job for fifty years. They found me my
phenomenon without stepping outside the hotel. He was the elevator
operator. Through two international wars, one civil war, a couple of
revolutions, the collectivization of the peasants, countless pogroms and
purges and a five-year plan or two, he had minded his own business and
kept the lift moving. I suppose I should have guessed where to look for
stability, for returning to Europe after the war, I found everywhere the
same faces in the old hotels. Others might have suffered a sea change
and be in the armed forces or the maquis or working in factories or
government departments of charities. But the maître d'hôtel and the
hotel porter were at their familiar posts, with the same ingratiating stoop
to their shoulders and on their features the same deferential concern. As
rabbis acquire a rabbinical vocal delivery, as if godlike serenity had
somehow become mixed with crude oil, so the hotel porter acquires a
manner whose complaisance bears him safely through conquest and
liberation and the rise and fall of regimes.

There was one less comfortable episode, the only glimpse vouchsafed me of the quicksands through which my new friends must constantly pick a wary way. Before leaving for Russia I had asked Grisha
Piatigorsky, the great Russian cellist, if I could see anyone or do anything for him in Moscow, for I knew he had never been back to Russia
since he had left it. When I offered to carry any messages he might have,
he told me of his worries about his father: through all these years his
letters, parcels and gifts of money had remained without acknowledgment; would I, if possible, look his father up? I promised to do my best,
and, arrived in Moscow, asked the help of my Russian colleagues.
Coming out from rehearsal one morning, I saw in the foyer of the building a fairly aged man, pointed out to me as Piatigorsky's father. Before I
could do more than frame a greeting, the old man launched into a
passionate outburst.

"You bring me messages from my son?" he shouted. "What kind of
a son do I have? What kind of a son is it that forgets his father?"

"He hasn't forgotten you; he's worried about you: that's why I
asked to see you," I managed to interpose.

"Why doesn't he ever write? Why does he never send me anything? Not so much as a word!"

"But he does! All the time! Letters, money, parcels. They can't have got through." Far from softening his wrath and distress, my explanation served only to deflect him to a new target.

"This cursed miserable regime! It doesn't care about its old people. It leaves them to rot. It has no heart, no pity!"

He made not the slightest attempt to muffle his rage, but declaimed it for all the world to hear. The musicians standing around were terrified. Addressing him by first name and patronymic, they implored him to stop: "Be quiet! Please be quiet!" and when these appeals failed, dragged him, still shouting, away. I did not see him again. It was the only ominous crack in the happy surface of my Moscow days.

Not that tranquillity was a feature of my sojourn, which was, rather, packed brimful with introductions, hospitality, talk, sights, a super-MGM-style production of *Cinderella* which sent its heroine on a world tour to participate in every style of dance against every type of décor, presentation to Ulanova afterward, a gypsy opera, my own and other concerts before impassioned audiences, and underlying it all, the sense of penetrating a world of music and manners which, had history not wavered, would have been my own. My greatest pleasure, of course, was to make contact with Soviet musicians—nonetheless my colleagues for the belated beginning of our acquaintance—some of whom I was repeatedly to meet again, either in Moscow or the West. I had misconceptions to correct and findings to establish: the classicism of a Russian interpretation of Tchaikovsky was a welcome surprise after some of the unleashed Tchaikovskys of my experience; the excellence of Russian musical training duly impressed me.

But neither then nor later could the run of approved Soviet music altogether seduce me—though it might intrigue, as did a musical celebration of Lenin a few years ago. One could only call it an oratorio, not simply because it was a sacred ritual, Lenin cast as Jesus (or rather Jesus cast as Lenin) and proceeding through suffering to apotheosis, but because the techniques were borrowed from the Passions of Bach: the evangelist-narrator, the solo recitatives and arias, the hymns for full chorus. In one scene Lenin, visiting a factory, causes a girl worker to swoon, at the end of which mystical experience she offers him a rose. It is an extraordinary example of socialist religion, which I would dearly love to present in the West. Such oddities apart, Soviet music is immensely competent, but its deference to mass taste, or Kremlin taste, its appeal to a narrow range of broad emotions, sound somewhat commonplace and tiresome to foreign ears. No doubt direction from above is to blame for much, although I suspect that even allowed the emancipation and sophistication Stravinsky enjoyed, Soviet composers of the caliber of Kabalevsky or Khachaturian could never have matched his originality and power for all their skill in bringing off effects. Among the directives and prohibitions governing Soviet composition, there lay at least one tragedy, however.

To anyone who knew his music, a first encounter with Dmitri Shostakovich could not fail to be startling: in contrast to the elemental force, bombast, grandeur of his works, he was a *chétif* figure, the perennial student, unassertive and shy, who looked as though all the music could be wrung out of him in a couple of song cycles. For a long time he was under a cloud, then he put his neck beneath the yoke, wrote to move the multitude, and received every honor. He gave the world marvelous works, but I feel that in his heart of hearts lay concealed many other masterpieces which he took unwritten to the grave in August 1975. Had he been free to develop as he wished, I imagine his music would have been more subtle, more harmonically experimental, repudiating the blatant effects which can coarsen his best writing. I see this as the greater pity because I personally owe him much, for his brilliant Violin Concerto offers violinists most gratifying opportunities to bring the house down.

Of course, my greater debt in this regard is to David Oistrakh, for whom the Concerto was written and who gave me the facsimile score in 1955, to present to the world at the same time he did: an example of selflessness which summed up this kindest of friends and colleagues. On my first visit to Moscow I did not hear him play—and curiously enough, though later we performed together in half the capitals of the developed world, we never did so in Moscow—but notwithstanding this notable gap in my 1945 Russian experience, from the start Oistrakh incarnated my own Russian-Jewish inheritance. I felt very close to him, sharing as well as a background and an instrument, a taste in performance. At that moment my playing may have been, thanks to Enesco and Busch, a fraction more classical, and his a touch more academic-romantic, but if so, the difference was scarcely noticeable and quickly bridged as our styles drew closer after the war. Although Oistrakh was not yet conducting, he clearly had all the makings of a musician who could turn his hand to anything: his cultivation as deep as it was wide, his musicianship as penetrating as it was flexible and red-blooded. He came, of course, from Odessa, the son of a poor bookkeeper who played the violin for pleasure and early introduced David to it. After graduating from the

Odessa conservatory in 1926, Oistrakh soon won himself fame and affection. When I met him he was both a professor at the Moscow conservatory and Russia's darling. As such he had in that drained country the tremendous privilege of an apartment for himself, his wife, Tamara, and Igor, his son: two or three rooms, crowded and cozy with instruments, music, books, mementos. I loved him immediately. Not only was he the gentlest, staunchest, most warm-hearted of men, but he was also simple and ingenuous. He never felt the need to appear other than he was or explain what might be difficult to grasp, but presented himself candidly, without second thoughts or self-consciousness or doubts about his reception, a complete human being.

Some commitment called Oistrakh away from Moscow within two or three days of my arrival, so although I already felt I knew him, it wasn't until we met in Prague to play together in May 1947 that our friendship had a chance to flower. The occasion was distasteful enough, one of those official celebrations when the gold chairs and the diplomats are lined up to applaud selected talent. Commands to perform were a feature of Oistrakh's life, as of any Soviet artist's—of any artist's in any autocratic regime, I suppose. I don't think they enjoyed being summoned to the Kremlin and ordered to impress visitors, but it was a way of life which Mozart and Haydn also submitted to, not to mention Enesco in the service of the Rumanian monarchy. Brought up an American, free of courtly obligations, I was always a little embarrassed by the civil power's presumptuous disposal of its artists, but I came to Prague at Oistrakh's own invitation, and therefore with much to look forward to and nothing to resent. For the first of untold times we played together with, as I recall, only a piano for accompaniment. If anyone had hoped for a gladiatorial contest deciding supremacy and defeat, he was due to be disappointed: then, as always, David and I could not have been more devoted to one another or played together in greater harmony.

I think it was on that occasion that David made me a gift of Prokofiev's Violin Sonata. This was a courtesy returned, for wanting to leave something in Russia, I had brought with me in 1945 the orchestral scores and solo parts of two violin concerti, the Elgar and the Bartók (only to find that both were already known, by means of the BBC, to Russian musicians although both score and parts were unobtainable). My gift was not universally appreciated. Novello, the British publisher of Elgar, was particularly irritated to think that Elgar's harmonies might echo through the length and breadth of the Soviet Union and the publishers not a penny the richer; for those were the days when communists scorned the performing-rights scruples of the capitalists and the bourgeois. Novello need not have worried: to my knowledge the Elgar has never been performed in Russia, and thirty-odd years later, the score must still be gathering dust in the library of the conservatoire. Nor did Bartók fare much better. His concerto too would have gone unheard in Russia had I not performed it in Leningrad in 1962, when, considering the audience's musical unpreparedness, it went down well. When Oistrakh gave me Shostakovich's Concerto, we introduced it simultaneously, playing it first in Johannesburg in 1956; when he gave me the Prokofiev Sonata, however, he was still confined to the Soviet bloc, and mine was the sole privilege of presenting it to the wider world. I chose New York for its debut.

Too soon for liking, I had to say farewell to Moscow and board the plane back to Berlin, for a flight very different from the lonely splendor of the outward journey. This plane was full of Russians traveling to reunion with their spouses serving in Germany and making a party of the occasion. They knew I played the violin, and play the violin I had to, in return for tidbits from their oily paper bags (improvidently I was without a brown paper parcel of my own). They sang, singly and together and with my accompaniment; they recited Pushkin, Lermontov and other poets for each other, the whole company savoring the familiar beauties. It was extraordinary and heartwarming to discover what strength traditional culture still had. After a merry journey we reached Adlershof, where all my companions disembarked while I, at the pilot's instance, stayed aboard for an expensive hop across Berlin to the American airport. I perfectly understood I was a pretext: the Russian pilots seized any excuse to have their aircraft serviced and refueled by their lavish allies, and valued on their own account a few hours at Tempelhof. Once again, no sooner had I reached Berlin than all outward flights were canceled by fog, but luckily more important personages than I, a Soviet delegation including Gromyko, had urgent business in London and I was able to travel on their coattails. A convoy of some dozen vehicles set out for Bad Oeynhausen, a railway terminus in the British sector from where a train ran nightly to Calais, eleven of them black Soviet official saloons carrying the delegation, the twelfth a gray American army vehicle carrying me. Ahead and behind were scout cars and bringing up the rear a breakdown truck. It took our cumbersome procession most of the day to complete the drive, and this time I had no chance to sing for my supper: there were various stops, but I didn't feel it appropriate to go up the line of vehicles requesting a share in the packed lunches of Gromyko and friends, so stayed quietly on my generous physical reserves.

At Calais the next morning we unexpected passengers waited while a troopship was loaded, to the gunwales it seemed, with returning British soldiers. During the operation, which took a little time, the Russian officials addressed no word to me and scarcely a word to each other, but simply stood there, cold, grim, taciturn, radiating suspicion and unamiability and showing me a face of the Soviet Union hidden from me in all my days in Moscow. Eventually we were allowed aboard and allotted a few privileged square feet of space. I stayed on deck, fenced in by violins and booty: Diana's book, a case of Crimean wines for my mother, and three big drums of caviar given me by Oistrakh and the others. London in those days was only less austere than Moscow and the caviar seemed haloed with the prodigality of another age, if not simply a figment of hungry imaginations. Diana parceled it out in half-pound jam jars and distributed them among her friends, keeping, however, a respectable amount for ourselves.

Then I went home to the United States for my winter tour, with misery in my heart but no clarity in my mind about how the knots in my life should be untangled. The two years from autumn 1945 have left a blemish on my history. Some mistakes one makes are fruitful; one gains strength and wisdom by them; but this one I deeply regret, for nothing was gained by it and Diana, who asked nothing, was subjected to many months of agonizing uncertainty, committed to me yet never knowing when I might reappear or for how long. How far I had fallen from my childhood dream of universal peace and harmony! How helpless music proved to be in this personal defeat! I had estranged myself from parents, wife, even children. Many mistakes—today I am tempted to call them crimes—lay heavily on my heart and I was powerless to do anything about them. I did not realize at the time that what should be never would be, and so I caused endless suffering and postponed the right course of action. Without a doubt this was the worst period of my life, the most unfocused, the most imprecise, when I let things drift and myself drifted nearer disaster than at any other time.

In Rome in the summer of 1946 I met a young man, a British army officer then working with displaced people, who was to become very near and dear to me: Richard Hauser, who is now married to Hephzibah. Richard had, among other accomplishments, a talent for graphology. I tested his powers on examples of the handwriting of my father, my mother and Diana, and was greatly impressed to find his penetration agreed with mine. Examining a page from Diana's hand, he said, "This has been written by an extraordinary person, an artist of some kind, I would say. She could run a business, an institution, a country. . . . She could cope with any responsibility." He asked me to write something for him, studied the lines for a few moments and then pronounced in his blunt way, "Well, you'll either make the grade in the next few months or you'll be finished." It was not a comfortable alternative.

The winter before that disconcerting encounter Diana had taken her sister Griselda, gravely ill with tuberculosis, to a sanatorium at Davos in Switzerland; racked by anxiety for Griselda, unwilling to work until her sister should recover, lonely up in the Alps, Diana needed all her personal resources to survive. Then, if at any time in my life, I blessed the invention of the telephone. Every evening after the concert I telephoned her from wherever I was in the United States and we talked for, literally, an hour at a time. Toward the end of one such hour the operator (in Seattle, as I remember) cut us off in mid-dialogue, whether from impatience or absence of mind, putting me into a fury: I hate things not to be carried to their natural conclusion. At my insistence the operator made the connection to Switzerland again to let us say goodbye. The following spring, still leading two lives, neither of them properly, I rented a house near Montreux for Nola and the children, thus remaining for many months as cut off from Diana as if I had stayed in the United States, and as dependent on the telephone.

Antal Dorati and I had been invited to Vienna and Budapest to give some concerts in the summer of 1946, and as had become my custom during the war, I negotiated our transportation with the U.S. forces in return for a recital for the troops. Two little open planes with room enough only for a pilot and a passenger were sent for us—in fact, there was a third one intended for our luggage, but we were traveling light. Since American military aircraft could not use neutral Switzerland's facilities, Dorati and I joined the planes at Friedrichshafen and flew along the Alps in the sunshine to Vienna, where a central street had been cleared for our landing. Vienna was then under four-power control, each of the Allies housing their headquarters in a different hotel. The Americans were in the Bristol, so to the Bristol I went to telephone Diana. So soon after the war it was difficult to make international calls in Europe. Three tariffs existed: the ordinary, on which one had to wait for weeks; a more expensive one, requiring only days of patience; and the "blitz" or "lightning" tariff, which connected one more or less immediately at a straight ten times the basic rate. I always rang "blitz," but even so, telephoning wasn't easy. With the help of the U.S. Army's "magic number," however, all delays and difficulties evaporated like dew before the sun. Naturally I memorized the number, used it every day in Vienna, and every day was in touch with Diana. In Budapest the frustrations reverted to normal but another two or three days in Vienna made up for this, at the end of which I had to return to Friedrichshafen and Montreux.

We set off from Vienna late one afternoon. Fearing the daylight would not last as far as the Bodensee, my pilot suggested our spending the night at Salzburg; which change of plan suited me very well, giving me an extra opportunity to dial the army's priority number and talk with Diana. All went happily for about forty minutes, when a gentlemanly English voice interrupted us: this was not a military conversation, and much as he regretted it, he would have to cut us off. However, he was kind enough to let us bring the call to a graceful end. Very early next morning, when the sun was about to rise, the pilot and I set off again, confident that we would have a perfectly lovely flight (there are few more exhilarating experiences than taking off from a tiny airfield in a tiny plane at dawn: I have had the pleasure quite often in different quarters of the globe). But when we reached it, the Bodensee was lost in fog. I proposed we land at Zurich—which, although it would be fine for me, confronted the American airman with possible arrest and internment. "Do you know the Swiss language?" he shouted back, over the noise of the engine and the wind. There was no time nor had I sufficient lung power to give a lecture on the four languages of Switzerland, but I assured him I could talk him out of the hands of officialdom. Zurich too was invisible behind banks of fog, however, whereupon the pilot directed his machine to a little place on the Swiss banks of the Bodensee which in his experience was usually clear, even in the foggiest weather. Sure enough, it was clear that day, hardly more than a turnip patch but big enough for our little plane. We landed, I got out, and before I could thank him or say goodbye he was off again, his clandestine mission accomplished.

By then it was about half-past six in the morning. I walked to the nearest farmhouse and knocked at the door. Eventually the farmer came downstairs, still in pajamas, ushered me in and, without posing awkward questions, let me use his telephone to summon a taxi. I awaited its arrival outside. At that part of the Bodensee an embankment has been built to protect the surrounding fields from flooding. As we drove up onto it we were stopped by a border guard on a bicycle. Had we heard the sound of an airplane engine? he wanted to know. Regretting that we could not help him, the driver and I shook our heads and were waved on. It was the only time I entered a country illegally.

While I returned to the United States in the autumn, to tour as usual, Diana—her beloved sister better and now married to Louis Kentner—took herself alone to New York in an attempt to start her career again; and finally, after a winter of disappointments, was invited by her, and my childhood friends "the boys," to stay with them at Cathedral Oaks. Meanwhile Hephzibah, who had been in Australia throughout the war, arrived at Los Gatos with Lindsay and their two small sons, Kronrod and Marston. Hephzibah and I had not played together since 1940. In 1947 we were to give our return performance in the Metropolitan Opera House, New York, in preparation for which event I gathered the clan, Yaltah and her son Lionel included, eight of us altogether, at Saint Petersburg, Florida. I took a house there for a month and, little thinking how I was exploiting her, persuaded Diana to join us and put her in charge of it. I had recently read Walter B. Price's pioneering book, *Nutrition and Physical Degeneration,* and chose Saint Petersburg because there was a dentist there, Dr. Page, who was a fellow pioneer in preaching the noxious effects of sugar and white flour. Dr. Page put us on a diet excluding these substances but not otherwise stringent, and unhampered by his limits, Diana produced fantastic meals for all the household. Persuaded by her brother, Nola had accepted separation, she was willing to trust Zamira and Krov to Diana and myself for the summer holiday in 1947, and at last Lindsay won her over to take the step I could not bring myself to take against her. She divorced me.

Diana and I wanted to marry quietly in Copenhagen, but were foiled by the punctilio of the minister at the British embassy there, who saw no reason to dispense with the bans and issue a special license. So London it had to be. Fortunately Mr. Marsh and Mr. Stream—for so the gentlemen in charge of Chelsea Register Office were improbably named—proved more humanly aware of our predicament than the diplomat in Copenhagen. By their kind subterfuge, the press were about their business elsewhere when we were married on Sunday, 19 October 1947. Straight from the wedding breakfast, given by Louis and Griselda, we went to the Albert Hall, to rehearse the Paganini Concerto Number 1 in D Major.

10

Diana

Almost thirty years later Diana still chides me, half ruefully, half teasingly, for my mournful looks on our wedding day. I had not the smallest doubt of her, you may be sure, but doubts about my own maturity I had in abundance. I had proven myself a pretty quarter-baked husband, unpossessive, uncommanding, possibly unprotective. In my morality one did not win rights by defending them against others; one deserved them, so that it was difficult to feel proprietary about anything and impossible to feel so about a human being. My uncertainty that I deserved Diana was reason enough for a worried face; it seemed a defiance of fate to celebrate a victory not yet earned.

Since then I have learned a few useful lessons. I am less inclined to suppress natural reactions, I hold inviolable principles in suspicion, and I have discovered it in me to be possessive of my wife.

"She could cope with any responsibility," Richard Hauser had predicted of Diana, and if I didn't then need graphology to support my admiration of her capacities, how much less do I need it now! There has never been a moment when my wife hasn't carried the event, however strange, painful or unremitting its demands upon her imagination and endurance. The control learned in the overlapping disciplines of childhood flows in her bloodstream, has become her nature, and brings everything she does to the perfection of a performance, so that what *is* cannot be separated from what *should be*. She has been a constant inspiration, a stimulus, an expression of animated beauty in my life and in our children's lives; and thus it has been from the beginning.

Our first week of married life was, I must acknowledge, a paradigm of all the weeks that followed: after the wedding breakfast a concert; after the concert a one-night honeymoon in a country cottage lent by Diana's friends Madge and Cyril Ritchard; after the honeymoon several appearances in the British provinces; after which we crossed the Atlantic for the winter tour. Not until the tour was over, in spring 1948, did we come to rest at Alma, for eight years to be our home—or rather our headquarters, since tranquil domesticity must always be the victim of a career such as mine. Summers were spent at Alma, spring and fall in Europe, winter in the Americas. In the flux and reflux of these seasonal migrations Diana bore our sons: Gerard in 1948 at the Edinburgh Festival, and Jeremy in San Francisco in 1951; traveling and travailing, as she put it, and giving birth wherever the violin happened to be in the ninth month. A third child was born to us in 1955, only to die: the saddest event we have shared.

Even before Gerard and Jeremy came to claim her attention, however, Diana had taken family duty to heart, interpreting this call upon her with generous inclusiveness and fulfilling it with loving integrity. Before our marriage she had not hesitated to look after Zamira and Krov, and now again they were absorbed into our Californian summers. Diana is not only fit for any responsibility, she is incapable of not responding to a need. She early won my parents' affection and respect. During and after the break with Nola, I felt at ease neither with my father and mother nor with myself, but Diana restored the naturalness to our relations, and so in a way confirmed me as an adult: for this status is not truly established until parent and child meet on mutually loving and respectful terms, and sometimes it needs an outsider to clinch the adjustment. Seeing in Diana a person of real presence and quality, my parents could not but meet her on her level and rejoice in my happiness. They evoked in her a response no less heartfelt.

Coming to California from the tensions and deprivations of wartime London, Diana found in its beauty and plenty the perfect framework in which to unfold mind and spirit, but even had our schedule encouraged it, lotus-eating could be only a temporary indulgence to a nature such as hers, and when the children's formation became an object, we decided to give our sons the advantages we had ourselves enjoyed. San Francisco could not provide such advantages; New York undoubtedly could, but I still couldn't bring myself to live there. Los Angeles, for its part, had, as it has, all that the human being could possibly want and much he never suspected was desirable, but all imported, packaged and displayed hugger-mugger, a sort of surreal bargain basement rather than a way of life: Chinese lessons cheek by jowl with all-night gambling, a dogs' beauty parlor, a Zen Buddhist reading room, a bicycle shop, a liquor store, a fortuneteller's booth, a midnight massage clinic, a shooting gallery, all jumbled together in a zany juxtaposition of mysticism and materialism defeating coherence and at any rate my powers of digestion. So Europe it had to be.

Diana was too shy to propose settling directly in London, her preferred city, and our choice fell on Switzerland, for its sanity, schools, healthy climate and central location. There was financial good sense too in the move, because in those days American residents abroad did not have to pay tax on earnings outside the United States. As it happened, my recording contracts were with London, not by any initiative of mine but because, years earlier, in the 1929 slump, I and other financial embarrassments had been offloaded by the American recording company Victor onto its more secure English sister, HMV, the forerunner of EMI. Other American artists retransferred their allegiance after the crisis, but I left mine where it was, and could now enjoy the tax-free benefit. This piece of good fortune permitted us to buy a house in London and build a chalet at Gstaad, acquisitions which before or after that moment of liberal tax allowances would have been impossible. At first we lived in a rented house at Gstaad until, in 1958, Bernard Berenson persuaded us to come to Florence. The Italian interlude proved one of the most delightful of our lives. As many good things do, it came about unpremeditatedly.

We had long wished to meet the king-usurper of Florence, and when we did a warm friendship developed, particularly between Diana and BB, which expressed itself in a very regular, almost biweekly correspondence. BB's high-handedness and vanity were said to irritate many people and I know that some harbored very unfriendly feelings toward him. As a musician, however, I didn't compete in his territory, and as a Jew I had a natural respect for his age and experience. Had he been any younger, no doubt our relationship would have been completely different and I suspect I wouldn't have stayed long under his roof, if at all. But in the circumstances, I found in him only generosity and a certain stimulating worldly wisdom.

Once or twice a year Diana and I would visit him from Switzerland, taking an overnight train and staying the best part of two days. On one such visit he offered us the use of the Villino, a charming farmhouse opposite his I Tatti. I knew we would eventually return to Switzerland and probably at some point establish a home in London, but such decisions have their timing and the time was not yet ripe. So we accepted.

Like my mother, I love Italy and rejoice in the direct, uncomplicated, basic humanity of the Italians. I remember an incident from the first time we went to Rome as a family. At a market stall my mother bought some persimmons, a favorite indulgence of mine, but as the grocer put them in a bag it seemed to her that there were not quite the dozen she had ordered and was about to pay for, so she asked him to recount. Sure enough, there were only eleven. Why had he tried to cheat her? *"Ma, signora,"* he explained disarmingly, *"era tanto facile!"*—"It was so easy!" A great quality of the Italians is that they form few theories. After the war men of good will bent their minds to the task of re-educating the Germans, because what the Germans had done was clearly deliberate, the result of theory, system, drill, indoctrination. But no one spoke of re-educating the Italians, and in fact they have much to teach us all: to take events with a grain of salt, to look upon the human comedy with an eye accustomed to the theatre, aware that the line between the theatrical and the genuine is, though real, hard to draw.

Berenson was a tireless walker. We roamed the hills with him. No landscape is more enticing to the walker than the trails leading into the surprisingly wild regions above Florence—indeed along the whole spine of Italy. Despite a considerable population, the Italians have managed to preserve this wild streak of mountains and forests running down the length of their country—the counterpart, providing health, strength, virility and spontaneity, to the almost overly civilized Italian society. It also provides good things to eat, as the market in Florence bore witness, its stalls heaped with delicate young fruit, vegetables, game and lamb. The farther one travels east, the younger becomes the animal served for dinner, until in the Middle East even the unborn lamb is shorn of its fleece. Without going so far in infanticide, Italy offers youthful tenderness—suckling lamb, new peas, just sprouted wild asparagus.

Finally the time came to leave Italy. Early in 1959 we settled in Highgate, an ancient leafy London village, now encircled by the sprawling metropolis and scarred by highways, but still retaining on its perch overlooking the dense mass of the city a trace of once compact individuality.

Everything seemed to point to London. For Diana England was home, for the children it meant educational opportunity, for me, ever since my first sight of it thirty years earlier, it had been the most livable country in the world. Of all countries, England offered me the greatest scope for the gratifying of nonmusical interests; for unlike vertically structured societies such as that of the United States or, particularly, the Soviet Union, England is socially "horizontal"—at any given level various professional circles are open to you. You happen to be a violinist; you happen to win recognition; and this, you find, wins you acquaintance with scientists, sociologists, painters, captains of industry, actors, statesmen. Whereas in the United States the social thrust is toward the pinnacle of a particular profession, and the highly paid physicist (or historian, or violinist), holding on to his pinnacle for dear life, must shout across to the man atop the next one if he hopes to be heard and get an answer. In Russia, of course, once set rolling on your chosen track, you stay on it, even living in the same building as your confreres, spending spare time with them, going on holiday to the same resort, protected from chance collision with anyone of a different expertise. Only the dissidents mix disciplines in the U.S.S.R., it seems.

Diana has an artist's eye. Any problem of proportion, color, visual effect, surrenders itself immediately to her sure solution. She draws, she knows and loves painting and allied arts, she counts artists among her friends. I don't know anyone in the world who dresses as elegantly as she does, or as cleverly. She may look as if she has just emerged from spending a fortune in a Paris couture house; in all likelihood she has pieced an outfit together from a *trouvaille* purchased in New York and its perfect mate discovered in a sale in Melbourne, Australia. For Diana makes a virtue of necessity and shops as she travels. In a traveling life, she has kept a record of what clothes are required for each climate at each season, and I am sure that if some quirk of touring unexpectedly mislaid us in Angkor Wat or on Popocatepetl, Diana would issue from her tent perfectly groomed.

In the domestic scope where for too long her talents have been confined, she has employed them to transform our surroundings. Ideally a beautiful home is created by long labor, but time being a luxury Diana has had to do without, she has learned to furnish houses from plans, at long distance, in snatched moments. Alma offered her imagination small range, for it was furnished already; even so, she contrived to raise it to a new level of elegance. Her great achievements, however, were the house

at Highgate and the chalet we built at Gstaad in 1960, each allotted two
spans of ten days each between tours and in that space of time equipped
to the last tea towel. Much of the furniture of our London home was
inherited from Mulberry House or brought from Alma, but Gstaad had
to be done from scratch, and Diana did it single-handed. Off she went to
Gstaad to keep the builders building; got up each day before dawn to
catch the first train to Bern or Zurich; slid down the January ice to the
station; arrived at the city as the stores closed for lunch; window-
shopped, planned, chose, discarded, decided; made her purchases, and
returned in the evening, drawing sketches in a school exercise book.
When I brought Gerard and Jeremy to our new home, Diana met us at
Spiez, the railway junction where the mountain route begins, for she
wanted the joy of showing us her handiwork. All any of us had so far
seen was the site; here we found ourselves in an enchanting house,
complete in every detail, furnished with Austrian and Swiss rustic
pieces, with dough-kneading benches serving as tables and three-legged
stools as chairs. A purchase of my own has pride of place there—a Lurçat
tapestry depicting the beasts, birds and insects of the field. Made during
the war, it carries one rebellious patriotic message, for the owl's eyes are
woven in the *bleu, blanc, rouge* of the tricolor.

Two years later, through the good offices of my friend the composer
Peggy Glanville-Hicks, we bought an abandoned peasant's cottage on
Mykonos—as near Asia as might be without actually leaving Europe—
and in correspondence with a gifted young American, Jim Price, who
stayed to oversee the repairs, Diana made it livable by remote control.

Mykonos architecture is like melted vanilla ice cream; every year
new coats of paint and plaster are applied, so that edges and right angles
disappear beneath lovely bulbous curves. We have respected the simplicity of our little peasant house. Built of stone, the roof insulated with
straw and seaweed between narrow beams (for wood is precious on the
island), with a distinctive little chimney, it is cool, white, clean and
totally unspoiled. For a few years it was an idyllic summer holiday
hermitage where one wore one's oldest clothes, swam in the empty sea,
daily collected steaming loaves of black bread from the baker's brush-
wood oven, and took evening walks in what Diana called our supermar-
ket—our three terraces and the adjoining vineyard where grapes, figs,
pomegranates, prickly pears, tomatoes and quinces grew, these last
usually full of worms. Then in 1967 the colonels made their coup and
that was the end of our idyll for seven years. At the time of writing,
although the colonels are ousted and Greece has an elected government

once more, we haven't been back to our little house on Mykonos. One day soon we will go there again.

One thing Diana does not have is any device to spare herself. Whereas I am a perfectionist in music and accept that I cannot aim at perfection in any other sphere, she is a perfectionist *tout court*. The result is that three details left undone—and one can always find three details—are as important as if existence depended on them. Her standards are such that every button has to be in place, everyone in the house happy, every lapse of mine from faultless order to be hoisted up beyond reproach—though she is philosophically indulgent even when her husband defeats her best efforts; and since I leave any amount of debris to be cleared behind me, she has her work cut out. She shares qualities with my mother—the high standards, the self-discipline, the sensibility to language above all. But our children's upbringing was vastly different from my own. Whereas my parents were hardly ever separated from their children, we had constantly to leave ours to their nurses and later their schools. Diana divided her duties as best she might, alternating a month on tour with me and a month at home with the boys, keeping always in mind the member of the family whom she was obliged to leave to his own devices. Exacting of herself, she makes allowances for others and is not at all possessive of her children. No more than myself has she ever felt they were her private property, nor striven for the intense closeness of the traditional Jewish family; but from the start she treated them as individuals, talking to them before ever they could respond in kind—for she trusts in the efficacy of verbal communication and if anyone could reform the world by words (or for that matter example), it is Diana. I think it has been a source of some frustration to her to discover that words do not work with everyone. Some ears are deaf.

Not, however, the ears of our boys, whose rapid conquest of language vindicated Diana's methods. She turned my constant absences into an asset, for I was hardly ever there to belie the Promethean, Augustan, Herculean qualities I was credited with. As a father I have probably spent less time with my children than any man not sentenced to life imprisonment. In the prewar summers when I was free, I saw more of Zamira and Krov than I did of Gerard and Jeremy at a like age; even so, my daughter and eldest son remember me as a rare visitant in their early lives. Whether or not the children lost anything thereby, it was a loss to me, but an inevitable one. Too often Diana had to be both parents. She managed admirably, seeing to it that I remained ever present, however distant in fact, and stiffening my image with an authority which very likely I could not have maintained in the flesh. Present or not, I found ways to express parental concern. Regretting Zamira's unfortunate infant diet of Karo syrup, I interested myself in the boys' nourishment, and when I was at home baked them supplies of whole-wheat biscuits, very hard and lasting, which took the place of the pacifiers I objected to and that left great brown dribbles down their bibs.

Because I spent so much time away from them, I was curiously detached from my children when they were little, and have made close contact with them only as they grew up. Zamira and Krov, Gerard and Jeremy had no preconceived tracks laid before them, and certainly none was thrust into music. In fact, I probably enjoyed an earlier introduction to music from my father's Chasidic songs than my children did from my violin, and none of them was taken in infancy to concerts. When Jeremy wanted to leave school to devote himself full-time to the piano, I discouraged him. These tactics only pushed up the pressure of his ambition, and the resulting determination added to his talent won achievement. Having done little to launch his course, I now have the keenest pleasure in making music with him. He is the only musician of the four, but all are musical, especially Zamira.

To begin with, Zamira and Krov lived with their mother except for the summer holiday, until, when she was twelve, Zamira asked if she might come to us. She was a brave, self-reliant little girl who had more or less looked after herself in New York, taking herself to and from school and so forth. She knew Diana and I could not give her a home for every day, as we were constantly traveling, and agreed to go to boarding school in the high mountains of Switzerland, a salubrious situation and a good school, if rather old-fashioned, which did her, I hope, a certain amount of good. I remember her courage when we saw her off for the first time at Zurich station. She joined us for all her vacations and sometimes, when vacation and travel coincided, made a trip with us. After school in German-speaking Switzerland, she lived in Paris, later in Florence, ultimately in London, acquiring thereby the fluent use of four languages. Drawn to the artistic, she has always admired Diana and emulated her aesthetic awareness, of painting and music as well as of appearance and dress, although she has not practiced the performing arts.

For a time she was married to the pianist Fou T'Song, an experience that gave her, as well as my first grandchild, Lin Siao, a thorough knowledge of piano literature and style, and a sharp critical appreciation. Fou T'Song introduced me to a people, a mentality, a way of life that represents one of the foundations of human history. His father, an eminent French scholar, sent us from China letters we shall always treasure: in the most cultivated French, written (or drawn) with a brush, expressing his happiness that two of the oldest races in the world, the Chinese and the Jewish, should be thus united.

But the marriage did not survive. Zamira is now happily married to Jonathan Benthall, who comes from an English family which still lives in the Elizabethan manor house, now owned by the National Trust, where his forebears have lived since the sixteenth century. Apart from his talents as a writer, anthropologist and computer expert, Jonathan has all the kindness and devotion I could wish for Zamira. It is a great joy to see such tender love. On December 8, 1976, a son, Dominic Gabriel, was born and I became a proud grandfather for the second time.

If Zamira has been drawn to and formed by the aesthetic, Krov has been charmed and formed largely by the out of doors. When his mother moved to the Bahamas, he swam a great deal and drove fast cars, and it was perfectly natural that after a variety of schools and the University of Louisiana, he should volunteer for the Special Forces in the American army. He distinguished himself in various hair-raising exploits parachuting from forty thousand feet, diving around submarines, exploring the floor of the ocean, raising sunken aircraft from the depths of Lake Michigan, blowing up bridges, and taking on secret missions whose details he has never revealed. If I found it astonishing that a child of mine should be so athletically adept and venturesome, it was, I suppose, no more astonishing than that Jewish fathers who spent their lives locked up in schools and offices should beget the Israeli soldiers of today. Krov, moreover, had his Australian heritage to fulfill. I was worried that his skills might involve him in the Vietnam war, but he was so highly regarded that he was kept at home to train others and finally was released, the United States having spent thousands of dollars on his preparation for life. I can assure the government that the money was not spent in vain. He is a credit to his country and his parents.

Krov has brought his gifts to a very wonderful evolution: along with his physical fearlessness, he has a sense of moral obligation to the natural world. Some years ago he sold all that he had and set off, with his lovely young wife, Ann, and a certain amount of secondhand film equipment, for Patagonia, spending some months in that inhospitable land to film whales, penguins, cormorants and other species. Their film on the right whale, for which I commissioned Edwin Roxburgh to write a score, was acclaimed on British television and in 1975 the BBC sent

Krov and his wife on a second adventure, to Central America. After further rigorous months in tick-infested jungles, a second superb film, on the flora, fauna and Mayan civilization of the area, was shown in Britain. As I write, Krov and Ann are in Queensland on an ABC commission. For six months they will live with and film hitherto unrecorded wildlife on the Barrier Reef and inland.

Gerard's family nickname is Mita, whereby hangs a tale. Before his birth we referred to him as "Smith," Diana being determined to preserve the child, sex as yet unknown, from any more outlandish flight of fancy. Eventually he was christened respectably—Gerard Anthony, in memory of his grandfather and his godfather, Anthony Asquith—but Smith or Smithy he unofficially remained, and Mita was his own first attempt at it. Comparing him with his brother, Jeremy, I find something of the same contrast that I once made between my mother and father: Gerard with a high sense of style, complex, exclusive, conservative, and with a fiery temper; Jeremy flexible, investigative, self-analytical, and with a mercurial temperament.

Gerard has Diana's literary and dramatic sensitivity, which her strategy of talking to him in infancy greatly fostered. At the age of three he always had a book in his pocket. Although he doesn't particularly appreciate its being recalled, he stole the show when he was twelve years old in Bernard Miles's production of *Emil and the Detectives* at the Mermaid Theatre in London. He has since worked in related fields, but has not chosen to become an actor. Both he and Jeremy are self-contained individuals, and what they don't choose to reveal, Diana and I don't choose to pry into. Leaving Eton, Gerard rejected the university in favor of "real life," but a year passed before we learned that he was working in the editing department of a movie company. In 1971, when his company was all set to begin production in Italy of a film on the life of Trotsky, we received a telegram from him in New York: "Am here, not there." No questions were asked, but we learned the answers in time: Gerard had fond recollections of California, where he had spent his early years, and no doubt in addition wanted to put a certain amount of space between his parents and himself; but the crucial motive for his flight from Europe was that having been born abroad of only one American parent, he was required by law to spend four consecutive years between the ages of twelve and twenty-eight in the United States to establish his citizenship (born of the same parents, but in San Francisco, Jeremy remains an American whether he ever sets foot there or not).

Now as solid and unchallengeable an American citizen as they come, Gerard has spent his qualifying years at Stanford University, regularly visiting my parents in nearby Los Gatos to drive them about, look after them and become my mother's favorite grandson. Alike in many ways, they recognize each other's qualities and defects and are devoted to each other. The years away from the parental home have brought Gerard a great measure of philosophy. He knows what he wants. He has fashioned a way of life to his selective personal requirements. He is perhaps too exacting of his fellowmen, so that he does not easily gather a circle of indiscriminate acquaintance. Like Diana, he is caustic, intolerant of falsity, affectation or stupidity, and he, again like Diana, provides a stimulating balance to my own nature, which is in a way too selfish to trouble about improving individuals. His great virtue is honesty. His critical faculty spares no one, including himself. When he can reconcile his complexity with his basic integrity, he will have achieved the crystallization of his character. He and I are now closer than ever before.

After Gerard's birth and before Jeremy's we engaged an excellent Swiss nanny, Schwester Marie. The effusion of her devotion went to the new baby, whom she regarded as her own, but when in the course of time she left us, it was not Jeremy, but Gerard, who shed tears. Gerard has my mother's fierce, exclusive loyalties; Jeremy is gregarious. He is universally liked and finds everyone interesting.

His musical gifts declared themselves early. He wrote music before he wrote words, embellishing his crotchets and quavers with little branches so that they resembled Christmas trees. At the age of five he began studying the piano in Florence with Madame Nardi, a first-class teacher who gave him a good grounding, and very soon thereafter Jeremy and I were playing our first piece together. In London he was sent to a progressive school where the children had a wonderful time upsetting the desks and the timetable and throwing ink pots at the staff; then— from one extreme to the other, it may seem—to Westminster Under School, upon which he reported after one day's trial: "This is a real school—we're not allowed to throw things and we have to call the teacher 'sir' " (one of the teachers a school mistress!). Finally I decided he should join Gerard at Eton: he was leading an indoor, coddled life and becoming soft. I had some resistance to overcome, from Diana and especially from Jeremy, but the plan was vindicated by its success. Jeremy grew hale and hearty, and what was of greater consequence, closer to his brother.

By that time I had started a school of my own, for which Jeremy's musical attainment certainly qualified him, but as I have said, I wanted to dissuade him from burning his boats so young. However, after about a year and a half at Eton, he wrote to ask if he might go to Paris to study music with Nadia Boulanger, and when the school granted him three months' leave of absence I let him have his way.

Nadia Boulanger's reputation as a teacher of music needs no boost from me. Her summer academy at Fontainebleau has spread her name wherever music is listened to. Her hold on my heart dates from a confidence I offered her at a banquet in Paris when I was fifteen, was consolidated when I met her in the United States during the war, and confirmed by her committing a handful of her violinists to my temporary charge at Fontainebleau in 1954. I forget what was being celebrated at that Paris dinner at which I made her acquaintance, but I do remember my pleasure at being placed next to this admired authority, and my humming to her the theme of a Bach fugue in defense of my interpretation of it. She is an extraordinary person, with both the French and the Russian qualities of her forefathers—a warm, spontaneous, generous, hospitable, party-loving, Slav nature from her mother, and from her father a French clarity of mind. All her life has been devoted to the memory of her sister Lili, a talented composer who died young, some of whose works I have recorded. It is a measure of Nadia's successful tribute that the crossroad outside her home in the rue Ballu, Paris, is now named Place Lili Boulanger. Nadia is devoutly Catholic and conservative, valuing order in all its manifestations, giving to Caesar what is Caesar's no less than to God what is God's, acknowledging the respect due to pope, king or president by virtue of their office. In practical terms there are no barriers to her attention and love. It is remarkable to see her handling young people: they tremble before her and adore her; she demands and gets their best. In many ways she reminds me of my mother.

If music was indeed to be Jeremy's destiny, he could have no better teacher. His three months away from Eton were extended to six, then to nine, during which his progress was so remarkable that there could be no more talk of his not being a musician. He was greatly privileged, of course—given daily lessons by Nadia, housed in a room adjoining her apartment, benefiting in addition from Marcel Ciampi's teaching several times a week; but he responded ardently to his opportunity—he seized it in both hands. He made himself a schedule which stipulated forty hours' work each week on the piano, apart from other musical studies, and yet found time to read newspapers, go to theatres and concerts, make friends, and altogether lead a most interesting life.

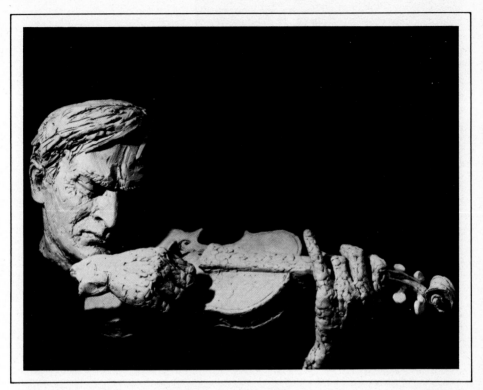

David Wynne's sculpture

With Margot Fonteyn,
Bath Festival, 1962

With Rudolf Nureyev,
Bath Festival, 1964

At a rehearsal of the Philadelphia Orchestra, Eugene Ormandy conducting

Practicing

Conducting

Playing with Ravi Shankar

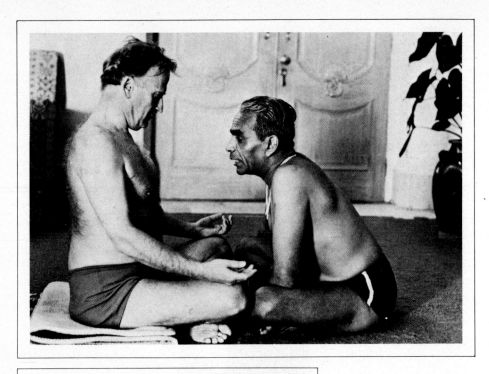

A yoga lesson with his guru,
B. K. S. Iyengar

Following a BBC television
program on yoga

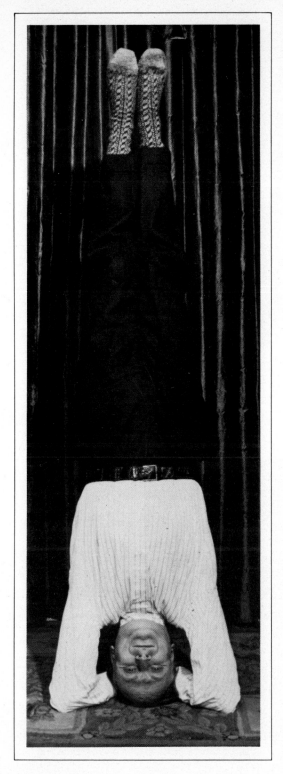

Headstand (*sirsasana*)

With Queen Elizabeth,
Queen Mother
of the Belgians

With Mrs. Gandhi when
Yehudi was presented
the Nehru Peace Prize, 1968

Nehru and Diana

The International Music Congress, Moscow, 1971

Robert Masters rehearsing with Yehudi

Rehearsing the orchestra

Sixtieth-birthday concert in Carnegie Hall, April 13, 1976.
Yehudi, Ernst Wallfisch, Jeremy, and Mstislav Rostropovitch

Maurice Gendron, Marcel Ciampi, Yehudi, and Jacqueline Gazelle
before classes at the Yehudi Menuhin School

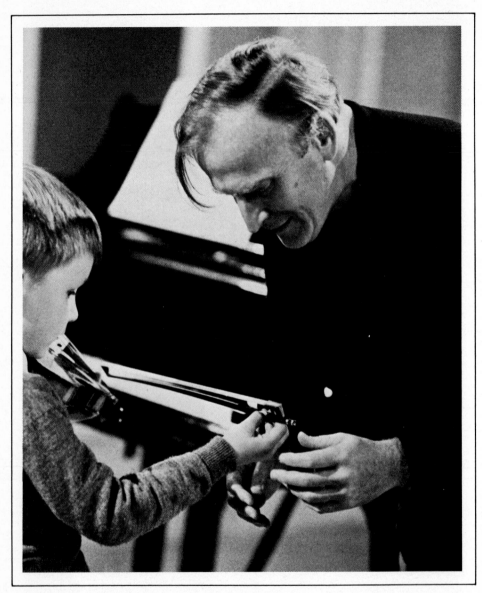

Teaching

After some eighteen months I sent him to Vienna to study conducting with Hans Swarowsky. For one thing, pianists, even the best of them, are too numerous; they propagate like rabbits, for those who can't make a soloist's career take their revenge by teaching innumerable other pianists, who failing in turn to succeed as soloists, in turn become indifferent teachers. . . . Secondly, I knew Jeremy had the gifts of a conductor, not only musical gifts but human ones—natural movement, co-ordination, tact, charm, a talent for getting along with people and getting the best out of them. Thirdly, the tendency of our day is for conductors to be pianists or composers as well, as are Boulez, Barenboim, Previn and many others.

Jeremy's Viennese interlude did not sway his determination to be a pianist, however, and already he is an extremely good one. We have played many concerts together, in particular touring Germany several times and appearing in Israel, while in Holland he has won himself a reputation without any help from me. It is a great satisfaction to talk music with him and to make it. Although I have spent precious little time on his musical formation, except on such works as we perform together, he and I seem to feel identically. He brings me a measure of corroboration, and has himself sensitivity, insight, firm attack. Having made his debut and accepted many engagements, he suddenly decided in 1974 to cancel them all and give up public performance for a time, so that he might work quietly by himself, building up his repertoire and technique. I think he was wise, for when can one do that again, when one is properly launched in public life? At this date I can confirm that he has made splendid use of the time, and is committed to a new round of engagements.

It is a joy, a comfort and an inspiration to know beauty in many different forms: the sound of a violin, the objects around one, above all the beauty of one's wife.

In 1975 a portrait was painted of Diana, one more to add to my collection, and I saw it grow from the canvas. We were guests of the artist Niko Ghika and his wife, Barbara, in their house in a remote and beautiful corner of Corfu, with no one to see all day but each other and nothing to do but please ourselves. The experience of seeing my wife's features, her character and her history emerge from streaks and blobs of color (almost as if everything were painted except the subject), of being admitted into a mystery, of hearing explanations and offering reactions, was among the most tender and enthralling of my life. In the normal way, one cannot speak from the heart about one's wife: another woman will suspect comparisons, another man bragging, so shyness and convention keep one's mouth primly shut on sentiment. Suddenly, through the making of a picture, sentiment was legitimate and effective.

It was appropriate that a painting should release expression of my feeling for her, because Diana herself is supremely an aesthetic achievement. That she should become a dancer was utterly predictable, for the ballet is, if it is anything, the basic discipline of the human body, subjecting every nerve, bone and muscle to the aesthetic principle. Her whole response to life bears witness to this priority. She herself claims to observe no moral precepts, only aesthetic proportion, but that in practice proves to work quite as well as the Ten Commandments in the avoidance of vicious behavior and the encouragement of virtuous. Brutality, impatience, envy, greed, suspicion, are certainly ugly, and equally certainly love and generosity are beautiful. Beauty's laws are more definable, more exacting, and assuredly more comforting than the laws of morality. Beauty is both intoxicating and sobering—intoxicating because it gives inspiration and invites abandon; sobering because it demands an exceptional degree of discipline. Morality in contrast is too often associated with hypocrisy, suppression, prejudice; with the self-righteousness that true believers show, who fanatically invoke theri sanctions, regardless of whether they produce pain or pleasure, good or harm. Diana's morality would never produce harm unless in the service of beauty, and then she might well resort to stringent measures. Seeing everything in terms of aesthetic meaning, Diana opened up to me a multitude of new dimensions. Among them, one which has since given me constant delight has been, precisely, visual art.

I like to see around me the distilled expression of human dreams, worries and fantasies, and in my time have bought many a painting and other beautiful object. But my interest in such things developed late. Neither of my parents had much concern or gift for the visual and until I was seventeen or so I lavished my admiration on such objects as cars, cameras, and so forth. More than anyone, Diana trained me to appreciate painting and sculpture and spurred me to acquire examples. An early painting which we bought together was by Marie Laurencin, on a visit to her Paris studio soon after the war. The first time we were in Israel, Diana spotted one of the country's most talented painters, Moshe Castel, who has since won wide recognition; we bought several of his works. Alone in Berlin one day, without Diana's immediate encouragement, I fell for the work of the German artist Jaenisch and bought three of his canvases. Jaenisch had spent some years in North Africa, and his works are flooded with light.

The draftsman's hand draws a line across the paper at once precise and free. This coupling of discipline and abandon, this essential paradox of beauty, seems to me the supreme human achievement. Any art must illustrate it, a great musician, a great painter, no less than an Edmond Rostand improvising in alexandrines. Indeed it is not confined to human creation: the gulls that disinter clams from the sandy beaches and drop them with unerring precision on the rocks, the cat whose spring lands it with unerring precision at its destination, make that balance between spontaneity and discipline which for me expresses life at its highest. Hence the painter in his studio fascinates me very particularly; I am privileged to count a few among my friends One for whom I have a special regard is the great artist-humanist Oskar Kokoschka, happily a neighbor of ours in Switzerland. I admire equally his paintings of London and of the mountains, and note with interest that, a massive person himself, he has become ever more concerned with masses, of color, weight, form, eschewing detail. Every year I look forward to seeing him at my festival at Gstaad unless, of course, he is spending the summer at his school at Salzburg.

Although Diana's world was furnished with music from the beginning, music was but one muse among half a dozen, all meriting devotion. She inherited poetry from Ireland, wit from France, and a passion for language from both. Devout generations bequeathed her a religious attitude, a metaphysics bred into the bone, and when she escaped from home tutelage and gave up the institutional forms of belief, left her with a sense of infinity looking over her shoulder. No more than my parents or myself would she act without the approval of that unseen presence, the eternal eye which is within or without and probably is both.

Since our boys have grown up and gone, I live in a female household with every opportunity to do justice to the strength of the "weaker sex." Apart from our housekeeper, Millie Lowe, the pivot of our lives, as reliable as sunrise and as intelligent as she is devoted, our supports are Kathleen Smith, who for two decades has borne much of the secretarial burden, unfailingly reliable and sweet-natured, from the postman's first appearance in the morning to the last telephone call late at night; and Eleanor Hope, who has lately joined us, who humanizes the image of the perfect secretary, bringing humor and imagination to the burdens I lay upon her, however tedious, however difficult.

I long regretted that my preoccupations lent Diana's talents only limited and self-denying perspectives; indeed I knew it was immoral that such gifts should not have free opportunity to fulfill themselves. In recent years, with family responsibilities declining and my activities diversifying into the conducting of orchestras and the running of festivals, it has been possible to find an occasional outlet for her abilities, thus giving me much satisfaction and, I have to admit, relieving me of an edge of guilt. In 1969 she got her first chance since our marriage. At that year's Bath Festival, Mozart's *Impresario* was to be presented, produced by Wendy Toye, but as the original story is rather feeble, Robert Morley, the actor, was asked to rewrite it; which, most successfully, he did, not only making it a worthy vehicle for Mozart's music, but working in a part tailored to Diana's great gift for comedy, in the person of a crotchety washroom attendant, and even finding me something to do onstage before I descended into the pit to conduct. I loved to see her back on stage, working with other actors again and enjoying it, able after all the years of staying in the background on my behalf to shine on her own. But this was just an appetizer for what followed.

The next year, first at Bath, later for BBC television, Diana was asked to recite the poems of Ogden Nash for a performance of Saint-Saëns's *Carnival of the Animals,* took one look at them, and wrote her own. I could well understand her reaction: just as Diana could not bring herself to say these lines, I have found myself unable to play certain cadenzas—they are things with which one cannot identify. She gave herself two or three days to prepare the verses—we were at Gstaad at the time and comparatively relaxed—and in that brief interval produced the fifteen poems required. The production was a great success. Two years later, asked by Humphrey Burton to contribute to his Aquarius series on London Weekend Television, she recited various poems of Edward Lear, to music specially written by Edwin Roxburgh; and the following Christmas, 1973, did a program on the poetry of E. E. Cummings. I had thought I knew Diana through and through; still she managed to astonish me. To see her completely emancipated from subservience, giving herself to the production of the poetry, projecting it, shaping the lines, encompassing a range of emotional, dramatic effect from satire through comedy and bawdy to tragedy, was a revelation. The programs were eventually shown in Canada, although, to my sorrow, not in the

United States. No American television channel could be found to show a program on an American poet.

I trust Diana has further relevations in store for me; that in the more leisured years ahead she will have a chance to create herself anew, in poetry, in painting and in acting; for her fulfillment and my pleasure.

11

Adventures
of
an Ardent Neutral

Alone among the lands of the world, Hungary and Rumania clothe nationhood in music. Where other little countries newly alight with conviction of identity exalt themselves in the figure of some despot or revolutionary who sets fire to a citadel or wreaks vengeance on neighbors, the Hungarians and Rumanians choose musicians as national heroes. In Hungary Zoltán Kodály shares the honor with Bartók, but in Rumania Georges Enesco's primacy in his countrymen's devotion is beyond division or dispute. The strength of Rumania's musical traditions, even in our urban, streamlined, computerized international civilization, is something to marvel at and offer up thanks for. Every little corner nourishes its own style, and a connoisseur sampling this villager's flute playing or that gypsy's performance on the cymbalom can, like a wine-taster placing a vintage, locate it on, say, the north slopes of a particular valley or the west bank of a given river. In a country where music has roots so vital, it is to be expected that musicians should be held of some account; nor is it surprising that a nation should take pride in having fathered the greatest all-round musician of the century. But for all that, there is at first view something charmingly unlikely in the translation of the servant of a courtly, stately, feudal order long gone into the figurehead of a present-day people's republic.

The dead, it might be said, can safely incur veneration; any construction can be laid upon their lives and utterances without fear of repudiation. I feel, however, that Enesco's socialist canonization was right and admirable, for if he served the court, if he took his princess away from Rumania forever when the communists came to power, his musicianship was nonetheless a native plant, vigorously accepting grafts from Paris and Vienna but feeding them with vital juices extracted from Moldavia's soil, air and water. He justly bridged the transition from monarchy to people's republic because his significance underlay both. Had he stayed to witness the old order giving place to new, he could hardly have been happy; I doubt, however, that he was happy in exile. He had, of course, no option to stay: the Princess Cantacuzène could not adopt the manners and enthusiasms of the comrades and it was necessary to take her and her reduced entourage abroad. I think that without her to consider, he might have gone back to Bucharest, to accept the homage which was his due, to repay it with music, teaching, conducting operas and orchestras, to serve his people and fulfill himself.

The monarchy was still in place (with Michael, he of the white ponies, occupying the throne I had once tried for size) and Enesco's exile yet to come when, in May 1946, I paid a first postwar visit to Rumania. The country was under Allied occupation, and Russian and American troops in evidence, but such foreign encumbrances had not discouraged a great upsurge of peacetime activity. Bucharest was bustling, food was plentiful and good, traffic comparatively thick in the streets, the air electric with life and enterprise. The always obliging Americans lent me an army car to revisit Sinaia, there to find the magic consecrated in memory as potent as ever, binding forest and mountain, animal and plant and the whole range of human expression into the unity of the golden age (since 1946 Sinaia has suffered the common degradation of tourism: new concrete buildings tame its pristine wildness now, and crowds shatter the coherence of centuries). King Michael gave me luncheon, and further gave me, when I finally left the country, a guard of honor, obliged to stand to attention at the airport for two hours or more while we waited for clearance from the countries on our route to Switzerland. I must have been one of the last foreigners thus royally noticed, for Michael's days of state were numbered and the communists who would displace him already marshaling their forces. Any event could be woven into their grand design, including my visit: agreeing to a request to play for workers, I found music was not the principal object of the occasion, but a photograph which lined me up in apparent amity with Party leaders and was widely published next day.

Such currents and conflicts were visible enough, but naturally had less relevance to me than reunion with Enesco, last seen in Paris in the spring of 1939. We met at the airport and drove together into Bucharest, which, as it happened, I had never visited, Sinaia being some way short of the capital. Built Paris-fashion with elegant stone houses along boulevards and avenues radiating from *étoiles,* it is a handsome, substantial city. I said as much to Enesco. "Hush!" he whispered, covering his mouth with his hand in a gesture of mock-furtive confidentiality. *"C'est la Boue-qui-reste!"*—"It's the mud that remains!" Dear Enesco! Although the seven years since our last meeting had bent his back, his humor was as ready as ever. Indeed no matter how much I idolized him, he never disappointed me, humanly or musically. He took me to Princess Cantacuzène's town house, a small palace where, in constrast to her becushioned quarters, voluptuous with divans and hangings and decorations, he occupied a monastic cell: whitewashed walls without so much as a picture on them, a narrow metal bed, one window. Having fallen in love with the princess when he was a boy and she an established and married member of the aristocracy, he crowned a lifetime's fidelity by marrying her in the mid-1930s when her husband died and she was ill and wretched, in a condition demanding constant care. He would leave his little room to appear in her large ones, the court minstrel bringing music to delight the cultivated appetites of his lady and her circle. The private spectacle was all the more touching because in public *he* was the grandee —the idol and ideal of his country.

No other sojourn anywhere matched that one in Rumania for sustained rapture. It was an Enesco festival, an Enesco orgy, an Enesco delirium, promoted by my coming. He and I gave concerts every day for nearly two weeks, with public rehearsals in the mornings, going through a good part of the violin literature, every day a different program, Enesco either at the piano or conducting the orchestra. At each concert and rehearsal, we had to have police help to forge a passage from car across sidewalk to stage door, and after a couple of nights under siege from well-wishers I was forced to flee the hotel to a private bolt hole (a very kind couple exchanged their apartment for my hotel rooms, with attendant perils). I came clothed in triple symbolism. As Enesco's disciple, I was in a special category for Rumania and benefited beforehand from every possible favorable presumption. As an American, I stood for a generosity which had spilled its blood in Europe's cause and presaged hope and freedom for the future. Thirdly, I was a Jew. Bucharest was then the Jewish capital of Europe, offering refuge to literally thousands who had contrived to escape capture, not only in Rumania but in all the countries roundabout. Two hundred thousand of them were in the city at that moment. Many were soon to disperse to Israel or elsewhere, but meanwhile they pressed to give me a welcome of almost messianic proportions. When a service was held in my honor, all the streets for blocks around the temple were dense with Jews, moved to exaltation at thus affirming their existence, they who so lately had left the valley of the shadow of death. Rumania was to continue their friend; to ʾhis day it has maintained good relations with Israel, the only socialist country to do so.

Enjoying so overwhelming a reception, Enesco and I succeeded in amassing a fair sum of money, which was divided among the Red Cross, Jewish charities and young Rumanian musicians. I was a little put out to discover that the hire of the private plane which brought me to Rumania and took me away again was first deducted from the total.

Enesco had nine more years to live; sad years, of exile, of hardship, of a progressive weakness of the spine which permanently bent his back. Once more based at 36 rue de Clichy, he toured to make a living for the princess and himself, but, his money and property in communist hands, could not earn enough to keep the handsome second-floor apartment where, twenty years earlier, he had taught me. Gradually the furniture was sold off, the grand piano gave place to an upright, the household moved to a small, dark apartment at ground level. Here the princess kept her court, shrunken now as were her circumstances, less assured, with the taint of banishment and pointlessness upon it, but still observing the old rituals. I recall an occasion in New York where Princess Cantacuzène received just such a reduced, diluted circle and Enesco played for them. Although by this time he was severely stooped, his performance of the *Geistertrio* had a size and vitality of spirit that matched Beethoven's. It demonstrated a very important mystery of violin playing—that vision can overcome technical disability. The number of violinists who play beautifully with faulty left hands is legion, but because they have something to convey they find ways to convey it. That was not Enesco's case, of course: he exemplified the related truth that conviction and inspiration, once possessed, remain. Having known the elation of communicating through the violin, Enesco, although crippled and with his hearing slightly affected, could yet give a performance hardly to be surpassed; just as an old man no longer capable of the act of love may understand love better and better convey its meaning than an ignorant lusty youth.

In Paris, Queen Elizabeth of the Belgians, whose admiration for Enesco would have surrounded his stricken grandeur with comfort, set

afoot with me and others a conspiracy to aid him, all the time fearing
that his pride would not permit him to accept a penny. Alas, before long
it foundered on Balkan rocks, sabotaged partly by the princess, partly by
the untrustworthiness of some of those attending him. Whenever Diana
and I were in Paris, we visited him daily, anguished that we could do so
little for him, humbled by his dignity and humor in the debased surroundings he chose to ignore. Whether with reason or not, he feared that
his Guarnerius, purchased many years since by the Rumanian court and
people between them, might be inveigled away from the princess and
returned to the state, so one day he summoned me into the little room
that served as bedroom and music room and put the Guarnerius into my
safekeeping. "I'm never going to play again," he said. "This will be safer
in America than here." (Ultimately the Guarnerius did return to
Rumania, and rightly.) He also gave me, as a gift, his first good violin, a
Santo Serafino, bought with his earnings as a student in Vienna; I still
keep it zealously. Thus, without ceremony or many words, he took leave
of the companions of his life, stripping himself of the last splendor, the
last affections, the last claims, in preparation for death. He died in Paris
on 4 May 1955.

I have been back to Rumania several times, always, on Enesco's
account, welcomed as a favorite son. For my part, it may be imagined
how great the pleasure is to find my own love shared by a whole nation,
to see that Enesco, whose figure is fading from memory elsewhere, whose
works go tragically unheard, here at least is accorded towering stature.
(His second homeland has not quite forgotten him, I am glad to say; at
the time of writing there are plans to found a conservatoire in Paris in
his name.) Rumania's tribute is formalized in the Enesco Museum,
which has gathered together manuscript scores, letters, pictures, instruments and all manner of mementos; but he is Rumania's *genius loci* and
permeates all its life. The conservatory is the Enesco Conservatory, the
violin competition is the Concours Enesco, and his most important composition, *Oedipe,* is in the repertory of the Rumanian State Opera Company. Perhaps one day it will be produced in other opera houses; it
deserves no less, for it is the masterpiece of a master, nursed into shape
over decades, the score traveling everywhere with him and growing
bulkier by the year, gaining pages on holidays, during weekends, and in
hotel rooms late at night after concerts.

If Enesco sponsored me in Rumania, in Hungary Bartók post-
humously discharged that office on my return to Budapest after the war.
By 1946 Hungary's national hero had been dead several months but I

had known him personally, I played his works, he had written the Sonata for me, and these evidences of friendship were quite sufficient passport into Hungarian hearts. Sometimes at heavily subscribed concerts loud-speakers were fixed up for the benefit of the overflow standing in the square outside.

I always think that the richest culture comes from cross-fertilization between east and west. Hungary, along with the Austro-Hungarian empire as a whole, was cause and effect of just such a cultural ferment, drawing on the folklore of Hungary itself, originally Asian; on the Turks, who came to the gates of Vienna and left much behind them when they retreated; on the Balkan tradition, the German, the French, the Italian; and, like the Jews, on the Khazars. Vienna in particular was the result of east-west, north-south crossbreeding, a city where there were few who didn't in one fashion or another make music, and nobody who didn't know at least something about it. Even today music gives Vienna its core, a truth demonstrated somewhat negatively perhaps in the fact that Viennese intrigue neglects politics, diplomacy and commerce to focus on the opera house. As Vienna in its long heyday attracted Mozart, Beethoven, Brahms, and then enriched itself with their contributions, so in our century Budapest has been the city of musical pilgrimage, but altogether gayer and madder and more exciting than one expects a place of pilgrimage to be, headily combining the most exquisite musical refinement with a certain abandon in social mores. To my regret I didn't thoroughly know Budapest in its interwar *épanouissement*, when Bartók's greatness gave musical substance to independent nationhood. On my first visit, in 1930, I was too young, too briefly there and not sufficiently my own master to explore its many layers, and afterward the ups and downs of history rather diminished, though they could not quench, its charm.

From 1946 one of my clearest memories, shamefully enough, is of gormandizing at a luncheon given in the park by the city fathers and prepared by the great caterer Gerbaud. Budapest was still war-battered, there was not much in the way of goods to be had, but undaunted, the Hungarians took problems for challenges and produced a meal to be recalled in after years with nostalgic gluttony. Across the Danube's pontoon bridges strutted the ragged people of Budapest, their carriage such as never a victorious people had, let alone a vanquished, as if in hard times and grim prospects they inherited the earth. Not to know when one is beaten can be a valuable ignorance, making it possible to raise phoenixes from the cinders of one's dreams, but without some other quality, moderation or preferably cunning, the phoenix is condemned to the flames again in a brief fatal flare of glory. Unlike the Poles, taught the trick of survival by centuries of foreign domination, unlike the shrewdly calculating Rumanians, who can twist even misfortune to their advantage, the Hungarians always go too far. I was again in Budapest a few months before the 1956 uprising and at a press conference answered questions of a daring and impudence which simply refused to acknowledge Hungary's lowly place in the balance of power. When the Russians installed a docile regime, I was in two minds about returning: part of me wanted to express solidarity with the defeated, another part counseled that performing in Hungary, I would have no means of dissociating myself from the new leaders. I listened to the second part and stayed away for some years, but finally abandoned a protest which lost relevance as time passed (when eventually I did go back to Budapest, I was offered a state decoration, but diplomatically turned it down). No doubt Kadar's regime was the only possible one in the circumstances; it has evolved humanely, all things considered, and although Rumania as a nation has won a greater degree of independence from Soviet tutelage, the irrepressible Hungarians enjoy an individual freedom which Rumanians do not know.

The music of Zoltán Kodály helped trigger the 1956 revolution, but in the payment of accounts after its suppression he remained unassailable, protected by the people's reverence. He was a redoubtable man, soft-spoken and sharp-witted, the smiler with the knife under the apparently harmless remark, suave, elegant and practicing a chivalry almost as ideal as Enesco's. In 1946 his extraordinary wife, Emma, was still alive, about a hundred years old and admitting to ninety-two, I think. She was lovable in the most literal sense—half the musicians of Europe had been her lovers and an adoring circle warmed her old age. She would talk about the golden days of the past and bring out albums of photographs taken in summers in the mountains when she and Bartók and Kodály rock-climbed in the nude. When I went to luncheon, Emma would sit at the head of the table and Zoltán would serve her and look after her in the most touching way. She had to go to hospital once, so he went too, to stay by her side. He bought an American car, no cheap purchase there and then, to amuse her convalescence with country outings. Emma repaid his cherishing by naming her successor, choosing as his next wife a girl as many decades younger than Zoltán as Zoltán was younger than herself. But it was he who made the typically Hungarian proposal: "Would you be my widow?" After Emma's death, her place at table was always left unoccupied, not to be trespassed on by any young usurper.

Meeting Kodály at the airport in 1946, I straightaway asked him to compose something for me. He accepted the commission, adding that a cruise then in prospect would offer him the chance to fulfill it. I knew he composed slowly, so was not unduly disappointed when the years slipped by without bringing me a manuscript, but every now and then I would jog his memory. Once he wrote to say that the first two pages had been written. Like an insurance assessor, I sent him my calculations: so many years to complete two pages; so many more years he could expect to survive (he kept himself in immaculate physical shape, swimming every morning); it seemed to me (I wrote) that I had every reason for optimism, and would he please find check enclosed for the work so far? The check came back, however, with the message that enough people played his "bad music" to raise him above financial embarrassment, and meanwhile he would try to finish the work. Sadly I had no occasion to send another check: the composition was never finished and even those first two pages are not mine.

Is it possible to ask too much of music? As a child I saw it as an irresistible force for good, uniting the human race at its universal depths beneath the divisions, working that magic which Schiller describes in his "Ode to Joy" as "binding together what Custom pulls asunder." A twentieth-century lifetime cannot preserve such hopes from the battering of disappointment. The barriers of custom remain in place and music itself has too often celebrated them. If my own ambition to bring about an occasional reconciliation on humanity's behalf has dwindled with failure, it has not been discarded. I have run my head into a few brick walls of sentiments I could not share, but the experience has neither proved fatal nor taught me that music must be weak before human implacability and the wise musician should dumbly fiddle while the world burns. Indeed I contest both heresies: music has been my *laissez-passer* to foreign lands, I am at ease wherever I travel, I esteem the people and values of countries other than my own. Such is my good fortune, no doubt; I would that more shared it, even if, in my experience, general benevolence has sometimes seemed to deny particular loyalty, thus offending many, involving me in lively controversy, and exciting the very passions that I mean to soothe.

I have never regretted stirring up hornets' nests, however. What does this make me? I wonder. An amiable fool blundering into delicate situations which the angels of prudence suspend their breath to contemplate? A self-righteous prig who believes everyone else is marching out of step? A man perfectly aware he has no monopoly of rectitude who yet pits conviction against received opinion? Naturally, I hope that evidence will be found to support this last interpretation. In the first polemic I provoked, I believe the verdict has already been pronounced in my favor (unless the rueful truth is that time wears out the bitterest quarrel). This was my defense of Wilhelm Furtwängler after the Second World War.

Furtwängler was at the time a conductor honored from a distance. I did not play with him until 1947, but I knew enough about him from report and recordings to guess that performance under his baton must be an exceptional experience. Such in due course it proved. Although different from Bruno Walter, Furtwängler in my personal pantheon ranks with Walter as an exponent of the German tradition at its most exalted. I still had not met him, however, when, after an early visit to liberated Europe, I returned to New York and, as a witness newly arrived from the field of victory, was met there by a press conference eager to know if German culture was to be discredited along with Hitler. Seeing no future in keeping war wounds open, believing it my duty to report good things if they happened to be true, I passed on the judgment of Paris: French musicians had told me, I said, that of all their colleagues who had remained in Germany, Wilhelm Furtwängler was the one to whom the heartiest welcome would be accorded; not only, or primarily, for his unequaled gifts, but because he had refused to accompany the Berlin Philharmonic on propaganda visits to occupied France. So far, so simple; little did I foresee that this straightforward factual piece of information would be translated into a weapon for a war I did not know I was fighting. Next day's tabloid headlines announced that I wanted to see Furtwängler in America, and American Jews were in uproar.

Furtwängler's fault, like my own perhaps, was to overestimate the power of music. If he did not expect it to absolve original sin, he did believe it proof against contamination. Shortly after the Reichstag fire, he had invited Schnabel, Huberman and myself to appear as soloists with the Berlin Philharmonic. All three of us refused. As director of the Berlin State Opera, he decided, again in 1934, to stage *Mathis der Maler,* knowing that Hindemith, a "decadent" composer, did not officially exist; when Göring canceled the performance, he resigned. One might have thought successive rebuffs sufficient to convince him that the middle ground he held was no man's land, a glorious place by some discarded nineteenth-century measure, but no longer defensible. If he was convinced, then he chose to become a kind of living suicide. His prestige proved only great enough to let him go on being an aristocrat in the jungle, committing humane misdemeanors, registering vain protests and throwing down gauntlets with impunity: he could neither accomplish his own demise nor get himself sent to the concentration camp. In 1936 Richard Wagner's granddaughter Friedelind, who fled Nazi Germany three years later, witnessed a meeting between Hitler and Furtwängler at her mother's Bayreuth home.

> I remember Hitler turning to Furtwängler and telling him that he would have to allow himself to be used by the party for propaganda purposes, and I remember Furtwängler refusing. Hitler got angry and told Furtwängler that in that case there would be a concentration camp ready for him. Furtwängler was silent for a moment and then said: "In that case, Herr Reichschancellor, I will be in very good company." Apparently Hitler was taken aback by the conductor's defiance, because he went into none of his usual rantings but simply walked away.

Yet in the same year, Furtwängler turned down an offer to succeed Toscanini as permanent conductor of the New York Philharmonic when Jews voiced their indignation, saying that he could not conduct in New York "until the public recognizes that politics and music are apart." Neither Hitler nor Jewry could drive home a message he didn't wish to believe, the result being that he found himself nowhere, a foreigner in Nazi Germany and a Nazi in the eyes of foreigners.

I wish I had had the inspiration (or perhaps courage was the missing factor) at the supper in Milan in 1946, when Toscanini dismissed his fellow conductors, one after another, to the rubbish heap of cultural history, to ask his rating of Furtwängler. Furtwängler was at that point, if not an unknown, an unmeasured quantity to me, but I knew enough to know that this would be a home question. These two were great rivals, representing mutually exclusive values, human and musical, in a climate of feverish partisanship, like gladiators avoiding confrontation in the same arena to assert each his own claim before his own supporters. Both had conducted in Vienna, both had conducted Wagner at Bayreuth, and where either superseded the other there were immediately factions. Toscanini, I believe, was partly responsible for New York's resistance to Furtwängler. The gulf between them comprised not only nationality, not only temperament, but birth and upbringing: Toscanini the child of a poor farming family whose musical promise ensconced him at a tender age in the opera pit, there to receive his education; Furtwängler, son of an archaeologist, who spent his childhood in classical diggings and classical studies, for whom music was not the first, last and only activity, but life's crown. Furtwängler was self-willed, but by natural endowment, by inheritance from his class, and possibly therefore less securely armored than Toscanini in his self-made will. He flinched from criticism—whether arrogantly convinced he was above it or from an insecurity reassured only by admiration, I don't know. In contrast, Toscanini—whose eminence in New York, however, put him out of reach of all but occasional flights of adverse comment—had too sure a view of his place as the servant of music to resent anyone misguided enough to disagree with him.

All these differences of character, circumstance and sensibility produced, as they were overshadowed by, their contrasting approaches to music. Once when we met in Lucerne, Furtwängler compared music to the flow of a river which the conductor must follow, taking account of the topography, whether it thrust the flood through narrow gorges or gave it space to broaden out in tranquil meadows. He rejected method, metronomic rigor, the weights and measures of musical grocery, to rely on intuition and dream his way through the scores. Happily, intuition did not lead him astray: it was shaped by the music it was shaping. Furtwängler, after all, was old enough to have known Brahms. His performances were never twice the same, as his recordings show: each time he surrendered himself to the river, which might have changed since he was last there—perhaps it was spring and the river in spate with melted snow, perhaps a dry summer had reduced it to a trickle, or a sudden thunderstorm set the water racing. Carl Flesch conveyed his sense of searching:

> There is no dead moment in his music-making; it all lives, loves, suffers and rejoices. . . . Furtwängler's pursuit of immediate acoustic satisfaction, his Don-Juan-like emotional restlessness, his striving after continual renewal of feeling, result in the listener being excited rather than moved by his conducting. . . . He will probably reach the zenith of his powers simultaneously with a certain erotic appeasement, attaining serenity with the transmutation of earthly into heavenly love.

"Furtwängler," Flesch added, "is nearest to my heart of all conductors. He is quite free of megalomania and self-glorification, the hallmark of his caste; his genuine modesty manifests itself at times even in the form of an inner uncertainty. Above all, his is the child-like naïveté that always distinguishes the true artist."

His capacity for ecstasy through abstraction was not his alone, but the common capital of German culture; deformed and degraded, it spawned the grotesque myths of National Socialism; allowed to expand in the disinterested pursuit of truth, it fathered philosophy, music of Beethoven's universality and musical interpretation in kind. Wilhelm Kempff maintains that tradition today. Toscanini's greatness lay elsewhere. For the Germans a thing might be a symbol spanning the universe; for him a thing was a thing, a composition was not a winding watercourse but a Roman road, not an unpredictable force of nature or mysticism to the mercy of whose currents he must abandon himself, but an expression of the human spirit which Latin clarity could penetrate and illuminate.

If in our day Wilhelm Kempff can observe German tradition wherever he finds himself, Furtwängler was so deeply rooted in his past that he may have believed expatriation imperiled identity, that there existed an ethnic or national soul which belonged to the country as much as its hills or plains, that his musical vision could best be made to exist in Germany, by a German orchestra before a German public. Where Toscanini's pulse was nothing if not transportable and imposable, Furtwängler's quibbles with pulse, his incomparable blurring of edges, his quest for "flow," did in fact require almost telepathic intimacy with an orchestra. Of his "secret," he wrote that it lay in "the preparation of the beat, not in the beat itself—in the brief, often tiny movement of the downbeat, before the point of unified sound is reached in the orchestra. The manner in which the downbeat, these preparations, are shaped determines the quality of the sound with the most absolute exactness. Even the most experienced conductor is forever astounded by the unbelievable precision with which a well-coordinated orchestra reflects his most minute gestures."

His "most minute gestures" appeared only somewhat minuter than his broadest. Such was Furtwängler's abhorrence of junctures, markers, articulations, beginnings, endings, it cost him anguish just to bring down his baton; he would do so, according to one musician who played under him, after "the thirteenth preliminary wiggle." For all the service such scruple renders to music, it leaves one defenseless before the moral dilemmas imposed by tyranny.

It was his greatness that attracted odium. There is justice in that, I suppose, for the greater should be held more accountable than the lesser, but Furtwängler was caught, and most unfairly, by the timing of the world's indignation. Musicians more compromised than he, who furthered their careers with party membership and favors to the Nazis, have since risen to acceptance and acclaim, and not a slur remembered. Furtwängler, without their guilt, stood large in the public eye and therefore a target for vilification. In the event, he was easily cleared of suspicion. Had it not been for him, Carl Flesch would not have made his escape from occupied Holland to Switzerland; several Jewish musicians who reached the United States testified to his efforts to preserve them from deportation. But he had held office in the Nazi regime and until he was acquitted of anything worse, he could hold office no more. At the invitation of the American military government, I played in Berlin in 1946 and 1947. I much wanted to go, as a Jew who might keep alive German guilt and repentance, and as a musician offering something to live for. On the first occasion Furtwängler was still suspended and the orchestra still under the baton of Sergiu Celibidache; but in 1947 Furtwängler was back in the place of honor.

As I had imagined, to play the greatest German music with this greatest of German conductors was an experience of almost religious intensity. I came down from the clouds to find myself a traitor.

In 1947, Berlin, like many another European city, still harbored camps for displaced people, most of them Jews. I wanted to play also for them. The American authorities obligingly organized a recital—not at the camp itself, which was known as the Deuppel Center, but in the Tivoli, a cinema still standing in one of the suburbs—and arranged for buses to ferry the audience to it. To this cinema, with capacity for well over a thousand, fewer than fifty displaced people chose to come. The explanation was supplied by a camp spokesman signing himself "Jonas of Lemberg."

> When I read of your "human deeds" towards "distressed German youth" and of how your new worshippers applauded you, I knew that in your audience there must have sat those two passionate lovers of music, Eppel and Kempke—SS men from the Jurewitz camp near Lemberg, who liked to have us sing while they shot our brothers down. . . . Wherever you travel, our newspaper will follow you like a curse until your conscience awakes.

Diana and I resolved to go to the camp itself. When we reached the wire fences and guarded gates of the Deuppel Center, it was to feel with the keenness of personal experience how slow was its inmates' return from the tomb. The car drew up at the entrance to a long, low hut and was immediately surrounded by an unsmiling crowd. Diana got out first. She offered her hand to the nearest man and greeted him: *"Guten Morgen."* He stared and hesitated, but she kept her hand out until he was forced to take it. In my turn I shook hands with him. Two military policemen escorted us into the hut and, with some difficulty, pushed us through the dense crowd inside to the stage. Boos, hisses and imprecations followed us all the way. Since the noise showed no signs of abating, I stood up to confront my judges. Packed shoulder to shoulder, crouched on shelves and window sills, hanging on to pillars, they waited for my defense, sallow-faced men and women in threadbare suits and babushkas who felt themselves outlawed among outlaws, lost in the interstices of real nations, the condemned who had not quite died.

"I cannot blame anyone for his bitterness," I recall saying. "You have suffered too much. And still I do say that you simply cannot rebuild your life on your suffering. Don't let it be said that we have only learned the worst of our enemies! We Jews don't beg; we work! We are the best cobblers, the best tailors, the best doctors, the best musicians. That's what it means to be a Jew! I have come to Germany to restore that image, to show how false was Hitler's caricature. That's why I'm here. . . ." They began to cheer and shout, "Our Yehudi! Our Yehudi!" like shades who had not at first recognized Orpheus in Orpheus, hell being hell.

Jonas, who was also on the platform, stood up to speak against me; but they would not give him silence. The confrontation, so grimly begun, broke up in friendliness and forgiveness, and in appeals for a second concert. Unhappily, it could not be: I had no free hour until I left Berlin the next day. The most moving moment was yet to come. That evening Jonas of Lemberg came to find me and apologized for his accusations. Later he told American reporters that had another concert been given, everyone would have gone. "Perhaps it is too much to expect that those who have not experienced persecution and camps should understand our feelings," he commented.

In truth, his hatred of his oppressors was as easy to understand as theirs for him was difficult: what is more comprehensible than hunger for retribution? Jonas was right, however; we are the creatures of our experience. I had not myself lost anyone in Germany. Had I then been mourning wife or child or parent, would my words have been so bravely conciliatory? Probably not. But I believed and still believe that insistence on vengeance, excluding all other response, was, however understandable, a weakness. Patriotism cannot be enough if it puts beyond consideration most of the human race. I too was a creature of my experiences, and they had shown me my fellow man the world over, even in Germany. There was also, as I had pleaded at the Deuppel Center, a certain joyfulness in representing my people there precisely where they had been the despised and rejected of men. However, the episode had its somber lesson: as Furtwängler had found before me, music does not always guarantee communication; in some circumstances another means has to be found.

On that visit to Berlin I was greatly struck by the humaneness of the Americans. It may be said that no more than I had my fellow Americans suffered German occupation, bombing or reprisals, and that therefore they were not there in bitterness, to punish or to exact revenge; but the truth went deeper than such negative arguments. In spite of interventions which have miscarried, in spite of a diplomacy bred in business —on what can be seen, foreseen and contracted for—rather than in the skills of navigating a continuously shifting sea, the United States stood, as it stands, for a great deal that is free and generous. I still believe it is the hope of the world.

Winning the understanding of the wronged men and women of the Deuppel Center proved both more painful and simpler than outfacing the protests of the Jews of America. Accepted by those who had suffered most, I found, however, a stimulus in displeasing others on a point of principle. A boycott was organized of a tour I was to make in Central and South America, but through no merit or enterprise of mine, it failed, to the extent of provoking counterdemonstrations. In Buenos Aires the Jewish community put on a special service and invited me, to assure me of my welcome among them. But the real test was not Europe, not America, North or South, but Israel.

Israel was almost two years old when, in 1950, I reached its shores, by then flooding with new immigrants bringing from the mills of Germany, Russia and Poland the fiercest and most exclusive passions. My friend and impresario Baruch Gillon, himself Russian, invited me to come, then wrote suggesting second thoughts: news of the proposed tour had brought assassination threats from a terrorist group. I wired that I was coming anyway: "Precisely because I played in Berlin I wish to play in Israel." There wasn't any particular courage in this reaction, although perhaps some obstinacy: I knew I could trust myself to the Jews, who, if they have temperament, have also a lively sense of justice. A crowd of newspapermen at Tel Aviv airport was the only untoward feature of our arrival, and this was conjured away with the promise of a press conference next day. Next day came. It was the Deuppel Center all over again, again with Diana at my side but this time with Hephzibah as well. Indeed my first statement to the Israeli press consciously echoed Jonas of Lemberg's to the American: "I realize that it might be asking too much of those who have suffered beyond human endurance that they share my convictions now or ever. I also realize that I may have inadvertently reopened old wounds and caused pain. This I regret most deeply, and I offer my apologies to all those whom I may have hurt. But I cannot renounce the principles by which I live." Someone prompted me to say I would never return to Germany; I said I probably would return.

The gauntlet of universal peace thrown down, I proceeded to wage twenty-four recitals in half that many days, going from cities to kibbutzim to military hospitals, with Diana and Hephzibah my outriders. Hephzibah, only recently returned from Australia and umarked by the controversy, no doubt helped smooth my rapid passage, but in the event little smoothing proved necessary. At the first concert the audience was searched, no car was allowed within a block of the hall, and we played under the eye of an armed guard. Within a couple of days all precautions had withered away in a climate of unambiguous good will, and my long, sometimes fault-finding, always sympathetic involvement with my fellow men of the State of Israel had begun.

Before Israel was Israel, the Promised Land was part of the landscape of my imagination, looming, somewhat mistily to be sure, in the family prehistory, an episode in both my parents' lives and not the less powerful for their having spurned it. We think we can renounce our past, only to find ourselves all the more bound to it by the very act of renunciation. In Jerusalem I visited the restored, polished shell of just such a college as my father had attended, perhaps the very one, where the boys had rocked and recited themselves into a daily trance of piety. I could picture him, wearing long side curls, walking the narrow streets shoulder to shoulder with his Arab friends, fellows in common disapproval of the Turkish overlord. Incapable of lukewarm idealism, my father, once he abandoned Zionism, abandoned it utterly, while continuing to espouse the cause of the weaker against the more powerful; were the Jews the underdogs today, and the Arabs in command in Israel, I have no doubt that he would be violently pro-Israeli. My father is very Jewish. He understood the yearning, the dreams, that preceded Israel's foundation, but when it came to the machinations employed to establish the state, he balked. He could not come to terms with the panoply of statehood—the army, the militarism, the flag-waving—nor with the narrowing of a vision that had once measured mankind as to the small limits of a single country.

As for myself, I could find no virtue in exclusivity at either end of the argument. No more than other visitors, however, was I proof against Israel's extraordinary dynamism, either on that first visit or on the many visits since. To meet a tolerance that accepted the odd man out, that understood even my father and accepted me, forgiving my stubborn partisanship of Furtwängler, was a heartwarming experience. So was the discovery of uncles and cousins. Severed from the past by geography, I nonetheless had a strong sense of ancestry—perhaps the stronger for being fed on semi-mythical forebears rather than on the obstinate flesh and blood of known and present ones. Israel, however, gave me not ancestors but a collateral line, cousins of my own and younger generations, working in kibbutzim, in a workshop making musical instruments, in the tourist industry, representing the range of Jewish energy which the creation of Israel released. In two weeks which crammed my past and the infant country's future into an explosion of impressions, a memorable incident was an invitation to Israel's White House at Rehovoth, near Tel Aviv, to meet President Chaim Weizmann and his wife. He a product of English Jewry, the least persecuted and most nearly dispassionate Jews in the world perhaps, she of rich, emancipated Russian Jewry, neither damaged by deprivation or suffering, they had to make no effort of imagination to understand my preference for a middle way both sympathetic and critical.

Vera Weizmann had retained the autocratic manner born of her family's position in the old Russia. I recall her showing us round the garden, followed by an aide-de-camp, and breaking off the conversation to exclaim, without so much as turning her head, "Captain Bergman [if that was indeed his name], you will not use my garden as an ashtray! Pick up that cigarette and put it in your pocket!" Later, when we lived at Gstaad, she several times visited us there, and always invited Gerard and Jeremy to lunch at the Palace Hotel; Jeremy adored her. In 1950 the president was already aging and ailing. His life's work crowned with success, he could have been forgiven for relaxing on the laurels of the first victories and achievements. Instead he cast his hopes, and some doubts, into the years to come. He confided to us his fear that the opportunities offered by the Jewish state—to be a soldier, a farmer, a builder—might sap the strength of Jewish excellence in philosophy, scholarship, music, the abstract accomplishments of the Diaspora. I think he was wrong, or at any rate has not yet been proved right: the founding of the state not only opened up new paths but fueled a tremendous upsurge in artistic activity and other traditional Jewish modes of expression. In the quarter century which has since passed, however, much of Weizmann's vision has indeed been eroded; but not, alas, by the competing claims of peace.

In the summer of 1947, when the odium of having played with Furtwängler was still freshly upon me, I drove to Prades, near Perpignan, at the eastern limit of the Pyrenees, to see Pablo Casals and—although this was not the object of the visit—to request his aid and comfort for Furtwängler.

That summer was to be spent in Provence. We had been lent a farmhouse and Diana had spontaneously offered to share our holiday *à deux* with Zamira and Krov, then aged seven and five. The farmhouse lay between Gassin and Ramatuelle, near the coast of the Var. There we camped out with neither hot water nor other tourists to blemish the idyll. So shortly after the war, commercialism and its attendant pollutions had not yet tainted the Riviera, whose beaches, some still mined, stretched serenely empty on either hand along the Mediterranean. After some time we were joined by Pierre Bertaux (by now Préfet at Lyons), his wife, Denise, and their three boys, the eldest of whom was six years old, a child whose command of language and ideas left me dumbly humiliated: in the manner of the Bertaux, he was an *académicien* born, a master of the polished phrase before he went to school.

Leaving the children with Diana and Denise, Pierre and I set off for Prades. En route he offered me a wager: "I know what Catalan nationalism means," he said. "Before you leave Casals you will hear that the first parliament in Europe was Catalan, that the first mountainclimber in the world was Catalan, and that the Catalan flag once flew from every Mediterranean citadel."

Casals was in his seventy-first year, revered for his refusal to capitulate to Franco not only by fellow Catalans but by exiles and patriots from every region of Spain, a constant procession of whom beat a path to Prades. I had first heard him play many years earlier in San Francisco, and had met him before the war when he came backstage after a concert I gave in Paris; I remember a slight embarrassment at overhearing his and Enesco's mulling over my prospects as they nodded their wise old heads together. In London in 1944 we met at the house of Elena Gerhardt, the lieder singer, for an evening of trios with Gerald Moore. But it was only now that I really began to make his acquaintance.

He had survived the war in a modest little house fronted by a yard where the exiles and patriots gathered. An outside staircase led to the second-floor apartment, which he rented, while his neighbor on the ground floor was a Catalan poet with whom he was then collaborating on a Catalan Mass. He had been through not exactly desperate, but hard, cold, hungry, anxious days, collecting twigs and debris to keep himself warm; once he was picked up by the SS and questioned and in the end released. He spoke about these hardships and adventures, then sat at the piano and, with tears on his cheeks, played us excerpts from his Mass. Then came the moment of parting. As Pierre and I were picking up our coats, Casals solemnly said, "You know, there was a time when Catalonia commanded the sea, when her flag flew at every mast, when she founded Europe's first parliament. . . ." It was all I could do not to laugh, carefully avoiding Pierre's complacent eye.

As was demonstrated by his resolve not to set foot in his native land while Franco's dictatorship remained in power—a resolve which never wavered, condemning him to die in Puerto Rico in 1973, still in exile— Casals was a man of sustained commitment to a cause. He showed the same implacability in his violent hatred for Cortot, who had accepted an official musical position under the German occupation, living in luxury as a result and traveling by car while other musicians of his caliber collected driftwood and struggled to reach their concerts by métro. Subsequently Cortot was forbidden to play in France for a time but continued his career in Germany. Like Pétain, he had made his choice, convinced himself it was the right one and lived to see it proved wrong. He remained a distinguished old man and a great musician, but no hero. I asked Casals his opinion of Furtwängler; although he would never play again with Cortot, he said, Furtwängler he admired, not only as a conductor but as a German: he had been right to stay in Germany and do what he could for music and musicians. Reassured, I suggested that I might try to arrange a recording of the Brahms Double Concerto to be made by Casals, Furtwängler and myself. He accepted in principle.

I made several attempts to pursue the matter; EMI, who treated Casals generously, advancing money when he needed it against later earnings, were interested; for Furtwängler it would have been a most valuable accolade, given by the foremost antifascist musician; but all approaches were deflected by Casals—he would love to make the recording but couldn't at the moment. Finally, some two summers later, after perhaps the third prodding, he sent me a letter which with disarming frankness betrayed the limits of his independence: he assured me that he personally had nothing against Furtwängler and could envisage few greater pleasures than playing with him, were it not for the fact that to do so might compromise his antifascist stance and dismay his followers. In other words, he was prepared to let me know he didn't have the courage of his convictions; so long as those convictions were approved by his admirers, they were strong convictions indeed, but in other circumstances not strong enough to withstand guilt by association with a man wrongfully accused. It was an honest letter and a disappointing one. Casals similarly disappointed me when he lent support to the New York boycott of his most beloved pupil and "heir apparent," as he himself had nominated him, Gaspar Cassado. Cassado had sinned by continuing to live in Italy during the war and performing, once, at his mistress's urging, for Mussolini—courses of action which, however inept history might show them to be, could hardly be considered criminal. In those days of revulsion against anti-Semitic barbarism, Jews had greater encouragement than ever before or since to presume that all mankind would stand up to protest against their suffering, but even then the expectation was extravagant. Cassado was a political innocent, a lovable, simple man who played the cello magnificently, a good human being; which was much to his credit. The boycott, reinforced with threats of physical violence, prevented him from performing in New York and accomplished his deportation from Ellis Island. Casals's approval of these sanctions of course broke Cassado's heart.

And yet Casals's own heart wasn't in it. He had become, in a way, the prisoner of a coterie of my New York colleagues who more or less ran the first few festivals at Prades, making wonderful music with Casals but also using his prestige for their own purposes, including punishment campaigns against suspect musicians, which, because of my championing of him, came to focus particularly on Furtwängler and on me. They demanded heroism of such as Cassado; they were not heroes themselves, but, protected from the dilemmas he had faced, buttered their prosperous bread and called for vengeance on the erring. As I have said, the great Bruno Walter refused to join the pack: Jew though he was, and refugee from Nazi Germany, he never gave his name to the calumniation of Furtwängler, his rival. Meeting Walter again, at the second Edinburgh Festival in 1948, I told him how grateful I was. For some years after 1947 I didn't visit Prades, but thereafter I went frequently, and believe I was welcomed as the bringer of fresh air into an atmosphere by then somewhat claustrophobic with mingled flattery and exploitation. For my part, nothing could exceed the pleasure of playing with Casals, and our relationship was warm and disinterested. On one visit, before I left I asked to speak to him alone, told him of Cassado's unhappiness and my own view of the injustice done him, and begged Casals to offer the hand of reconciliation. He did so immediately, bringing Cassado flying to Prades to be embraced and giving that story at any rate a happy ending. Gaspar Cassado died in Barcelona in 1966.

Once the fitful postwar fevers had subsided, the Prades Festival was, humanly as well as musically, a cure for the frayed spirit. I love that part of France, where the mountains rise up from a countryside which is sleek, plump and glossy with the earth's fruits—even more so in those days, before over-irrigation and chemical fertilizer took the taste out of them. One warm early morning I walked some miles through the apricot orchards which mount the slopes of the Pyrenees behind Prades and along the line dividing the plantations from the uncultivated heath. This is marked by a water conduit, some three feet wide, which follows the contour of the mountain, with gates every now and then to permit the farmers to tap its flow. I took my clothes off and lay upon the water, to be carried passively at its gentle pace, around the ins and outs of the slopes, from time to time branches passing over my head, with nothing to disturb the sunlit silence except bird calls. It was a sensation of utter blissful wholeness, bodily and spiritual, such as one is rarely granted. Almost every time I went to Prades I would devote one day to climbing the Canigou, the peak which dominates the region and must once have been its sacred mountain (it was on the Canigou that, according to Casals, a Catalan had founded the sport of mountaineering). I have always longed to climb, but never sufficiently indulged the longing. Other musicians have been superb rock-climbers: Dmitri Mitropoulos used to go each summer to the Rockies, and now his successor at Minneapolis, Stanislaw Skrowaczewski, follows him in this too, tackling vertiginous faces with rope and pitons. The ascent of the Canigou, however, is no more than an extremely arduous walk, which rewards success at the summit with a magnificent panorama of mountains, foothills, plain, coastline, and sea shimmering on the eastern horizon. This climb I made each time with Casals's friend and physician, Dr. Puig.

At various times in my life I have benefited from "peaks" of human achievement, which rise above the ordinary level of performance as the Canigou rises above the eastern Pyrenees, and set a standard for all subsequent occasions. Such was a Furtwängler performance of Brahms's

Fourth Symphony, never to be surpassed; others, less exalted, were gastronomic: the best *épinards en branche,* for instance (at the George V in Paris just after the war); the best duck (in Denver, shot as it crossed some particularly rich grain area); the best meringues (in Tel Aviv, made by the Israel Philharmonic's housekeeper, Madame Chaoul); the best coffee (in Havana, Cuba, where for once the taste lived up to the smell—I have never since cared to taste any lesser coffee). The last time I climbed the Canigou I had my unique, unchallengeable experience of champagne.

Puig and I were joined by Alberto Lysy, a young Argentinian violinist whom I was teaching when and where I could; Alberto felt ill and lagged behind, Puig forged ahead, and I ran from one to the other, multiplying by three the distance to be covered. As a result I was in a state of advanced dehydration when, descending from the summit, we reached the rest house where we were to lunch. Instead of prudently slaking my thirst and stoking my energy with water, I slaked and stoked with champagne, about two bottles of it, chilled, exhilarating and beyond my powers of description adequately to convey. I did contrive to descend to Prades again and play chamber music with Casals that evening, but only to postpone my suffering until later, catching a tenacious cold which culminated in a tonsillectomy. I have never really enjoyed champagne since.

Gradually Casals became disillusioned with Prades. The town was proud of him, but more possessively than gratefully. There was the inevitable provincial myopia which tried to keep his vision to heel, a short-sightedness I too have encountered in running festivals. Then, in 1956, the beautiful, intelligent Martita came, they fell in love, and she took him home to Puerto Rico, where the government treated him with a deference France never seems to show its musicians. In Puerto Rico the festival prospered undiminished, and there finally I met and made friends with some of the New York contingent.

Sasha Schneider, violinist, conductor and Ur-Russian (although he was in fact born in Poland), was the driving force behind these festivals, as I daresay he had been at Prades before I went there. A man of immense vitality and irresistible enthusiasm, he wrings from life the utmost in depth and breadth and quality of sensation. To see him galvanizing an orchestra into producing the last iota of conviction and expression is an experience indeed. He would collect the best musicians in the United States, forming them into a company of pilgrims who would devoutly gather in San Juan to play with and for and conducted by

Casals. I came to love Sasha dearly. It was a particular pleasure to know individuals, not to have to accept them as representatives of a group; to appreciate someone without being obliged to label him.

The greatest Puerto Rican pleasure was, of course, making music with Casals. Enesco apart, there has been no one in my lifetime who better inspired one to play chamber music. In my enduring picture of him, he is at rehearsal, humming like a bumblebee, his gold spectacles perched at the end of his short nose, his bow raised to attack the strings, to prod a point at one of us, to flick away a fly, as need demanded, presiding over his disciples like a benevolent, jolly father superior. Working with the narrow precision of a jeweler and the vast experience of a life rooted in music, he had a very special contribution to make. His acute awareness of accent and timing, his insight into pulse and counter-pulse, his sense of dynamic rhythm, were a revelation. I remember his advising me to stress the upbeat in the last movement of Bach's E Major Suite, a gigue in six-eight time, the better to reveal the character of the phrases. Like Nadia Boulanger, Casals believed in paying more attention to upbeats than to downbeats: downbeats, being on the beat, could safely be left to make their point; upbeats were an indication of will and decision, as in Hungarian music where the counter-rhythm provides much of the excitement. In Hungarian ensembles, the second violin has often nothing to do but maintain the m*pa*, m*pa*, m*pa*, of the counter-rhythm, the challenge to the main rhythm, the element of vitality; and does this with a speed and accuracy beyond belief or my capacities. In default of documentary evidence of his conviction that Bach had Hungarian blood, Casals would play Bach's improvisational preludes in such a manner as to persuade one that a cymbalom accompaniment, changing harmonies every so often, was intended. Casals did not play the piano well, but well enough for his purposes, which were more prayerful than self-glorifying. Every morning at the piano he made his reacquaintance with Bach: the revent daily launching of a supremely dedicated life.

When I was young, one had the illusion that European music was an indigenous growth in the United States. Now it can be seen to be only part of the picture, and perhaps a grafted part at that. The great American production is the musical, neither opera nor vaudeville but deriving from both genres and, what is more to the point, deriving from American lives. It is only right that a country with two centuries of independence to its credit should bypass the manners of the mother continent to fashion its own; but how sad it is that when my countrymen were still colonizers, not yet natives, they scorned the wisdom of the first Americans! Had the settlers been willing to intermarry with and learn from the Indians, the United States would be a more balanced country today, its people more attuned to their earth, more acclimatized to their climate; and American music would not have taken so long to produce distinctive modes.

Tragically, the opportunity was lost. I fear that many South American countries are now re-enacting the tragic sequence: destroying the very element which would give them security, mental balance, survival capacity, a contact with their land. This is a great sorrow to me, for I love South America. I made a first visit to this subcontinent, way back in 1938, with Nola and my father, traveling from New York to Rio de Janeiro by ship. From deck level all docks present a confused picture of bales, crates, trucks, cranes, and men rushing around like mad intoxicated ants; Rio on this day added sweltering heat, shirtless hairy chests, and an enormous amount of sweat and smell to the general excitement. As we disembarked into the midst of this lively scene, perhaps the swarthiest, hairiest, sweatiest longshoreman on the quay came up to me, grabbed my arm, pulled me aside and hissed confidingly into my ear: *"Moi aussi, je suis coupé!"*—"I too am circumcised!"

During the war I went several times to Central and South America, returning more than once to Brazil and carrying away from there on one occasion a highly prized souvenir. Impressed by the works of the great painter Portinari, I wanted to buy one for myself, and went one night to his house to have my portrait painted. Since my plane was to leave at five o'clock next morning, Portinari had to work concentratedly through the night, and even so could not quite complete his task: to this day the ear remains a rough sketch, a circumstance which, let us hope, has no particular significance.

Although in South America Western music belongs to the "Europeans," the level of society least rooted in the land, the intermingling of cultural traditions is such that I find audiences nearly everywhere. Of the many tours I have made on that continent, one of the most memorable occurred in 1949.

We were in Peru, most fascinating of all countries, when Diana suddenly rebelled against the tyranny of the schedule. "Look," she said, "we come to all these lovely places, and what do we see? We see the airport, the concert hall, the hotel—and the concierge's outstretched hand. We're not leaving Peru until we've been to Cuzco." An ultimatum is an ultimatum. We awarded ourselves three days' vacation and took a little plane up into the Andes. Few sights are more beautiful than the earth's surface from three thousand meters, especially when, as here, plain gives way to rolling hills, and hills to the awesome mountains. The plains and hills were a patchwork of unimaginable vividness—fields of yellow, orange, red, lilac, purple, black neighbored one another. Not until landing did we learn what we had seen. It was maize drying in the sun, but maize of a dozen or more varieties in a peasant agriculture which had never tried to standardize nature.

Such beauty alone justified the escapade, and Cuzco too was worth the detour, as the guidebooks say. We reached this gracious little Spanish town in time to witness a Corpus Christi procession, in which most of the participants were Indians whose fine aquiline features and slanting eyes bespoke their Inca blood. Having got me thus far off the concert circuit, Diana tempted me further—to Machu Picchu, the ancient Inca city whose jungle-swallowed ruins were discovered early this century. Perhaps today Machu Picchu has a postcard kiosk and a Hilton hotel and dancing girls; I have not been back to see; but in 1949 a tourist had to be hardy to get to it at all. From Cuzco the route led steeply downhill for perhaps a hundred miles, across a valley, and then steeply uphill for a further mile or two. We accomplished the first, downhill, stage in a car whose tires had been removed, leaving the iron rims to run on rails; a method of progress which risked dislocating every bone in one's body and inhibited speech lest one bite one's tongue in two. One circumstance saved us from being bounced bodily out of our unlikely chariot: with six passengers (the other four being a company of cheerful young Chileans to whom every misadventure was new cause for merriment) and a driver, we were wedged in too tightly to move. After four lively hours we disembarked in the valley, at a very sketchy village composed of some ten or twenty mud huts. Where the village stopped, the jungle began, lush with orchids, begonias and other vegetation, which I could not recognize.

According to our program, a string of mules should have been waiting in the village to carry us up to Machu Picchu; but the arrangements had broken down, and from this point we were on our own. With the presumption that the river must flow from the top of the mountain, we decided to climb up its course and, in the deepening dusk, started the ascent, at first singing and chattering, later silent and puffing and exhausted. It was, I believe, the severest physical test I have ever undergone. Machu Picchu made one concession to sightseers: there was a guest house offering the Spartan comfort of wooden-plank beds, sandbag mattresses and one rough blanket each. After our exertions, it seemed all we had ever wanted. As the sun rose next morning we came out on the mountain, and there around us lay the ruins of Machu Picchu, the beautiful, enigmatic witness to a vanished civilization.

For such reward one ought to travel painfully, expending the effort of one's own legs and lungs; the beauty which requires no greater forfeit than stepping into a car or switching on a television set is too easily undervalued. But mankind—and not only in the industrialized West—has lost the capacity to adapt to nature. That marvelous human flexibility which raised families and created cultures in the Arctic, the desert, the Amazonian jungle or atop the Andes, is in a fair way to disappearing and in its place we substitute capsule living, our capsules air-conditioned, heated to such and such a temperature, furnished with encapsulated food, encapsulated information and even encapsulated religion, in churches, sermons and catechisms, communist, Christian or other. Very little comes to us directly from the source, and thus anonymously standardized, we are improvised human beings.

Peru in 1949, however, had still some way to go to reach this sterilized sameness. Back in Cuzco, we had the not altogether gratifying experience of being recognized by a man who overbore my protest that I was on holiday by claiming that refusal to give a concert would offer grave offense to the city and its citizens. A recital was arranged for the evening. Arrived at the hall, I was somewhat taken aback to find the piano, a cottage upright, disemboweled, its inner workings exposed on the floor, and someone busily groping inside the carcass. My face must have expressed my feelings. "He's tuning it," I was assured. "No one has played it for five years." Across the subsequent recital accompanied by an approximately tuned piano a veil had best be drawn; but one thing I remember with affectionate respect: throughout the eleventh-hour tuning and thereafter, the audience displayed only patience and appreciation. Clearly such little contretemps were to be accepted gladly.

From Peru we went to Ecuador to play at Guayaquil. Here another sort of hazard came between the audience and me. At the hotel, Diana and I were met by a very charming man and wife, the organizers of the concert, who had come to take us to the hall. They led us downstairs into the open air, whereupon from all sides we were immediately assaulted by flying missiles. Retreating into the safety of the hotel, we asked what this could be. The lady apologetically explained, "It is the time of the locust. We must run for the car." And that is what we did, with heads down, through an aerial barrage. In fact, they were not locusts, but perfectly harmless large grasshoppers, whose only inconveniences lay in their quite ridiculous numbers and their mindless habit of flying into obstacles at high speed without looking where they were going. With the car windows closed, we reached the hall unmolested and made another dash for the shelter of the artists' room. Half a dozen grasshoppers contrived to come in with us. Each member of the audience must similarly have introduced his or her quota, for the recital was enlivened throughout by their darting hither and thither and crashing into people and furniture; but no later hitch had power to disconcert me, for at the beginning, as I raised my violin to my shoulder, lifted the bow, concentrated my mind on the music—I found a grasshopper amiably regarding me from his perch upon the strings.

Our next engagement was at Maracaibo, in Venezuela, after which we were due to go to Caracas, and thence home to the United States. Once again, however, as at Cuzco, I was persuaded to give a concert beyond the line of duty, this time at Barranquilla in Colombia. I cabled my agent, Quesada, that I would not be arriving in Caracas on the Saturday night as planned, but at lunchtime the following day. Then we went to Barranquilla, had a lovely concert, stayed the night and flew to Caracas on Sunday. Quesada was waiting at the airport. Civilly Diana hoped that the change of plan had not discommoded him in any way. "Not at all," Quesada replied. "The only pity is, the concert should be now." We met his announcement with dismay, horror and apology, but Quesada's equanimity showed such emotions to be quite out of place. "I told everybody. They will come tonight," he promised cheerfully. And they did. The Spanish understanding of *mañana* undoubtedly has its uses.

12

A Sense
of Time

One blessing which a traveling artist quickly learns to value is a good agent. So fortunate have I been in mine—one per country, or continent, or area of cultural influence—that the connections between us have lasted all my playing days. In the United States, Laurence Evans and Jack Salter, who had taken me on as a boy, survived independently until 1938 when, with other managers, they formed themselves into a co-operative establishment called Columbia Concerts. To this day it is my American management. Mr. Evans and Mr. Salter are dead, and Kurt Weinhold, who inherited me from them, has more or less retired (although not from our lifelong friendship), passing me on to the good offices of Tommy Thompson. In Britain, Harold Holt acquired me from his predecessor, Lionel Powell, and bequeathed me to his successor, Ian Hunter. Thus things change, but the changes are not of my making: lacking good reason to do otherwise, which my devoted agents have never given me, I stay put.

There was of course one bond which horribly broke. As I have said, Louisa Wolff and Emil Sachs were swallowed up in Hitler's death camps; their agency vanished with them; no one survived to re-establish it. When eventually I came back to Germany, the concerts were at first arranged from France, but in time I came to know and like Hans Adler of Berlin, and it seemed unreasonable not to deal directly with him. He has managed my German affairs for over twenty years now. In the Netherlands in 1929 I came under the protection of the de Koos Concert Agency, which, although its founder has died, still operates under his name. Sylvio Samama, who now runs it, is an unusual manager: he has a certain margin of private fortune which he uses to launch young artists on their careers. He has taken on several at my recommendation and succeeded with them all. My first visit to Spain, in 1932, forged a connection with Ernesto de Quesada and his sons, under whose aegis I have traveled Latin America, from the Mexican border to the Argentine. Ernesto, a strict vegetarian from his youth, died only recently at the age of ninety-five. I am still loyal to his far-flung sons.

Meanwhile in France I have been handed down from father to son to a third generation of Dandelots and am currently represented in Paris by Yves. Yves's father, Maurice Dandelot, used sometimes to travel with Diana and me, and thus we had a mild adventure or two together. One such occurred on my first visit to North Africa, in 1951. After a concert in Tangiers, with another in Casablanca scheduled for that evening, we were driving serenely along when, on the outskirts of a village, the car rounded a corner and all at once plunged into a veritable lake covering the road and the engine died. We were not the only travelers to be incommoded by the flood, the result of a freak storm, as we afterward learned. As far as one could see, the road and surrounding land lay under a sheet of water, in which a dozen half-submerged vehicles gave mournful witness to the limits of man's power over nature. An excited throng of villagers, in and out of the water, regarded the stranded cars and assured their drivers that there was no hope of rescue.

At Diana's suggestion, she, Maurice and I climbed onto the running board and thence waded through the water to the higher ground to ask for help. Very reasonably the villagers pointed out that they could do no more for us than for the shipwrecked drivers ahead of us. Was there a railroad? Yes, indeed there was, but the flood had put the trains out of action too. Was there at least a telephone by which we might alert Casablanca of our predicament? Before this hope could be dashed in its turn, salvation appeared in the unexpected shape of an urchin on the edge of the crowd. "Oh, look!" he suddenly squeaked in French. "That's Yehudi Menuhin!" That an Arab village child should recognize me was astonishing enough, but no more astonishing than the effect his recognition produced. Something must be done, everyone agreed; then, wasting no more words, half the village plunged into the water and by sheer force of numbers pushed our stricken car up a side street to dry the engine out. From somewhere a truck was brought, its tailboard lowered, two planks propped against it to form a ramp, and with another mighty corporate heave, the car was lodged on the back of the truck. Diana, Maurice and I climbed aboard, and from our high, swaying perch waved the villagers goodbye. For a kilometer or so the truck splashed through the flood, then set us on the dry road again, and we reached Casablanca about a half hour before the concert was due to begin. As this story shows, there are advantages in having well-known features, but it is also agreeable to be anonymous. One day in New York I saved my anonymity by the skin of my teeth. A succession of disasters had left Diana without a pair of unladdered stockings to her name, so we went into a little store on Madison Avenue to buy some. Behind the counter stood an elderly couple. All the while Diana was making and paying for her purchase, the old man studied me closely, then, our business completed, he asked "Has anyone ever told you that you look *exactly* like Yehudi Menuhin?" I know an escape route when I see one, I hope. "Oh no!" I replied, registering pleased surprise to the best of my ability. "How very nice! He is someone I've always admired!" And we scuttled out of the store before anything more awkward might be said.

Maurice Dandelot was again accompanying us, in Switzerland this time, when the usefulness of having an identity was once more proved; although, as will be seen, only half proved in democratic Switzerland. Any traveler who has had to change trains at one of the smaller junctions will, I trust, endorse my contention that the Swiss railway timetable was devised by a clockmaker, and understand that the concert artist transporting his paraphernalia through that country can sometimes feel like a desert nomad trying to herd camels across swiftly clashing ice floes. The train from Chaux-de-Fonds on this particular day deposited us at one side of Neuchâtel station; the train which would carry us to an engagement in Geneva started from the other side, five minutes later. So, while an aged porter, accompanied by Maurice carrying the violins, shambled off on the round tour of the station with our trolleyload of luggage, Diana and I dodged across the tracks, found the stationmaster, and won from him (as I thought) a few minutes' lenience. Poor civil servant! Was he to betray me or his country? At the last moment respect for punctuality got the better of him, and Diana and I found ourselves aboard a moving train, severed from Maurice, the violins and the luggage. Without second thought I pulled the emergency cord, bringing train, passengers and catastrophe to a shrieking halt. We were still alongside the platform.

What thereupon broke out was, in a word, bedlam. One would have thought oneself in Sicily, not sober Switzerland. Amid the cries and plaints of the outraged passengers, against the deafening bellow of the train's alarm system, the scandalized stationmaster hurried down the platform, mounted our carriage and dragged us off. We were at once surrounded by a crowd, jostling and arguing and advising my summary consignment to prison. In the middle of the uproar Maurice appeared. Seeing the train in movement, he had abandoned the porter and the trolley of valises and leaped into the last carriage; had I but known it, I could have kept my appointment in Geneva with no greater inconvenience than the lack of concert clothes. Anyway, the alarm was finally silenced and, at Diana's suggestion that afterward the timetable was sacrosanct, we were allowed to board the train again, there to be dealt with by the conductor. I was fined the statutory sum. This episode, no doubt equivalent almost to a revolution in the annals of Switzerland, came to a graceful conclusion at the next stop, Lausanne, where yet another gold-braided *chef de gare* made his appearance—to refund *half* the fine.

In fact, had I been charged the full sum, it would have been cheap at the price. Well-behaved all my life, at least in public, I had long been thwarting two desires. One was, precisely, to pull a train's emergency cord; the other, which was to abandon myself to anger without compunction, like Toscanini wreaking destruction on the telephone but preferably with graver cause, was granted fulfillment in South Africa in 1950, when, for the first and only time in my life, I came into conflict with apartheid and, hearteningly, emerged the victor.

When Diana, Marcel Gazelle and I arrived at Johannesburg early that year, I had just read *Cry, the Beloved Country* by Alan Paton and wished to tell him how much his book had moved me. I telephoned him at his school at Diepkloof, asked if I could be of any use, and was invited to play to the boys. On the *stoep*, as the veranda is called in those parts, stood an old broken-down piano, which Marcel did his best with, while ranged in lines in the sunshine, the boys squatted on their haunches. We played very light pieces, which they seemed to enjoy, then exchanged roles to listen to the children's lively rendering of various Christian hymns. To round off this domestic little outing, my South African management rang me up and complained that it wasn't allowed for in the contract. As I have said, my relations with my different agents have been and continue to be excellent. The exception proving the rule, the South

African agency also differed from the others in being a vast and wealthy combine controlling cinemas and theatres as well as performers and performances. The combine's man detailed to look after me was a Mr. Dick Harmel.

Accused of breaking my contract, I suggested to Mr. Harmel that he must be talking nonsense, for black Africans, certainly black African boys at a reformatory school, could not attend my concerts. "Or can they?" I added innocently.

"Of course not!" he said indignantly, falling neatly into the trap.

"Well, then," I said, "I'll arrange to give duplicate concerts for the Africans on the mornings of my regular concerts." Before apartheid was thoroughly formalized, blacks and whites could, if not simultaneously, use the same premises, at least in Johannesburg, where the city hall in which I played was open to everyone. Thus it was arranged (although not by my disapproving management), and the morning audiences were brought in by bus with their children and their babies. Johannesburg had at the time a public-spirited Jewish mayor who further lent me the services of the municipal orchestra, with whom I went one day to Sophiatown, a sprawling shantytown for Johannesburg's black labor force. In the middle of acres of huts stood a single solid brick building, more serviceable than beautiful, a gift of South African Scots. This served as a social center, providing reading and games rooms, refuge from the rain, and a small theatre. The concert we gave there was one of the most affecting of my life. Speaking the English of Oxford or possibly Cambridge, two spokesmen for Sophiatown welcomed us; this was a great occasion, they said; had they control of their country and its treasures, they would mark it with gifts of gold and diamonds, but as their rights were denied them, they hoped we would accept the traditional greeting—whereupon they put a necklace of beads on my neck, another on the conductor's, and carried a third down to Diana, sitting in the audience. Then everyone stood to sing what in other circumstances would have been their national anthem (and may yet be, although one hesitates to envisage the preliminary bloodletting). In 1950 the Africans' solemn and exalted singing had something of the same electrifying effect of, say, the *Marseillaise* sung in German-occupied France. I played a Bach Concerto and the Mendelssohn. Whenever some passage struck the audience's fancy, a reaction rippled over the sea of black faces, in which the faces of Diana and one or two others who had come with us pointed up the contrast. The performance over, I suggested that musicians from the orchestra might come regularly to Sophiatown to give lessons. I believe it happened for a while.

Between Johannesburg and the continuation of the tour, Diana, Marcel and I made a brief sortie to Lourenço Marques, upon returning from which and on the point of catching the Capetown plane, I was summoned to see Mr. Schlesinger, the overall executive of the combine which at some lowly echelon of its complex operations managed my appearances. I did not guess that this summons was to usher in one of the great moments of my life. Across a length of floor suitable to his imperial importance, behind a desk whose glossy mass soothed favored clients and intimidated importunate ones, as occasion demanded, sat Mr. Schlesinger. "I am afraid," he opened, "that we shall have to sue you. You have given all these concerts without any permission from us. You are in clear breach of contract. We find this situation quite unacceptable and must ask you to forfeit your fees."

Here was my cue. Accumulated decades of wrath simmering away beneath a decorous exterior found at last their righteous outlet. The moment being too heady for any tamer posture, I stood up to deliver myself of my sentiments: the people I had played to outside the framework of my contract (I said) would not and could not have attended the supplemented the paying audiences. There was no moral justification organized concerts; in no way did they detract from or could they have whatever for his action and I would make sure the world knew the whole story. And I stalked out and slammed the door with most liberated abandon. The extraordinary thing—which I have never followed up sufficiently, I think—was that the strategy worked. Of course, it wasn't in fact a strategy, in that I responded impulsively to provocation without second thought, but it might have taught me for future confrontation the uses of unrestraint. When the plane landed at Capetown later that day, an abject delegation of Schlesinger's local representatives met us, wringing their hands in contrition, submissive to any further whimsical jumps my temper might make. Regrettably, by briefly famous victory left no lasting mark on South African history.

We were to return to South Africa once more, in 1956. Thereafter I decided I could not in conscience perform in a country where a powerful minority treated a powerless majority so inequitably (something no more and no less reprehensible than a powerful majority's inequitable treatment of a powerless minority). Many another artist made a similar decision, as well as sportsmen, churchmen and some statesmen. The South African regime remains in place, its colors unchanged; but for how much longer? Are there perhaps straws in the wind today, indicating that pressures are gathering which may yet bring genuine equality?

Nineteen fifty-one found me in another, and very different, outpost of the British Commonwealth, where two events occurred which were to change both Hephzibah's life and mine.

One morning, when Diana, Hephzibah and I had gathered in our hotel in Sydney, Australia, the telephone rang. "This is Richard Hauser," the caller announced. "Do you remember me from Rome?" My memory for chance-met people is, I have to confess, not spectacularly good, but him I remembered effortlessly and with no particular sympathy either. Might he come over? Hauser wanted to know. I was sorry, but I was too busy. Was I free for lunch? No, I had an engagement. When? At five to one. Very well, he would be at the hotel at a quarter to. And he rang off. Promptly at twelve forty-five he arrived, very cheerful and disheveled, to explain that he had come to Australia at the behest of the Sydney authorities to investigate the social conditions of workers in the public transport system. The ten minutes he had requisitioned from our schedule were soon over; Diana and I left for our appointment, but Hephzibah pleaded a diplomatic headache and stayed with Richard.

Twenty-five years later she is with him yet. As well as bearing him a daughter, Clara, in 1955, Hephzibah put all her heart and energy into her husband's social work, both in the field and in the books on their experiences which they have written together. So unremitting is their commitment to the disadvantaged of society that were it not for concerts, I doubt if Hephzibah and I would meet at all. Richard's approach is to set the lame to lead the blind: he sees the abandoned child, the battered wife, the delinquent, the convict, the addict, the helpless aged, and all the other deprived human beings he cares for, as a network of interacting need, in which, as one problem derives from another, one victim can help another. I greatly admire his and Hephzibah's lives—not only are they devoted to their fellowmen, but they express devotion in the most practical, humane and real ways.

My own important encounter on that journey in 1951 took place in Auckland. Hephzibah and I had come to New Zealand for a few concerts, leaving Diana, who was expecting Jeremy at the time, to take life as placidly as Lindsay's sheep station permitted. One day in July, in an osteopath's waiting room, to fill in time while Hephzibah had a treatment, I leafed through the books on display and came upon a thin volume on yoga. Yoga, whether physical jerks or philosophical system, I had never so much as heard of, but this little introduction to Hatha Yoga—that is, the bodily postures, or *asanas*—struck me with the force of a revelation. Without even knowing that I was searching for it, I had stumbled across a key to unlock old enigmas, to make me aware of my capacity, encourage the physical ease missing from my upbringing, point the way to further comprehension of violin playing, and perhaps—if I persevered—stand me on my head in long-delayed fulfillment of child-hood ambition (I used to envy children who could walk on their hands). Intrigued by so much promise, I asked the doctor if I might take his book on tour with me and return it at the end of the week. All that week, when not traveling, rehearsing and performing, I shut myself up in various hotel rooms to experiment with the *asanas*—finding much pleasure in exercises which demanded no strain but on the contrary inner quietness, which were neither aggressive nor competitive but to be done in solitude, which required no equipment but a few feet of floor space. When the tour ended and the book was restored to its owner, I had learned enough to continue with the practice, however crudely.

So it came about that seven months later, I arrived in India with something Indian to my credit. To anticipate encounter with a new culture has always pleased me, even if the anticipation has to be trivial, as when, between New Zealand and India, I paid a first visit to Japan (my first Asian country) with Adolph Baller. In 1951 the flight from San Francisco to Tokyo took two days, a good part of which I spent practicing to eat with chopsticks, achieving a measure of competence and greatly amusing my Japanese hosts. In the same way I prepared for India by practicing yoga, and news of my interest in it preceded me there. On our first evening in Delhi, challenged by Pandit Nehru to show what I could do, I stood on my head in a somewhat rickety and unsatisfactory fashion, under the critical gaze of his daughter Indira, his sister "Nan" Pandit, and a few members of the government. "Oh, that's no good!" said Nehru in his sharp way. "I'll show you." He took off his little Gandhi hat and very elegantly—although not more elegantly than I can manage it now—upended himself on the drawing room carpet. Dutifully I did my best to emulate my first guru, and we were both on our heads when the splendid turbaned and sashed butler threw open the door to an-nounce that dinner was served.

No sooner had news of this event traveled the grapevine into the newspapers than gurus began to queue up wherever I went, each recom-mended by some prominent patron. On the day Diana and I were to leave Delhi for Agra, I was taken at four o'clock in the morning to witness one of the most venerable, a bearded sage of perhaps eighty, naked but for a band about his loins, go through his exercises on a leopard skin in a forest clearing, surrounded by disciples. As did much else in India, the reverence of this little ceremony compelled recognition of an acceptance of life in all its expressions which we in the West have lost, if we ever possessed it. We debase the body, we shame it and cover its shame, whereas Indian wisdom—with erotic temple sculpture as with yoga—offers grateful tribute to the body and rejoices in it. If our predicament is partly Christianity's responsibility, it is not Jesus Christ's: anyone who cares to read the Gospel According to Saint John in the Nestorian record will see that Jesus, like the Hindu, preaches care for the body, insisting on its need of air, sun and water; but fanatical puritans among his followers had to cleave body and spirit asunder and set the barriers of heaven and hell between them. In the cool of the early morning wood, I took off my clothes to learn respect of the body from the old Indian saint.

There were other gurus and other lessons, but not until I met Iyengar, no bearded ascetic but a good young man with a wife and children, did I take lessons regularly. We made each other's acquaintance in Bombay. Having traveled to see me from Poona, at the behest of a mutual friend, he appeared in my rooms one morning and straightaway made it clear, with a kind of rustic authority, that the "audition" to follow was mine as much as his. My prominence he did not doubt, but in fact Iyengar had never heard of me before. If I was a name to be reckoned with, whose favor he could imagine redounding upon him, I was, for all my celebrity, another Western body knotted through and through. I could allow him only five minutes of a busy schedule, I warned him. He bade me lie still, touching me here and there. One hour later I awoke, feeling more refreshed than I had felt for ages. Like the other pedagogical "recognitions" of my life, this one too began with the casting of a kind of spell. Iyengar has since won acknowledgment outside India, the author of an exhaustive treatise on yoga, a lecturer in demand at foreign universities. As the weight of activity came to press upon his life, as upon mine, we saw less of each other, but for some fifteen years he traveled every summer to Europe on my behalf and whenever I went to India, he would be there throughout the stay to put me daily through my paces.

"Yoga" means "union." Its goal is union with the infinite, a goal which can be reached by any number of routes; but just as there is one ending, so there is one beginning, the *asanas* of Hatha Yoga, which are the precondition of every advance. It would be possible to make yoga a life's occupation, giving up more and more of one's time to its refinement. This has never been my intention. For me yoga is primarily a yardstick of inner peace: if one is afflicted by despondency or envy or overeating or any of a hundred other human miseries and temptations, if one fills one's lungs with nicotine and one's belly with alcohol, one cannot breathe deeply, evenly and quietly, as yoga teaches. It begins with a certain peaceful concentration, and when the breathing is quiet and the body pliable, it is time to start the *asanas*, rejoicing in the balance, flexibility, consciousness of oneself, awareness of one's potential that they bestow. In my life yoga is an aid to well-being, permitting me to do more and to do better.

First and foremost, of course, yoga made its contribution to my quest to understand consciously the mechanics of violin playing, a quest which by 1951 had long been one of the themes of my life. As a child, able sometimes to surpass my teachers in the performance of a specific work, I knew that I did not know how I did it, and not being by nature fraudulent, was later embarrassed to assert on forms demanding my occupation that I was a "violinist." That I had played the violin was a fact safely embalmed each day in the past, that I should be able to play it tomorrow a claim savoring of recklessness in my woeful ignorance of what "playing the violin" signified. Long before my search for enlightenment became systematic, I groped for partial understanding, usually unsuccessfully, as an incident from my tenth or eleventh year illustrates. There was in the San Francisco Symphony Orchestra a brilliant violinist called Piastro, who was eventually to succeed Louis Persinger as concertmaster and later to become concertmaster of the New York Philharmonic under Toscanini. I knew Piastro well and much admired, among other brilliances, his staccato. One day I asked him how he did it. He picked up his violin and rattled off a few incisive bars. "I do this," he said, "and this." As a demonstration it was impeccable, reproducing exactly the staccato I found so satisfying, but as an explanation it left me as baffled as before. He did not explain for the simple reason that he could not. He could not unpick the mechanics of muscle and motion that produced his staccato—or my own, for that matter; and it was this which I needed to know. In the year and a half of idleness in California which closed my first decade of touring, my worry reached a peak: having left my violins in their cases for some weeks, I found on unpacking them again that I could not be sure of promptly re-establishing intimacy. One day my fingers had their old reassurance, another they fumbled. Fortunately the outcome was happy, critics and audiences declaring I played as well as before, if not better, and I agreeing with their verdict. But beneath surface mastery lay quicksands of doubt. Inevitably one faltering step would have me floundering in them; equally inevitably, my step faltered under the wartime burden of domestic difficulty and an exhausting schedule which together allowed no leisure for renewal, physical or psychological.

Another artist, trusting to his musical gift and ignoring what he could not understand, might have negotiated this marshy patch securely upright, but blessed or cursed with inherited Talmudical tendencies, I had to comprehend the inherent nature of my stumblings before I could regain confidence. What had happened was a break in sequence. Between musical vision and its communication, a transition hitherto made intuitively, there occurred—not always nor predictably but ever present as a threat—a rupture which brought all to naught. Intuition was no longer to be relied on; the intellect would have to replace it.

Was mine in fact a singular predicament due to an inquiring cast of mind? Experience persuades me that many people must follow the same circle from intuition through intellectual analysis to restored spontaneity, and indeed that the circle is implicit in learning and its completion the saving grace of true civilization. Some individuals or societies exist contentedly at an early stage of the journey—the primitive at the intuitive, where without intellectual effort he achieves harmony with his environment; the ideologue at the stage of intellectual abstraction, where theories don't depend on intuition and need never be tested; and most of us some way short of either in a limbo of semi-deprivation. Violin playing should be—can become—a "natural" activity, but having said that, one has not said much, for how many "natural" or even automatic activities are successfully accomplished in our unnatural times? How many people walk badly, breathe badly, chew badly, digest badly? Such is the price of a civilization which has left intuition behind and not yet discovered the way back. The loss is grave for everyone, not least for artists, whose wisdom must be a tree, its roots spreading in darkness and its branches reaching to the light of consciousness.

The intuitive aptitude I displayed as a child was, if you like, my doing and my undoing, my making and my unmaking. But there is an advantage in establishing the top story of one's constructions first: one has seen the heights, one knows what one is building for and what must be sustained. If the structure can remain suspended long enough to permit the gaps to be filled in, building from the top proves more efficient in the end. To be able to walk onstage with as much pleasure and as little self-consciousness as one might walk along a street has been my ambition. Having done so many times, having played with exaltation and *élan,* I knew what I was aiming for. It was half the battle. Another contribution to ultimate victory was the sure conviction that motion held the clue. I have always been fascinated by movement—a bird's flight, acrobatic children cartwheeling in the park, a painter's hand moving across the canvas. In mid-adolescence I "invented" an aircraft consisting of a wing divided into segments, each driven by its own engine so that, if need be, it could detach itself from those to either side and fly independently. Whether or not my idea had any bearing on aeronautics, it had much bearing on my dominant concern—the wing a hand, each engine a sinew, each segment a digit capable of flying in any direction under its own auspices. In such ways I began groping toward enlightenment long before embarking on the conscious search for basic principles. Once discovered, basic principles seem self-evident—the principles of violin playing as those of aerodynamics; but it took mankind many centuries to learn to fly.

Undoubtedly I had lost time in balking at scales, arpeggios, *études* in youth, but tackling the problem as an adult, scales could be but a hit-or-miss remedy, treating symptoms, not finding causes, hammering mechanical responses into place, not explaining the mystery. Robbing me of some measure of intuition, adult life more than compensated for the theft, however, with the gift of insight. Just as musical vision had long required justification by conscious analysis of each composition, so now it was essential to trace with equal thoroughness the process which translated thought and feeling into action, vision into innumerable muscular reactions. The direction of the search established, every experience pushed me further: my own practice, exchanges with other violinists, the laws of physics, a passage to India, and of course and specifically yoga, which taught me lessons it would have taken years to elaborate for myself. All influences pointed toward less tension, more effective application of energy, the breaking down of resistance in every joint, the coordination of all motions into one motion; and illustrated the profound truth that strength comes not from strength but from the subtle comprehension of process, of proportion and balance.

Thereafter, with a compass to keep me on course, rejecting counsels which led only to time-consuming detours or dead ends, progress was steady. But first I had to discover that acquiring a skill consists as much in unlearning as in learning. Those of us who develop bad violin-playing habits must, before we overcome them, experience a point of zero tension which might correspond to the purgatorial middle ground where sinners shed their old identity. The wrong strength must be let go and a period of "no strength" endured. Mine, it can be said, began with the sleep induced by Iyengar.

A quarter of a century has passed since then, time enough to see his lessons, and the lessons built on his lessons, evolve into an item on the day's agenda as routine as bathing. It has been a long labor performed in mid-career, an achievement of which I am now moderately proud. Some people would choose privacy to confront relearning their trade, but the lonely vacuum of the research laboratory is not my native element. At the most crucial times I needed the demand, or reassurance, of public performance. Today I don't fear indolence, confident, as I was not in 1936, that the gift is not an *ignis fatuus,* there one minute and gone the next, and altogether outside one's control or understanding. What announced itself as a forbidding challenge has taken its beneficent place, yielding inestimable dividends; not only in technical control, the service of music and teaching, but in general human experience. My search has been one of the main lines of my life, a stabilizing element, an ongoing effort, a lasting satisfaction. The sureness of childhood has been regained, with added intellectual stiffening. Given a half hour to warm up, I know I can play; given a few days to master new music, I can expect to do it. I have learned that harsh whips of determination cannot drive one to performing pitch, but that one is led there by the quiet exercise of principles grasped by the mind and absorbed by the body over stubborn years of faith. I have understood that no experience can be isolated from violin playing, that the flexibility with which one holds violin and bow, the mastery which does not grab or dominate, has illuminating parallels in human relations. I am thankful to have been obliged to discover and assimilate so much, for the experience has given me something of value to impart to others.

That India should offer me at once a homeland and a new-found land with lasting power to astonish seemed only right, for it is precisely the reconciling of contradictions within an all-accepting unity that is the country's genius and its abiding appeal for me. There is, of course, a ratio between the expectations one brings to a new experience and the fulfillment won from it; and, moreover, it will by now be clear to the reader that reaching the answer first and gathering the evidence afterward has been a *leitmotiv* of my life, and not only in playing the violin before I knew what I was doing. Thus, adolescent attempts to hold my breath—attempts first made at the age of thirteen at Basel, when I clocked up four minutes—presaged trust in yoga, and thus, when Diana and I set off for India in 1952, I was perfectly ignorant of it but nonetheless sure the journey would strike deep responses in me.

Although one doesn't know how many generations atavism endures to link descendants with their remote ancestors, my conviction that the father I traveled east, the closer I came to my origins guaranteed I should find India the primal ocean whose waters flowing westward across the centuries fed my familiar streams of ideas, attitudes and music. And so it proved. At a more deliberate level, the philosophy of Constantin Brunner prepared me for the encounter. Brunner, a German Jew captured by the Nazis when Holland was overrun and sent to die in a concentration camp, had come into my life by the anonymous gift of his writings in 1938 (not the first or the last time that submission to another's initiative deflected my direction). My German being more adequate than expert, I made heavy weather of the first hundred or so complex pages, but thereafter became increasingly attracted to the beauty of his prose and to a *Weltanschauung* of inclusion. I was later told that Brunner had studied Hinduism; it may have contributed to his belief in the one force binding creation together, inanimate as well as animate. Certainly it was the Hindu's glorious indulgence in life in all its shapes, an indulgence delightfully new to me yet responding to some profound sentiment, which forcibly struck me within minutes of first standing on Indian soil.

Diana and I had flown to Delhi overnight, so that we drove through the sparkling early morning from the airport to Lutyens's viceregal lodge, the erstwhile headquarters of the British raj, where we were to stay. I shall never forget that drive across a landscape exuberant with life: throngs of people, men in white dhotis, women billowing along in saris of brilliant red, green and yellow; birds of every feather maintaining an uninterrupted cacophony in the trees; monkeys in chattering dozens leaping from branch to branch above the traffic; oxen everywhere, gentle white creatures with long, elegantly curved horns, ambling into the road, along the sidewalk, through adjacent fields; and among all this wealth of existence, none seeming to dominate.

There were, it occurred to me, two views of creation: one competitive, holding that everything exists at the expense of everything else; the other cooperative, believing that the broader the circle of life, the more it would sustain. Both were valid, neither could be held with puritan strictness, but the emphasis was all. Having grown up in competitive America, where survival was by will power and pesticides, I could not find other than marvelous a world which drew its strength from the encouragement of so much life and the destruction of so little. The cattle on the sidewalk, around which the human stream formed little eddies, were not simply tolerated but venerated, and not only as a form of life with inalienable rights, but as contributors to the rest of the circle: a main source of protein, giving milk and cheese, a producer of dung (surely man's as well as animals' first repayment to the nourishing earth), which precious substance provided fertilizer, binding for mortar, and fuel. Made into neat pancakes and stacked on flat, round trays, it was carried proudly aloft on the heads of the ladies. Indeed the United States was not like this. I am always sorry that these two of my several homelands should fail to comprehend each other; that the Muslim mentality, dynamic, sometimes aggressive, should prove so much more understandable to the American than that of the gentle Hindu, whose resignation is the fruit of a yearning to encompass the paradoxes of existence—matter and energy, life and death, pleasure and pain, himself and all creation—in one harmonious whole.

Over two decades and more Diana and I have visited India half a dozen times, traveling the length and breadth of the land, seeing folly and corruption as well as wisdom, recognizing that the clock turns there too and not inevitably to advantage, but ever anew delighted by a culture so dense, varied, rich, which manages to coordinate elements we have given up, supporting all its layers and contradictions on millenarian values. India, I feel, has softened my Talmudical adjudications between right and wrong, upheld innocent acceptance of the lovely things of life, given me much that was new yet welcome, understandable, waiting to be experienced. The first invitation came about at the proposal of Lady Nye, wife of the first British High Commissioner to independent India. Nehru, having gone to prison in opposition to the raj, was, however, happy to maintain friendly cultural relations with the old colonial power and chose to invite me, not yet the honorary Englishman I seem since to have become, but already linked, as he in his way was, with Britain. I played a series of concerts for the famine fund.

It did not in the least surprise me that a lively friendship should straightaway spark between Diana and Pandit Nehru. Not that she wooed him; on the contrary. In Nehru's house in Delhi that first night, we saw a bust of him, dramatically lit and reverently adorned with fresh flowers. "Is this, by any chance, a memorial?" said Diana; by the next

day it had been removed. At dinner Nehru led the conversation, prosecuting in retrospect the sins of the raj, as if to prick us to its defense or to
acknowledgment of its blame. "I had thought," said Diana sorrowfully,
"that I was to meet a great Indian Brahman. And what do I find? An
irascible English lawyer!" And Nehru rose with animation to meet this
irreverence.

Outstanding in his distinction of mind and nobility of character,
Nehru was also one of the few honest men of state our times have
known. No matter whom it hurt, including himself, he would not hesitate to speak the truth. There was some vanity in him, in his awareness
of being Gandhi's heir, in the fresh red rose he always wore; but there
was no hypocrisy, no decent veil drawn over difficulty. After that first
dinner (an English menu, to my slight disappointment), he took us out
onto the balcony in the half-sultry, pungent Indian night, mazy with the
light of more stars than one knew existed, silent but for the occasional
bark of a wild dog. While we breathed the spicy air, he sighed a little
with wistful resignation. To govern India was an impossible task, he
said; no one could cope with it; but neither could it be abandoned. "All I
can do is hope and work and pray." I think that when the mantle of
government descended to his daughter, so did its inescapability. Indira
Gandhi knew as much as anyone about the evolution of India and the
business of state, yet for years she disclaimed ambition to be prime minister. Fate has its pressures, however, and the obvious person to hold a
country together cannot easily see it fall apart. In 1952 she was an
enchanting young woman, her father's disciple, formed by him, returning devotion for devotion. I did not guess her strength, but I might have,
for even then it was clear that she disclosed only those thoughts and
feelings she believed would be to good purpose.

On that first visit Diana and I stayed for several weeks, with concerts in Delhi, Bombay, Calcutta, Madras and Bangalore. Fearing we
would be exploited by charitable organizations, and eager to show us yet
more of India, Nehru sent us here and there and particularly to Kashmir,
his own beloved Kashmir, whose separation from India he simply could
not countenance. Without his personal commitment, I too felt Kashmir
belonged to India, the roof of its world, complementing its heat, the land
of refuge and of monasteries where man seeks ultimate union with the
infinite. Thus geography echoed society and the highest was the highest.

Under Nehru's and others' tutelage we saw more than I could ever
relate without resorting to the exclamatory litanies of a travelogue or to
the pious snapshots of the family album, which must remain dim and

unexplained to strangers: the languid Hindu; the Bengali, who is nothing if not a born volcano; the archaic, least invaded south; the Parsees, whom I call the Jews of India (but who are in fact Zoroastrians, self-exiled from Persia), whose monotheism has bred a judicious, pragmatic race and given Indian finance, industry and commerce its backbone; the genuine Jews at Cochin, perhaps the oldest Diaspora community in the world, some of whom had emigrated to Israel and returned again. And the work of all their hands, an art—in music, dance, painting, sculpture, architecture—which channeled eruptive emotions into subtle, disciplined forms. I retain an impression of immense contrasts cohabiting without strain: the renunciation of a Gandhi with the voluptuousness of the most skilled massage I have ever had, or of the oldest of the Jaipur palaces, where streams of water bearing rose petals used to flow through the rooms, at once cooling and perfuming the air; a range of human culture which stretches from half-Pygmy and other primitive peoples practicing animal sacrifice in the forests, through the purity of the unchanging village, to a nuclear scientist like the late Homi Bhabha, one of the rare all-round human beings I have known, a Leonardo da Vinci of our day, whose knowledge of culture (ours as well as his), whose skill as a painter, only completed a physicist of genius; and yet whose scientific eminence was profoundly Indian, in that nuclear physics is a discipline natural to a people who have never drawn a distinction between body and spirit, matter and energy.

Mine was the good fortune to be shown not the India which self-consciously sells its exoticism to foreigners, but the thing itself, at its most authentic and cultivated. I found it a ladder with religion on every rung, linking the remote past with the dawning future, intuitive man's immediate responses with cultivated man's most abstract concept of a disembodied, unnameable power unifying creation. The enchanting discovery was that India had not pulled up the ladder on its journey through the ages, but only lengthened it. Nothing had been annihilated, no bulldozer had obliterated the past.

All my life I have longed to feel underfoot the solid ground of the past, and this, among all India's gifts to me, is the one I receive most gratefully. Just as in space all life coexists, so the tenses of the universe are not sharply differentiated, but time is elastic, morning merging into afternoon, the past indistinguishable from the present. I have two parables—two among a hundred others—which incarnate for me India's sense of time.

The first comes from Calcutta. Nehru himself took us there, having business at an assembly of state governors, and granting himself an hour's leisure, escorted us to a park such as I had never seen. Its clearings and pathways, its sun and shade, covered many acres, and all this wide extent was in fact one single banyan tree! Here was a work which only time could accomplish; here was confirmation of my belief that patience is all, that whether one considers a banyan tree or a marriage or a culture, one must wait to reap the fruits. Another time we were taken to see a statue of a Jain Buddha in Bangalore, at the summit of a huge rock dominating the plain. Innumerable steps lead the pilgrim to the top, where the statue, perhaps fifty times life-size, sits in serene contemplation of the landscape. Once a year, I was told, it was anointed with milk and honey. That ceremony I did not witness, but while I was there a lesser ceremony took place. Just before noon we walked to the edge of the rock, where the overhang measured some thousands of feet to the plain below, and looking to the far horizon eventually discerned a speck which grew bigger as we watched and some minutes later took shape beside us, an eagle coming to be fed. That in itself was adventure enough for a sunny morning, but remarkably, this eagle was only the latest in a long line of eagles which from time immemorial had flown at noon each day to find sustenance at the statute of Buddha. It is the Indian's sense of time which lies behind the doctrine of reincarnation, the belief in a continuity so unbreakable that what is present belongs to the past and future, to earth and heaven; and it is this sense which, until now, has given India its stability. I had seen hereditary eagles; they were only a further commentary on a lesson Nehru himself had taught me. So strong had the principle of heredity been, he said, that in the past there existed hereditary ear-cleaners, fathers and sons in unbroken succession whose skill raised the soothing of an ear itch to the heights of ecstasy. The penalty of such a society is, of course, that its stability precludes any movement whatever. Well, since I have known India there has been movement—toward ever-swelling cities, toward growing industrialization, down the dubious road to "progress." I cannot think it a happy change.

The Parsees, for all their likeness to the Jews (I was present at a wedding and at a boy's coming of age, both of which ceremonies reinforced the claim to similarity), practice one very different custom: the remains of their dead are exposed on the Tower of Silence to the vultures. Thus, nothing is held back, whatever small value the corpse still has is returned to the earth, and the cycle of life which spells continuity is maintained. To belong to such a continuity relieves the individual, I think, of much of the burden of uniqueness. Life and death are not all and nothing, but stages in a process, episodes on an infinite river to which one trusts oneself and all other phenomena. So it is that Indian music reflects Indian life, having no predetermined beginning or end but flowing without interruption through the fingers of the composer-performer: the tuning of the instrument merges imperceptibly with the elaboration of the melody, which may spin itself out for two, three or more unbroken hours (or which, nowadays, for the purposes of broadcasting, can tailor itself to a thirty-minute slot).

Despite predisposition in India's favor, I have to acknowledge that Indian music took me by surprise. I knew neither its nature nor its richness, but here, if anywhere, I found vindication of my conviction that India was the original source. The two scales of the West, major and minor, with the harmonic minor as variant, the half-dozen ancient Greek modes, were here submerged under modes and scales of (it seemed) inexhaustible variety. Even the arcane rules of dodecaphonic composition had been anticipated and surpassed, for where the dodecaphonic system requires—somewhat arbitrarily, in my view—all twelve notes to be sounded in a given sequence and forbids their repetition within it, any given Indian *raga* chooses five or six notes, never more than seven or eight, while the hundreds of *ragas* between them exploit all possible notes in permutations of a subtlety and flexibility we can scarcely conceive. Melodically and rhythmically Indian music long ago achieved a complex sophistication which only in the twentieth century, with the work of Bartók and Stravinsky, has Western music begun to adumbrate.

What Indian music has not, and Western music richly has, is, of course, harmony. This is not fortuitous. Just because the Indian would unite himself with the infinite rather than with his neighbor, so his music assists the venture. Its purpose is to refine one's soul and discipline one's body, to make one sensitive to the infinite within one, to unite one's breath with the breath of space, one's vibrations with the vibrations of the cosmos. Outside the family, the Indian's concern does not easily fasten on the group. Europe's genius, on the other hand, has been to form individuals into communities, each accepting loss of freedom in the interests of the whole. Hence collective worship, hence armies and industries and parliamentary democracy, and hence chorales in which each voice has a certain independence but is nonetheless severely constrained by other voices.

When I was invited in 1965 to collaborate in the Commonwealth Arts Festival held in several British cities that autumn, I was granted a first close view of the music of yet another culture which added perspective to the links between social and musical organization. If Indian melody and Western harmony had seemed to provide matter for comparison, Indian individualism and African collectivism set the poles of the issue further apart. The African music was tribal, the music of a society which worked, worshipped, celebrated, mourned, and brought up its children together, without any European compromise between the one and the whole, and without need of a harmonic structure. Complexity of rhythm, equally a mark of Indian and African music, is based in an African ensemble on a division of labor, different players keeping their own beat against each other, and contriving to pull off this difficult feat by playing in a kind of hypnotic trance. The sum of the divisions is a subtlety of rhythm which so far not even jazz has reproduced.

In contrast, Indian rhythmic complexity is primarily one man's doing. Before beginning to play, the Indian group—consisting of some combination of three solo players providing drone, melody and rhythm (in order of sound)—chooses a *raga* and a *tala*, the warp and woof of the fabric about to be created. A *raga* is a scale-cum-melody, a given sequence of notes whose interrelationships are already determined, so that each note may be approached only from particular directions and in particular ways. The *tala* is the rhythm. Dozens exist. The Indian pulse beats to our basic 3/4 and 4/4 time, and beyond that to every conceivable odd and prime number (some variations of which were also discovered by Bartók in Hungarian and other folk music and given by him to the world at large). To make the whole exercise more intricate, the Indian, having chosen a *tala* of, say, eleven beats, will then improvise in groups of ten, leaving to the audience the responsibility of beating the basic rhythm; which, unperturbed, it does with unfailing accuracy. It becomes a game in which each tries to put the other off his stroke, a sort of intellectual motor race in which concentrated precision keeps apart two rhythms which start close, separate, then converge. The excitement mounts until, at the 110th beat, when at last the two rhythms meet, there is a tremendous Ha! of glee from the audience. As if the Indian rhythm player's task were not already complicated enough, he also contributes to the melody. The tabla, or Indian drum, is an almost melodic instrument, the pressure of the player's hand altering the tension of the skin and therefore the pitch; the player can slide between notes with precision-tool accuracy, asserting the rhythm with inflections of pitch, attack and volume, varying from the most delicate to the most powerful.

Indian music thus accommodates the group, but the individuals within it remain soloists, never coalescing into a harmonic statement. To form orchestras of Indian musicians would be to run counter to nature. I have been spared such bastard growths, but I have suffered the excruciating experience of hearing the Indian sitar or vina or violin accompanied by a harmonium, a relic of Christian missionaries' misunderstanding of the culture they were attempting to change.

The West had to invent the tempered scale, each note adjusted up or down from its true center to reconcile the different keys and permit modulation from one to another, thus advancing the development of harmony. I can't pretend to regret a development which has fed my whole musical life, but equally it is impossible to deny that the tempered scale corrupts our Western ears. The perfect fifth, set by the drone in Indian music and established as the overture to performance, is the criterion of all the other intervals, its continuing presence preventing absent-minded sliding out of the given key. As a result of such meticulous preparation, Indian musicians are sensitive to the smallest microtonal deviations, subdivisions of tones which the violin can find but which are outside the crude simplifications of the piano (or harmonium). I once enjoyed a striking object lesson in Indian musical priorities. It occurred in Delhi, at a congress assembling musicians from all parts of the country. Most venerated of all participants were singers of eighty years of age and more, whose voice, in our meaning of the word, had gone, but whose accuracy of intonation would have shamed celebrated coloraturas, and whose intelligence in improvisation was, of course, a virtue which Western singers are not generally called upon to display. These ancient singers joined the ancient gurus in my mind, joint symbols of a system of values which put time at the service of accomplishment.

If not necessarily an inherited trade in the manner of ear-cleaning, music-making is something to begin practicing early, say at three years old, with the prospect of a measure of excellence before one is thirty. As with other improvised music, a rigorous structure must be mastered if creation is to flower at the moment of performance. Otherwise, to improvise would be to invent a language on the spur of the moment. Grammar, syntax, vocabulary must all be known before the everyday miracle of speech occurs. So it is with improvisation. It presupposes a path between the mind's dictation and the fingers' obedience so short that it can't be measured, but the laying of the path is the work of technique and discipline developed in years of training. I have heard Indian music played by the untalented and the insufficiently trained: it is the most tedious thing imaginable, safely strait-jacketed within the laws and observances of the *raga,* never straying from the worn banalities of the cliché. I have also heard, and indeed helped introduce to the West, the masters—Ravi Shankar, who plays the sitar, Ali Akbar Khan, whose instrument is the older, perhaps less brilliant vina, Chatur Lal, the tabla player who took the United States by storm, then died tragically young of cancer. None of the instruments in the Indian classical range, developed for temple performance to the greater glory of God, has great carrying power, a shortcoming which nowadays is got the better of by electrical amplification permitting performance in stadiums holding several thousands of listeners. But to be present, as I have been, at a "chamber music" recital by Ravi Shankar and Ali Akbar Khan, each goading the other to new heights of invention, is an experience more magical than almost any in the world. One is in the presence of creation.

Given his form and meter before he starts, like a poet commissioned to write a sonnet or a ballad, the Indian musician resembles more a medieval troubadour than a composer sitting before blank paper at his desk. He does not interpret; he *is.* An oral tradition is a wonderful thing, keeping meaning and purpose alive and accessible. As soon as an idea is confined to the printed page, an interpreter is required to unlock it. The Indian musician requires no intermediary; he creates in public and does not keep a record. Naturally I am a novice in the matter, having neglected at the age of three to begin the necessary schooling and to anchor myself in the tradition; when I play with Ravi Shankar I must learn my lines beforehand. But even at this subordinate distance from genuine improvisation, participation in Indian music means much to me—urging in sequences which will never be repeated the savoring of each note; heightening the ear's perception of the notes, the rhythms and the flexible tensions between them; increasing, as some drugs are said to do, awareness of phenomena; safeguarding against the staleness of repetition. A great artist, a Rubinstein or a Rostropovich, does not repeat, but relives his repertoire, assisted by orchestra and audience and the urge to live life to the full with the means at his disposal. But repetition remains a hazard for us all, in the office, the factory, even the concert hall; and perhaps it becomes more crucial as one reaches an age to indulge in fewer adventures, to find acceptable less new music.

I have said that Indian music sprang surprises on me, a statement which, while true enough, requires qualification. There had been a long apprenticeship in my devotion to gypsy music, one European debouching of the Indian stream. Among the earliest pieces to move me was Sarasate's "Gypsy Airs," a predictable enthusiasm for a Jewish violinist of Russian provenance, but also an augury of later passions. The phrase "It's the gypsy in me," generally offered in extenuation of disorderly conduct, bears witness, however, to a need wider than mine alone for the refreshment of living with the moment as if one had never known it before. Perhaps because I was by temperament or training inclined, even at the crest of a wave, to calculate its amplitude and momentum, I have always thirsted for abandon. Just as yoga promised release from physical impediments, so improvisation promised abandon to musical impulse. Thus, Ravi Shankar followed the gypsies and, in course of time, Stephane Grappelli, the great jazz violinist, followed Ravi Shankar, successive mentors on a journey to spontaneity. But the desire to travel that path was always latent; as probably it is for other violinists.

I was introduced to Grappelli through his recordings, which so impressed me that a few years ago I persuaded him to play with me. Again, my part was prepared in advance (by Max Harris, an excellent musician), but in our recording sessions Grappelli never repeated himself; each "take" he played differently, as the inspiration of the moment suggested. He is a man I envy almost as much as I love him, who off the cuff can use any theme to express any nuance—wistfulness, brilliance, aggression, scorn—with a speed and accuracy that stretch credulity. If we pursue our joint sessions long enough, I may, even at my advanced age, learn the knack of improvising. It is a process that cannot be hurried, however, nor can I give it the time it requires; so at present I am content with the role of novice, happy to take what jazz can teach me. To reach our apogee, we have to subjugate our natures, then to free them. In the venture, each tradition, the extempore and the interpretative, can help the other, and those musicians who synthesize the two are the most complete, the worthiest of our admiration. That is perhaps why I have always adored Enesco. As I have suggested, the lines of my life are mostly simple, rounding the circle where they are not straight.

Soon after our first visit to India, Diana and I renounced airplane travel for the better part of nine years. Since the birth of our sons, Diana had flown with teeth gritted, although without complaint until confession was wrung out of her. There had been many difficult, uncomfortable, dangerous flights in the interim, such as the occasion at Lisbon, in 1951, when our light aircraft, attempting to land in an Atlantic gale, plunged repeatedly at the runway, only to bounce up again, tossing its passengers about like peas in a bucket; and was finally pinned to the earth only when its wings were gripped by hooks on the end of long, man-handled poles. Twenty-five years ago flying was a more chancy business than it is today. I remember in particular a transatlantic crossing which Diana calls our "gremlin flight."

On 27 January 1950 I was due at the Albert Hall, London, where Sir Adrian Boult was to conduct a program including the Elgar and the Mendelssohn Violin Concerti. Diana and I left New York on the evening of the twenty-fifth, with ample time, as we presumed, to keep our appointment. With everyone secure in his safety belt, the plane shot down the runway, then halted with a tremendous screeching of brakes just short of takeoff. This was twice repeated before the shaken passengers were unloaded and told to return to the airport in the morning. (The unplanned night in New York had its reward: we went to a brilliant concert by Heifetz at Carnegie Hall.) Next day we set off to England again. To begin with, so thick was New York traffic that we almost missed the plane, which might have saved everyone a great deal of trouble. Disaster avoided, we took off at eleven-thirty, and shortly afterward the pilot made his rounds. Wanting to reassure Diana, I stopped him and suggested that the untoward incidents of the day before hadn't been too serious. In that wonderful calm bluff English way, he answered, "Airplane engines, you see, are made up of thousands of individual parts, and it is quite impossible to tell when any one of them may cease to function"; with which Job's comfort he passed on. A short while later one of those many parts did indeed cease to function: oil began blowing over the wings, and back we went to Idlewild, as it then was. At the third try, later that afternoon, we succeeded in crossing the Atlantic, making one stop to refuel in Newfoundland and another at Shannon in the Irish Republic, for one flew from landfall to landfall in those days.

Here the English weather blocked further progress: fog had closed London Airport. It was about 6:30 a.m. local time when we arrived at Shannon, too early to despair of reaching our destination. We telephoned my agent, Harold Holt, and I borrowed an airport office to practice in. However, as the hours passed and the London fog failed to lift, I grew anxious enough to try to charter from Aer Lingus a plane small enough to land in conditions which our big Stratocruiser could not cope with. For some reason Aer Lingus was not allowed to rescue us, so after more endless hours, we took off in the transatlantic plane, first at three forty-five—when the radio was found to be out of order and we had to turn back, then, finally, at four-fifteen. All hopes of rehearsing had long been abandoned, but the concert itself still seemed safe. The fog had yet a couple of tricks up its sleeve, however. After circling over Heathrow a few times in a vain attempt to find a break in the blanket below him, the pilot landed at Manston on the east coast. Diana and I were delivered to earth through the luggage shaft in the plane's belly, hustled through customs at a trot and thrust into a waiting car, which roared off the airfield with most gratifying drama. One mile farther on, the gentle fog of the countryside rolled toward us in thick, soft, totally opaque clouds, and we crawled the rest of the way at hardly more than walking speed, Diana shivering in the unheated car, for she had sacrificed her fur coat to my violins.

We were of course late. Adrian Boult had been unable to delay beginning the concert, which, among other motives for urgency, was to be broadcast. It seems he announced to his audience, seen and unseen, "We are without our Hamlet; we shall begin with the symphony." The symphony was still in progress, although nearing its end, when our car drew up at the artists' entrance, and no sooner had Diana and I reached the artists' room than Adrian summoned me to come onstage. There was no time to warm up the violin, nor to change. I went on as I was, in a tweed suit, and but for Diana's last-minute intervention, would have played the Elgar with a boarding card dangling from my lapel. After all the near misses, it was a good concert. At Claridge's later, the doorman scolded us for the fright we had given him and showed us successive editions of the evening papers: hour by hour the stop press had reported the checkered progress of the gremlin flight.

Such ordeals, even when happily concluded, were not calculated to soothe Diana's nerves. Then, as it happened, plane crashes in the late forties and early fifties made terrible inroads on musical talent, particularly violinistic: first Ginette Neveu, then my dear friend Jacques Thibaud, shortly afterward, William Kapell, the American pianist, whose plane came down on 29 October 1953, not far from our home at Los Gatos. At Kapell's death I called a halt. I was playing in Indianapolis that day, and asked the audience to observe a minute's silence in his memory, then, the concert over, telephoned Diana in California to say there would be no more planes, at least until they could avoid flying into mountains. (The recent accidents had apparently been caused by lack of knowledge of the contour of the land; more precisely, by lack of radar in civilian aircraft.) One newspaper columnist found my conduct lily-livered, and said so, provoking many an indignant letter in my defense, among which I fondly remember that of a Wiltshire colonel, who exhorted me: "Dammit, Menuhin, travel by camel if you want to!"

Our renunciation of aircraft gave us a slower tempo for a time. As long as it lasted we enjoyed it. But much as we might wish to, it would be difficult to repeat the gesture now. The glorious American trains, the transatlantic liners, are no more.

13

Spokesman for Myself and Some Others

Already David Oistrakh and I had met several times in different European cities when one early summer day in 1955 Diana and I invited him with the Soviet composer Aram Khachaturian to dinner at Claridge's in London. Oistrakh urged me to return to Moscow; nothing, I said, would give me greater pleasure, but such a journey was not to be undertaken at the drop of a hat (in fact, it took another seven years for this particular hat to reach the ground), and meanwhile wasn't it about time he made a first excursion to my own home country? "America!" exclaimed David: that was completely out of the question; he would never be allowed to land. Stalin was dead, McCarthyite hysteria was on the wane, but Khrushchev had not yet spoken to the Twentieth Party Congress and the cold war was taking its time to thaw. However, I thought I discerned enough cracks in the ice to justify boldness. I proposed, and he accepted, a wager of a pound or two that the United States would invite him to perform.

What I then did was not perhaps in the best sporting tradition, but there were at stake more important considerations than gambler's honor. That evening I sent two cables, both pressing for Oistrakh's invitation. One went to the State Department and asked the authorities to waive the fingerprinting requirement (Russians, I had found, did not take kindly to fingerprinting, associating it no doubt with the pursuit of criminals; there was *a priori* no reason to exclude violinists from the potentially criminal classes, but I could vouch for Oistrakh's respectability). The other cable was sent to Kurt Weinhold at Columbia Concerts, proposing that he arrange a tour in the autumn at the same fees I earned myself. This last stipulation was delicate: clearly David's fees should not be lower than mine, but should they be higher? Within twenty-four hours I had affirmative answers to both requests, and turned up in triumph at David's hotel to claim my winnings.

As luck would have it, I was in the United States when he arrived. Ten years, give or take a day, had gone by since he had met me on the runway at Moscow airport. I could do no less for him. A telephone call to Washington granted me authorization, and at Idlewild I walked past the waiting Russian diplomats, through immigration and customs, to stand alone on the tarmac and welcome David to America. As we entered the airport building, he said with faint embarrassment, "Look, will you forgive me? I think I must ride into town with my people. They wouldn't quite understand if, on top of being made to wait inside, they were to go home empty-handed." We talked until the baggage came up, then I surrendered him to his escorts. During his American tour, which was, predictably, a triumph, we met often, of course, and it was then that he gave me the Shostakovich Concerto.

My attempt at even-handedness in the matter of fees came to grief on the Soviet regulation which transferred foreign earnings to the state's pocket and paid the performer in rubles, at the going Soviet rate, when he returned. Within the Soviet Union, however, great musicians are doubly favored. In return for a measure of compliance, the regime treats them liberally, providing excellent training in their young days and handsome salaries, housing and other material privileges to reward achievement; in addition, they are loved by the people, whose devotion blends gratitude for pleasure received with submission before the god-like, which, while out of reach, yet suggests that divinity can be won. Music, I suspect, has a particular sway over Soviet hearts, striking an echo from the long-buried Russian past and offering solace for a work-aday reality, providing an escape for the confined human spirit. One of my favorite Russians—indeed a general favorite—is Mstislav Rostropovitch; no spirit could less properly be described as confined than his! A few years after Oistrakh's pioneering American tour, it was no longer exceptional for Russian musicians to travel to the West, and thus Slava and I found ourselves together on the same stage in New York, at a benefit concert at which Eleanor Roosevelt was the guest of honor.

We did not perform together, however. The Soviet leash may have been lengthened, but it was still firmly attached, and Hurok, the impresario who had contrived to bring Slava to the United States, was taking his Moscow instructions very seriously. I much wanted to play a trio with Leonard Bernstein and Rostropovitch on this gala occasion, but Hurok would not risk going beyond the letter of the agreement with Gosconzert. He had a personal motive to stiffen his intransigence: he had often tried and as often failed to persuade Lennie Bernstein and myself to quit our respective managements and come under his protection. "I'm not letting Rostropovitch play with those bums!" he grunted, and so saying, concealed Slava in some retreat until he could safely be produced. When Slava did turn up, at the general press rehearsal, he was warmly apologetic about the missed chance of a trio, but we hadn't supposed for a moment that it was his fault. I came to like Hurok. He was one of the last great pirate impresarios, for whom there was much to be said. They took risks, they launched artists, they were admirable entrepreneurs. My last view of him was in Moscow once, in a great fur coat, patiently pursuing some interminable negotiation with Gosconzert. I hope he concluded it successfully.

My experience of the different countries of socialist Eastern Europe owes more to the character of the individual nations than to the character of the regime they have in common. Thus, though I have often been to Rumania and Hungary, I have visited East Germany only once, finding the experience too oppressive to be tempted to repeat it.

Twenty years and more had passed since the concerts with Fritz Busch and Bruno Walter first took me to Dresden and Leipzig when, in the mid-1950s, I returned with my new German agent, Hans Adler, and was deeply moved to find myself remembered by the public. In Leipzig we were accommodated in a big hotel built for foreigners attending the trade fair, a pretentious building liberally furnished with the bloated square columns beloved by fascist architecture, which now gave cover, or at least somewhere to lean and lurk, to the informers of the secret police. There seemed little attempt to make surveillance unobtrusive: one was aware of being watched and felt on edge in consequence. In one way the concert compensated for the chilly preliminaries, in another way it underlined their bleakness. Two or three members of the orchestra recalled playing with me in 1931, and although the rather ugly new hall which replaced the ruined Gewandhaus was full to the roof, outside were crowds of young people still clamoring to be let in. From the stage their rhythmic chanting was quite audible. Adler, sitting in the audience, caught my eye and signaled a question. At my nod the doors were opened and the youngsters poured in to fill the aisles and stand at the back. When the scheduled program came to an end amid emotional ovations, I played a solo encore or two, then remarked to the conductor that the orchestra might have joined me in the Beethoven Romances, if only they had had the music with them. "We can send someone on a bicycle to fetch it," he quickly said. And all the while the messenger went and came, pedaling furiously, I imagine, the audience kept up its applause. The music was put on the stands, we played both Romances without rehearsal, then finally I tore myself away, just in time to catch the train to Munich, where Diana was waiting for me.

The German Democratic Republic has most likely changed since then, the more relaxed manners of the present possibly removing some of the nostalgia for the past which the Leipzig audience displayed; but my small experience of the country belongs to those depressing years and their shadow remains in my mind. A year or two after that concert, when I was crossing the GDR from West Berlin to West Germany, there occurred a particularly unfriendly encounter. Being supplied with a return railroad ticket at Frankfurt and a transit visa at the same time, I assumed, wrongly, that the visa, like the ticket, would function in both directions. On the return journey, therefore, at the frontier some half hour or less from the Berlin station, I was found to be attempting an illegal crossing. By this time I had undressed, settled down in my sleeper and begun reading, relishing the prospect of a quiet night ahead and arrival at Frankfurt in the morning. The border police knocked, entered, discovered my lack of a visa, and ordered me to leave the train. Not yet understanding what was amiss, I took this for a bad joke, shut the door again and went back to my bed and book. The train remained stationary. Minutes passed. Then the police returned, the more peremptory for my ignoring their instructions. Clearly I would have to do as I was told, but with the age-old resentment of impotence, I took my time to dress and repack my bags. I was ushered off the train and into the office of the station police chief. Two other passengers were similarly made to disembark.

There we sat for several hours. The police chief looked at our papers again, and if my name was known to him, he did not admit it. Nothing further happened. I consoled myself with the reflection that there was still half the night to go before my failure to arrive at Frankfurt alarmed Diana. Then, without explanation vouchsafed us, another passenger and I were put into an automobile such as I have not seen before or since, designed presumably for the transport of suspects: it had a capacious back seat but, without doors at the back, discouraged hopes of a leap to freedom. Such drama was anyway not required. We were driven to an outlying station on the West Berlin suburban network and left there with our luggage. Fortunately a late train eventually arrived, returning empty to the city. Without a ticket, or anybody to worry whether I had one or not, I was carried to the Kurfürstendamm, whose lights, after the dismal dark of the German Democratic Republic, seemed the friendliest things in the world. Next morning I took a plane, the only one in the nonflying years.

Although in Poland too I have performed only once, the strength of the Polish character has long impressed me. If they can be cruel and anti-Semitic, the Poles are still a great people, gifted, brave, surviving interminable occupations because their values, unlike ours, lie not in the immediate and the material but in what is necessary for their spirit, in their sense of origin. After the war the old city of Warsaw was rebuilt, detail by detail, before housing estates and public transport were tackled. The Poles needed to feel at home.

The one journey which Diana and I made to Warsaw, in 1956, was memorably eventful in the manner of those days (indeed, giving up aircraft, we did not give up adventure). En route from Vienna, our comfortable old Austrian train was stopped in Czechoslovakia and all its passengers decanted onto a far from comfortable Czech train with seats so narrow and slippery that the force of gravity kept tumbling one to the floor. Here we spent sixteen hours. The change of trains, on the pretext of some technical shortcoming in the Austrian rolling stock, was—we were given to understand—a common occurrence, a covert little gesture of hostility in the ongoing cold war. Tired, dirty and disheveled, we arrived at last, and found half musical Warsaw awaiting us at the station.

Just as I had debated with myself about returning to Hungary after 1956, so, twelve years later, Czechoslovakia confronted me with my conscience. Before the Russian invasion turned the "Prague spring" to winter, imposing the only order the Soviets know, which is brute order, a benefit concert had been arranged. Should I keep the engagement? Some Czechs at home and abroad very decidedly discouraged my going, others were equally sure that I should go. I went, and thus experienced one of the most moving occasions I have known. It was far more than the music which spoke to the people; it was the fact—as in 1945—that I was an American, representing freedom, hope and salvation (that salvation which we did not provide). It was a demonstration of defiance, courage, solidarity with the higher values of life. Had Czechoslovakia been allowed to continue its experiment, the world might have seen a new sort of civilization, one reconciling the best of communism and the best of the West, one which might have pointed the way for mankind.

In a lifetime before the public one develops antennae for their responses. Like a dog who knows it is evoking sympathy or fear or impatience, one senses an emanation of good will or otherwise, as unmistakable as it is intangible. In my experience the anticipatory emanation has nearly always been sympathetic, a welcome established over the years which I look forward to and rely upon. But sometimes the warmth has been missing and the recital a failure. There was one such occasion on the Aleutian island of Adak during the war. Baller and I were stopping there over the midday hours on our way farther west, and since there was a hole in our schedule, the local officer suggested we fill it with an impromptu concert at the camp cinema, the advertised film being postponed to make way for us. It was a disaster. Half the audience stayed on from an earlier showing of the film, idly curious to hear this violinist thrust upon them; the other half resented having to wait for their favorite star. After two or three numbers it was obvious there was no forging rapport with these listeners; I signed off with the "Ave Maria" and left. A similar failure occurred in Puerto Rico. Here the organizers, opting for spectacle, had me play out of doors and assembled an audience of respectable magnitude by ferrying in truckloads of conscripts from a nearby army camp. The young servicemen didn't know me, had never heard my kind of music, and couldn't hear it now anyway, the amplification being so poor that the sound hardly reached beyond the third row. So the captive audience talked and fidgeted and wondered what they were there for, and again I cut the blunder short.

Normally such debacles are avoided. The business of advance announcement and ticket selling selects one's audience and predisposes it in one's favor, a sifting process more valuable than idealists may be willing to admit. Almost always a free concert brings an audience without commitment to the occasion, fretful sultans waiting to chop off Scheherazade's head unless she seduces them into listening. An exception is the audience in Central Park, in New York, at summer concerts. On the other hand, the charity audience which pays inflated sums has often made me feel the music was dear at the price, that having done their duty they could scarcely be expected to display enthusiasm as well. One city can contain many audiences, differences reflected the world over, but it is nonetheless possible to speak of national audiences, not only in that they appreciate the music of native composers—Elgar in England, Fauré in France, Reger in Germany—but in their different responses in general.

Of all audiences, the German and the Japanese are the most disciplined and polite. The Japanese especially are reverently inaudible beyond belief—one simply doesn't know they are there. Two Americans appropriate more space and effect more distraction than a thousand Japanese, whose rapt attention and quasi-invisibility are such as might unnerve the unaccustomed artist. It used not to be the manner of their country to applaud, but applause like other Western habits, good and bad, has taken root in postwar Japan and ovations now are respectably enthusiastic. The Germans' love of music prompts a reaction I have found in no other country: at the end of a piece, applause never comes immediately, but a fractional pause is made, balancing the pause before the music starts, framing it in silence; then the hall applauds as one man, for there is no dissenter in a German audience. In Israel, in contrast, there are only dissenters. As one looks along the front row of the Fredrick Mann Auditorium in Tel Aviv, one sees as many varieties of expression as there are people. Someone is madly applauding; his neighbor, arms folded, remains unconvinced. A whole recital usually contrives to weld these unrepentant individualists into a unity, but one feels one must win from each his personal surrender.

Unfairly in my view, the English audience has the reputation of saving its coughs and sneezes for slow movements. This has not been my experience. I have found, even in the smallest British towns, a very touching genuine response, a vein of true sentiment which resists pretension. It may be that I am biased toward the English: so many tributes have reached me, backstage and through the mails, that I play to the English audience persuaded they are already my friends. I have, too, a special tenderness for the Moscow public, associated in my memory with students who seem to be familiar with corners and crevices of the auditorium unknown to other people, whose heads, like the Baron's illegitimate children in the last act of *Rosenkavalier,* pop out of the most unexpected places. The Russian audience can also surprise: once in Odessa—in a hall, therefore, full of as many Jews as Russians, all of them cognoscenti—the well-wishers gathered in the artists' room after the recital offered few compliments on my playing, few comments on my interpretations, but, to a man, demanded to know how I fingered this or that passage.

After the Israelis, the greatest individualists in my view are the

French. Shortly after the war, Louis Kentner and I gave a recital in the Salle Pleyel in Paris. The hall was full, right down to the *strapontins* which fold down in the aisles, and to this mass audience we proposed to present Bartók, then scarcely known in France. The Sonata Number 1 was heard in considerate, or possibly considering, silence, and as it finished a fair volume of applause broke out. From the gallery, however, came shouts of *"Ridicule!" "Absurde!"*—the only spontaneous negative reaction I believe I have ever encountered. No tomatoes were thrown; in fact, the gallery's thumbs-down only incited the rest of the hall to redouble its applause, which went on so long that finally it brought Kentner and me back to replay the last movement. Now, the last movement is relatively long. The prospect of being subjected to it again was more than one man in the hall could tamely countenance. He was seated on a *strapontin* in the central aisle—that is, in full view of the stage. Taking from his pocket a newspaper (the French can fold newspapers smaller than any other people), he patiently unfolded it, spread it to its full width, and read it with flamboyant concentration until Bartók, Kentner and I were done with. I had wondered if he might leave the hall, but the French know the value of money. He had paid for his ticket, made his gesture and meant to hear the rest of the program.

The American audience's great virtue is, as I have suggested, its openness of mind. It was no accident that the first Indian musicians I contrived to bring to the United States—Ali Akbar Khan and Chatur Lal, in 1955, at the invitation of the Museum of Modern Art—should win immediate appreciation, for Americans have few barriers of prejudice to demolish but rather a predisposition in favor of the new. Undoubtedly such a cast of mind reflects national experience. So too did a reaction to a controversy I provoked in December 1957, a reaction which displayed all my countrymen's preference for the exercise of spontaneous initiative over the regimentation of authority or tradition.

The *mise en scène* was provided by the New York Philharmonic, with which I was to give four concerts on four successive days. At the first, on Thursday, December 12, I played the Bloch Concerto, an overlooked, underplayed work whose inclusion in the program I had insisted on as a tribute to a great, neglected and stricken composer (already ill then, Bloch died in 1959). So warm and sustained was the ovation that I asked the conductor, Previtali, if I might give an encore, and, with his permission, played a short piece of unaccompanied Bach, which was well received. All very routine, you may think; but as I promptly learned backstage, my encore, far from being routine, had broken—nay, dese-crated—the traditions of the New York Philharmonic Orchestra. To this day New York's elevated musical standards rule out encores as mere self-indulgence for soloists, this high-mindedness gaining further support from conductors who wish to keep the program to schedule, and from orchestra boards who don't wish to pay musicians overtime for sitting idle while (as they see it) a soloist plays to the gallery. Previtali, being a guest conductor, could be excused for failing to grasp this New York peculiarity (and *agreeing* to my encore, for I always ask the conductor), but I, as an old touring hand, should have known better, or so it seemed. In the warmth of the moment I responded to the audience's emotion as I would have done in Paris, Rome, Vienna, Berlin or London.

Next day's reviews left no doubt of the enormity of my offense, but while some critics roundly deplored my manners, others enjoyed the drama, and the humor, of the occasion. Among these was the critic of the *Herald Tribune,* which headlined its account "Menuhin Fiddles While Orchestra Board Burns." The result of this publicity was to electrify the second concert, held on Friday afternoon, an event which at any other time would have passed unnoticed by the wider world. Friday afternoon is subscription day, attracting an audience which attends with something of the same dutiful regularity as it attends its hairdresser, its dentist and its club, and which never permits its applause to pass the bounds of seemliness. Not this Friday. The auditorium was as full as possible, and everyone in it seemed determined I should have my encore. It was not a question of pleasing or moving them: if I had stood on my head or whistled through my teeth, they would have done as they did; which was to clap and call and stamp and shout until they brought me back for a third, a fourth and a fifth time. Like theirs, my blood was up. Encour-aged by the orchestra, I played an encore for them.

This pushed the question beyond a musical dispute to a moral issue, even prompting newspaper editorials. To my gratification, the vast majority, perhaps ninety percent, championed the assertion of individ-uality against the rules laid down from above, the compliance with the public's wishes against the regulations of the stuffed shirts. With all these troops behind me, I risked a bolder defiance at the Saturday eve-ning concert. Once again the hall was full; once again at the end of the Concerto an extraordinary volume of sound broke from the audience; but this time I did not let my violin speak for me, or for them. I made a speech (today, I trust, I would not succumb to the temptation). "I am not allowed to play an encore," I told them. "Soon *you* won't be allowed to applaud. If Bach could have known the irreparable damage to the traditions and budget of the New York Philharmonic that only two minutes of his music would cause, I am sure he would be deeply grieved. In spite of the fact that these concerts, unlike those of other great orchestras, seem to be directed by extramusical forces, I would like to assure you on behalf of my colleagues on the stage, and myself, how much we love and are grateful for your enthusiasm and support. You may applaud as long as you like and whenever you like." Diana scolded me for the unwisdom of this speech; so did my agent Kurt Weinhold; and I was sufficiently chastened by their distress to attempt no gesture at the fourth, and last, concert on Sunday night. But the ovation went on, and on, and on. It lasted as long as any encore I might have given, as no doubt the audience intended.

As a musician, well aware that art must have local roots if it is to convey universal meaning, I view evidences of national difference, even the perhaps insignificant ones I have cited, with approval as well as interest. The yearning to preserve a distinctive culture which sets the Basque against Madrid, the Scot against Westminster, the American Indian against Washington (however vastly these examples differ in degree), wins my sympathy. Undeniably the aspiration is legitimate and worthy. But is it possible, given human nature, to separate good from bad, the wish for cultural autonomy from the wish to impose one's way of life on one's neighbors? For me—the product of an upbringing not exclusively Jewish, not exclusively American, nor exclusively any other thing; one who has lived in many parts of the world and established ties with Asians, Africans and Europeans, as well as his beloved Americans; one who has spent his life bridging gaps—exclusivity as expressed in nationalism is not enough. I find it stifling. I also find it dangerous, for it carries within itself the seeds of its destruction. The first premise of existence is interdependence—not at the level of human organization alone, but throughout that cycle of activity embracing man and microbe, the worm and the swallow, in a complex of interlocking functions, all moving to the complementary rhythms of life and death. My ideal world would express its interdependence in a burning desire for understanding, a true sympathy, a readiness to pardon, which would sacrifice no strength, spare neither itself nor its enemies, but through its even-handed honesty would win universal trust—like a good doctor who is rigorous with his patients while healing all alike, saint or sinner, enemy or friend.

I understand the appeal of exclusivity, its virtues, even the need for it. But it is not my way.

In music there is a temptation to view technique and interpretation as distinct, or—if so artless an antithesis is resisted—to see interpretation as already existing, needing only a vehicle, and limited or released by the lesser or greater perfection of technique. Faced some years ago with conducting the *Eroica* Symphony, I demonstrated the error of this notion in a rather singular way. Some half century of *Eroicas* had naturally fostered a conception of the music, but when I came to prepare it for performance, I played through the first-violin part and found my fingers suggesting ideas which listening and study had not prompted. Such interplay of means and ends seems at least as true of human endeavor in general as of artistic striving. Thus, the call for equal justice in the American Constitution, which yet permitted the massacre of Indians and the enslavement of blacks, is now acknowledged to apply to those excluded minorities, and will one day, let us hope, be extended beyond bipeds of whatever ancestry to quadrupeds and every living thing, if only in self-preservation. Similarly, Christian ideals survived to condemn in retrospect the Inquisition, and communism feels obliged to present oppression in terms of ideal claims. Vision hauls practice upward, and in rising, practice pushes farther the boundaries of vision.

Some visions prove more fragile than others, however: if the Constitution (or Christianity or communism) has still power to inspire, the American dream has lost its confidence. In my lifetime I have seen my country stir to consciousness of strength and mission—and subside, battered by repeated failure and the world's abuse, into a new uncertainty. There is something both pathetic and sympathetic about the American of today, a touching quality which his fathers did not have. One is tempted to advise him to be less willing to wear sackcloth, to point out that other dreams—the French and Russian as well as the American revolution—have also fallen short, that to be no better than others is to be at least their equal.

Britain, which of all countries of the world has evolved with a minimum of revolution and the guillotine, is supremely fortunate in its daily acknowledgment of a value higher than power. Just as in a coral reef the remains of previous generations constitute the physical protection of the species, so in Britain the fossilized heritage of the past gives checks and counterchecks to society, most strikingly in the vestigial, symbolic presence of the monarchy which commands a loyalty owing nothing to power. Power must always be partisan; it belongs to money or the military, to Republican or Democrat, left or right, capital, labor or bureaucrat—to those in power. To have a nonpower above power seems to me the ultimate safeguard.

So, I, who once jibbed at kissing a royal hand, have come to admire constitutional monarchy, while never being tempted to reject my American inheritance. I am a passive sort of person: put me somewhere and I grow roots which no amount of traveling can wrench up. Just as I have kept the same managements throughout my professional life, so the recording company with whom I signed a contract as a child is still the company I record with. At a more positive level of commitment, passive acceptance of the *status quo* becomes conscious loyalty. I see no point in pretending to be other than I am: as I would not change my name, or be baptized, so I remain an American.

There was, briefly, a moment when my American identity came under threat. In mid-November 1970 I applied for renewal of my passport at the American embassy in Bern, only to be told that under what was called "a preliminary decision" I must lose my citizenship for having accepted some months earlier honorary citizenship in Switzerland. Two Swiss cantons had proposed the honor: Bern, where I had long organized the annual Gstaad festival, and Solothurn, in recognition of a foundation established to help young musicians of the locality. Having (like the United States) no titles to bestow upon civilians, the Swiss sometimes offer this greatest of all marks of appreciation—one which carries considerable weight, for not only is it accorded to one's family but, once Swiss, one's descendants remain Swiss forever, a fact which saved many a Central European Jew with a knowledge of his forefathers.

Other countries apparently are not dismayed to see one of their own so honored, but in the United States, it seemed, a second allegiance was held to displace the first. However, stay of execution on the "preliminary decision" was granted and my passport extended to allow me to fulfill engagements in London and New York. Meanwhile I addressed a protest to the secretary of state, William P. Rogers, pointing out that Winston Churchill had been granted honorary American citizenship without anyone in London casting doubts upon his loyalty, and asserting, as vigorously as I could word it, that if my American citizenship was to be taken from me, it would have to be the government's doing, without my cooperation. The affair soon reached the newspapers, and the consequent publicity settled the issue in a couple of days, during which newspapermen supplied me with bulletins of events as they happened. It appeared that Mr. Rogers was in Brussels at the time, on diplomatic business, and

that directly after disembarking from the plane which brought him home
he signed a letter to me, apologizing for the misunderstanding, hoping I
would always be an American, congratulating me on Switzerland's gesture. A *New York Times* reporter told me of the contents of this letter
that evening and, sure enough, some days later it arrived.

By way of footnote to this story, I should perhaps recount the
moment of my greatest humiliation. Licensed to drive in the United
States from the age of twelve, I had later acquired a British and an
international driving license (having passed a test in Edinburgh), and
was therefore, as I am, qualified to be in charge of a motorcar anywhere
on earth; but I thought it would show a sense of the honor done me by
the grant of Swiss citizenship to drive in Switzerland on a Swiss license.
So I applied for a test. It took place on the appointed day in Thun, the
administrative center nearest to Gstaad.

The examiner put me through the most difficult requirements of
urban Thun and its neighboring mountains, made me back up inclines
and into narrow spaces, park on hills and show all the other essential
skills of a Swiss driver. All went perfectly. Then we came to the oral part
of the test, and to the highway code. Now, the Swiss have innumerable
cabalistic road signs of every variety, some seemingly delivered from
druidical or runic sources, others from ancient Egyptian hieroglyphs,
some in one color, others in others, and all these nuances expressing a
wealth of meaning. I had of course neglected to master the complexities,
and the upshot was I failed. Gerard was with me at the time and hadn't
words to express his view of the injustice done me. I knew there was no
injustice; road fatalities being what they are, the examiners cannot be too
severe. But such reflections were small consolation for my awful fall from
grace. I continue to drive in Switzerland—indeed I drove, quite legally,
away from the debacle—but so far I have not ventured to apply for a
second test. Honor demands that one of these days, before senility sets
in, I try again.

To choose is to reject, an action painful to those greedy for experience.
All my life I have had to renounce options in deference to the timetable,
plucking up little shoots before they flower so as to permit something else
to grow. Thus, touring the Soviet Union with Diana and Hephzibah late
in 1962, though I at last reached Odessa, mother city of Russian violinists and therefore my own grandmother city, as it were, the extra week
which would have granted me acquaintance with the Crimea could not
be spared. I have not yet seen the marvelous countryside of my mother's

tales. That visit, the longest I have so far made to the country, occurred at the high point of Khrushchev's liberalism, in the year when Aleksandr Solzhenitsyn's *One Day in the Life of Ivan Denisovich* was published, and took in a whole range of towns—Kiev, Minsk, Lvov and Kishinev, as well as Moscow, Leningrad and Odessa. Since then my standing in Soviet regard has taken a turn for the worse. My outspoken regret when the screws of censorship were tightened, when the Russians invaded Czechoslovakia, and when Jews lost their jobs for applying to emigrate to Israel, incurred displeasure, especially that of the late Madame Furtseva, the minister of culture. Matters came to a head when the biennial congress of the International Music Council was to be held in Moscow in October 1971.

Two years earlier in New York, I had been unanimously elected president of the IMC, an autonomous offshoot of UNESCO, and was expected to attend the Moscow meeting to preside over its deliberations and submit myself for re-election. Furtseva's antagonism, however, threatened to interfere with this program. We never had the dubious pleasure of making each other's acquaintance, but she proved quite ready to dislike me at a distance. During the two or three years before 1971 I had pressed for David Oistrakh's attendance at the Gstaad festival, using the good offices of the Swiss embassy in Moscow to plead my cause. After repeated disappointment, the ambassador asked for an interview with Furtseva herself, and was roundly told she would never allow a Russian artist to play with me again. In the circumstances I did not see how I could be present at the Moscow congress—unless by some unpalatable doublethink I pretended that the welcome IMC president and the unwelcome violinist were different people. These sentiments made known to the IMC secretariat, Furtseva relented sufficiently to send not David, but Igor Oistrakh to Gstaad in August 1971, a compromise I was happy to accept.

My years in office had added new friends to the long list of musicians from every nation met in the course of travel, so Moscow offered, among other pleasures, that of reunion. Shostakovich, Khachaturian and Dmitri Kabalevsky were there. Two missing faces, however, were those of David Oistrakh, then in Stockholm, and Mstislav Rostropovitch, who, accompanied by the redoubtable Furtseva herself, was in Vienna (I have no evidence that Furtseva had set up this excursion to avoid shaking my presidential hand). The first days were given to reports from the national delegations, after which the election of officials took place, the president's office being the last to be filled. I left the hall while the delegates voted, then was called back and told that my re-election had been unanimous, the Russians having proposed me and the Americans having seconded the proposal.

What more could one ask? It seemed to me, however, that I could not simply bask in the general good will, that on the contrary, unanimous election carried with it an obligation to say those things which people less securely positioned could not afford to say. What I said at the Moscow congress was not courageous, for what could be done to me other than banishment from the U.S.S.R.? Herein lay my duty as I saw it. I could speak in Russia as a free person, and as the only person in that situation in the position to speak, I must do so as if the world were normal, without barriers, without prejudices: not to condemn the Soviet Union, not to stand as a representative of capitalism (heaven forbid) and scold the Russians for undemocratic misbehavior; but to speak frankly and humanly, deploring all our faults, grateful for what did any of us credit, hopeful of a better future. And while I spoke no one would interrupt me.

The election of officers ended a morning session; the opening of the public congress was to occur at three o'clock in the afternoon. Between these two events I returned to the hotel and collected my speech, which I had learned in Russian so that I could dispense with an interpreter, and which I had also had translated into several languages for distribution to the press. Then I got up on the podium and began my address. I spoke of my feeling for Russia, land of my ancestors, of music's contribution to mankind, of Russia's contribution to music, of all nations' interdependence in today's shrunken world; I balanced the perils of political suppression of art with those of its commercial exploitation, and suggested that such abuses harmed victimizer as well as victim. There was more to come—about man's need to be himself, able to live where his heart called him; compliments to Russian achievement in musical education, and so forth—but whatever was said in the second half of my speech, whether covertly reproachful or overtly enthusiastic, broke uselessly against the Russians' stony faces like waves breaking against granite. My crime was to have named Solzhenitsyn, along with Shostakovich and Yevtushenko, as present-day illustrations of the vision and profundity of Russian art. At that rejected name, the ice age descended upon the hall, and nothing I said subsequently served to lift it.

Normally, I gather, a speech by a foreign dignitary, a guest of the Soviet Union, would have been noticed in the press, but neither *Pravda* nor *Izvestia* nor any other newspaper, nor television, nor radio, carried so much as a word. But the channels of contraband information were in good repair, it seemed, and by that evening and throughout the following days I was enjoying lightning encounters with anonymous Muscovites who knew all about it. In the street, in theatre cloakrooms after concerts, I would feel a hand touch me, or a gift slipped into my pocket, and hear a whispered congratulation. Yevtushenko, a fine poet and a very likable fellow, whose name I had so dangerously coupled, scorned secrecy. He came to see me with his poetry teacher, a charming old man, and congratulated me openly in defiance of possible hidden microphones. I did not know what to make of this: was it Yevtushenko's initiative? Was he just a court jester licensed for nonconformity to prove Soviet tolerance? Was it some curious devious official assurance that all was forgiven?

Before I could come to a conclusion, Jack Bornoff, the invaluable executive secretary of the IMC, told me that Soviet officialdom was deeply angry with me; but for the moment they kept their displeasure to themselves and the congress continued on its predestined course without further incident.

I had come to Moscow hoping to intervene on behalf of two Soviet citizens whose grievances had been brought to my attention in London: one had been imprisoned for his politics, one had defected to the West and wanted his family to join him. Requests for help for such people often come my way and I would in normal circumstances send an appeal or sign a protest. This time, as I was coming to Moscow myself, I resolved to make the appeal a personal one, and asked therefore to speak to a member of the government. Whether my petition was out of the ordinary, I don't know, but it took the authorities to the eleventh hour to grant it. On the last morning, a few hours before our plane was due to leave, I was summoned to Gosconzert to see not Furtseva, still in Vienna, nor her deputy Kukharsky, also out of Moscow, but the number three in the ministry, Supagin. It was a bit like being interviewed for a job. On the official side of a table long enough for a board meeting sat Supagin, flanked on one side by another functionary, who occasionally interposed a remark, and on the other by yet another, who kept his mouth shut and took notes. On the petitioner's side I was joined by the guide-interpreter assigned to Diana and me, a splendid Wagnerian blonde whom we nicknamed Brünnhilde, who spoke English as well as I did myself and knew the highways and byways of English literature rather better.

The conversation began amicably enough. After an exchange of civilities I said I had a question which the ordinary Russian wouldn't be able to answer: I had been most impressed by Soviet education and foresaw that in ten or fifteen years Russia might have the most informed and cultivated population of any country in the world; if so, did the government think it possible to continue running the country in the manner it was run now? Supagin's reply was no doubt sincere. He recognized that the West laid greater emphasis on the individual and his liberty than did the U.S.S.R., but now the West was paying for this choice in violence and drug abuse. "We can't afford to let people do what they want, because we have great plans," he said.

Well, I had my answer, such as it was, and was ready to move on to the real motive for the interview when he suddenly said, "You think we are having a very pleasant conversation, don't you? But I am German-trained"—meaning, I deduced, that he elevated thoroughness above amiable chat—"and I have a question for you: Why did you mention Solzhenitsyn?"

Taken aback by this turn, I had, however, sufficient presence of mind to say I had wanted to pay tribute to the greatest Russians.

"Solzhenitsyn," he pronounced, "is neither a great Russian nor a great writer. He does not deserve to be free. If the laws of our country were effective he would be in prison." (As everyone knows, the Soviet penal system not being proof against international outcry, Solzhenitsyn was subsequently sent not to prison, but into exile by force.)

"I don't agree with you and neither does the world," I replied.

"Have you seen him?"

Happily I had not—happily, because if I had, it would have done Solzhenitsyn no good and Rostropovitch, who had lent the writer his dacha, some harm. The interview, now becoming an interrogation, went on for some time, growing ever more hostile on Supagin's part. At one moment he said a word in praise of Stalin, which didn't surprise me: I could see he was a man always to be on the right side and that Stalinism was becoming respectable again. However, I had no more time for sparring. I had to catch the plane, so abruptly brought up my two deserving cases. As I began to read the details of the first one, Brünnhilde suggested it would be quicker if she translated into Russian off the page. I handed her the document. Until now, through all the increasingly harsh turns the conversation had taken, Brünnhilde's equanimity had remained unimpaired, but as she detailed the injustices suffered by one Soviet citizen she began to be upset.

"Capitalist propaganda!" commented Supagin acidly when she had finished: his equanimity at any rate was not to be disturbed by such trifles. The second case fared no better. I stood up, keeping exasperation in check, to take my leave. "If I have offended you," I said, "it's only because there is no one in the world who would more like to be friends with you. The world will be a sad place if we cannot speak to each other. I've done my best. I don't know that you have accepted it in the spirit in which it was meant. But there we are. Goodbye."

In the car I let my control give a little. "If there's any type of human being I hate, it is the bureaucrat who butters his bread at the expense of people in his power," I began, then lost my powers of indignation, and went on, "I suppose this is all absolute nonsense. I've wasted my breath. It's not going to make the least difference." "Oh, no, no!" said Brünnhilde. "It's terribly important!" Neither she nor I opened our mouths again for the remainder of the drive. Boris Yarustovsky, head of IMC's Russian national committee, came to the airport to see us off. He contrived to have the last word. "If only you hadn't said that!" he complained, mourning my tribute to Solzhenitsyn. Well, if I hadn't said "that," things would have gone beautifully, on oiled wheels, but maybe the forgotten would have been more forgotten. I had no triumph to celebrate, but I wasn't repentant.

About three years later I met Aleksandr Solzhenitsyn and his wife in Zurich. After a concert Diana and I invited them to supper at our hotel—a supper which included a large drum of excellent Iranian caviar. In one respect at least we had something worthy of our guests.

As before from a distance, so now in person, Solzhenitsyn impressed me tremendously. Here if anywhere outside *Parsifal* was a *heilige Tor,* a Prince Myshkin, a "blessed fool." One recognized that good too had eternal roots, that there could be in man a strength which simply refused to compromise or to accept the unclean. One might not always agree with his tactics, but it is precisely because he is not a tactician that he is important in a world of degrees and accommodation. He is more than a writer. He is a cleansing personality, a prophet with a mission to his own country and to us all.

Slava Rostropovitch, as all the world is aware, had his knuckles rapped for championing Solzhenitsyn. Having known Rostropovitch many years, and finding him an enchanting character as well as a great musician, I would have been heartily sorry for his predicament in any case, but as events fell out, I was marginally involved in it.

Early in January 1974, IMC's twenty-fifth anniversary was to be celebrated in Paris with a concert, among other festivities, at which Rostropovitch, Dietrich Fischer-Dieskau, Wilhelm Kempff, Régine Crespin, and others including myself were to perform. The arrangements were made, the program printed, the television broadcast set afoot, when, just before Christmas, I heard that Slava had suffered a heart attack. Straightaway I telephoned his wife, the singer Vishnevskaya, in Moscow to say how distressed I was. "A heart attack?" she exclaimed. "Whoever told you that? He's in the best of health. He's conducting in Georgia at the moment, but I expect him in Moscow by the weekend."

Excellent news though this was, it confirmed my suspicions and laid bare a sinister design. The rumor of Rostropovitch's illness, reaching the IMC secretariat by way of Czechoslovak musicians returned from the Soviet Union, indicated in roundabout fashion that Slava was to be prevented from appearing in Paris, while the punitive nature of the ban was concealed from outsiders. Already for two years he had been refused permission to go abroad and had suffered other penalties—rarely allowed to perform in Moscow, directed to the provinces instead, withdrawn late in the day from conducting an operetta he was preparing on the grounds that the work of this foremost musician was "not good enough." Pinpricks, no doubt, in comparison with what the undocile artist had suffered a generation before, but nonetheless wearing to the spirit. The ham-handed furtiveness of Soviet tactics told me what line I should take.

I was in Berlin at the time. From there I sent a telegram to the Ministry of Culture to say that, contrary to report, Rostropovitch was in good health, we were not imbeciles to be taken in by lies, and we expected him to play at the Paris concert as had been agreed. The return telegram attempted bribery: the ministry proposed sending in Slava's place Shostakovich with a new quartet he had written and the Borodin Quartet, their best, to play it, all expenses to be borne by the Soviet government. "Very kind suggestion," I cabled. "Shostakovich heartily welcome, but we will accept no substitute for Rostropovitch." Their response was to repeat the offer, requesting official invitations for Shostakovich and company. The correspondence might have continued for another half-dozen exchanges without further progress, so I addressed my third telegram over Furtseva's head to Leonid Brezhnev, and threatened to release to the press the whole story of Rostropovitch's punishment and the exchange of cables, pointing out the harm this might do to détente. That afternoon Slava got his visa.

Arriving in Paris on 6 January 1974, he reminded me of those dogs kept in kennels on transatlantic ships who, let loose on land, romp crazily around, not knowing where to put themselves. He was like a little boy, laughing, shouting, pinching himself to make sure these really were the streets in Paris. In recognition of my part in bringing him there, he offered to play with me at my sixtieth birthday concerts, arrangements which at the time of writing still stand.

To leave one's country is at best an unsatisfactory solution for an artist, who must draw life from his culture. Since music crosses cultural barriers more easily than literature, expatriation for a Rostropovitch is a less dismaying prospect than for a Solzhenitsyn, but though Slava makes the most of freedom, he has sacrificed much, not least his teaching career at the Moscow conservatoire. One of the many admirable features of Russian musical education is the duty laid on great virtuosi to pass on their skills. The only exception I know of is Sviatoslav Richter, whose eccentricity makes him a law unto himself.

I first met Richter in London, on which occasion he and his distinguished wife came to dinner at our house at Highgate, but long before I or anyone in the West knew him, his reputation loomed large. In the early postwar years other Russian pianists would confide, "We are just pale shadows of the best of us, and he is Richter." His visit to Highgate coinciding with a lovely autumn evening, we took the air in our little garden and I made laborious attempts at civil conversation.

"You're going back to Moscow now?"

"Yes."

"Will you be performing?"

"Oh, no! I never play in winter."

"Will you be teaching, then?"

"I never teach! I hate teaching!"

"Perhaps you prefer the south, the Crimea, in winter?"

"I detest the Crimea."

"Do you go out much, to the theatre, the opera?"

"I never go out."

"What *do* you do, then?" I asked, defeated for further suggestions.

"I hibernate. I will give as many concerts as you want in summer, but in winter I hibernate." He became quite animated as he described how he contrived to do this: apparently he had been allowed to build a little house by a river near Moscow, in a region normally reserved for fishermen, which (he claimed) had walls as thick as the span of his arms and windows no larger than the circle made by finger and thumb. Protected against the weather's worst, it was also protected against human society, for there was no road, only a jeep could reach the house, "and then not always." However, as the evening wore on, and when we played the Brahms G Major Sonata together, it became ever more difficult to believe him the misanthrope he made himself out to be. He had just come from the United States, and upon Diana's asking how the country struck him, volunteered the information that he particularly liked Chicago. In response to our astonished looks, he explained, "In Chicago I had the feeling, whenever I left the hotel, that *anything* could happen." A few years later I witnessed a happening that perhaps satisfied Richter's thirst for unplanned excitements.

In New York in the early 1970s, Diana and I attended a recital given in Carnegie Hall by David Oistrakh and Sviatoslav Richter. The opening sonata, the Beethoven Number 6 in A Major (beautifully played, of course), passed without incident, then, in the first movement of the Brahms D Minor, a young man raced down the aisle, leaped onto the stage and shouted, "Soviet Russia is no better than Nazi Germany!" The music halted and Oistrakh left the stage, but Richter sat on at the piano, observing with interest the thin, taut, fanatical young fellow still screaming protests against Soviet treatment of the Jews. That New York militants plotted a demonstration was known, but the two or three policemen in the hall failed to forestall it. One plump officer, his hips bulging with weapons, lumbered after the demonstrator and was levered by members of the audience onto the stage, where he took the youth in tow. Oistrakh came back, the Brahms Sonata was begun again and reached its last movement before a second young man sprinted toward the stage, this time to be neatly intercepted by the audience. At the intermission Diana and I went backstage. Richter was gleeful, but poor David sat on a divan, drained and miserable, while his wife, Tamara, hovered anxiously about: with a couple of heart attacks on his medical record, he could not be expected to benefit nor she to be reassured by such shocks. "Yehudi," he asked, looking up with a rueful smile. "*Waren das deine Juden oder meine Juden?*"—"Were those your Jews or mine?" "*Das waren unsere Juden,*" I replied—"They were ours." It was nothing but the truth.

I think I have sufficiently protested my interest in what survives. The obverse of this enthusiasm is a certain lack of trust in the new, a skepticism about revolutions and other sudden departures, which from Israel's foundation, has caused me concern for its future. For two thousand years we Jews survived without a land to call our own, only strengthened by pogroms, inquisitions, holocausts, only rendered the more resilient for having nothing to defend, and, by the same token, obliged to handle the abstractions of ideas, words, money, mathematics,

music, which escaped the blunt materialist categories of oppressive laws.
We were the salt of the earth, giving savor to all countries for having a
claim upon none. I regret to see this image reduced to the small measure
of a single state, and while I regret, I fear it. Eternally victims of some
authority or another, in the past we fought our battles in a different
dimension and for a different victory from our persecutors. Now we must
fight the same war as the enemy and may win it or lose it. The Jew
has suffered for his religion and his race; now he must suffer for his
nationality. It may be the greatest peril yet.

And yet, though I can never be a Zionist, nor concur in a purely
nationalistic destiny, Israel has taken me by storm. It is in itself extraordinary that one of the world's oldest civilizations can be reborn to such
vigorous youth. Perhaps, for all the shortcomings I ascribe to national
movements, a jolt such as a revolution or the winning of independence
or a country injects life as no other historical process can; a life which, in
Israel's case, was flooded with elation by reason of what went before—
the belief, nourished over long centuries with blood and patience, prayer
and dreams, that the Promised Land would be Jewish once more, and, in
the short term, the terrifying chain of events which made it possible. No
one can deny the apparent paradox of this determined dynamic nation—
created out of the emotional intangibles of devotion and faith over two
thousand years; nurtured by persecution, prejudice, and fitful opportunity; welding hundreds of thousands of wretched refugees (the most
heterogenous assembly of bloods and races ever), with the support of a
very advanced world community, into a stable modern state unique in the
Middle East, outstanding in its arts, crafts, sciences and freedoms. And
all this whilst the surrounding neighboring states long peopled by related
indigenous populations enjoying the benefits of vast lands, raw materials,
tremendous wealth, solar heat, and a unifying religion as well seem
unable to turn these tremendous assets into policies both farsighted and
generous. Perhaps this is an additional reason to fear the ephemeral
character of power, of property, and even of nationhood.

However, the result has been a torrent of zeal and activity which
submerges the niceties of balanced judgment. To lift one's head from two
thousand years of books and find one can wield gun or plow, to disinter
the language of one's forefathers and give it currency in kindergartens, to
absorb into a little strip of land thousands of poor broken people from
every corner of the world and build from them a society clamorous with
life and energy, cultured, democratic, and for the most part civilized—it
takes a cooler head and a soberer heart than mine to resist the attraction.

Each visit since 1950 has renewed the excitement, giving me innumerable friends in whom the country's special genius is made flesh and blood. Although they were born abroad, composers such as Ödön Partos or Paul Ben-Haim, painters such as Reuven Rubin or Moshe Castel, already show in their work the development of a native Israeli style. Israel resounds with piano and violin practice and youngsters throng the conservatory, and—while wondering if this represents the last flowering of the Russian gift or the first of the Israeli—I note with pride that Israel has given the world more than its share of great performing musicians; among them Daniel Barenboim, Gary Bertini, Pinchas Zukerman, Itzhak Perlman—one of the most generous, lively, gifted and beloved of my younger colleagues. Artistically, historically, ethnically, philologically, even medically and in numerous other ways, Israel is a fascinating experiment. I understand from medical researchers, for instance, that so great is the variety of blood groups in this little country, it forms an ideal laboratory for exploring resistance and vulnerability to disease. If only Israel survives, the Jew will offer the world yet more new contributions.

This most youthful of countries contrives both to honor its past and to not be shackled by it, making research in history, archaeology, custom, language and art a springboard for present endeavor, as if the Diaspora had only interrupted a destiny. David Ben-Gurion in particular impressed me as living out in the twentieth century the history recorded in the Bible. I met him several times, once at En Gev, the settlement below the Golan Heights, where the concert hall, pockmarked by regular bombardment, was regularly visited by the Israeli Philharmonic Orchestra. Ben-Gurion was the second statesman in whose company I stood on my head, for he too practiced yoga. Scholar and writer as he was, the hint of eruptive force in his character recalled Ernest Bloch, while his strength and presence, his integrity, which rejected the soft diplomatic word and brought him in retirement back to the land, suggested an Israeli Abraham Lincoln.

In the course of time I also had the privilege of meeting Golda Meir, an enchanting personality of true Russian spontaneity, big-hearted enough to be the world's mother, but constrained by history to reserve maternal devotion to the Jewish world alone. Early in 1974 I tried to engage Mrs. Meir's sympathy for the Palestinian refugees, believing that common sense, if no nobler motive, counseled against raising up enemies; but her commitment could not reach so far: her refugees were the Jews, come, understandably enough, to fulfill themselves, not liberate others. All the same, I grieve that chances of magnanimity should be lost. Anxious for the good name of my people, I would have Israel an example to others, extending Jewish ideals to those beyond the borders and minorities within. I would like to see Jerusalem a capital city of a new sort, serving as a spiritual focus for Muslims, Protestants, Greek Orthodox and Catholics as well as for Jews. Exclusive ambition has too often crucified Jerusalem; it must not happen again; it would be too terrible.

Is it reasonable to expect of Israel a tolerance no other country has ever shown—more especially in her present phase of ecstatic nationalism and while under threat from her neighbors? If any country can make this leap to wisdom, I do believe that it is Israel.

I have reasons for expecting much of Israel and the Jews. Take a good Israeli like Teddy Kollek, mayor of Jerusalem: an outstanding man, fully alive to the responsibilities of his position, he puts his native energy to the task of bringing together the peoples of the city. Or take a figure of world Jewry such as Nahum Goldman, who has occupied the highest positions without ever becoming a slave to any faction. A man of independent mind, great culture and unfailing humor, he seems at home in every country and persists in seeing Israel in the light of her international relationships rather than simply as the haven of the Jews. He realizes that tomorrow comes. It is no accident that he is a skilled negotiator.

Another man whom I particularly admire, who is strong in his convictions and yet meek, courageous and yet perhaps not courageous in the ordinary sense, for he does simply what he feels he must, is Joseph Abileah. Formerly a violinist in the Haifa orchestra, he is now a campaigner for a confederated Middle East. On one of my early visits to Israel he recruited me to his cause. Speaking Arabic as well as Hebrew, as welcome among Arabs as among Jews, a realistic idealist who seeks other people's solutions and does not impose his own, he works tirelessly to spur people to renounce blind nationalism in favor of a perception of common humanity, forming task forces of Israeli boys and girls to rebuild Arab houses destroyed by the army. Were the Nobel Peace Prize mine to give, it would be his: once in a while it should go to those in obscurity who devote their lives to reconciliation.

So there are hopeful elements. May they prevail. But meanwhile the Jews, outside Israel as well as within it, must identify with a state, ensuring its defense by politics and military might, and in consequence, in a short thirty years, we have worn out good will and become scapegoats to the world. It is an achievement to unite the world, no doubt, but what a price it may yet exact! My greatest dread is that the Jews of Israel may have to pay this price; my dearest wish to see the Jewish state enjoy a viable relationship with its neighbors. I am determined to be of use; but it may be my fate to defend the nation against my own ideals.

In 1975 the horns of the dilemma became for a while uncomfortably sharp. The story began when UNESCO's general assembly in November 1974 passed resolutions censuring Israel for not granting cultural autonomy to the Arabs on the occupied West Bank, for destroying Arab houses in Jerusalem and replacing them with new developments, for desecrating Muslim holy places by archaeological excavation, and so forth—genuine grievances, but couched in the war cries of international vituperation which betrayed that these issues were being exploited for political capital; that discussion ending in agreement was not the object of this antagonistic exercise. With sinking heart I saw UNESCO developing in the UN's wake into a sterile political arena. Although, like UNESCO, constituted of national delegations, the International Music Council has greater freedom of action than its parent body, and need not abide by UNESCO resolutions or, indeed, play politics at all. Directed once to expel Taiwan in the hope of tempting China into the IMC, we refused: a culture cannot be expunged from the face of the earth by political directive. So now, in the dispute over Israel, we were prepared to go our separate way—although not to the extent of severing connections with UNESCO, a course of action urged by two hundred musicians in a protest published in New York, Paris and London.

Leonard Bernstein had signed this demand. Lennie is an extraordinary musician, a cultivated, brilliant, clear-minded, socially responsible and beloved colleague—I don't know whom I find the more endearing, his wife, Felicia, so lovely, poised and wise, or Lennie himself. He is one of those generous people deserving of respect who stand up for their friends in public, but he admits other points of view than his own, and though he disagrees with me on Israel, he still trusts my basic intentions. When IMC's executive committee unanimously rejected the suggestion of a break with UNESCO, I wrote him a letter elaborating my own attitude:

. . . [J]ust as a musician must be absolutely convinced of his interpretation, or a composer of his creation, so am I, as a friend of Israel and as a colleague of artists everywhere, obliged to voice an opinion which I firmly believe my colleagues will in fact themselves adopt, for they too are guided by the same concern for humanity at large and for Israel in particular.

The UNESCO vote of censure against Israel served undoubtedly as a rallying point for the same chorus of national delegates which had already joined for this very purpose at the United Nations. This time, a cultural justification served the same end.

My contention is that this exaggerated condemnation is ill-served by the equally exaggerated response of my fellow Jews and will merely obscure the issue. . . . The issue is simply: general war or peace; simply: the survival of Israel. This depends on the extent of support which firm, moderate opinion can command in Israel, echoed in the Jewish communities of the world and among the peoples of the world, including Israel's neighbors. Every wise and courageous friend is a precious asset to Israel. . . .

. . . [I]f she showed herself prepared to listen to censure and criticism in a mature way (as we musicians always must), Israel would win many friends who now either condemn her out of hand, or who are only limply reluctant to offend their Jewish friends and colleagues. I cannot repeat emphatically enough how important it is for Israel to remain present and represented at all conferences and deliberations. Challenge is endemic through our long history and the dignity to meet it our destiny. . . .

Few peoples of the world have known more deeply the pains of the uprooted, the dispossessed, or the unrepresented. The only way the Jewish people can put their immense historical experience and perspective to work for the benefit of Jews everywhere, for Israel and for the world, is to apply to others that understanding and compassion that they themselves have rarely received, thus reversing the disastrous chain of events which again threatens to engulf them and the world. . . .

By then Israel was boycotting both UNESCO and IMC, refusing to meet UNESCO's new director general, Amadou Mahtar M'Bow of Senegal, sending back the money—small amounts but nonetheless symbolic—which had been forwarded despite the resolutions, and generally showing itself to be intransigent. Much as I deplored the stubborn unhelpfulness of the beleaguered, I found it understandable: to be at once a cornered animal and an armchair philosopher is a difficult feat. I did what I could to unblock the impasse. I wrote at the director general's request to various acquaintances in Israel, pressing for a meeting, even in secret, to launch negotiations. My last card, however, was a gesture of helplessness: unless the UNESCO executive took a stand against the vengeful spirit of the resolutions, I would resign the presidency of the IMC. It was not a happy position to be in, able to offer only a negative response as one was dragged into the maelstrom; seen as a Zionist for offering it, or an anti-Zionist for abstaining; but the alternative was that antagonism would, with success, become yet more fiercely political and UNESCO decline into a club for exchanging the abusive clichés of propaganda.

Throughout the confrontation I was much heartened by the brave, humane, principled and skillful diplomacy of the director general. Mr. M'Bow spared neither patience nor energy to reconcile Israel and UNESCO, efforts rewarded when Israel accepted visiting UNESCO missions in July and September 1975 and when the executive board voted to soften the anti-Israeli stand in October. Hence my threatened resignation was not put into effect: I completed my six years of office by presiding over the IMC's sixteenth general assembly in Canada in September 1975.

More fundamental than his resolution of the crisis, however, was M'Bow's recognition of UNESCO's inherent weakness in its being composed of national delegations afflicted with short-sighted national aims; and his convening reinforcements in the shape of a panel of counselors, nongovernmental individuals who meet regularly to provide an independent critical and constructive assessment of its work. I was among those asked to serve, and our three meetings in 1975 gave me another forum in which to plead for a morality of tolerance and the separation of culture from politics. Every parliament, I suggested, should have voices for the speechless, deputies who represent the fowl of the air, the fish of the sea, the unborn generations. Similarly I would have UNESCO an organization where all cultures might find expression. Who, for example, speaks for the Kurds in the international assemblies of our day, or the Indians or the blacks of America? Raising the Israeli issue to a general level, I proposed that, in UNESCO at any rate, the nation-states' representation might be replaced or at least complemented by a more authentic structure of the cultures of mankind. I shall continue campaigning for this dream.

As the IMC delegates gathered in Toronto in late September 1975, I found them apprehensive that national bitterness would leave its mark on our assembly. The Israeli delegation—Joseph Tal, a saintly man who lost his only son in the 1967 war; the warm-hearted Madame Smoira-Cohen of Jerusalem Radio; and Israel Adler, a distinguished and humane musicologist—had brought with them a statement rejecting the UN's condemnation of Israel, which they meant to put to the congress. Already it had been distributed privately. Clearly the musical causes we had come to consider were in danger of being forgotten while the delegates found themselves obliged to adopt the old alignments, reacting like so many Pavlov's dogs to the old loaded words. I was determined that under my presidency this would not happen.

The night before the congress began I told my Israeli colleagues that I would take issue with any delegate—Soviet or American, Arab or Israeli—who used one such word, intended only to injure and insult. I would ask him or her to leave. "You know what it would cost me to have to ask the Israeli delegation to leave," I said. "I beg of you, let us make this congress a harmonious one. Let us give an example to UNESCO and the United Nations. Let us show them that musicians know how to keep harmony." My opening address gave me a chance to make the appeal general:

> . . . Different kinds of music, unlike politics, however different in theories they may be, are not mutually exclusive. Music is like earth, air, fire and water, a great basic element that belongs everywhere; like bread and compassion, mankind cannot live without it. . . .
>
> Never forget we are not here as national delegates *only* representing political states, but as musicians representing humanity's cultures. It is our solemn and noble duty to conduct ourselves in a way which can give comfort and hope to humanity at large and as would befit the dignity and dedication of our calling. . . .
>
> In this spirit I am personally inviting my colleagues from Egypt, Iraq, Syria, Tunis, together with my colleagues from Israel, for a quiet get-together so that we may profit by this unique opportunity of trying to understand each other sensitively and sympathetically. We are free agents, we are musicians. At least we can compose a Middle East federation of cultures and peoples which politically belongs, I pray, to a not too distant future, but which humanly and musically may already be within our reach. . . .
>
> Many are the individuals I have encountered at UNESCO in Paris who already have developed alongside their loyalty to region and state a loyalty to humanity. I have met Europeans, Africans,

Arabs, Jews, Indians, and others who are now true citizens of the world. We all know what anguish is the conflict between private and public loyalties; between business and society, between profit and morality. Without losing loyalty to our nation, our era demands the addition of this newer, wider loyalty and allegiance. We have learned to our cost that we can no longer hope to create exclusive heavens. However, neither should we want to iron out our differences to the point of dreary anonymity. . . .

Let us be ourselves. Let us be loyal to those of our kind, but not at the expense of others. And let us add this greater loyalty which embraces not only all other men but the animals and the plants as well, that organic life of which we were all consciously a part before technology engulfed us.

Over the ensuing days we achieved harmony—only within our own ranks, to be sure, for the politicians have not yet chosen to profit by our example; but however modest, it was an achievement. No political machination, no word of abuse, interrupted our musical discourse, and at two luncheons Arab and Israeli delegates met to celebrate what united them and to ignore the divisions. On the last day, with the business complete except for the election of officers, an Israeli asked for the floor. Such a request at such a moment was out of order; nonetheless, I gave him his way. He stood up. He and his fellow Israelis, he said, had been so moved by the co-operation of their colleagues from all over the world, even from countries which considered themselves Israel's enemies, that they wished to make a contribution to the good will. "We would like publicly and officially to retract our statement of censure."

It was my moment of greatest satisfaction. If ever my childhood wish to bring peace and solace to mankind was granted, it was then. But how short, ephemeral, illusory. Is it useless, or even worse than useless, to try?

It seems fitting to end this chapter with the confession of a failed attempt to deflect the course of history. Arriving in Athens in late 1974, at the express invitation of the new Karamanlias government—a gesture of gratitude, confidence, and trust for Diana's and my resolute determination to have no truck with the colonels—some months after the Cyprus adventure had brought the colonels down in Greece and just before the country was to pronounce its verdict on the monarchy, I determined to make a plea for reasserted continuity, for the nonpower above power which would guarantee stability in change. As I might have foreseen, my intervention had no effect whatever, but caused much anxiety to Diana, to our hosts at the British embassy (the British being only less distrusted in Greece nowadays than the Americans), and to the Greek authorities, put to the trouble of providing police protection. I must quote the sporting and excellent Minister of Culture, Mr. Trepanis, who came backstage at the intermission and accepted an apology for my misbehavior: "You are perfectly within your rights—this is a free country!"

The incident began with a press conference on the day of our arrival. I was not so politically naïve as to suppose my cause had an overwhelming chance of victory, and despite my agent Cretas's tugging at my sleeve to restrain me and the umbrage discernible on the faces of the newsmen, I persisted in saying my piece. The result was a couple of articles in the next day's papers urging the country to organize against the outsider come among them, and a lively overture to that night's concert. As Louis Kentner and I walked onstage the storm burst: shouts of "Fascist!" "Apologize!" "Go home!" and a confetti of tracts littering the hall, while the uncommitted majority of the audience applauded to express indignation or cover embarrassment. Emotional outbursts have their own momentum. This one lasted five minutes or so, during which Kentner sat patiently at the piano and I regarded the uproar before me on the principle that fierce animals should be faced head-on and approached. Accustomed to standing in front of audiences, I found no great hardship in waiting until the commotion ran out of steam. When it did, I expressed admiration for the students' pioneering resistance to the dictators, explained that the proceeds of the concert were to establish a scholarship for music students, suggested we get on with the business of the evening and invited the hostile element to a powwow afterward.

That was the end of the incident, but my invitation to debate was sadly not followed up, and an offer to play next day for students who (apart from the handful of rumpus-makers, not primarily interested in music) could not afford tickets to the recital was countermanded by the authorities for fear of further disturbances. Which was a pity: a chance to talk to them would have been cheap at the price of a little abuse. A couple of days later, Greece rejected the monarchy.

14

Rules
of Conduct

Explaining a love choice is difficult. How much more difficult when, to explain it, one would have to describe the sound of one's projected voice! In that respect one always loves not wisely but too well. Some seventy years ago the distinguished British violin-makers, William Hill and Sons, observed in their classic study of Stradivari:

> As celebrated players have either lacked proficiency with the pen or the inclination to use it, we must, in the almost total absence of any written record of the opinions of the many great performers who used Stradivaris and owned much of their fame to the superb tone of their instruments, attempt to supply this regrettable deficiency. . . . [I]n spite of the much-vaunted advance in education during the nineteenth century, the supposed greater tolerance, interest, and breadth of view of our latter-day players, we as yet do not know of any instance where a celebrated player has taken the trouble to soberly put down on paper his views of an instrument, as Mozart did, even in the midst of a busy life, when he made the acquaintance of Stein's pianofortes.

Their rationalism having come to grief on the Strad, these gifted gentlemen, whose implements, measurements and chemical analyses had demonstrated that a violin is more than the sum of its parts, turn to the violinist. And how do they address him? Why, of course, like rationalist schoolmasters chiding a delinquent pupil whose instinctive life they fear and resent. "Come now," they appear to say. "You've been at your desk for a century! It's high time you learned how to reason and record your thought," as though the virtuoso could, if only he bestirred himself, use other words than the poor ones at *their* disposal. True, Mozart recorded his views of Stein's pianofortes, but to state the obvious, if pianists were to embrace their voices, they might find themselves tongue-tied.

A piano, however superb it may be, is inanimate and neutral; though it respond to the pianist's intentions, it responds on its own percussive terms, making seven octaves available to him and not the least enharmonic, giving him notes but stripping them of vocal embellishment, as though this were the flesh it exacts for its servility. A great violin, on the other hand, is alive; its very shape embodies its maker's intention, and its wood stores the history, or the soul, of its successive owners. I never play without feeling that I have released or absorbed or, alas, violated spirits. For the pianist to set down his thoughts about the quality of a mechanical virgin is one thing; for the violinist to perceive "soberly" his totem, quite another.

I could recount my entire life in terms of a dialectical argument between the Stradivarius and the Guarnerius del Gesù. Not to say that each Strad or Guarnerius does not have a personality distinct from its siblings: my Khevenhüller Strad delivers a sweeter tone than my Soil Strad yet does not quite match the Soil's power to ring out above a symphony orchestra. Transcending such idiosyncrasies, however, is a generic temperament, a nature common to all the instruments of either family, which must, I feel, reflect the hand that carved them.

As Stradivari's career followed a remarkably straight course, bringing him wealth and eminence, so his violins possess great formal beauty. Having lived to biblical age, siring numerous children and numerous instruments, for fifty-seven years in the same house like a sun so confident of its position it does not feel impelled to move, he made brilliant, burnished sound that conveys, for me at any rate, moral notions of loftiness. One must rise to a Strad before it will speak from its craftsman's soul. It spurns the man who lets his hand exert too much pressure or his finger fall ever so slightly wide of its mark. As master, there is ultimately no pleasing him except by faultless workmanship, for he shines upon one's blemishes. As mistress, there is no winning her except by incessant victories over oneself, by demonstrations of perfect control.

From Bartolomeo Giuseppe Guarneri's instruments, whose label bears the initials IHS (*Jesus hominum salvator*), one can infer quite the opposite, a man at once passionate and compassionate, bull and saint, a temperamental nonconformist, a holy criminal who brawled, found no conjugal happiness, engendered no children and died rather young when he was beginning to enjoy prosperity. Their wood is on the whole poorer than the Strads'. Their f-holes were obviously gouged by some rough measure of the eye. Curiously, a stain or sap mark, parallel to the fingerboard on both sides, appears on the bellies of many of his instruments, as though his identification with Christ were sufficiently strong to leave stigmata. A phenomenon of coherent asymmetries, a fellow human mercifully absolving the player of his gaffes, the Guarnerius, whose earthier voice belies the fact that it is often slightly smaller than most Strads, sings through its pores and sings *de profundis*. One need not rise above oneself, for it appeals to the natural man. Although Strads have been the dominant instrument of my life, at regular intervals I have played Guarneri; finding the first gold while the second brings to mind the red of Sainte-Chapelle stained glass.

I made my first tour with a borrowed Guarnerius called the "Bâle," so that choosing a Strad shortly afterward under the benevolent eye of Mr. Goldman was a deliberate decision. Equally deliberate was my decision some five or six years later to borrow the Ysaÿe Guarnerius from Emile Français. I recall feeling a dullness or staleness in the 1933–1934 concert season, an adolescent *Weltschmerz* which dogged me on tour and made it exceedingly difficult to do more than go through my familiar motions. Where Ysaÿe's taurine presence (not to mention his ominous advice) had intimidated me, now that he was dead I could absorb his lessons instantly, magically, through his violin; where learning proved foreign to me, my animist conviction that the spirit which dwelled in that Guarnerius might resuscitate mine had the most remarkable effect, for so long as I played it I felt myself to be a virile man capable of greater attack than ever before. (With the great violin there is a thin line between animism and science. If one believes Emile Français, who used to contend that badly played instruments could clam up as if their very molecules had been set in discord, and not open again until patiently appeased by expert hands, may one draw the inference that any given tone will in time impress itself upon a violin as some molecular arrangement, that its wood embalms the artist's soul?)

Why, then, did I not purchase it or another? No, owning Strads and borrowing Guarneri cleverly accommodated my desire to assert myself and the fear that unless I did so in the Master's name I might be doing so at his expense, very like that childhood dream of doubles in which Kreisler gave me his violin—a Guarnerius—but kept it. (In the end he bequeathed it to the Library of Congress, which circumstance permitted me to play it at last some years ago.) In the same month Zamira was born, my first wife made me a gift of a beautiful Joseph Guarnerius del Gesù, made in 1742; I rarely played it and, some years later, gave it on loan to my first protégé, Alberto Lysy, who has used it these many years. Round about my fiftieth birthday I found myself studying Hill's catalogue of exceptionally fine Guarneri, with an eye to those available. Kohansky's, which I had always admired, was not, alas; but another, the "Count d'Egville," belonging to a collector from Braunschweig, captured my fancy; I boarded a plane for Germany at the earliest opportunity. It may seem odd that the owner of two Strads and a Guarnerius could feel so excited at the prospect of playing still another great eighteenth-century instrument; or perhaps, on the contrary, odd that I had not hitherto admitted my desire to preside over a seraglio! Instruments had always come to me as gifts or loans, by circumstance or favor—all save the Soil. But I could buy a Strad more readily than a Guarnerius, secure in the knowledge that to possess one was to be possessed by it, that it assuaged any guilt attending on pride of ownership with its own intrinsic retribution. I borrowed the d'Egville and played it with rapture for eighteen months, then returned it to its owner. In 1971, at last, I found a supremely beautiful Guarnerius that had belonged to a cousin of Charles Munch, Mlle Ebersholt, whose father had given it to her when she was fifteen years old, in 1880; and I bought it the next year.

Having in my conception a life of their own, all wooden objects have therefore rights to be acknowledged in tributes of wax and polish. I like to be surrounded by the sympathetic faces of old chairs, cabinets and paneling, and feel proportionately solitary amid the clinical anonymity of modern furnishing. My violins above all have a vote in determining their future, translated into a sense of obligation on my part and expressed in the lavishing of care and affection. (Who could lavish affection on a piano? Or cuddle it, or carry it in his arms, or put it to bed in silk and velvet?) I clean my violins and give them their rightful luster with preparations made by Étienne Vatelot of Paris, who also shares the responsibility of repairing them with the venerable firm of Hill and Sons and with Charles Beare, a dear friend. I string them with strings by Pirastro of Germany, or, in the Americas, with Kaplan strings, which are well-suited to the climate; preferring to the all-metal string of current fashion—clear, brilliant, reliable, practical in all the wrong ways, exerting painful tension—the compromise of metal wound on gut, occasionally reverting to the simple gut strings which Stradivarius and the Guarneri had in mind when they carved the instruments in my trust. What now decides the selection of one or another violin is a silent colloquy between them and myself, too profound to be intelligible even to me, but not dictated by the music, fleshly or spiritual, to be played. Each instrument has its rest periods, upon emerging from which it and I must make each other's acquaintance again. It takes us a couple of weeks to become accustomed to one another.

Natural selection, it seems, sometimes calls a halt to ambition. I understand that ants, surely the most resilient and numerous of species, have not troubled to evolve further for several million years. So, give and take the differences, with violins: the eighteenth century marked an apogee; change could mean only decline. But behind and beside the perfection of Cremona, the violin has flourished in a thousand crude shapes since it first emerged as a popular means of making music in the Middle Ages. It was to win social acceptance and courtly music to match its new status; it was to learn community discipline in chamber groups and symphony orchestras; but it survived these adaptations to remain the supreme solo instrument, subjective enough to have meaning, anonymous enough to be universal, mobile as the man who cradled it from settlement to settlement, from concert hall to opera house. Generations of such musicians built the tradition I belong to and those who were not gypsies tended to be Jews.

The Russian-Jewish monopoly of the violin is less total now than it was sixty years ago, when any musically gifted Jewish child of Russian background was more or less fated to end up a violinist. Should this observation seem rueful, let me add that I count myself supremely fortunate in the circumstances of my birth; I bless the destiny which guarded me from the piano and delivered me to a lifelong embrace with a Strad. There was in our house, from about the time that I too was there, an upright piano, a Mathushek, upon which my mother when the mood was propitious would play a certain Chopin waltz, in C♯ minor (the piano was the one possession my parents had shipped to San Francisco from New Jersey). Later one Mason & Hamlin grand, then a second, were added to the household effects to serve my sisters. But none of these instruments cast doubt upon my violin, and, as a family, we did not go to piano recitals; to recitals by Jascha Heifetz, Mischa Elman, Toscha Seidel, Fritz Kreisler, Georges Enesco, we went as naturally as breathing. The man who carries his voice with him has, it would seem, a relationship with his listeners more romantic and focused than that which the pianist enjoys. Would I judge differently after a lifetime before the bared denture of the keyboard? I think not. The piano speaks with many voices, the violin is the individual voice, proved throughout history to speak to and for the multitude more effectively than any number of majority decisions, however harmoniously arrived at.

Curiously enough, ugly violinists marry beautiful wives. This is not a matter to be pursued too nicely, precision in judgment, like comparisons, being odious when applied to one's colleagues and fellow creatures; but without overly troubling about the evidence, I contend that violinists can be ugly and their wives beautiful, and further, that the phenomenon bears witness to the violinist's possession of a magnetism denied other mortals. Typically, he is also more sensual than intellectual, somewhat narrow in outlook, and probably vain. He takes a pride in the sound he produces comparable to the pride his beautiful wife takes in her good looks, a pride which in neither case may be permitted to subside into complacency. He is romantic in the sense of having sentiments to express "felt in the blood and felt along the heart," and thence overflowing; and (despite the affinities which take no account of uncomeliness) not at all in the popular interpretation which would see him as all wings and freedom and unfettered impulse. On the contrary, he is an animal shackled to a treadmill of his own devising, on which untold hours of labor grind out grudging rations of satisfaction that may, if he plays well, last the length of a performance but are exhausted almost before the applause. Given that most of mankind wear out their days on one treadmill or another, for lesser reward or none, the violinist is, finally, privileged. I once had a chance to gauge how privileged I was by at least one man's calculation.

Visiting Chicago in the postwar years, I often stayed at the home of Edward Ryerson, head of Inland Steel and president of the Chicago Symphony Orchestra, a slim, trim American of the old school in contrast to the more or less balloon-shaped object which is the American businessman today. (Our friendship had an unlikely beginning: after the war the Chicago Symphony invited Furtwängler to conduct it, he accepted and a contract was signed. However, when the anti-Furtwängler lobby threatened to boycott Chicago, the agreement was abrogated and Kubelik appointed instead. In the middle of this dispute I announced a counter-boycott—which I observed for some years—in protest against the slighting of Furtwängler. Thus, Ryerson and I became fast friends through my refusal to appear with his orchestra.) On one of our visits Nora Ryerson gave a dinner to introduce Diana and me to the meat-packing gentry of the locality, and when we were taking leave at the end of the evening a gentleman—whether Swift or Armour or Cudahy, I don't remember—took my hand and held it consideringly as if weighing it; for a moment I wondered if by any chance he mistook it for a pig's trotter. "When I think," he said with solemn emphasis, "of all the money this has earned . . ."

It is unarguable that during my lifetime the violinist has seen his stock devalued; not by some other instrument's upstart pretensions to supplant the violin, but submerged beneath the sheer quantity of musical experience poured over our heads from the bottomless cornucopia of technically conveyed sound. Even in San Francisco, a western Odessa in the engendering of musicians—even, very likely, in Odessa itself—the ardent melomane of the 1920s hardly ever heard an opera and his regular musical nourishment was limited to dear Alfred Hertz's Germanic menu figuring mainly *plats du jour* of Beethoven, Brahms and Wagner. In the explosion of music reverberating across the intervening half century—music rescued from the past, borrowed from other cultures, fathered in backyards in Johannesburg, Rio, or Kingston, Jamaica, or amid the mixers and consoles of an electronic laboratory—no wonder the violin's treble seems muffled. However, if its once single-minded following has dispersed to rival attractions, the violin also draws a better-informed audience today, one which spices love with critical awareness. The Beethoven and Brahms concerti are still the most popular music I play, but nowadays Bach and Bartók—of all composers those who, in my view, best understood the violin—have also a passionate following.

Perhaps what we have lost is the courage to appreciate the violin at something less than its most exalted. I don't view the eclipse of salon music with satisfaction, nor rejoice in the discrediting of the style which purveyed it. Not long ago I played at Pamplona, Sarasate's native town in northwest Spain, and seeing the honor in which he was held—squares, buildings, institutions bore his name—I concluded that here was sufficient commitment to light-heartedness to launch a Concours Sarasate, directed to presenting the violin as a salon instrument, in contrast to the general run of existing *concours*, which increasingly stress size, in solidity of works, big tone, huge—rather than elegant—technique. No sooner had the idea dawned than I passed it to the city fathers, enumerating its advantages: it wouldn't be expensive to mount, for no orchestra would be required; it would command an immediate

audience, for concert managements were wrong in thinking entertainment at a discount—on the contrary, the public responded to such music
with hungry fervor; it need not limit itself to the nineteenth-century
repertoire, but could include the jazz improvisations of today's musical
entertainment. Whether or not the stone dropped into Pamplona's pool
will have a lasting ripple, I think it a pity that an instrument so versatile
should lose even one of its many facets.

In an inextricable confusion of cause and effect, along with the
disappearing music, a breed of violinists who shaped everything they
touched with elegance has also disappeared. Sarasate was an outstanding
exemplar, and so, in different ways, were Kreisler and Thibaud. Thibaud's elegant playing was part of his French genetic code, an inborn
faculty for handling a phrase which asked no by-your-leave of the metronome. Although the French have the worst street manners in the world,
their salon manners are exquisite, they know the courtesies. I recall
noting as a child that even a less than first-rate French orchestra could invariably do justice to Mozart, whereas all but the best German orchestras
punished his delicacy with a heavy hand, a comparison which taught me
that Mozart could be appreciated only in a chivalrous tradition. Thibaud's Mozart was without rival in my young days. Acquaintance with
Kreisler did not blunt the worshipping regard of my youth, but rather
the reverse; he remained for me the player who above all others *spoke*
the music, as if each piece was a poem recited to the beloved. In addition, I had many chances to value the gentleness and sweetness of his
character, and his generosity. Kreisler had a particular knack of giving a
little more color and variety to the classical pieces he adapted—occasionally he might overdo things, but on the whole he supplied just that
measure of conciseness, elegance and richness of harmony which rescued
the music from convention and restored it to the repertoire. His arrangement of Viotti's Concerto Number 22 in A Minor was especially successful; he gave it to me to use as I pleased.

By nature indulgent, he ensured discipline in his life when he
married Harriet, a rather bossy woman who kept him sternly on the
straight and narrow path. He loved her dearly, bewailed her absences,
repeatedly volunteered how much he owed her; when he was on tour,
I had to reconcile these obviously genuine tributes with Harriet's dismissive treatment of him. Once, at a luncheon Diana and I gave in New
York, he and Thibaud were exchanging anecdotes of youthful escapades
—in and out of bedrooms, late for rehearsal or concert because other pur-
suits were more tempting, standing in for each other at crises, and so on—

Diana

Diana in her dressing room
when she danced for
the Markova-Dolin company

Griselda and Diana
dressed as the
Misses Gunning
at a charity ball

Krov and Zamira

Zamira, Jeremy,
and Gerard
with their father
in Switzerland

Playing with Jeremy,
age six, at Bernard
Berenson's I Tatti,
Florence, 1958

Gerard and Jeremy listening, 1954

Hephzibah, Jeremy, Yehudi, and Yaltah rehearsing for
Yehudi's fiftieth-birthday concert, at which he conducted
them in the Mozart Triple Piano Concerto, the Royal
Festival Hall, London, April 1966

The younger generation: Krov and Ann,
Jeremy, Zamira, Lin, and Gerard

Zamira and Jonathan

Hephzibah, Yehudi, and Yaltah, Bath Festival, 1963

when Harriet slapped them down. "Oh, Fritz!" she said. "Who's interested in old men's senile recollections?" When he had to repair his fortunes, he would arrange a tour of England, thirty-two concerts in thirty days, for the English loved him and he returned their devotion. It was about England—more precisely about the scale of fees and price of tickets at London concerts, information of no present relevance but nostalgic charm—that he spoke when I last saw him. It was a summer afternoon in New York, not long before he died in 1962. The city heat, my dear old friend at ease in an open-necked shirt, his leather chair which was losing its stuffing, his agent and friend Charles Foley making desultory conversation, Foley's office, three or four floors up in an old building on one of the narrow streets off Fifth Avenue, an office no longer the hub of an active career but itself in retirement—all combined to give an impression of gentle lassitude at the end of the road.

The performing violinist continually reviews the hours, days and weeks preceding a performance, charting the many elements that will release his potential—or put a brake upon it. He knows that when his body is exercised, his blood circulating, his stomach light, his mind clear, the music ringing in his heart, his violin clean and polished, its strings in good order, the bow hair full and evenly spread, then—but then only—he is in command. But neglect of the least of these elements must gnaw his conscience. The audience, even the critic, may not suspect his troubled conscience, or may ascribe a blemish to an irrelevant cause, all unaware of the player's silent admission of insufficiency, his self-disgust, his begging to be given another chance. Even if no fault is noted, the audience's plaudits, their stamping and standing, are of no comfort to him then.

So a violinist (like any other artist) lives in training. He makes his body his vocation. His stance must be erect yet supple so that, like a graceful reed, he may wave with the breeze and yet remain perfectly self-aligned from head through spine to feet. He is a living structure stretched between the magnets of sun and earth. Just as only a stretched string can vibrate, so before a violinist's body vibrates he must feel drawn upward, his head delicately poised on the vertebrae, his diaphragm raising him on a cushion of air, while the working parts of his anatomy—shoulders and arms, hands and fingers—float and balance at different levels. Elegant management of the body is among the qualities civilization denies us, and too often the violin, inviting surrender, only makes rigidity more rigid. I remember my disappointment one day in the 1960s when some young violinists played for me in San Francisco. Among them was a black youth who predictably carried himself with lanky flexibility. I awaited revelations; but, violin in hand, he was as awkward and stiff as his white counterparts. In contrast, many of the Asian players now infiltrating our concert halls demonstrate a body-mind coordination that is halfway to technical mastery.

Before I begin my daily stint, which now consists less of pieces of music than of a drill of basic motions, there is, therefore, something even more fundamental to be done. Violin practice starts with me on my back (or in diverse other positions) on the floor, exploring the laws governing the working of the human anatomy.

Lying flat, I raise both arms, both legs, separately and together; I rotate them, let them dangle, check each joint, feel its individual weight, search for the minimum tension required to resist the pull of gravity, note the body's adjustment to it. These gentle movements are accompanied by breathing exercises: an inhalation as a limb is lifted, the breath suspended at the apex of the stretch, as the limb falls an exhalation on a tone hummed through the lips, whose vibration can be felt throughout the body if no untoward knot or tightness interrupts it. I raise, say, my left arm, consciously noting that the initiative of this movement is first felt in the shoulder and, further, that even before the arm leaves the ground it is being carried, the body rolling slightly to the left in anticipation of loss of support and of extra weight to bear. What the eye sees—the raised arm—is but the last link in a chain of events originating in the mind. To be conscious of these events as they happen, before they are apparent to the eye, is a lesson in the subtlety I believe to be a cardinal principle of violin playing; but just to awaken oneself to them is enough. Not for the violinist the exhibitionist and fiery springing from seat or keyboard of a virtuoso pianist, or the acrobatics of certain conductors. He is part of his violin, his left hand fingering its way, without any margin for error, over the millimetric subdivisions of a space that varies like a slide rule, and his bow never leaving the string but under precise, controlled conditions. There is no allowance for him, no possibility of vagaries more exorbitant than a swaying of the hips, a balancing from leg to leg, a shaking of the head, a wiggling of the toes. Of all instrumentalists, he must learn to catch motion on the wing, to perpetuate impetus and gather momentum, finding static support nowhere, and indeed seeking none. From the first he must learn to float and carry, to drift with the stream, to initiate a motion and push it along subtly, as he does the rhythmic pulse of a musical idea.

To play the violin one must form a clear image of the interplay of six directions within, as it were, a sphere. These are toward and away from oneself, horizontal push and pull, vertical carrying weight from above and vertical supporting weight from below (likewise, bridges are built upon the opposing vertical principles of arch and suspension). All six must be experienced separately in the two hands and ten fingers, along the length of the fingerboard, and at each point of the bow, before they will cooperate kinetically. Each is worked in each position and into each is built its countervailing force, so that there may exist between the two a regulated tension which lets us support weight in motion and adjust speed in weight. The latter we carry into our very fingertips and sustain upon resilient arcs, arches, circles and spirals. At the moment of playing one does not calculate one's orbits, but to prepare the automatic impulse I have found it useful in practice to think of these basic elements, three times two.

Over the years a drill has evolved which is at the same time specific, time-saving and teachable to others. Each item has been individually investigated, individually tested, but in course of time the basic exercises, involving both hands, have been put together in ways susceptible of infinite permutation: coordinating the hands in opposite or the same directions, matching or staggering fingering, bowing and breathing, working on the independence of the fingers of the left hand while experiencing the numberless variations of the feel of the bow in the right; to dissolve what I call adhesions, in computer language, involuntary synchronizations which are the equivalent of prejudices in daily life. The weight of the bow on the G string is very different from its weight on the E string, and this difference demands a compensating alteration in the play of the fingers, giving on the G string more responsibility to the third and fourth. Naturally, it entails a different movement. These infinitely varied movements any violinist must make; my exercises locate them and bring them to awareness. For instance, what is the minimum hold of the bow? Can it be held by merely the first finger and the fourth? If one leans forward, the thumb is scarcely needed; if one leans backward, it must take the weight. Similarly, as one presses the string with a finger of the left hand, the whole hand and arm should feel the effect, rising in sympathy with the downward pressure. Otherwise the sound is dead, and no expenditure of will power can avoid the pain, the rigor, the dissatisfaction, and produce a beautiful, communicating sound.

For these abstract exercises I mute the violin and put a piece of tissue under the strings, tucking the flapping ends into the f-holes. I could say that to practice with a heavy mute, or, as I once did, with a soaped bow, saves my ear from being dulled by a surfeit of sound, that this self-imposed continence (especially where familiar pieces like the Brahms Concerto are concerned) makes the pleasure of performing aloud all the keener. Beyond that, however, mime obliges me to internalize the music until I can "hear" it in my digits, muscles and joints, until the body becomes a kind of aural intelligence, an instrument perfectly tuned and playing independently of me, a "pure" voice. Assuming, as I do, that beautiful sound has a visual coefficient, I would, if that were possible, make myself its form or statue, I would cut a figure intrinsically capable of hitting a note exactly as I please, with percussive effect or with vibrancy, leaping to it or sliding, sliding quickly or slowly, like the Zen archer so self-aware he will hit his target blindfolded.

If there is time I will spend an hour or so thus practicing, frequently making new discoveries; for enlightenment has not been a once-and-for-all event, a miracle on the road to Damascus, but a continuing exploration. Perfection cannot be achieved unless its pursuit becomes a way of life. My goal has been so to play the violin that whatever I play is an exercise for whatever I might play. Concentrated observation and practice of minuteness are gradually absorbed; the conscious brain is short-circuited; but I make a point every so often of retrieving these least movements from the subconscious to give them an airing. The legend of Paganini's practicing gives encouragement: for many years a jealous admirer followed him on tour, determined to lay bare the secrets of the Maestro's practice and never catching him in the act, until one day, through the keyhole, he saw the violin taken from its case. His heart leaped—and fell: after a few motions Paganini laid the instrument down. Whether this story is true or not, the moral remains to edify us. There comes a time when, if everything is mastered, integrated, co-ordinated, absorbed, it is only necessary to reassure oneself that the integration is still complete.

Although my life is governed by a schedule, the days themselves are mine to order. Sure enough, there has been many a train to catch, but never the seven-forty commuters' train to town. My great luxury, in days which parcel out minutes to this or that occupation, is to cheat the clock of the duties it lays down. When circumstances allow, I get up before the pressure of other people's lives makes itself felt, do my yoga in the expansive quiet of the early morning, and go back to bed for a delicious hour when the rest of the world is waking up. Washed, fresh, stretched and eager, I am ready to approach the violin, to which, by preference, the morning is reserved. I am not a slave of routine, however, not even my own. As high as I put the priority of performance, I put higher my fellowmen, whose claims sometimes overtake the violin's. But I have learned to make use of short spaces of time: I can quickly bring myself to performing pitch, or catch up on sleep at almost any hour of the day or night.

There is one temptation which I don't always resist. Ideally a free day occurring after, say, two weeks of daily performances should be a day of fasting, spent largely in bed, with only a little work to keep the body limber. But the urge to depart actively from routine is always there, and the free day too often misused, to the disadvantage of the next concert. A sabbath to keep holy, in the old sober fashion, would be an excellent thing for violinists. The greatest enemy to performance, however, is too much food.

I was brought up on a healthy diet: my mother served us salads, much raw fruit and vegetables, a moderate amount of meat, never fried foods or sauces, and rarely sweets. Not having a scientific interest in the subject, she was once persuaded by a friendly grocer that canned spinach was a great improvement on the fresh variety, so troublesome to wash. We went round to his store in our car and carried off a case of canned spinach. My mother cooked it once, we all tasted it, and that was the end of canned food in our house; unopened, the remaining cans went into the garbage. Today it is known that the spinach can act on the tin and become a very poisonous food indeed. So from childhood, I have had a predisposition to healthy eating and, as already recounted, Dr. Walter B. Price confirmed it. In accordance with his findings, I changed my diet and that of other people within my sphere of influence.

At my school white flour and white sugar are not bought, and the children rarely suffer ailments, are always of good cheer and ready to work or play energetically. I also, in my zeal, contributed to the founding of Wholefoods, a store in London set up by the Soil Association to sell food grown or raised organically. It is one of my regrets that I don't have an organic farm of my own, but to compensate for this gap in my life, I visit Sam Mayall's farm in Shropshire. I remember his once giving me a most striking object lesson: next to each other were two fields of wheat, one artificially fertilized and twice the height of the other, which had been treated only with natural fertilizer; but a violent storm had swept the countryside, laying the tall wheat low while the short, sturdy organic crop survived undamaged. After some bad financial moments, Whole-foods is now making money, which, since it is a non-profit-making venture, is destined for the founding of other stores and the education of the public.

Meanwhile I personally am well on the way to vegetarianism. It seems there is a consumer's path to travel from the four-legged animal to the two-legged fowl to the no-legged fish, and thence to fruit, vegetables and cereals. I am not there yet; in company I sometimes succumb to fish, more rarely to meat; but all my convictions point the way to vegetarian scruple. Not simply is it more humane or more healthy, but its rectitude is supported by economics: if everyone fed directly from the land, instead of from the land through animals, there would be land to feed us all. For me, however, the clinching argument is the effect on a concert of a heavy stomach which hasn't quite digested the lunchtime pâté and the so-different effect of a light stomach that has taken the best out of a good, easily absorbed meal. Immediately before a concert, I will if necessary supplement such healthy nourishment with a tisane in which are mixed the vital core of grains, powdered yeast, a variety of vitamins and honey, or with one of the life-promoting preparations which are increasingly on sale today.

I trust the reader will not underrate the importance of these intimate details. Indeed I believe there is satisfaction to be found in even the basic functions of our bodies. You will find no reference to digestion, urination, defecation in political philosophies or annals of state; nonetheless all life is subject to these processes, and they surely provide a first lesson in the consideration we owe the future, as well as in the importance of a pleasure delayed. The Chinese, I understand—who, like the Indians, have a sense of time—take account in their cuisine of the delayed, as well as of the immediate, satisfaction. Would we all did so! Much of the world's dis-ease stems from the discomforts we bring upon ourselves, while looking for someone else to blame; for human nature resists being separated from its unwholesome, pleasant habits. But the musician knows there is no one else to blame: he carries the burden of his own wrong notes.

Sometimes there isn't even gluttony to blame. One such occasion was a matinee concert in Milan, which at the time I wanted only to forget but can now look back upon with fair composure.

Diana and I had traveled to Milan from the south of France, in a fearsomely overcrowded train full of Italian matriarchs sharing loving-kindness and garlic sausage among their families and making the nonparticipating stranger feel the more isolated by contrast. Early in the afternoon we arrived, and assuming the concert to be in the evening, took to our beds to undo the stiffness of the cramped journey. Almost at once the telephone rang to announce that I was due onstage in an hour. Up we got again, bathed, dressed and set out to meet the audience, without so much as a minute to look at the music. I knew I was to play the Paganini B Minor Concerto, which I hadn't played in many months, but going over it in my head, I completely forgot that the soloist faced some cadenzas in the first movement.

We reached the Teatro Nuovo, an underground hall in which I have since refused to perform. Much as I approve of underground factories, underground concert halls have proved—so far at least—a disaster. The atmosphere, the clamminess, the closeness, the lighting, the acoustics were all depressing beyond words. In these gloomy surroundings, the need for the cadenzas I was lacking burst upon me, and all I could find to do was a few arpeggios up and down before going directly to the last trill. I wasn't very proud of myself that day, all the less so when Rafael Kubelik came backstage, as warm and encouraging as ever. As a young boy he had traveled a great deal with his father, the great violinist Jan Kubelik, and I suppose he knew very well that every artist's career must include a few shameful incidents.

Straight from the concert we fled back to the hotel to ask the porter when the next train left for Venice; dashed upstairs; threw our possessions into the valises; raced to the station, made the train, and so escaped. Some hours later we were drifting in a gondola up the Grand Canal under a summer night sky. The concert was lost in the misty past, the magic of Venice soothed the present. I was never happier.

The sensation of escaping from the scene of one's crime is a recurring blessing in the life of a traveling violinist. Even when a concert has gone without hitch I enjoy disappearing to be quiet and alone. Once the job is done, I want to move on to the next obligation unless I find myself in a city of many friends.

A concert hall contains a vast assortment of people, rich and poor, simple and socialite, noble and dissolute. It is one of the pleasanter by-products of a musician's life to be on good terms with such a wealth of human types, whatever incomprehensions flourish between them. It is possible that I value it particularly because of the contrast it represents to my unpeopled youth; but however that may be, I now enjoy many friendships which have generated without benefit of contact, expressed in messages or gifts repeated over the years until they become little traditions. Sometimes a degree of real closeness is reached. I would single out one lady, Angela Marris. Miss Marris attends all my concerts in England and not a few abroad—some years ago we celebrated our one thousandth joint appearance, so to speak. She owns a completer collection of my records than I have or EMI has, and she has knitted her fidelity into sweaters made to all the family measurements.

I am very conscious of the bonds with my fellowmen grafted me by music, but I admit that I value most highly the bonds with women, and the older my ladies are, the more dearly I cherish them. It is perhaps life's greatest accomplishment to live to old age, maintaining one's wits, one's sense of humor, one's health and one's charm. I enshrine my old ladies in a gallery in my mind, and visit them there to pay my dues of admiration and gratitude. They, for their part, fill the gaps in a grand-motherless life.

Queen Elizabeth of the Belgians was one of them, not only a violinist and patron of music; not only a monarch of sterling purpose, defending her subjects against German occupation for all that she was born a German, traveling after the war to Russia and Poland in the face of domestic criticism; but also a student of yoga, a pupil of my own guru Iyengar. So youthful was she in her eighties that she learned to stand on her head.

From my childhood there were the Godchaux sisters, the queenly Mrs. Koshland, Mrs. Casserly, my first great lady in New York, Mrs. Leventritt, whose charming laugh her daughter Rosalie inherited. A little later I added to the gallery Emma Kodály, Nadia Boulanger and Magdalena Kash, a disciple of Constantin Brunner who to this day, at the age of ninety, works at the Brunner Institute in The Hague. In Britain I collected Lady Cholmondeley, Lady Meade-Featherstone-haugh, a herbalist who knows the secrets of mixing a bewitching potion, and Princess Alice, the Duchess of Athlone, who was a marquise out of a fairy story. It was Princess Alice's royal authority which persuaded our then nurse not to interfere with our son Jeremy's left-handedness. Others of my grand old ladies are Margot von Hausenstein, wife of a former German ambassador to France, and Nesta Obermeyer, a wonderfully ebullient American lady. At Gstaad I have a contraption for relaxing on: one fastens rubber belts around the ankles, leans back and upends oneself for as long as one pleases, thus painlessly taking the weight off one's feet. No sooner did Nesta Obermeyer see it than she tested it, enjoying the experience enough to repeat it whenever she comes to Gstaad. There are not many eighty-year-olds who have such a spirit of adventure, I think.

15

View
from the Stage

In the late 1940s an American tour took me to the small mining town of Wheeling, set incongruously amid West Virginia's rural beauties. Lacking urban graces, Wheeling had, however, an orchestra, an orchestral society assembling local patrons, and an energetic, talented young conductor named Henry Mazer (now assistant in Chicago), who carried the brunt of the enterprise, functioning—it seemed to me—as janitor, ticket seller, money raiser and publicist as well as conductor. While driving me to my hotel after rehearsal, he asked me to a supper party to follow the evening concert, and overcame my commitment to going early to bed with the information that one of the orchestra's principal patrons was to give it.

"There's one thing I must warn you about," he added.

"Yes?"

"He doesn't like Beethoven."

"Ah!" Upon inquiry, I learned that our host's annual donation was two hundred dollars, in Mazer's view a sum worth the expenditure of some tact; I promised to keep a check upon my feeling for the Master. After a program on which of course Beethoven did not figure, my contribution to it being Lalo's *Symphonie Espagnole*, Mazer and I were delivered at the elevator's last gasp to a penthouse apartment where, as we entered, I received a blow between the shoulders and, recovering my balance, heard a hearty, beefy gentleman demand, "Well, Mr. Menuhin, and what do *you* think of Beethoven?" "Many people," I ventured cautiously, "seem to like him."

"Ach!" snorted our host. "No guts!"

Between Beethoven and myself, I felt I knew which at that moment better deserved the rebuke, but a promise is a promise. Wheeling apart, however, so many and so constant are Beethoven's admirers that the Violin Concerto has become over the decades my yardstick of rising standards and changing fashions in orchestral playing, and I wish he had written two or three more—it is one of a violinist's enduring regrets that the great Romantic composers each left him only one concerto, as if accomplishing a *pro forma* exercise before concentrating on the "real work" of writing symphonies and, it must be added, piano concerti! Unlike the Brahms Concerto, which is soft clay to be molded in performance and therefore needs a conductor and orchestra of great talent to do it justice, the Beethoven is an already finished beautiful object, to present which requires, at the lowest, only scruple. This truth was demonstrated to me with some force shortly after the war.

A month or so before I was to start a South American tour which included a recital in Guatemala City, a letter reached me in San Francisco from Guatemala City's resident conductor, a man called Paco. Its substance was: "Forgive us if we seem presumptuous. Knowing you were coming here, we wondered if you would consider performing the Beethoven Concerto with us. We shall perfectly understand if you refuse. We are not very good but we will work before you come, and if, at rehearsal, you find us impossible, you must say so honestly; it will already have been a privilege to go through it with you. . . ." Such a request could not be denied. I suggested that if the rehearsal went well, we would perform together in the second half of my scheduled concert. When I arrived I was touched beyond words. Not only had Paco rehearsed the orchestra every day for a month; he had rehearsed every section and every individual player. Each detail was in place, each note in rhythm and in tune, each *piano* and each *forte* observed. Yes, there have been greater performances, but here was utter conscientious integrity and Beethoven shone through it undiminished.

Paco's orchestra was modest enough to take nothing for granted. At the other end of the scale are the Berlin Philharmonics of the world who equally take nothing for granted. But there are many degrees of skill and complacency in between. To offset Beethoven in Guatemala there was, some ten years later, a desperately bad Beethoven in Texas, in a small town which must be nameless, less from charitable concealment than because I have forgotten which small town it was. I have said that Beethoven is served by scruple. Whether he is to be so served is apparent to the soloist from the first bars, indeed from the first notes on the timpani, which are often neither in tune nor in rhythm. The four short notes of the first string entry, admittedly awkward to handle immaculately, are another sign of what to expect. When the Texas orchestra began the tutti at rehearsal I was so appalled that, for once in my life, I seriously considered canceling the performance. I felt thoroughly ashamed of myself: did thirty years of work, travel, thought, discipline and commitment to music lead only to the massacre of Beethoven? Eventually fellow feeling for the musicians, who clearly had no idea how disgraceful their playing was, overcame the call of conscience. As inoffensively as I could, I asked the conductor if I might rehearse the orchestra in the opening tutti, and improper and humiliating though the suggestion was, he made no resistance. We got through the Concerto somehow.

In general I have enjoyed excellent relations with conductors. As a child I did not offer comment, but even now discussions between soloist and conductor don't appeal to me. Music is its own language, not to be shored up by words; the interpretation should speak for itself; it is a matter of sensitive ears, not persuasive arguments. The basic assumption is that the conductor accompanies the soloist, but on either side of this premise there is room for maneuver, depending on the authority and experience of both and on the license which the music leaves the soloist. It is primarily his responsibility to decide tempi, and as there is often a tutti before his entry, a conductor, having begun at a tempo he considers appropriate, will sometimes look for the soloist's approval rather than pursue futilely what must later be corrected. If he does not, and is playing, for instance, faster than I wish, my deliberately slower entry will persuade him to adjust. There can be, however, no rigid structure of command and obedience. The conductor is responsible not only for tutti, but for passages of accompaniment where the orchestra has faster notes than the soloist, for these notes determine the basic speed. I have favored points of interpretation which sometimes I cannot forbear urging upon a conductor—for example, the crescendo on the first violins' two upbeat notes in the recapitulation in the first movement of the Brahms Concerto, one of the great moments of music, which is frequently overlooked. Attempting such interference, one must observe the courtesies. Obviously one should not contradict a conductor in front of his orchestra, and if, as a violinist, I am tempted to suggest a particular fingering or bowing to the first violins, I must first ask his permission. It is always granted.

One such instance occurs in the Beethoven Concerto. When I was a boy, the first violins opened the statement of the main theme with a down-bow, thus:

To my way of thinking, there is a classical inevitability about this arrangement, for one no more naturally starts a statement on an up-bow than one lays down the law with an upward motion of the arm. However, some fifteen years ago the practice began to creep in, now adopted by almost all orchestras, of beginning with an up-bow so as to underline the pattern. It is almost pedantic to lament the change, for if the visual effect is unfortunate, the difference in sound can scarcely be discerned. Moreover, the choice of an up-bow is well meant and one therefore hesitates to condemn it. Though I wince at it, I usually leave that up-bow, but with my own orchestra I insist on returning to the manners of my youth.

The great orchestras of the past had noble standards. What has risen is the level which second-, third- and fourth-ranking and even amateur orchestras now set themselves; even youth orchestras sound professional today. No doubt recording, which allows us all to hear ourselves as others hear us as well as providing authoritative performances, should take much of the credit, but another factor may be the period of respect for the composer's intentions through which we have passed. The profit does not exclude loss, however, and both factors come together in my mind as aspects of the mechanical age which puts the legalistic, the controlled, the planned in advance above what an individual feels. Marcel Ciampi used to tell me that before the First World War an artist could silence challenge of his interpretation simply by declaring, "That's the way I feel it." By the time I listened regularly to music, romantic latitude was being replaced by "correctness," obsessive evenness of tempo, the conviction that one should play music on the instruments for which it was written, with the forces at the composer's disposal and in the manner of his day. When I was first in Paris, in 1926–1927, I attended a concert by the Capet Quartet, whose devotion to correctness led them to play without vibrato. To play without vibrato is an excellent check upon one's intonation and useful therefore in testing an ensemble's accuracy, but so intolerable did my ears find it in performance that I left the hall (I have regretted my flight ever since: the Capet Quartet were superb musicians from whom I could have learned much). In recent years there have been signs that the pendulum is swinging back again—not to the extent of denying respect to the composer, but sufficiently to make emotion acceptable once more. I have the impression that my own playing has not followed the pendulum's lurches, but I may be deluded: does the fish know whether he swims in salt water or in fresh? Of course, the salmon must.

Some conductors are synonymous with their orchestras, at once their creators and their creation, as Eugene Ormandy with his Philadelphia Orchestra or Herbert von Karajan with his in Berlin. Inheriting a wonderful instrument, they have known how to maintain and even improve it. Karajan follows a long line of great conductors, but he is more than a conductor, he is a leader of men. He protects his musicians, sees they are well paid, ensures the quality of their instruments, encourages them to divide into smaller groups to play chamber music, and in all manner of ways boosts their morale. It is, in fact, a German virtue to respect native talent, in contrast to the French, who despite French chauvinism, tend to be unappreciative of their own great men. Thus, the Orchestre de Paris was not entrusted to Paul Paray, Pierre Boulez, Ernest Bour, or any other Frenchman, but offered to foreigners not necessarily equal to understanding the French orchestra—though Paray is, at ninety, as active, sharp, and effective on the podium as he was almost fifty years ago when he conducted my first European concert, and Boulez has a grasp of the score, a clarity of mind beyond belief (it was a singular experience lately in New York to introduce this man who knew inside out the intricacies of Berg and Webern to Brahms's Violin Concerto).

The balanced English strike, as so often, a compromise between French and German attitudes, honoring their own musicians while opening their hearts to musicians from abroad. This magnanimity is exemplified by Sir Charles Groves, who instituted at Liverpool an associate post to give the younger generation a chance to try its wings. It was at Liverpool that Zubin Mehta, for instance, first proved himself. I too have benefited from Sir Charles's selflessness. At the Carl Flesch Concours in London, with which I am connected, he conducts all the finalists in their concerti—which, more than a labor of love, is an exacting, exhausting grind. It is not by chance that England (along with Israel) has produced the most promising crop of young conductors; nor perhaps altogether by chance that for a few years Britain had a musical head of state. With all the respect I have for Edward Heath's integrity and intelligence, I feel that he is most fulfilled and relaxed among musicians. Early in 1976, he, I and four others were awarded honorary degrees by the Sorbonne in recognition of our contributions to the European entity—I don't know which gave me greater pleasure, my being the first musician to be named a doctor by the Sorbonne, or the generosity which allowed an American to be a good European too. On this occasion I played a piece of Bach for violin alone and Edward Heath ended the proceedings by conducting the Sorbonne choir and orchestra in the Hallelujah Chorus from Handel's *Messiah* (as long ago as Handel's day, outsiders were welcomed in Britain; like the plays of Shakespeare and the King James Bible, *Messiah* is now part of English consciousness). Even more impressive, however, was a dinner Heath gave at Downing Street in 1972, when he was prime minister, to celebrate Sir William Walton's seventieth birthday, when he arranged musical interludes between the courses, introducing each with a few well-chosen words. It was, and remains in retrospect, reassuring that so civilized an evening could take place at the hub of state. Could any other country do likewise? I wonder.

The professional musician, for instance myself, can take a work and study it dispassionately, reserving exaltation for the moment of performance. But among the many professional conductors whom I have come to know over fifty years, there is one who has somehow preserved the freshness of the amateur. This is Edmond de Stoutz, conductor of the Zurich Chamber Orchestra. He occupies a niche in the world of music which is quite his own, carved out by the completeness of his dedication to his orchestra. In it there are first-rate musicians and musicians who are less than first-rate, but under his guidance the *whole* becomes first-rate. Hardly a day passes without his rehearsing them, and he conducts a rehearsal with the same zeal and excitement he brings to a concert. He shares the rigors of bus and boardinghouse with his players and yet retains his authority by virtue of the fact that he carries the burden. I have never known a person with less vanity; which may sound a contradiction in terms, for the conductor without vanity almost does not exist.

In the postwar years I gave up employing a regular accompanist although the two last, Marcel Gazelle and Adolph Baller (who overlapped, Baller touring with me in the Americas and Gazelle in Europe), remained welded into my life, and it was with Gazelle that I was to embark on my great adventure of starting a school. Once in a while I would employ an accompanist for a particular tour, most notable of whom was Leon Pommers, a charming fellow who still speaks with a Russian accent, one of the best accompanists in the United States and now a professor at Brooklyn College. He plays jazz very well too.

Increasingly, however, I have played with the pianists in the family and with other accomplished pianists of our day, such as Vladimir Ashkenazy, whom I invited to the Windsor Festival in 1972—a primary advantage of organizing festivals is the license given to invite the musicians one wants to meet and hear. Ashkenazy returned the courtesy by bringing me to play in Iceland, the strange and beautiful homeland of his choice. Another outstanding pianist who unfailingly inspires me is Wilhelm Kempff. Our acquaintance had a comic overture.

Late in 1955 I was asked to perform at a concert in Athens to be attended by King Paul and Queen Frederika, the diplomatic corps and "all Athens." Wanting neither to bring an accompanist nor to perform Bach solos, I inquired whether by chance a pianist would be there and learned that Kempff was due to perform; it was arranged that we should play together. Diana and I arrived by train—for this occurred during the nonflying years—and on reaching the British embassy, where we were to stay, found that our luggage had not caught up with us. Various embassies were rummaged for suitable clothing, but without great success: the trousers (French) were seemingly ironed sideways, the boots (Spanish) were too big, the tailcoat (German) trailing in the dust, the shirt (Italian) bulging out to give me the splendid frontage of a diva, and the overall sartorial effect such as to prompt the Italian ambassador to ask Diana who my tailor was. Only the Soviet representative saw nothing amiss.

Kempff and I hardly rehearsed on that occasion. We just skimmed through the program, discovering straightaway that we understood one another. This pattern was to be maintained: when he and I recorded all the Beethoven sonatas, we played without rehearsal, often choosing the first "take" of any particular movement. As I have suggested, Kempff is today the noblest exponent of the German tradition, who has remained true to the age when clock and metronome had not yet taken over the organic rhythm of the music and who is at the same time true to our age in his self-discipline. He achieves a supreme integration of the natural and spontaneous on the one hand and, on the other, rigorous respect for the composer's intention.

No twentieth-century musician could help but appreciate one of the great accompanists of our time, the Englishman Gerald Moore. Moore—now regrettably retired—used always to surprise me: given the size and width of his fingers, the extraordinary delicacy of his playing could not be foreseen; judging from his appearance as he sat at the piano, one felt it would be heavy and solid, but I doubt whether a more sensitive accompanist has ever existed. The two English accompanists whom I know best, Ivor Newton and Gerald Moore, have great virtues in common, but at opposed ends of the national spectrum: Ivor is the urbane, cultivated salon figure, Gerald represents the countryside. Artists who belong to the landscape seem an English specialty—just as London's parks have never been thoroughly citified, but remain rural fingers thrust into the heart of the metropolis. Elgar and Britten were two such artists, Moore is another. Unlike the completely urbanized musicians of Germany or France, the English musician will as often as not look to the countryside for refreshment, will own a farm if he can, or raise animals, or like Gerald Moore retire to Box Hill, to feel himself part of the life of plants and trees and fields.

The pianists with whom I most often play nowadays are my brother-in-law Louis Kentner and my sister Hephzibah. Louis, a Hungarian by birth, is a very great musician, one of the last of the grandiose pianists from the world of Liszt, Busoni and the early Rubinstein. Even before we were formally related, we played together often, and have since performed the Beethoven cycle twice in Paris and once in London. Louis enjoys the admiration of connoisseurs everywhere, as well as possessing a contented disposition which envies no man's circumstances. He has a loving and beloved wife, Griselda, Diana's sister, his books, his music and his teaching, and he loves his life. He has performed wonders at my school: in the time since he took over as head of the piano department the children have begun to play with a command, a vision, a spaciousness which only a great artist can convey. I know he too finds satisfaction in the work.

With Yaltah, although she too now lives in London and has occasionally performed at festivals organized by me, I have played very little. Yaltah is a very feminine person, sensitive, delicate, fragile, whose approach to music is deeply emotional. When my sisters were little girls at Basel, Rudolf Serkin (who taught them) considered Yaltah the more talented. It would be more just to say they have different talents. Hephzibah is a Rock of Gibraltar with an aesthetic unyielding to triviality, vulgarity or exaggeration; Yaltah, although less commanding of the key-board, has remarkable musicality and her performances are more reveal-ing. Living for a long time in Los Angeles, where she came to know many modern composers, she has been more in the stream of contempo-rary music than Hephzibah, who developed her independence and authority playing the classical repertoire in Australia during the war. I doubt whether Yaltah could cope with the rigors of the concert tour; unlike Hephzibah, she has not been trained to its army discipline, nor perhaps has she the physical strength to meet its punishing demands. In a destiny not notable for its indulgences, the piano may have been her refuge. Yaltah is a ministering angel, handing out remedies, crutches, comfort to the ailing who come to her door, reaping the rewards in kindness and gratitude that life has otherwise denied her.

Rightly or wrongly, I imagine that I know a human being from his or her musical performance. Performing, an artist lays himself bare, he exposes the secret temperament, the hidden motive, he risks the psycho-logical revelation. My sister Hephzibah is a case in point. Her playing has a clean, clear, somewhat no-nonsense approach, abjuring frills. It has as little cosmetic as she has, as little patience with the gaudy, eye-catching gesture as she herself is free of ambition to attract attention. Hephzibah's *pudeur* has its negative side, in that she has never cared to produce herself—in appearance, dress, performance, or in creating a public image. She could have been a leading virtuoso touring three hun-dred days a year. She chose otherwise.

She is fascinatingly like and unlike my mother. Like Mammina, she is so balanced, methodical and reliable that confronting a duty she will do it, unaffected by the pressures of immediate past or immediate future; in a house in turmoil, with a program to prepare and only ten minutes every two hours to spare for it, she will use each one of those random minutes to advantage, just as she once effortlessly mastered all the French irregular verbs. Like Mammina's, her taste abhors exaggera-tion. But unlike Mammina, Hephzibah has nothing to suppress. She has found utter fulfillment in her life, her husband, his social work, and her own music, and wears self-discipline, not as a rein upon an explosive temperament, but with joyful equanimity as if it were the most natural garment in the world.

Hephzibah's fondness for company is an old family joke—on tour with her, I daily look to see whom she may have invited to early break-fast. But behind such frivolities lies a truth. Just as Richard Hauser's social preoccupations awaited her commitment, so she prefers chamber music to the lonely glory of solo playing. In the main her appearances have been with me. She needs an object of inspiration, preferably her brother, in addition to the music; as in another sphere she needs to know she is fulfilling her husband's intentions. Hephzibah is quite clear about her nature. She admits that she requires other people's convictions to bolster her own, that she is not self-propelled, that she prefers to shine by reflection. However, with a rhythm behind her and a purpose to aim at, she holds nothing back. I think she falls into the third category of the proverb: He who knows, and knows not that he knows; awake him. And I believe she is awaking to her own gifts. Other musical influences than mine now work upon her: those of Efrem Kurtz and his wife, the wonderful flutist Elaine Schaffer, that of the Italian viola player Luigi Bianchi, have fired her to new expressiveness; and lately (and it would seem paradoxically) she has espoused women's liberation—perhaps to compensate for the handmaiden in her character, perhaps because her character permits self-assertiveness only in a larger cause.

Touring together, Hephzibah and I have our rituals. As experienced nomads who have learned to avoid unnecessary displacement, we prefer not to visit the hall during the course of the day, finding the time wasted on dressing, taxis, to-ing and fro-ing better spent in striking brief roots in the hotel room in order to sleep, exercise and work. About two hours before the public is admitted, we reach the hall, to practice first separately—she onstage and I in the artists' room—then together. I like to bring myself to performing pitch in this gradual way, but the hour spent onstage before blank rows of seats has also a humbler purpose: that of testing the acoustics. If one thing more than another can be labeled the bane of the traveling musician, it is poor acoustics; builders and managers of halls have found a dozen ways of ensuring them.

Built into our difference to technology there is a sort of perversity which embraces aberration with especial fervor. The perfect concert hall exists; it was invented by our forefathers and still stands in many a fortunate city to prove its virtues in performance. Yet how often clever architects, engineers and acousticians ignore such object lessons from the past to invest their combined expertise in a modern disaster! Such an enthusiasm for asking and cunningly answering the wrong questions raised London's Royal Festival Hall beside the Thames and New York's Lincoln Center in Manhattan. The acoustics built into the Festival Hall derived from the same obtuseness which designed recording studios twenty-five years ago without any echo whatsoever, as if music, like surgery, were best practiced under a light casting no shadow, allowing no depth, configuration or perspective. Less utterly antiseptic in conception, the RFH had, however, before modification, exactly the dry, mean acoustical effects the engineers had hoped to give it.

When Lincoln Center was in the planning, I sent to John D. Rockefeller III, who was promoting it, the plans of Stuttgart's Lieder-halle, which, born of an artist's drawing, not an engineer's blueprint, is one of the most imaginative and acoustically successful modern concert buildings. A structure of flowing, asymmetrical lines, the Liederhalle places its irregularly oval parterre between a curving wall of wood and another of streaked stone, and threads it with winding aisles which, like the river system they resemble, start narrow at the stage end and widen to accommodate increasing numbers toward the exit doors—the sort of common-sense arrangement it takes a designer of genius to think of. However, my attempt to influence Lincoln Center came to nothing. In contrast, Zubin Mehta, advising at every stage of the planning of Los Angeles' Dorothy Chandler Pavilion, ensured a rich, appealing sound, sufficiently median for lone singer or full orchestra. As in Festival Hall, so in Avery Fisher Hall at Lincoln Center, vibrating vessels installed in the roof have rendered the last state of the acoustics more glamorous than the first, but at a cost, on the occasion of each improvement, of a million dollars, the statutory sum, as it were, of American expenditure (at the time of writing, the spending of further millions is in process in a third attempt at rehabilitation). Technology can do much; it can seem to absolve the architect of responsibility; but the elegant economy which observes physical laws in achieving an objective remains the ideal.

For the happy accommodation of sound, a building must be high, spacious, and not too deep from back to front. Meeting these require-ments, the opera houses of the nineteenth century are, without exception and irrespective of size, perfect. Their horseshoe shape brings all the audience within reasonable earshot of the music; with shallow balconies and boxes, none of the public is hidden away in muffling shadows; the sound bounces off the walls and soars to the decorated roof. What the acoustical sophistication was that fathered these buildings, I don't know, having a pragmatic rather than a historical interest in the question, but I never cease to marvel that it should have been so wantonly discarded. Perhaps the answer to the puzzle lies in our epoch's preoccupation with the image and the eye, downgrading sound and the ear, and more par-ticularly in the presumption that new experience, pleasure and enter-tainment must reach us through the cinema. The cinema has done great

harm to concert halls, grounding the lofty roof, straightening and lengthening the auditorium, burying the audience under massive jutting balconies, reducing it to mere passive, comfortably cushioned spectators,
amplifying the sound to a deafening level of decibels. A ray of light can
illuminate a tunnel, but sound demands height, and with height can
communicate in a whisper. A recital in a tunnel is indeed a laborious
business, like swimming against a tide of molten toffee.

If Venice's little jewel, the Fenice, pleads for the cantabile strains
of Mozart or Paganini; if some great ecclesiastical edifice such as Canter-
bury Cathedral or the Münster at Basel seems built for the sonorities of
Bach; then the traditional European concert hall—Amsterdam's Concertgebouw, Leipzig's bombed Gewandhaus, or Boston's surviving
replica of it, Symphony Hall—is equally completed by the music of the
nineteenth-century masters. No less than the opera houses, these beautiful rectangular halls, with their elegantly proportioned height and spaciousness and with narrow, unobtrusive balconies, provide faultless
acoustics without fail.

One of their virtues is the lavish use of wood. Born in an age when
wood was the universal material and forests flourished in regions which
today offer only the bare earth's contours to the eye, the violin responds
most happily to a wooden echo chamber, as I repeatedly demonstrated to
myself during the war, in one standard wooden U.S. Army barracks after
another. Today the concert hall of Sydney Opera House, clad interiorly
in white Australian birch, provides further proof. Not many traditional
halls are paneled throughout, but within the building's noble proportions, the wood of floor and platform ensures warm and vital sound. Even
Paris's large, rather anonymous Salle Pleyel carries sound well from its
wooden stage. In a long acquaintance I have developed a fondness for
this somewhat ungainly hall and am prepared to overlook its faults. If I
cannot have wood, I like to play against rock, steel or—as I discovered on
my first visit to Mexico City in 1941—glass: the backdrop of the Bellas
Artes was heavy-leaded colored Tiffany glass from which sound bounced
with a brilliance and clarity equal to its lively hues.

Experience has given me reservations about performing out of
doors. Even in balmy regions, the three essential factors—stillness, no
humidity and perfect acoustics—too rarely come together. One of the
most dependable sites for such chancy concerts used to be the Robin
Hood Dell in Philadelphia, a natural hollow surrounded by grassy slopes
on which on summer nights the ladies' dresses looked like clusters of
wonderful flowers. Even in this pretty place, the sound had to be ampli-

fied for the further listeners, but it was discreetly done. Then improvement ruined the Dell. The slopes were bulldozed to enlarge the area, the floor concreted, benches installed, the amplification increased. Today it suggests a cattle pen. Perhaps the loss will be made good: in his untiring service to Philadelphia, Fredrick Mann has completed a new Dell in which I look forward to performing one day.

I have enjoyed successful concerts in ancient amphitheatres, the stone, steepness and shallowness of whose structure solve many an acoustical problem in the open air. But I have also known disasters, as at the first concert given in the Roman amphitheatre at Caesarea in Israel. Only trial can reveal error in these matters, and until then at Caesarea nothing had been tried. We were to give a program of chamber music—Maurice Gendron, Alberto Lysy, Ödön Partos, myself and Ernst Wallfisch, the violist (a student of Enesco's whom I met when he played at an official luncheon given in Rumania by the Gauleiterin Anna Pauker; and whom I contrived to bring to the United States). We sat down, opened our music, set it on the stands, raised our bows and began to play. All was going serenely when suddenly there came a puff of wind from the adjacent Mediterranean and, whoosh, the pages flipped rapidly over, landing some of us in the second movement, others in the last. We began again. The second gust was more considerable. Two lots of music flew right off the stands. Someone suggested clothespins, but as this solution required a pause at the end of each page while the music was unpinned, turned and pinned again, I finally asked for page-turners from the audience—or rather for holders down of pages. Among those who responded was Jeremy, then about ten. Thus we got through the first half of the program, each with his attendant acolyte. At the intermission our wives and friends came to offer consolation and commiseration—to all except me. Weak with laughter, Diana stumbled up to me and gasped, "I've never enjoyed a concert so much in all my life!"

Comedy or tragedy, that experiment taught the uses of screens and sounding boards for music in the open air. Nowadays excellent outdoor concert "halls" are built and Caesarea can be confident of its charms.

Very rarely does the traveling musician have to cope with too resonant a hall. The outstanding exception is, of course, the church. In my time I have played in many a church—for instance, at my yearly festival at Gstaad held in Saanen—and have come to know the problems and advantages of ecclesiastical architecture. For there are great advantages. Among the most exalted moments of my life was a performance of unaccompanied Bach in Westminster Abbey: it was an extraordinary and wonderful sensation, knowing that one's least note must wing and wind its way to every corner of the majestic building, and that the resonance of those vaulting walls, which would only clog a harmonic instrument, aided the single violin, underlying the implied harmonies as a pedal does on a piano, giving the sound radiance and warmth. In the resonance of a church one must alter one's playing: a fast movement, for instance, must be taken more slowly than normal; but such calculations are not often needed. In general, any divergence from perfect acoustics is not on the side of over-resonance but toward the dull, the flat and the dead. Worst of all is when the good ladies in some small town dress the stage with heavy velvet curtains.

I met the ultimate in the velvet curtaining of music at Mayagüez, second city of Puerto Rico (and birthplace of Martita Casals), when Adolph Baller and I played there in the war. In the little hall scheduled for our recital hung not merely one, but several sets of curtains between the wings and the open stage, among which we played bizarre games of hide-and-seek, blundering into one another in desperate attempts to find a parting amid the suffocating folds. It was like landing at Heathrow airport on some overcast London day when one penetrates a first layer of cloud expecting to see the land rising toward one, but finding instead a second layer and below that a third.

To find velvet barriers between oneself and one's audience an hour before the first note is due to sound is to be powerless: one can neither tear the draperies down nor mitigate their effect; one simply has to play as warmly as possible. In less disastrously decorated halls, however, improvements can be made. The position of the players *vis-à-vis* one another and the audience is a factor favoring or otherwise the balance of a performance. In a hall with little resonance, the piano is propped open on the large stick; where the acoustics favor the piano at the violin's expense, the small stick is used. Other things being equal, I prefer the piano full open and like to stand in its curve, whence the sound of violin and piano flows as a unit. The tests made and the decisions taken, it is time for the audience to begin arriving and for Hephzibah and me to disappear backstage. There I have the advantage over her. Few halls boast a piano in the artists' room, so she must twiddle her thumbs while I can continue limbering up until the last moment (actually, she practices on any table top).

There are three elements, it seems to me, in the design of a building which contribute to success in performance: they are the acoustical, the visual and the social, and all three were generally better served in the past than they are today. The doctrine that all men are equal appears to have led concert hall designers to assume that all men want armchairs for listening to music. Such an assumption is not only unrealistic in its estimate of costs to builders and audience; it also misconceives the audience's image of itself. Students avoid the stalls and throng promenade concerts not only on account of slender incomes but because of life style. Campaigning for informal concerts, Pierre Boulez, conducting the New York proms, has the seats taken from the parterre and replaced with cushions. It has proved a popular arrangement, but one would not need to go to such lengths were the halls not, to begin with, untenable for any but the bourgeoisie.

Then, an audience must be able to see and hear itself enjoying a performance. The failure to ensure a sense of corporate acclaim was one of the many original sins of the Royal Festival Hall, a hall which I sometimes think was designed to put the artist in his place and reduce his and everyone else's pleasure in the occasion. Hephzibah and I gave the first recital there, the day after it was opened with fanfares and orchestras. At that time the stage was no more than a foot off the ground, and as there are public exit doors also at this level, the performer coming back onstage to make his bow was screened from half the house by people streaming out to catch their last bus home. On the occasion of our next recital there, I asked to have the stage built up. It has now been permanently raised, but the Festival Hall is still calculated to reduce a concert to a street incident. Only less perfunctory is the Festival Hall's late-born sister, the Queen Elizabeth Hall, whose dark concrete walls have at least a certain somber glamour, as of a royal tomb perhaps.

These less than satisfactory buildings have made plain to everyone the virtues of the once much abused Royal Albert Hall in Kensington. Not only does it have ghosts, atmosphere and a sense of occasion, but its acoustics are at any rate no worse than its rivals'. Moreover, it brings on the performer at an oblique angle to the audience and into full view of the entire house at the same moment, the optimum conditions for establishing rapport. In contrast, at the Festival Hall (and at many others), the artist comes on from the side. The prime reason for his progress across the stage is to accept applause, but since he is progressing along a course parallel to much of his audience, he cannot easily face them, smile, acknowledge their tribute; and the whole exercise dwindles into a faintly embarrassing absurdity in which both parties valiantly display gladness, but from good breeding more than spontaneous sentiment. Quite the most uncooperative hall I have been obliged to cross was the old Shriners Auditorium at Los Angeles, where I often played in youth. Seating many thousands, it had a stage almost the length of a city block, to reach the center of which took so interminable a time that the audience's welcome, however genuine, exhausted itself before one arrived and the acclaim at the end of a performance could never stretch beyond a second return.

I enjoy the contrast which an artists' room presents before and after a concert. Before, it is a scene of earnest preparation (I can work in the presence of people if need be, but prefer to be private). Afterward it assembles a social throng whose compliments, if I have played well, are pleasant to receive. If I look forward most eagerly to Diana's return and to the comments of friends and colleagues, it is nonetheless true that everyone's contribution is welcome, even that of the inarticulate. But the after-concert ceremony has on occasion been awkward. I recall a recital which Hephzibah and I gave to a musical society in Vevey, Switzerland—a small society but a prestigious one, to which I have felt an obligation since the director showed me a somewhat brusque letter of refusal written by my father perhaps forty years ago. When I played there with Hephzibah, the well-wishers who came backstage included a lady whose poor face was distorted by a pronounced squint. She told me that I had given the first concert she ever attended, and added, *"Et cela m'a marquée pour la vie"*—"It marked me for life."

What is the interpreter's role? Certainly he is more than a simple transmitter. Between composer and audience he brings the living element and restores the pulse of life to the dry notes on the stave. What creates an interpretation is a very slight unevenness, originating in personal feeling, which recognizes that life does not proceed at an unchanging pace, but that blood and breath must quicken or slacken according to circumstance. As I am rather literal, I have tried to reduce the principle of distortion to a working technique, imitating instinct, as it were, or at any rate pinpointing under instinct's direction which notes are more important, which less, where a phrase rises and falls, which passages call for resignation, which for effort. Some works by their very nature bear less distortion than others. The noble unity of Bach's Chaconne, the greatest structure for solo violin that exists, is damaged by impulsive handling. The lengthened note, the hurry, destroying poise of progression, the vain ornament or indulgent change of volume, break the spell. With Bach's music in general, it is fascinating to note how by reducing volume, range

of dynamics, vibrato, attack, one often increases its power to communicate. Similarly with Schubert: perhaps more than any other nineteenth-
century composer's, his music suffers from an interpreter's temptations to
linger through a soft passage or accelerate a crescendo, but played
with almost metronomic strictness, its cumulative effect is overpowering.
Thus, although distortion is vital, it must be practiced on a knife edge,
and music made more dramatic than it was intended to be succeeds only
in being coarse.

The interpreter's duty is threefold. First he must master the numberless muscular pressures which in every position on every string will
produce every quality of sound. Then, having learned the phonetics of
his language, he must put them together to convey a message, and to do
this must have a fullness in himself to express before the composer's
fullness finds a response. Lastly he needs an understanding of the composer's style, a corrective to the urge to express himself rather than the
music. Thus, he puts all his equipment, his skill, the raw material of his
whole life at the service of another man's vision—a vision which has
become his own without, at the moment of performance, the need for
thinking about it. Technical mastery consists of automatic responses to
impulse, gathered over many years and fed into the instinctive computer
of one's brain, which then mysteriously translates impulse into the right
flexing and unflexing of the fingers as one draws the bow, the right width
of vibrato, the right speed, volume, pressure. It is as if one carried within
oneself a personal catalogue integrating instinct, experience, intellect and
emotion, at hand for reference at any moment under the guidance of an
interpretative conception.

The interpreter must of course create, but there are degrees of
creation and no doubt composition is the highest. My compensation is to
commission music, an activity which offers many pleasures. For the composer there is the satisfaction of working for someone willing to risk the
result; for the interpreter, to be associated with the act of creation fulfills
a part of his nature which may otherwise be frustrated. The creative, I
firmly hold, is the normal human condition, whether displayed in the
kitchen, in housekeeping, in violin-housekeeping or in any of a hundred
ways. That there is another definition of normality I am well aware, but
I combat strenuously the view that equates the normal with that state
of bodily and spiritual undernourishment in which most people have to
live. For me it is the height and perfection of normality to know the
painter in his studio, to greet the composer when the ink is drying on

his manuscript, to play his work for his first hearing. So from the time I first met Ernest Bloch, I have sought music when and where opportunity offered.

Bloch's last works, his Suites Numbers 1 and 2 for Solo Violin, were written for me; he had been my first composer, I was his last performer. He was already ill when I commissioned them in 1957 at Agate Beach in Oregon, a wild, forlorn stretch of coastline looking down upon waves coming all the way from Asia to break on the shore, a place which suited the grandeur and intensity of his character. His suites are beautifully written for the violin, expressive, melodic, classical in a manner that calls to mind latter-day Bach, and for that reason probably doomed to be underrated. It is curious that a work of art is not allowed to state its own terms, but must be judged by the canons of fashion. Were it possible, I would like to try a little experiment with these compositions, presenting them as the recently discovered work of a hitherto unknown contemporary of Bach—who was perhaps a Jew from Russia, or who had traveled in the East and come under gypsy influence, rejecting the ordered and fugal to write in a more episodic and improvised way; they would surely be considered the find of the century.

Without doubt Bartók is the greatest composer I have known. As man and as musician he had some kinship with Bloch. Both knew and loved the natural world; in music both express human pain, both have a heroic quality which goes far beyond the confines of ordinary mortals, both suggest power; technically, moreover, they share a liking for fourths and fifths. But points of similarity serve only to emphasize the distance between them. Whereas Bloch's outrage speaks perhaps too directly to the grieved human condition, Bartók resists such indulgence with un-Jewish ruthlessness. Bloch may be carried away by the Wailing Wall, as it were—railing against fate, shaking the columns of man's house, rebuking God for not having arranged things differently; Bartók is contained, his heroism rejects heroics, his compassion is forged in steel.

The Solo Sonata Bartók wrote for me was his last completed work, I believe. He later substantially completed two concerti, for piano and for viola—the latter a wonderful composition remarkably orchestrated by his *alter ego*, Tibor Serly, which I play. After Bartók's death I had the good fortune to present to the world another of his works, the First Violin Concerto, a charming piece in two movements, full of youth, tenderness and humor. He had written it many years before for Steffi Geyer, with whom he was then in love, but she never played it, and for that reason or another Bartók later used the first movement for his Two Portraits for

Orchestra, contrasting views of the same person. Steffi Geyer stipulated in her will that the Concerto's first performance should be given by her colleague the Swiss violinist Hansheinz Schneeberger; but thereafter, thanks to Bartók's New York lawyer and executor, Bator, I had exclusive rights to it for a year.

My veneration for Bartók once caused me embarrassment. Playing in Helsinki in the early 1950s, I made my pilgrimage to Sibelius, who, his life's work completed forty years earlier, was living in revered retirement. He received me on the balcony of his cozy wooden house, standing in its own stretch of forest, as must any self-respecting house in Finland. Who, he soon asked me, did I consider the greatest composer of the twentieth century? Thus challenged by one who had himself some claim to the title, I was at a stand between honesty and civility, but while I hesitated he rescued me. "Bartók is our greatest composer," he pronounced, adding that as a student in Berlin he had known Bartók. I could have hugged him—for casting me a lifeline, but more for his generosity and clear-sightedness. Sibelius's own achievement was admirable. It exemplified the power that music has above other arts to speak to and for a people's subconscious, giving expression to communal vision, experience and fantasy. Not only was Sibelius a spokesman for Finland at this profound level, but he was eminently exportable to the Anglo-Saxon world, sponsored in Britain by Sir Thomas Beecham and much played in the United States. On the other hand, he cannot speak to or for the Latins, whose Cartesian practicality rejects the Romantic ecstasy which turns fog into myth and darkness into long winter's tales.

On one of several visits to Helsinki I was invited to perform the Sibelius Concerto at the festival held in 1955 to celebrate the composer's ninetieth birthday. So honored, I did not dare confess I had never played the Concerto; I promised to perform, then settled down to work at it. Unable to attend the concert, Sibelius listened to the broadcast and afterward telephoned to express his satisfaction. It is always gratifying to have a living composer's approval; other considerations apart, it gives one a certain assurance that one is not distorting the dead.

After Bartók, perhaps the most important composer whom I have commissioned is the late Frank Martin, whose acclaim rose to match his stature only in the last years of his life. In preparation for the 1973 congress of the IMC, to be held in Geneva and Lausanne, it was suggested that the greatest living Swiss composer be asked to write a work for the opening concert to be performed by myself as president. Together, Edmond de Stoutz and I made the approach, the result of which was Martin's very moving *Polyptique,* a suite for solo violin and string orchestra, subtitled on Diana's suggestion *Six Images de la Vie du Seigneur*—Six Images from the Life of Jesus. While it was being written, and when it was recorded in 1974 in the presence of Martin and his wife, Maria, who helped in its composition, I came to know the composer and found him a man of utter goodness, pure, God-fearing, devout in the broadest, most tolerant sense, yet with a cutting edge. All his work is infused with deep conviction. He never followed fashionable trends, or wrote exclusively according to twelve-tone or any other theory, but evolved over the years a style which, while unmistakably contemporary, retains its individual harmonic character and withal has a human message to give. He told me that on receiving the IMC request he had not known what he would write, until one day he found himself in Siena and in the museum there saw a polyptych of scenes from the Gospels. In our correspondence Martin had already proposed writing a series of short movements rather than a concerto, a structure which admirably accommodated the inspiration of Siena. He chose six related scenes—Palm Sunday, the Last Supper, Judas, the Garden of Gethsemane, the Judgment and the Glorification. As I told him, I was grateful that he had spared me the Crucifixion; for the solo violin represents both Jesus and the Evangelist, while the orchestra supplies the apostles, the crowd and the atmosphere. Repeated performances in different countries since 1973 have only confirmed the music's appeal. *Polyptique* is one of the works which the twentieth century can be proud to bequeath to the future.

As I have suggested, an interpreter can afford to be more tolerant than a composer. The composer must assimilate only those influences which nourish his own creative gifts (influences which, of course, may be exotic and unexpected), and must by the same token spurn the unassimilable; consequently he tends to have strong dislikes. My own dislikes are not directed to the works of a particular country or century, nor to those of an individual, but in general to the cheapening of any genuine music from whatever culture. The more an interpreter understands, the more fortunate he is. Wide sympathies in the past, however, do not ensure comprehension of the present, which sometimes seems less a continuing experience of music than half a dozen new departures in as many directions.

Handling a two-hundred-and-fifty-year-old instrument and music much of which is scarcely younger, one may lose that sense of belonging to the present world which is as essential as regional or traditional roots to the vitality of a culture. I could wish that today's composers held the violin in greater affection, but recognize that melody or counterpoint, i.e., the blending of horizontal lines, to which the instrument pre-eminently lends itself, are not the first concern of most of them. Nevertheless, I have amassed many good and some outstanding works, and dare to hope for more from the current trend away from abstract experiment to renewed expression of feeling. But in one way the nonperformer has the advantage over me: he can spend instructive evenings with recordings and the study of scores, whereas all the time I have is given to preparing specific performances. As a result, I am not as familiar with the whole range of new composition as I would like to be; nor certain that my analytical methods, elaborated for the classical repertoire, can successfully dissect works so different—from those of the past and from each other.

Such is the diversity of a modern composer's means that, Balinese or Armenian in the morning, his work may be *à la* Mozart or electronic by the afternoon, and threatens surfeit by sheer richness of reference. When Viotti composed violin concerti (unlike the Romantics, he composed some twenty-nine), he spread invention thinly. It is reasonable to suppose that novelty had greater power to astonish early-nineteenth-century ears, before Brahms and Tchaikovsky, Strauss and Stravinsky, had complicated people's notions of the organization of sound. Today, in contrast, novelty is at a premium, requiring every can of baked beans to assert itself, every idiom to be personal, every person to be original, and every composition to startle by departure from tradition.

However, if I am glad to have my own world of music, a line of retreat from experiment, a shelter from which to make excursions along the wilder shores of new composition, I know that I return with a refreshed awareness of sound. I would be the last to deny the fascination of exploring either the other cultures now available to us or the structure of sound itself. The inquiring mind is surely one of humanity's most attractive features. Even in the past, of course, an innovator had to endure a time lag before his listeners caught up with him. The difference today is that the bemused listener must first choose which of countless innovators he will run after.

The innovator's first listeners will often be his performers. Curiously enough, Italy is particularly rich in little societies which cultivate interest in advanced music, perhaps in impatient reaction to the country's indulgence in operatic sentiment. For such societies, whose members are musicians and the richer intelligentsia, the more pioneering the music, the better they like it; but these are a tiny minority. In general, to announce even one work by an unknown composer is to keep an audience away.

In 1958 I commissioned a solo sonata from the American composer Ross Lee Finney for the opening of the American pavilion at the Brussels Fair, and shortly afterward included it in a recital my sister and I were to give in London. It being a rather difficult twelve-tone piece, we inserted it between safely familiar works, the sharp filling in the sandwich. About a week before the concert my London manager, Ian Hunter, reported disappointing ticket sales. My tactic was to remove Ross Lee Finney from the advertised program and replace his sonata with Beethoven's *Kreutzer*. The tickets straightaway sold out, as for the *Kreutzer* they invariably do. At the concert I gently admonished the audience. "I hope you don't feel you are here under false pretenses," I said. "You weren't going to come to hear the Ross Lee Finney which I wanted to play for you. We announced we would play the *Kreutzer*, and so we will. But first you must listen to Ross Lee Finney. . . ." By such contrivances, concert managements and artists try to broaden the pyramid's base. Perhaps we don't altogether fail, for it is a rare program today which only looks back to the past.

Among the prized new works composed for me are concerti by Lennox Berkeley, Easley Blackwood, Arnold Cooke, Ödön Partos, Andrzej Panufnik and Malcolm Williamson; a double concerto by the violinist and composer Stanley Weiner; a concerto for violin and sitar by Alan Hovhaness; sonatas by Paul Ben-Haim and Weiner; music for solo violin by Harry Somers; a duet for two violins which Darius Milhaud composed one night at my home in California, apparently unaffected by the lively conversation buzzing around him; incidental music by Edwin Roxburgh for Diana's television programs on Lear and Cummings; and works for orchestra, or for other soloists and orchestra, by Peter Maxwell Davies, Antal Dorati, Nicholas Maw and Oliver Knussen. One of the most talented of younger English composers, Alexander Goehr, wrote a trio which Hephzibah, Maurice Gendron and I first played at one of the Bath festivals. At first sight, passages in it seemed to me unnecessarily complicated, and I asked Sandy why he didn't write more simply. His disconcerting answer was that he had wanted to put me to the test! In fact, the piece stands on its own merits.

In addition, of course, from the Elgar Concerto onward, I have played or conducted much new music in the commissioning of which I had no part, including works by Enesco, Bartók, Britten, Hindemith, Bloch, Ravel, Ildebrando Pizzetti, and many others.

A further debt I owe to the twentieth century is friendship with that most exotic of my colleagues, the Canadian pianist Glenn Gould. It was with him that I first played a piece by Schönberg. Perhaps no one in the world knows as much about Schönberg as Glenn does, or more than he does about the recording and broadcasting of music. He is a paradox, choosing to lead a hermit's existence in his Toronto apartment, where even his secretary never penetrates, dining at some anonymous motel to escape recognition, but spending his summers in the northern wilderness, living rough with lumbermen and exploring gold mines. When we were rehearsing for a television program, I had the privilege of breaching the defended seclusion of his apartment. Apart from the piano, its furnishings had a somewhat unloved look. "Hasn't it occurred to you that you need a woman around here?" I asked. Rather indignantly he said that a lady came in once a week. I told him her visits left no obvious mark and wondered whether he had ever thought of getting married. "Ah!" he said disarmingly. "If I found someone like Diana, I wouldn't hesitate for a moment."

16

Promptings from Fate

Enesco's violin was too small to contain his powers; I, at sixty, know I have not yet explored the violin's limits. If I have not Enesco's musical diversity, my experience has, however, followed his in finding constraints as well as satisfactions in the life of a touring virtuoso. There is nothing odd in this. Some of my colleagues may travel the world with little baggage, but for everyone who contents himself with his instrument, others find ways to widen their scope. To impart what one has strived to learn is among the most profound of human urges, and in obedience to it, we violinists publish musical editions, write books, acquire pupils, found quartets, conduct orchestras. Meddling in such matters, I am happy to know that mine is a well-trodden path, but I suspect that personal history has pushed me somewhat further along it than most of my contemporaries.

In the democratic unit which my parents, my sisters and myself composed when I was young, none of us ever asserted himself or herself in an individual act of will which left the others out of account. Except for electing the violin at the beginning, I scarcely once disturbed the family pattern with a single-handed exercise of authority until I became an adult. Our days concentrated on duties to each other, to lessons and to music, and the wide various world across which we traveled so constantly remained at a certain remove, its problems real but theoretical. The result of my upbringing was not to stifle initiative, however, but to leave it in suspense. None of the important influences in my life was narrowing, and all of my teachers, Persinger and Enesco in particular, in the men they were as well as in what they taught, continually widened horizons. Consequently desires to explore, to make contact, to work with other people, to take initiative and exert influence were growing inside me before ever they found expression, like seeds germinating within their unchanged shells until at an appropriate moment the shells simply gave way to reveal not timid little shoots but, as it were, already sturdy plants.

The appropriateness of the moment has been a recurring blessing. Circumstances have repeatedly organized themselves to offer opportunity, even rescue. Such was the chance to break out of my platform personality in the wartime tours, or the discovery of yoga and its contribution to understanding violin playing, or the people or events which thrust me into festivals or onto the conductor's podium, or outside musical concerns altogether into preoccupation with health, education and ecology. It could be argued that apart from my immediate work, my school is the only achievement traceable to an unaided initiative, and that all the other obligations with which I crowd my life came about in response to suggestions or requests from others. These other interests are nonetheless mine, the furniture of the several other lives I would like to lead full-time but can't. I have seized what was offered with an appetite the more hearty for its long incubation, but—to anticipate the charge of obsession—I am as insatiable for leisure and holidays as for work and worry.

One specific gap in early experience, which the diverse activities of later years have helped to fill, was acquaintance with other musicians. To the outsider it may seem curious that someone who has spent his life with music should feel deprived of musical companionship; in fact, the soloist who fulfills an engagement this evening at Poughkeepsie and must travel to Kalamazoo tomorrow has no leisure to cultivate his colleagues. If there are compensations in such a schedule, in that renewed public stimulus helps to keep his playing alive, it also restricts lateral musical growth, as well as robbing him of the simple pleasures of talking shop. Part of the blame must be borne by that much-abused phenomenon the pace of modern life, a counterpart of monetary inflation, greedily swallowing ever larger expenditure of energy for no greater return. In the days when low taxation made a winter's earnings sufficient for a year's livelihood, and when engagements were spaced out by the relatively stately progress of ships and trains, it was possible to become acquainted with the musical celebrities of the towns one visited, to attend salons where they existed, to participate in an impromptu musical occasion, and to have the whole summer free for reflection, enjoyment and meeting one's colleagues. As a child I did not have such independence, but concentrated on my specific task, passed my musical life in front of either teachers or audiences, and went home to the family in the summer. Contact on an equal basis with other musicians almost never occurred. When I came to manhood, and after the war's dislocation, the pattern changed for everyone. Then, and even more so now, the functions of the salon, of summer reunions, of evenings without engagement in some noted center of music, were all encompassed by the festival. The many festivals I have been associated with in the last thirty years, as performer or as director, or both, have therefore opened doors on missing indulgences. But they are one outlet among others. At festivals each year, at *concours* less often, and most of all in conducting and in teaching, I have immersed myself in the wider world of music, made friendships of inestimable value with my kind, and gradually satisfied many an old yearning.

If, unlike Enesco, I don't find the violin too small, this has not prevented me from appreciating that the viola is larger! My involvement with the viola was, again, something I owed to another—to my dear colleague Nathan Firestone, who, as I have recounted, left me his Testori. To play the viola is to endow oneself with another voice. It is like growing a beard and finding one's weak chin suddenly authoritative. For many years after Nathan's funeral, at which I performed the slow movement of a Brahms viola sonata, I played the instrument only for myself until, in 1959, my newly founded orchestra presented the Brandenburg Concerti at the Bath Festival (in the Sixth Concerto there are no violins; the violas have the top line). Since then I have turned to it more systematically, not only for an occasional recording or public performance, but often using it as a practice instrument, especially on holidays. A fifth lower than the violin, and altogether a little heavier, wider, longer, quieter, it gives a feeling of strength and thus strengthens violin playing. It is not an instrument for the vain violinist showing off his pyrotechnics, but for the serious musician who takes his part in the inner harmony of orchestra or string quartet. To a violinist it offers a new repertoire and an extension of his experience without requiring of him in return an altogether new technique.

I have tried my hand at one other instrument, the Swiss alphorn; regrettably, the sounds I win from it are unpredictable, in pitch, in volume, even in occurrence. Without skills on drums, brass or wood-wind, I acknowledge my range to be limited, but console myself with the reflection that in a crisis I could probably acquit myself tolerably on the triangle.

I have never made up my mind whether musical competitions are more helpful or more harmful to young violinists. For an adjudicator they are very agreeable occasions, and give me a pleasure supplied by no other part of my life—a week, every now and then, in the exclusive company of violinists. In addition, they undoubtedly benefit violin playing, not only by raising standards, but by focusing public interest on a subject which usually escapes most laymen's concerns. It is gratifying to witness the fervor generated throughout Belgium by the quadrennial Brussels *concours,* perhaps the most prestigious contest of them all, where the candidates find themselves elevated to the unaccustomed and possibly intimidating position of national heroes, their chances of doing their native countries credit earnestly mulled over in homes and cafés and by taxi drivers. Perhaps one should deplore the fact that national sentiment adds piquancy to an event ostensibly only musical, but chauvinism tells only half the story. An adjudicator at Brussels is often stopped in the street to hear someone's views on this candidate's tone as against that candidate's technical brilliance, and can only be pleased to know that a whole country is, for the moment, taking the violin seriously.

Any event which serves to boost the violin must have my support; but my attitude to *concours* remains ambivalent. Indubitably they impose a tremendous strain upon candidates, yet victory does not necessarily guarantee a career; which may suggest incompetent adjudication but in fact simply demonstrates that a career is different from a contest. The failed contest which blights a career has occurred in my experience as an adjudicator, and I still wince at the memory. It happened in Brussels in 1967.

Since the Second World War the Russian contingent at Brussels had regularly scooped most of the prizes, a situation which, making success customary, only rendered anything less than distinction hideous to contemplate. On this particular occasion David Oistrakh spoke to me about his country's great hope, a young man called Sitkovietsky, who played brilliantly. The Russian team, teachers and pupils, adjudicator and contestants, all came together, and if such national solidarity permitted contacts between judges and judged which other competitors did not enjoy and seemed to betray the ideal of disinterestedness, the fault was overlooked because by any standards the Russians at that point were effortlessly superior. David's mention of his young compatriot was not intended to influence my judgment—indeed it occurred after the prizes had been awarded—but only to engage my sympathy. Sitkovietsky, he told me, could work with profit round the clock and had done so since the age of six, grooming himself through endless laborious years for world acclaim as a leading virtuoso. And then, at Brussels, he was rated second. For most aspirants this would have been a triumph; for Sitkovietsky it was a tragedy, and Oistrakh's despondency gave me the measure of it. To win meant to breathe, to travel; to fail to win meant relegation to some Siberian orchestra or provincial concert circuit; it was the difference between life and death. I myself had found a competing candidate more musical, but the poignancy of the situation gave me a revulsion toward dividing winners from losers—the more so when, a few months later, Sitkovietsky suddenly died of a brain tumor, his "failure" at Brussels doubtless still heavy on his heart.

The Brussels *concours* bears the name of the late Queen Elizabeth of the Belgians, who founded it with the assistance of her teacher, Eugène Ysaÿe, and it now continues under the patronage of Queen Fabiola. At the time of writing, the violin *concours* which would have been held in 1975 has been postponed for a year to coincide with the hundredth anniversary of the founder's birth. (Tragically it will also commemorate Oistrakh, who, until his death in 1974, was so inevitably a figure at it as to be part of the furnishings.) My own involvement with the *concours* dates from its postwar resumption, but unlike Oistrakh, for example, I have never been able to sacrifice a whole month to see the event through from start to finish, and have been obliged to confine attendance to the final week. By the time I come on the scene, the competitors have been reduced to twelve finalists, two of whom perform each night, from Monday to Saturday, when the results are computed and announced to a breathless nation. Each of these twelve, who have already been through several grueling rounds, must play a work for violin and piano, their own choice from the big concerti, and an *oeuvre imposée* written for the occasion, usually a short concerto, which is delivered to each finalist a given number of days before it must be played. Since the contest is broadcast, later competitors have the advantage of hearing this new work performed by the other finalists, but on the whole the *concours* is as fair—and as demanding—as human ingenuity can make it.

For someone like myself, who never attended a conservatory, as student or as teacher, who never played in an orchestra, these occasional weeks of prolonged contact with other violinists are particularly rewarding, granting acquaintance with those people with whom precisely I have most in common and least chance to meet. The one I used to seek most eagerly was Oistrakh, for the reasons of compatibility and friendship already given. We would talk about music, of course, and many other things besides; but politics we avoided: there was no point in stressing painful truths sufficiently evident of themselves.

Not all violinists, I have to admit, are good adjudicators. I recall one (he shall remain nameless) who scandalized the rest of us by giving favored treatment to his own pupils. But partiality in a jury is usually less of a problem than sheer subjective oddity of judgment. An offender in this respect was Joseph Szigeti.

Szigeti was a violinist whom I much admired and a man of whom I was very fond. From the accident of our both having houses in California and Switzerland, we saw a lot of each other, and I always found him completely generous, honorable and kind. Apart from Enesco, he was the most cultivated violinist I have known, but whereas Enesco was a force of nature, Szigeti, slender, small, anxious, was a beautifully fashioned piece of porcelain, a priceless Sèvres vase. Curiously for a Hungarian, from whom one expects wild, energetic, spontaneous qualities, Szigeti traveled ever farther up a one-way road of deliberate intellectualism. A young accompanist who had worked with Szigeti told me that two hours' concentration wouldn't get them beyond the first three bars of a sonata—so much analysis and ratiocination went into his practice. Had Szigeti worked in that manner as a young man, he could not have become the great violinist he was; I recall particularly a performance of the Brahms Concerto in New York and a recital in a small Texas town where we happened to meet, neither of which owed their impressive virtues to the plodding intellect. A similar pernicketiness marked his adjudication. Shortly before he died in 1973, he was a member of our jury at the City of London Carl Flesch Concours, which Yfrah Neaman and I organize every two years. I was struck not only by the sharpness of his intellectual grasp, but also by what seemed to me the perversity of his opinions. Some particular aspect of a competitor's playing would hold his attention, and he would take violent issue with it, to the exclusion of everything else. For him a violinist was made or broken, a prize awarded or withheld, on details that to me scarcely mattered.

Once out of Nazi clutches (with Furtwängler's help), Carl Flesch escaped to Switzerland, where in 1944 he died. Before his death he spent some time in London, and there, about thirty years ago, a small competition was begun in his name. It did not gain much amplitude, however, until Ian Hunter took it in hand and persuaded the City of London to incorporate the *concours* in its biennial festival. It was a simpler task to persuade me to be involved. Ian Hunter, my manager in Britain, is not a man to be satisfied with arranging concerts and negotiating fees, but has left his mark upon the musical world in the shape of many a festival launched or reshaped, many another event imaginatively undertaken, and at least one violin *concours,* the City of London Carl Flesch. Understandably, the new competition did not elicit much response to begin with, and still—despite Russian adjudicators—does not attract competitors from the Soviet Union; but gradually we have won renown and with it entrants from East and West Europe, the United States, Japan and Israel.

The Carl Flesch is, I think, conceived on more humane and possibly more musical lines than most contests. Each contestant has the opportunity, following the ordeal, of speaking for a half hour or more with two members of the jury, in recognition that he is not just a collection of skills which do or do not merit a prize, but a struggling violinist who may need advice, and a fellow human being committed to the same line of duty as oneself. There are other special features. Carl Flesch's son, who is an insurance agent, has offered a prize for chamber music performance, so that qualities wider than virtuosity are measured. Then, those members of the public who are present throughout the *concours* have a chance to name their own favorite. I think this a useful innovation. The musician plays for the public, after all, and must take into account that magnetism which will assure him a career. Furthermore, the results of the jury's deliberations are not confided to a secret ballot, as in Brussels, but to open discussion. It seems to me that one of the chief interests of the event is the chance given to violinists to discuss interpretation and technique, and that absolute discretion about the candidates' merits is forced and unnatural. So having reached our individual conclusions, we arrive at consensus in debate.

To avoid extremes of subjective judgment I plan to introduce (if the rest of the jury agree) a breakdown of items for consideration which I have previously used myself. Under overall headings of "left hand" and "right hand" are subheadings, each allotted the number of points which seem appropriate. Thus, under "left hand," points are given for "vibrato," "trills," "position shifting," "general clarity," "position of the violin" and so forth. There is a similar breakdown for the function of the right hand, and in addition, points awarded for interpretation, communication and musicianship. These points would serve as a basis for discussion, ensuring that no one aspect blinded us to the others and perhaps guaranteeing a more just verdict. Whether in fact the result would be any different, I can't be sure, but remembering poor Sitkovietsky, it seems important to be as scrupulous as possible.

Three promptings from fate may surely be taken seriously without charge of superstition. Thus, the Gstaad festival was launched in 1956 at the suggestion of others, leaving to me the graceful role of acceptance. It was in that year that Diana and I transplanted our family from the United States to Europe, and no sooner had we rented a house in Gstaad than the town's Kurdirektor approached us to hint that a festival might brighten the slack summer season. The other promptings came independently from friends.

As soon as the war was over festivals had started to crop up here and there. At first they were as rare and unpretentious as spring flowers, but holding promise of summer luxuriance in the future, when almost every town would wish to assert its identity in a festival and musicians would take in half a dozen in a season. Among the first was Aldeburgh in Suffolk, where in the midst of postwar austerities, Benjamin Britten found a way of playing his own music and other people's with his friends. After our joint tour of the concentration camps we remained in touch, and when Ben invited me to Aldeburgh, I jumped at the opportunity. This was Aldeburgh's infancy, before it gained its present prestige or Ben his international name, when arrangements were simple and one played for the love of it, there being, among other considerations, little or no money available. Once in a while the BBC would broadcast a performance and there would be fees for the musicians, but this was the unlooked-for bonus; the attraction of the event lay in meeting colleagues and making music with them.

Ben, however, wanted to show his gratitude in some positive way and, after several festivals at Aldeburgh, suggested discharging the debt in kind. If I were to start a festival of my own, he and Peter Pears would give the first concerts, he said. And why not at Gstaad? It had beauty to celebrate and the church at Saanen to play in. What seemed to confirm propitious stars for the venture was the coincidence that Antal Dorati, who had just visited Gstaad, also remarked on its festival potential and urged my taking advantage of it. Without further ado the idea became reality, Ben and Peter contributing as they had promised the two concerts which constituted that first festival in the summer of 1956: Vivaldi's *Seasons,* in which Peter narrated Vivaldi's own descriptions of the musical goings-on, and a Schubert song cycle. The scale could hardly have been smaller, but the new little shoot had life in it, and to prove it, celebrates twenty years of unbroken flowering in 1976.

Meanwhile countless other festivals took root in different parts of the world, so that summers quickly grew as thick with commitments as winters. Among the earliest was the Edinburgh, which I first visited in its second year, in 1948, an occasion triply notable—for Gerard's birth, reunion with Bruno Walter and a superb performance of the Mozart Concertante for Violin and Viola by Isaac Stern and William Primrose. Three years after Gstaad was started I became artistic director of the Bath Festival, a position I held until 1968, and followed this with four years at Windsor; thus learning that to be in charge of a festival is as good as a holiday. Music beyond the soloist's horizon or the ordinary concert repertoire is explored, colleagues gather in an atmosphere bubbling with camaraderie and cheerful purpose, one works seventeen hours a day, trotting from practice to one's own rehearsal to someone else's to a performance to a meeting, and feels at the end of it thoroughly retuned and restored.

Bath is an ideal place for a festival. No one could see this most beautiful of English cities without wanting to show it off. In obedience to the pattern of my life, I discovered its possibilities at the instigation of another, but, again in the pattern, found my own purpose served in falling in with the proposal. The Bath Festival had flourished somewhat uncertainly in the past, needing, it seemed, an outsider to stiffen local enthusiasm and not always finding such fairy godparents. During Sir Thomas Beecham's sponsorship of it, I performed the Viotti A Minor Concerto with him—the last time I played under Sir Thomas's baton and the first time I played at Bath—but this was the extent of my involvement with the festival until in 1959 Ian Hunter, who had taken on its management, suggested I try my hand at organizing the program. His imagination and energy brought Bath back to life, and if he felt that in giving me responsibility, he was also giving me an opportunity of realizing secret ambitions, he was quite right.

Some festivals take their character from a purpose, some from the celebration of a particular composer, some from the person in charge. My years at Bath and Windsor were of this last sort. There was no single center to the program planning, no mission to lead the public up an esoteric byway, no attempt at a distinctive and therefore limiting character. The programs reflected my history, preferences and aspirations, as well as what I held to be my responsibilities to contemporary music and musicians. I put my family, my friends and my past to use.

As at Gstaad, so three years later Benjamin Britten and Peter Pears helped inaugurate my tenure at Bath, but in addition Hephzibah and Yaltah were among the performers, both then and frequently later, and among the music played was Enesco's Octuor in C Major. At later festivals, there were further family contributions from Diana, Jeremy, my brothers-in-law Louis Kentner and Joel Ryce, Fou T'Song, then married to Zamira, and from Alberto Lysy, my first pupil and a colleague close enough to be part of the family. I tried to bridge gaps of place and period, bringing, from France, Nadia Boulanger and Pierre Monteux to conduct and my friend Maurice Gendron, the cellist, to perform, often in a trio with Hephzibah and myself; from India, Ali Akbar Khan, Ravi Shankar and others; from Iran, Hossein Malek to introduce the santour to Britain; from Greece, Gina Bachauer, whose good cheerfulness always calls to my mind those Central European stoves that warm huge rooms; and from Russia, Igor Oistrakh on one occasion and, on a couple of others, Rudolf Barshai with the Moscow Chamber Orchestra. In a wealth of events too numerous to summarize, a delightful experiment in 1963 was a "musical encounter" in which Johnny Dankworth, myself and assorted musicians, jazz and classical, improvised under Raymond Leppard's direction and played William Russo's Music for Violin and Jazz Orchestra.

Ravi Shankar's appearance at the 1966 festival briefly transformed our quarters at the Landsdowne Hotel into a corner of Old Delhi, and confronted me with one of the most scarifying challenges of my life. Ravi's *quid pro quo* for coming was that I should give a joint concert with his group: first I alone, playing a Bach sonata; then the Indians; then, for the finale, West would join East in a specially chosen *raga* to suit my inexperience. To ease me into public improvisation, a day and a half were cleared of other duties and devoted to rehearsal. Into our modest sitting room early one morning crowded Ravi, his tabla player, his drone player, and the cohort of fans that follows any Indian musician. A rug was spread out, incense sticks lighted, the lotus position assumed, and we began. I took the precaution of bringing a sheet of music paper on which to sketch my part as it came into being. Some exhausting hours later, Diana joined us, laden with bowls of curried vegetables and other delicacies, which were to be eaten without benefit of cutlery where we were, on the floor. The smell of curry, added to the smell of incense, gradually submerged the hotel's basic flavors of lamb and boiled cabbage. After lunch everyone lay down for a siesta, after which rehearsal was resumed. The concert was to take place the next afternoon. In the morning we transferred our rug, our incense and our labors to a committee room at the Guildhall for some last hours of practice under the portraited gaze of the city fathers on the walls. Came the concert. When I joined Ravi and the others (with rug and incense) on the stage, a burst of merriment from the audience greeted me. No doubt I did look a trifle incongruous in a borrowed Indian shirt and barefoot, but the laughter expressed only good will. Fortunately I made no obvious wrong turnings in the piece, at the end of which the audience called for more. "You're making the greatest mistake of your life," I told them. "I managed it once. I shan't be able to manage it again." "Go on," they urged. "Risk it!" So we risked it, and once again I got through my uncharted course not too inadequately. Just such warm-hearted concerts are a festival specialty.

At festivals I tried to establish a climate favorable to new music of other kinds, most years commissioning at least one work. To offer my contemporaries a chance to be heard seemed a duty to be shouldered, but it had its selfish side in that it furthered association with composers in the creative heat of composition. Nor did we overlook the amateurs or the children. A repeated feature at Bath was a public rehearsal of the local youth orchestra, and by the time I had transferred to Windsor, the students at my own school were ready to appear on the program and do their teachers credit. In a satirical moment Diana described our junketings as the "Bathfest." If "fest" suggests an occasion more cheerful and less solemn than "festival," her wit found the right word. I look back on those busy years with pleasure and gratitude, and rejoice that Gstaad still has its yearly "fest."

Over the years we have dared ambitious deeds at Gstaad, the B Minor Mass among them, but perforce our scope is limited to undertakings which accommodate performers and audience in one small church, and the emphasis is therefore on chamber or chamber orchestral music, whether classical or contemporary. I don't regret the restrictions. They preserve the village quality. Moreover, apprenticeship at Gstaad prepared us for larger ventures at Bath and Windsor, whose resources challenged us to make the most of them. Almost always ballet figured on the program, notably at Bath in 1964 when Margot Fonteyn and Rudolf Nureyev danced to my playing of a movement from Bartók's Solo Sonata; always the theatre was represented; occasionally we presented oratorios, including at my last Windsor Festival *The Creation* by Haydn. We did not confine ourselves to performances but, at Diana's suggestion, had each year a discussion to which, as to the more conventional items on the program, I invited my friends, Pierre Bertaux, Isaiah Berlin, Nicolas Nabokov among them. Subjects which were aired in an attempt to break down the barriers between too rigid specialization included the European Community, architecture, critics, and fringe medicine, as well as more directly musical topics. And finally we ventured into opera.

To conduct an opera was one of my secret ambitions. It was duly realized when *Così Fan Tutte* was presented in the Theatre Royal at Bath in 1966, with my orchestra in the pit and the parts taken by members of the Phoenix Opera Company, consisting of gifted young singers just embarked upon their careers. The undertaking was not without its technical problems, as will be seen, and it was also on the sands of operatic endeavor that my connection with Bath came to grief. After *Così* there were two further Mozart operas, *Die Entführung aus dem Serail* in 1967 and *The Impresario* in 1968; and the last of these I had to rescue by private donation when, at the last moment, the city authorities announced they could not meet my budget. When the town council refused to underwrite a fourth opera, I felt it was my cue to go. Ten is a good round number of years to hold a tenure, however, and perhaps it is wise to give someone else a chance at the end of them. I was pleased to be succeeded by the composer Michael Tippett, a generous teacher who has taken a hand in schooling the children in his neighborhood. Since he lived locally, I hoped Bath Festival would become "his," a counterpart to Benjamin Britten's at Aldeburgh; but he stayed with it only a few years, I believe.

Bath not only made me a Freeman of the City, but saw me off in style.

I have always adored the music of the Strausses, father and sons, of Vienna. I recall a 1929 production of *Die Fledermaus* by Max Reinhardt in Berlin which left me walking on air for three days afterward. Like Kreisler's, the lilting melodies of the Strausses had ideal shapes in my mind; I knew exactly how I wanted to hear them played, with a zest that whirled people off their feet, and if from time to time actuality measured up to my conception, it was not often enough. Then, on the last evening of my last Bath festival, my orchestra gave a program of Strauss waltzes, myself playing and directing in the manner of Willy Boskovsky, or of Johann Strauss, for that matter; and the audience, dressed in costumes appropriate to the music in the candlelit Assembly Rooms, were just as

exhilarated as Strauss and I meant them to be. Since then I have presented the program at a New Year's Eve concert with the Berlin Philharmonic. No doubt I shouldn't say so, but unrepentantly I thought
them beautiful performances.

The Windsor Festival, with which Ian Hunter and I were connected from its inception in 1969 until 1972 (when I decided I had too
much to do and sadly withdrew) staged a leavetaking no less splendid.
Windsor had been a delightful festival because the local people took its
fortunes so thoroughly to heart, but one regretted absence had been the
Queen's. Her Majesty had each year put parts of Windsor Castle at
our disposal—Saint George's Hall, the magnificent Waterloo Chamber,
decorated with portraits of Wellington, Saint George's Chapel—and we
had found it very pleasant to make music in such surroundings. Unfortunately the royal family had never been able to attend, as the festival
was held in September, when they were at Balmoral, in Scotland. Not
wanting to seem ungrateful for the Queen's generosity, I proposed in
1973 that I give a farewell concert for her in the castle itself. Not only
was the suggestion accepted; but she kindly turned it on its head, making
herself the hostess, naming the day, choosing the program, and giving a
party afterward to which she invited those who most loved music and
contributed most to it, from musicians themselves to those typically
British figures in public life and the military who are born musicians,
painters and poets. It was a lovely party in a lovely place; dawn was
breaking before it ended.

So, for many reasons, my involvement with festivals has been richly
rewarding. But their most important gifts to me I have left to the last: as
I had foreseen, they gave me better acquaintance with chamber music
and advanced my education as a conductor.

In 1958, some months before my labors at Bath began, EMI
wished me to record the Brandenburg Concerti and decided to assemble
a chamber orchestra for the purpose. Their first move was to contact two
noted musicians, Robert Masters and Ronald Kinloch Anderson, and
turn the task over to them. This accomplished, we met—in the recording
studio itself, as far as I recall—for what was to be, if not quite my first
attempt at playing and directing an orchestra, at least my first prolonged
experience of such music-making. Completed over several days, the recordings were so successful that there could be thereafter no question of
our abandoning the communal work, and the Brandenburg Concerti,
newly brought to performing pitch, were included on the first Bath
program. The orchestra still exists, still with Robert Masters as concert-

master, and now performs and records under my name; but while our connection with Bath lasted, it was known as the Bath Festival Orchestra and was the essential nucleus of our planning, whether we played in church, onstage or in the pit. Moreover, the section leaders formed an excellent quartet. At a stroke both chamber orchestral and chamber music were made available to me, as well as a superb, if unlikely, school of conducting.

That David Oistrakh and I shared conducting ambitions was a further bond between us. For almost thirty years I had the pleasure of playing with him, repeatedly if not regularly; yet of all the music we made together, only one record remains, a tape of the Bach Double Concerto played at UNESCO's tenth anniversary concert in Paris in 1958. I am glad it exists, but must rely on my memory for all the other shared concerts when we did the Bach together, or extended our partnership to include Igor Oistrakh in the Triple Vivaldi, or conducted for each other, exchanging roles from one concerto to another. Once I stood in for him as soloist. In October 1971 a heart attack compelled him to cancel a program he was due to give in London, and I returned from Madrid to take his place. After a morning concert there, Diana and I flew to Heathrow and went directly to the rehearsal at the Royal Albert Hall. It was one of the rare instances since the war of two concerts in one day, but concerts in cities almost eight hundred miles apart, which circumstance lent a spice of urgency. Afterward I visited David at his hotel and found him making the most of convalescence: with tape recording and score, he was studying a work he planned to conduct.

What activity can match conducting in fulfillment? The solitary study of the score, the corporate work of rehearsal, the final abandonment to a wave of sound, answer between them all one's needs, musical, intellectual, social—even physical. It is no wonder that conductors live to a ripe old age. For a violinist, who has spent a lifetime measuring millimeters on the fingerboard, there is a particular exhilaration in being able to fling his arms about and even jump, should it seem helpful to communication (so far I have kept my feet on the ground). A further attraction is the consolation it offers him when the effort of maintaining his mechanism against advancing age becomes a chore, rewarding past service by promoting him a grade in the hierarchy of manual workers and giving him orchestras of harmony to play with.

Tragically David did not live long enough to confine himself to conducting. He had undertaken a strenuous series of performances of all

Brahms's orchestral works with the Concertgebouw Orchestra in 1974, rehearsing every morning and playing every evening, and it was just too much. At the start of his career as a conductor he had a more assured technique than I began with, and I presume that competent coaching had supplied the means to put across his ideas, while his musicianship took care of the rest. As for me, I was thrown in at the deep end, but not left to flounder there alone.

My experience, possibly unique, was to be made into a conductor by the musicians I was conducting. When I speak of the technique of violin playing, I do so with the confidence of years of brooding on the subject. In contrast, my conducting technique has not undergone meticulous analysis and even now I can't claim to have evolved a thoroughly methodical approach. However, I believe I have made progress since the days when my only contributions were a conception of the music and a willingness to take advice. The credit for my improvement belongs to my orchestra and primarily to Robert Masters.

Two of the greatest joys in my life are my orchestra and my school, both of which owe their development as much to him as to anyone. Not only is he an excellent violinist, but as man and as musician he is sensitive, discreet, reliable and of sure judgment. There is no other person with whom I have shared as many ideas on the violin, on interpretation, and on music in general, whether in preparing performances of Boyce or Bartók, Schubert or Stravinsky, or in teaching children to enjoy playing the violin. He not only put the orchestra together with Kinloch Anderson's help, but has remained its concertmaster ever since and involved his wife, Noel, in managing its schedules and expenses, tasks which she ably carries out. Thus, with musicians and management taken care of, I need concern myself only with the pleasures and problems of conducting. That EMI should find me such a friend and colleague is yet another example of the serendipity which has blessed my life: met in the way of business in a recording studio, Robert Masters has become a pillar of strength upon whom I lean unashamedly.

It required his pivotal presence to encourage my experiments in conducting. He and the musicians he mustered handled the delicate matter of my formation with the greatest tact, and I can never be sufficiently grateful to them. I may not live up to their training, but certainly I could have had no better one. Relaxed, forbearing, determined to make a success of me, they contrived to be at the same time sympathetic tutors and obedient servants, submitting themselves to the beat of an amateur who knew what he wanted to hear but had scarcely any experience in expressing his demands, doing what I asked and instructing me how to ask them. Their good will merited my candor. I would ask how they preferred to be brought in, which gesture was clearer, how I could best communicate musical intention; and would always be guided without inhibition on either side. Dreadful tales are told of the revenges taken by malevolent orchestras on despised conductors; my experience was at the opposite extreme—a kind of noble self-sacrifice on the part of a group of outstanding musicians disguising itself under the easy face of comradeship. Their being outstanding musicians was vital to the endeavor, of course, but no less vital was the comradeship. Together we have had more fun than anybody can imagine, for there is no more exuberant, more boisterous company than orchestral musicians who are fulfilled and happy. There was never any question of naked authority based on rank, never the least reliance on a professional observance of hierarchy, but a flexible relationship which admirably accommodated the conductor who was learning his job; and that, I think, one could find only with an English orchestra.

With their encouragement my task became progressively easier. We began by performing works, the Brandenburg Concerti and others, in which I conducted from the first desk, leaving the orchestra largely to its capable devices once I had indicated the tempi, phrasing, and so forth that I wanted. I leave the reader to imagine the novice's thrill on first hearing his ideas made actual by other people, even when my double role did not permit exclusive concern for shaping the performance. Freedom to concentrate on this soon came, with the symphonies of Haydn and Mozart and with Bartók's Divertimento for Strings.

The Divertimento was an ambitious choice for a near-beginner, but I knew the work well, loved it, and in the spirit of advice Enesco once gave me to aim for a distant star (thus keeping oneself on course), determined to include it in the Bath Festival program in 1961. It was well received, but it took me another fourteen years to iron out a problem in conducting it, which derived, I believed, as much from my temperament as from pragmatic conducting techniques.

My temperament lies between those of my parents, on the one hand honoring my father's prudence, on the other rejoicing in my mother's repudiation of the forethought which restricts. In dismissing my father's attempts to control the future with her derisive "P-p-p-plans!" my mother not only caricatured the mistaken assumption that repetition aids clarity, she also expressed a truth about the artistic impulse. Granted, art is the product of long labor and stern self-discipline, verities which no one respects more than she, but when the time comes to draw bow across string, there can be no stuttering search for certainty, no "check, double check" that the note is right before one plays it. The sagacity which makes sure the bridge is safe, the road clear, the other party in the transaction not intending fraud, is the fruit of Jewish experience, well tried and necessary. It expresses itself in my life in minute musical analysis, vindicating intuition and defending me against challenge, my own or others'. But the nomad balances the Talmud. To liberate myself from prudence and reach the assurance of abandonment to impulse is my delight. These two sides of my nature in turn left their mark on the Divertimento.

The work opens dramatically, even roughly, requiring an extremely vigorous rhythmic attack. To be sure that the orchestra would come in as I wanted, I would give two beats in the chosen tempo and bring them in on the third. In theory no loophole for uncertainty was left, yet too often the opening lacked conviction. Then, as late as 1975, I decided on a wave of bold assurance that I would dispense with the preparatory beats altogether and launch the orchestra into action with one tremendous downward fist. The result was little short of miraculous: never had we opened it so well. We played it two or three times after that, and each time the miracle was manifested anew amid general rejoicing; for the more decisive I am, the better my orchestra is pleased with me.

In music of value there is room for many interpretations. While not condemning other people's, I naturally prefer my own and am always armed with arguments to justify them. It is possible that the heritage of the Law and the Prophets inclines me to explain too much; which would be a pity: having suffered Mengelberg's lectures, I would regret to expend vain words which clever musicians could perfectly do without. But even if anxiety to be seen to be right is a weakness measured in terms of worldly authority, I am unrepentant about my explanations. There exist people who lay no great store on the comprehension of others, and are perhaps the stronger for their insouciance. I am not one of them. I don't want power over machines, nor orchestras who react like perfectly drilled automata, theirs not to reason why, far less agree or disagree; I want companions who will join me in putting conviction into the music. For their part, I think orchestral musicians relish being taken into a conductor's confidence—indeed I have been told so by witnesses no less competent than the Berlin Philharmonic.

My relations with the Berlin Philharmonic date from 1929. Until only a year or two ago a few members of it who had played at my Berlin debut were still playing. Immediately after the war I did what I could in providing the players with instruments and strings, so a fair measure of closeness had been established when, some years ago, they thanked me for troubling to explain myself. Neither then nor earlier did I doubt, however, that an orchestra of this caliber could carry out the most taciturn conductor's wishes, or even play superbly in the absence of any conductor. It was with the Berlin Philharmonic, the first time I conducted them, that I found myself supervising another man's interpretation. The music in question was Beethoven's Seventh Symphony, which the orchestra had just taken on tour with Herbert von Karajan, and at our first rehearsal Karajan's Beethoven began beautifully. I took my courage in my hands and halted the symphony. "You play it wonderfully," I told the orchestra. "Probably you know it better than I do. But I have thought about the music a little. I have been carrying a few ideas in my ear and would be grateful if you would help me to hear them." They could not have been more prompt to humor me or more skillful in realizing my vision.

Curiously, it is one orchestra which never has to be encouraged to play slowly. There are orchestras, and artists, who have to be restrained, lacking the patience or the inner rhythm to hold a note or a pause. Not so the Berlin Philharmonic: it approaches a note with anticipation and leaves it with regret, and as a result, often has to be pushed; but what a privilege to play a slow movement with such players! It is one of the most wonderful experiences I have known.

I don't mean to give the impression that I find satisfaction only with my own orchestra and the Berlin Philharmonic. More great orchestras than I can readily name have submitted themselves to my direction. Equally some great conductors have helped me bear the responsibility. One, a dear friend and neighbor in Gstaad as well as an admired colleague, is Efrem Kurtz, who is always prepared to lend me his own scores and parts of the Beethoven symphonies, wherein Toscanini's, Furtwängler's and other great interpreters' markings have been carefully entered. Another is Sir Adrian Boult, doyen of British conductors, whom I have known since I was a boy. Only once have I seen him lose his remarkable sang-froid. That was in the days when television cameramen wheeled their machines right under their victims' noses to secure close-ups. Having suffered this interference for a time, Sir Adrian burst out in a tall fury and refused to pursue music-making under such conditions. I perfectly sympathized with him. When I was to conduct Berlioz's *Symphonie Fantastique* in Washington, I went to him for advice. Not only did he advise me, he also gave me his own baton, specially designed with a bulbous end wreathed in rubber bands to prevent its slipping from the three fingers supposed to wield it. Sure enough, it worked admirably, enabling me to control an immense orchestra with the minimum of tension, allowing the fingers to do most of the work, in Sir Adrian's own manner. Whether I matched his British composure, his gentlemanly detachment, I cannot say, but doubt.

As my tribulations with Bartók's Divertimento demonstrated, one of the thorny problems in conducting is to start: to bring from silence into triumphant existence, with the clearest and most economical gesture, the pace, volume and texture of the opening note. Basically a technical problem, it has perhaps been aggravated in my case by a philosophical obsession with the beginnings of things. As a child I used to speculate quite anxiously about where such phenomena as towns began and ended—to my legalistic mind there had to be an answer—and the need for a new start outside routine could paralyze me. When I was perhaps six years old, a family council concluded I should have a playmate, whereupon Max Kahn, the heroic Mr. Kahn's son (whom I still see in San Francisco), was invited. The two of us stood on the sidewalk regarding each other. To this day I remember how at a loss I was. I put the problem to Max: "What do we do now? How do we begin?" Well, I trust I have improved since then, in musical as in other beginnings, but the timing of them still challenges conducting finesse.

Important in all music, timing is crucial in opera, especially in the accompanied recitatives. To time one's gesture so that it brings in the orchestral punctuation at the exact fraction of a second is very tricky, and I cannot pretend that I always succeeded at my first attempt at Bath. Even when rehearsals had smoothed the difficulties, I continued to worry, and gained only a measure of confidence as one opera succeeded another. At the time of writing, Mozart's works remain my principal operatic experience, although at Windsor there was an excursion into Purcell's idiom when *Dido and Aeneas* was presented in 1969. I would much like to try my hand at opera again, to see what extra cunning the intervening years have brought and to venture into the Italian repertoire, the full-blooded excitements of conducting which I can for the moment only imagine.

Italian opera is but one of the new worlds I hope to explore. My conducting career has been charmingly topsy-turvy, casting unmerited presents into my lap with the eccentric benevolence of a rich uncle, while leaving for the years yet to come many first experiences which any normal conductor would have put behind him in his youth. Where most aspiring conductors labor through a conservatory, work their way up humble foothills to the heights, dream of the day, thirty years hence, when the Schubert symphonies will be entrusted to their practiced hands, I, with only a few years of part-time conducting to my credit, was given the opportunity of recording these great works in the mid-1960s. Of course, I invested every skill and sensibility I possessed in the enterprise, but nonetheless it was not the reward of achievement, but a gift. My own orchestra not having the resources for the later symphonies, it was expanded, onto its nucleus being grafted the concertmasters and section leaders of half the London orchestras, all content, for a recording at any rate, to take a back desk. The result was perhaps the finest orchestra that has ever been put together. With superb musicians at my command and superb music to play, what wonder if this was among the most intoxicating experiences I have ever had.

Coming late to the conductor's podium, I enjoyed an advantage not shared by everyone in my position: from long experience of recording, I had grown an objective ear, aware of balance, rhythm and obtrusive detail to a degree not normally developed in preparing straightforward public performance. Most people have at some point suffered the shock of hearing their recorded voice, and repelled by some unsuspected idiosyncrasy of pitch, timbre or accent, have questioned the machine's impartiality or wondered if they would ever again summon the courage to speak. A musician playing back a recorded "take" is in much this position of frank astonishment and threatened disgust. "Did I really do that?" he asks himself until repetition teaches him an outsider's dispassionate judgment. Occasionally—*very* occasionally—his performance surpasses his memory of it. Once on a transatlantic liner's public address system I heard the Beethoven Concerto played as I would dearly love to have played it, only to discover that the recording was one I had made with Furtwängler in 1947.

In the normal course of events, I would wish people not to be overly aware of the impression they make on others; we are subjective beings and should put up with the limitations of our condition. Nonetheless, recording is a tool beyond price to a musician, precisely because it cracks open the comfortable cocoon of subjectivity and furnishes him with a fresh set of critical faculties. I don't want to claim too much: clearly, before sound recording was developed, the great musicians knew what they were doing; but I believe that recording has contributed to the generally higher musical standards of today and telescoped the time it takes us musicians to reach them.

I have always enjoyed recording. I love the monastic dedication which is oblivious of audience, I value the lessons taught by playback. In my early experience, recording technique fell short of total candor. With a narrower range of vibrations than can now be captured, harshness was not registered, and the sweet-sounding records of Kreisler, Heifetz and my own youth owed some of their charm to technical shortcomings. However, postwar refinements in high fidelity removed this kind camouflage with the abruptness of a cold shower, magnifying the least roughness to terrifying proportions, as in the microscope's eye a hair becomes a log and the pores of one's skin each a separate volcano. Trying as it was to attempt to communicate feeling under these clinical conditions, it was nonetheless a useful discipline, exacting perfection beyond the ambition of ordinary ears. I am glad now to have undergone it.

If my agenda allows me more time to make records than to listen to them, this should not imply that recording is allotted ample place in my life. On the contrary, it must be fitted into the free hours between tours and other engagements, and generally involves an intricate shuffling of timetables to bring orchestra, conductor, soloist (if any) and engineers together in a studio at liberty to receive us, with music in a fit state to perform. I grant that commitments such as mine don't ease the problems of schedules, but the recording industry itself in growing large has grown cumbersome. As I have recounted, a record done with Louis Persinger in 1928 was made, processed and on its way to the music stores in twenty-four hours. Nowadays even the desire to profit from some great event can't hustle out a record of it in less than a few months. Each aspect of the industry's activities proceeds at the same deliberate pace. Months of market research justify the cutting of a disk, and sudden decisions are not allowed to disrupt the stately unfolding of the long-term plan.

I may prepare a work for a particular occasion and wish to record it immediately, but only rarely can unpremeditated recording relate to performance in this way. On the other hand, recording companies are increasingly reluctant to propose any works not intended for public concert, for in these circumstances the expense of study and rehearsal will be borne by someone else. Furthermore, studio time is cut as fine as possible. Having seen musicians price themselves out of the market—American orchestras displaced by cheaper English ones until the English, raising their demands, are in turn being displaced by the orchestras of Eastern Europe—I am sympathetic to the companies' dilemma; but not altogether. I am fortunate that EMI has resisted such "practical" accountancy to the extent of encouraging me to record many works never played in public—Bartók's Viola Concerto, Berlioz's *Harold in Italy,* Boyce's six symphonies among them—so widening my experience beyond what even festivals permitted. The Boyce symphonies presented a particular challenge. They were "virgin music" in that neither my orchestra nor I had heard them before, and the scores were not edited, musical convention in William Boyce's day (1710–1779) being of more account than editorial directions. With five recording sessions to complete the six works, we had to start from scratch, as far as possible indicating bowing, fingering and phrasing beforehand, forming an idea of tempi, volume, climaxes and proportion, then testing these prescriptions in the studio itself. Such work requires a special kind of orchestra, perhaps a special flair, but the recording process helps to make it possible. After each "take" we were able to listen, judge, correct, improve and replay, and an evolution that in the normal course of performance and reaction would have taken months or years was covered in a couple of hours. To hear oneself improve with such rapidity is not often granted in this short life.

I trust it will not be too short. I have compiled a list of future recordings which, if I am spared life and limb, will keep me busy for several decades yet.

17

A Legacy

My life has been spent in creating utopia. If this has been an ambition bound to fail—for utopia can exist only outside time; the tragic and the negative are built into the world we inhabit—it has nonetheless been achieved here and there, briefly and partially. Circumstances have conspired to help me, above all in giving me music and the chance to work at it, which, despite inherent frustrations and inevitable failures, is a blessing most people cannot know. I can only speculate on what I might have become had the circumstances been different or might yet become were they to change: were I obliged to suffer torture or live without sanitation in a room shared with six other people, I imagine any number of miseries would send me into a towering rage or reduce me to passive sourness and either way deprive me of the energy to do anything whatever. Nowadays happiness can be manufactured, so to speak, for the area of the brain which registers pleasure has been located and can be triggered into reaction by electrodes. I daresay there are situations from which I would be glad to escape by the simple pressing of a lever, but in general such artificial refuge from reality is anathema to me, for whom rewards must be earned if they are to be prized. My constant effort, therefore, is to mold reality into something that justifies happiness, that doesn't leave me with a bad conscience. I can afford to be satisfied if I play well because a lifetime's work has made it possible. I need, apart from well-being, a sense of purpose. It is my good fortune that I have never lacked for either.

Between the protected, directed isolation of childhood and the innumerable activities I now pursue there might seem to be only the connection of antithesis. In fact, as I have suggested, a straight line links the one with the other. An education concentrating mainly on languages, a youth spent traveling, a conscience taught concern for the world at large, were preparations for involvement, urging interest in people and readiness to be helpful where one could. The curiosity of my life, however, is that I can pursue only what I am committed to: I can learn the Verdi *Requiem* if I am going to conduct it; I don't have time to learn it if I'm not, and the reading of scores not intended for performance is an indulgence, as reading thrillers may be for other people. But there is another side to the coin, for if I have time to spare only on the useful, all the enthusiasms I cherish—ecology, the recycling of energy, medicine, education—turn out to have a wonderfully practical application within my sphere of responsibilities. For instance, it is legitimate to be interested in medicine when one has the welfare of schoolchildren on one's conscience. Hence the desirable and the possible are more or less reconciled and I have my cake and eat it.

Of the many causes to which I am committed, four are closest to my heart. One is Amnesty International's work for prisoners of conscience. The others concern education in its widest sense.

First is the Puffin Club, of which I am president, but whose dynamo is Kaye Webb. I am very devoted to the Puffins, a hundred thousand children in Britain who draw, paint, write poetry, design machinery, collect money to buy an island off the Scottish coast where puffins may live in safety and do many other wonderful things. The second is the college at West Dean in Sussex which alone in the country offers training in conservation crafts, such as furniture and clock repair, bookbinding, tapestry and so on, in an attempt to reverse the decline of craftsmanship and preserve a nation's heritage from the past. It was started and selflessly donated to Britain by Edward James, an amateur and benefactor of the arts whom Diana worked with when she danced in a company financed by him for Balanchine. Accepting his invitation to become a trustee of West Dean, I not only supported the college's aims but saw in it scope for much I was interested in, including windmills to supply electricity at low cost and the conversion of its farm to organic methods—objectives yet to be realized. Thirdly, and most importantly, there is my own school.

Not all children have two devoted Jewish parents as I did, and a psychologist might suspect that my school is primarily an attempt to fill that sad gap. More deliberately, it expresses my sense of obligation to life and to the society I live in. It is, after my own musical experience, the nearest I have come to molding reality into utopian shapes, a healthy, happy community of the young, not an elite but an example to others. To me it is a constant and increasing satisfaction, not least because its origin lies in the difficulties of my adult pilgrimage to comprehension of the violin. Having made the pilgrimage, I wanted to guide others; having learned, I wanted to pass my findings on. So my school crowns my life and will be, I hope, a lasting legacy.

In a sense, my career as a musical mentor began during my boyhood, in the years when Hephzibah and I played together in the music room at Ville d'Avray. Even earlier I had been obliged to be articulate in formulating my ideas to my accompanists—an experience which stood me in good stead: today, in front of an orchestra, I can convey by saying or singing the sounds I want produced. But making music with Hephzibah marked the real start of my teaching history, and the marvelous aspect of this start was its growing out of our relationship and family circumstances as easily and naturally as bread rising under the influence of yeast.

Even then, I am happy to recall, I kept a balance between technique and interpretation. Interpretation was the point of these practice sessions with my sister, but I could puzzle my way toward my imaged sounds only in terms of what our four hands were doing to our two instruments. I have never put much faith in injunctions to play "more gaily" or "more sadly," descriptions of achievement, not of method, but given the gaiety or sadness of the music, there were deductions to be made about tempo, emphasis, balance. All clarification starts in the dark and these were groping beginnings. One thing hampered me: such was Hephzibah's sensitivity that she did not need many words. She was an extraordinary instrument, almost an extension of myself. It was as if we did not bring our instruments together, but both played the-piano-and-the-violin. Later experience continued to spoil me: performing with musicians whom I knew and understood—Kentner, Casals, Toscanini, and many others—speech was not required.

It wasn't until the mid-1950s that I acquired my first violinistic protégé, and then in circumstances which allowed neither of us to play our roles very academically. For one thing, Alberto Lysy was no beginner waiting to be formed, but already an accomplished young violinist; for another, I was constantly traveling, and Alberto had to dog me to Gstaad, to London, to New York, if our meetings were to have any sequence at all. Before competing musical influences were so readily available as they are today, it was not too much to use the word "paternity" in speaking of the formation of violinists: a great teacher could create a whole progeny of fiddlers in his image. Even now there are recognizable family styles, as it were—I believe one is emerging at my school. But when Alberto Lysy came to me there was, for the reasons I have mentioned, no question of his being my creation.

He was sixteen or seventeen when he came from his home in the Argentine to compete in the Brussels *concours* in 1955. Not as schooled as some of the other contestants, he secured only fifth or sixth place, but played with a communicative passion far and away beyond all the others. Whatever he touched, one felt that here was a boy to whom music meant everything. He was very poor and in fact played on a borrowed violin, and everyone was very sympathetic toward him. Back in Argentina he wrote to ask if I would teach him. Because I couldn't give him all the time he needed, I took him to the United States, where he spent time with other fine violinists, notably Galamian, and at other times met my friends, shared my musical life and even my family life. He was a good friend to Gerard and Jeremy when they were children, playing football with them and taking them out like an elder brother. I don't know that I gave Alberto a great deal, but nonetheless something happened between us. His feeling about music is very close to my own. He has never set his sights on the narrow career of a virtuoso, but has chosen to combine solo performance with chamber music and teaching, activities which he now pursues with great success while his son Tonino studies cello at my school.

By the time Alberto was part of my life, the ambition to start a school was nearing parturition, an event prompted by our settling in London in 1959. I had not wanted to embark on the adventure sooner, not knowing what I had to give, but the idea had been gestating quietly for years. Ever since November 1945, when I visited the Soviet Union's Central School of Music, shining like a lone good deed in war-drained Moscow, I had wanted to establish something similar in the West.

I have been back to the Moscow school since, most recently in 1971, and on each occasion I have found it as wholesome, as serious and as hopeful as it seemed that first time. It consists of two adjacent buildings, one where the children study music, the other where they sleep and eat. Both buildings have a battered, serviceable, workaday look about them, with a suggestion of brick showing through plaster and those rows of tall plain windows common in Baltic public architecture. Within, the institutional impression is borne out—dormitory after dormitory with some ten precisely aligned beds in each—but from the neat bed linen in one building to the total dedication to the smallest beginner in the other, the conviction of care and concern is warmly conveyed. Despite the work, the ambition that must fire each child, the zeal of the teachers and the rigor of the training, there is no feeling of undue pressure. I thought it the one corner in Russia where I could myself have found a place.

When I first went there the junior boarding music school was unique to the Soviet Union, although not unique within it. Each considerable city had its equivalent to the one I saw, but graded in such a fashion that the best students found their way to Moscow—and to the best teachers. Children were accepted from the age of five and kept there until at sixteen or so they graduated to the conservatory (which only meant their moving a block away; for twenty years they lived their lives within a radius of about three blocks). After the visit to the director's office demanded by protocol, I was taken without much further ado to hear the children play.

What I saw was the end product of the teaching in various stages of finish, but not the teaching itself. Perhaps from pride in achievement, perhaps from a certain caginess, the authorities were reluctant to let me eavesdrop on a class at work, and instead produced a range of pupils from seven years old up. I was tremendously impressed by the quality of real performance shared by all these neatly turned out, eager, healthy children. Even the youngest, playing simple exercises, had an aplomb, a feeling for shape and presentation, that suggested they were performing in Carnegie Hall. It was not difficult to deduce the solidity, the security, the attention to detail of the Russian methods. Nothing was hurried or glossed over; only mastery of stage one allowed a child to approach stage two, and if at, say, stage seven a student failed to do something perfectly which belonged to stage three, back he went to climb the ladder again. And all must climb the ladder: talent or flair or genius is not sufficient reason to miss a rung. Remarkably, Russia produces almost no child prodigies—not by default, but by deliberate strategy. I was told that students did not play complete concerti until they were sixteen, but only passages or single movements. After completion of the courses at the Central School and the conservatory, the most promising are given another four years' training, and so don't emerge into public life until they are perhaps twenty-five. To a certain extent this thoroughness is wise;

but it obliges the students to fight their way up the hierarchy all their young lives, as if they were winning promotion in the army.

The children's nonmusical education was, as far as I could gather, limited to the basic elements of basic subjects, including the essential minimal political indoctrination and a moderate allowance of sport. As in my own upbringing, there was an emphasis on languages, for it was felt that this select group would probably grow up to travel; but all else was marginal to music. If this single-mindedness was partly to be accounted for by Soviet earnestness in grooming their elite, I could not help feeling it was also due to the fact that music remains one of the chief arenas for personal advancement and emancipation in the Soviet Union. I have often wondered what proportion of a country's dreams needs to be realized to give a whole society impetus. Perhaps it could be quantified at a casino: one winner in a thousand, say, is sufficient to keep nine hundred and ninety-nine on the rack of hope. In the United States, the rewards won by effort and talent have been high enough and widely enough spread to inject a sense of possibility into the whole population. In Russia, where the avenues of individual enterprise are closed, the hopeful symbols are different—great technicians, teachers, politicians, or the most productive coal miner in the U.S.S.R. But one of the most natural ways to personal fulfillment, one which can to a certain extent be home-trained and which depends on the individual heart and will, is music. Such is the reputation of Russian musicians that I imagine every achievement fosters a thousand ambitions. The curious thing is that there is no official system for teaching children to play the violin before the age of five, yet the Moscow school accepts only those five-year-olds who can already play; and there is no dearth of aspirants.

Since my Moscow visit in 1945 the rest of the world has been catching up with Russia in the business of teaching music. In Japan, in the United States, in Eastern and Western Europe and notably in Rumania, the standard is higher than it has ever been, and here and there boarding schools specializing in music have been opened. But until lately the Soviet Union led the world, and it was only right that in planning my own venture I should look to it for a model. In the spring of 1963, only six months before my little school opened its doors in London, I sent Marcel Gazelle and Alberto Lysy to spend a couple of weeks in Moscow learning what they could. No more than I had did they succeed in sitting in on lessons, but they brought back a pretty fair impression of how the children's days were organized, a blueprint we could alter to our own requirements.

For our school was not intended to be a copy. Moscow has three hundred students, I have thirty-eight. Apart from differences of scale, however, our priorities were different. Moscow was training soloists; we wanted to train musical all-rounders, fitted to moving on into teaching, chamber groups, orchestras or solo work, for whom, even if they were never to earn a livelihood from it, music would always be a source of mental and spiritual balance and of joy. What I disagree with in the Moscow school's approach (and find odd in a country which so honors the collective) is the tremendous stress on producing individual performers; this was the end product to which the whole school was geared, and too little was done to encourage the playing of quartets or other chamber music. Consequently chamber music does not flourish in Russia and the wonderful orchestras of Moscow and Leningrad consist largely of disillusioned soloists. At one of the Bath festivals I had a striking illustration of this Russian deficiency. One evening after a concert given by that Soviet rarity the Moscow Chamber Orchestra, the section leaders and I settled down for some informal music, including Schubert's Quintet in C Major; and astonishingly these young players who were drilled beyond belief, who played with a perfection which was fantastic, proved untrained to sight-read. Today Russia boasts several outstanding string quartets.

English orchestras, in contrast, are superb sight-readers, partly because they don't have enough time to rehearse, partly because they use their adventurous intelligence; the children at my school take painlessly to the discipline, as it was always planned they should. England is a land where the team is uppermost. Hence the English excel as viola players, in quartets, in chamber music ensembles, and in the art of living together. I am glad my school is under the protection of such an attitude; had it been launched in the competitive atmosphere of either Moscow or New York, my ambitions would have been much harder to fulfill.

It was only to be expected that the first people to coalesce around my hopes should belong to the family. Even before I had children to be taught I knew I wanted Marcel Gazelle and Alberto Lysy to teach them. As it happened, Alberto's performing career was too demanding to allow it, but Marcel, our first musical director, for long years our principal piano teacher, was the school's foster father, proving himself as apt at spelling out our dreams in terms of a working timetable as once he had grasped and rendered the music that we played together. It wasn't only that he ran the school remarkably, but that, from long intimacy, we shared a vision of what we were embarking on. To my great sorrow, Marcel Gazelle died in March 1969. As a little boy of six or seven he had started smoking, and it was that which caused his untimely death. I wish he could have lived to see more of the fruits of his endeavors. Today his widow, Jacqueline, my friend from Ville d'Avray, still teaches at the school. She too, it will be recalled, was a pupil of Enesco's. It pleases me to think that double lines of descent place Enesco in indisputable grandfatherhood to at least the violinists, and in some measure all the children, in my charge.

In a more literal sense my school is the offspring of a committee. In April 1961 the Music Academy Committee, as we first called ourselves, came into existence, and I persuaded onto it those of my friends interested in musical education: Sir Robert Mayer, Ernest Read, Ruth, Lady Fermoy, who is now a member of the school board, my lawyer F. R. Furber, my accountant Arthur Hollis, who had been sorting out my taxes since 1929. For two and a half years we plotted, at first doubting our ability to go it alone and hoping to attach ourselves to some existing enterprise, then acknowledging that if the school was to succeed, it would have to be *sui generis*. I found these months of discussion much too long. I wished to declare the preparations over and the adventure begun in September 1962. Cooler heads persuaded me of the unwisdom of starting out with an uncertain roster of staff and pupils and with insecure finances. I had to wait another twelve months.

The twenty thousand pounds needed for our first year's operations was provided by four benefactors, among them Lady Cholmondeley, one of my staunchest allies, and Dr. Günter Henle of Germany, publisher of perhaps the most reliable edition of classical music in the world. Oscar van Leer, son of a Dutch industrialist and philanthropist, was then and later repeatedly a benefactor. Thus one problem was solved. Then we needed students. Some were rounded up and auditioned by Gazelle and myself, including our youngest pupil, Rosemary Furniss, aged seven, who was to set another school record in being the first pupil to complete the ten-year course (I didn't know how well she would play the violin and I didn't greatly care: I was determined to have her because she was a delightful child; happily she proved a violinist too). Other students were furnished by my friend and colleague Frederick Grinke, an excellent violin teacher who joined the staff in the early years. On opening day we mustered eleven young musicians.

The wonderful thing about our beginning was that we were not obliged to do everything at once. How much more nerve-racking it would have been if, from one day to the next, one had found oneself in sole and total control of eleven youngsters—responsible for housing and feeding them, instructing them in the three R's and other, more arcane disciplines, in charge of their health and digestions, their physical exercise and their emotions, with a little matter of intensive musical education to be somewhere fitted in! Visions of the good and beautiful have a way of smoothing out knotty detail, perhaps with excess of light; but as one approaches the goal taking shape amid clouds of glory, its size and intricacy grow uncomfortably distinct. That we were only gradually eased into the awesome fullness of our duties is something I owe to a lady of indomitable assurance and courageous achievement, Miss Grace Cone.

Gracie Cone is retired now, but in the early 1960s, when my hunt for supporters brought us together, she was in dynamic control of a school precisely such as I envisaged, but for ballet and drama. The Arts Educational Trust had a hostel and specialist training rooms in Kensington and premises for general education a little way off at Hyde Park Corner. So the children lived, learned and trained within one orbit, just as it was planned mine should. Miss Cone offered to board and lodge our students, to give them regular lessons, and to rent us premises at Kensington for the musical end of the enterprise. It solved a dozen problems; we had a womb to develop in; there was no longer any reason to hesitate. "If you're ready, I'm ready," I suggested early in September 1963. "You may begin when you like," replied the magnificent Miss Cone. "We start," I said, "on Thursday next week." On that Thursday the pioneers gathered—Gazelle, Grinke and myself, and our eleven young hopefuls, full of trust and eagerness. The school existed. The endless planning had ended. New problems, of survival and expansion, were beginning.

The first problem was to find a place of our own. However useful as a foster parent, the Arts Educational Trust could not harbor us forever. Mrs. Langton, the school's first secretary, solved the problem for us, for it was she who found the estate at Stoke d'Abernon, on the Surrey side of London: two buildings on fifteen acres of Home Counties landscape. Staff and pupils took possession in September 1964.

We were blessed in our first headmaster, a man who met the challenge so well he must covertly have longed to pioneer all his life. Antony Brackenbury was a master at Bryanston School, one of England's public schools, when he chose to give up security in favor of an adventure then barely a year old. If I had filed the entire teaching profession of the country in a computer bank, I doubt I could have found someone better fitted for the job. In all teaching there must be a fusion of authority and humility—authority as an adult providing a stable framework for the children in one's care, and humility as another human being ready to educate an equal who may turn out to be a superior. In a specialist school, there is a particular demand for humility in the nonspecialist staff. Antony Brackenbury had to share his control of the school with a musical director of equal status and to accept that his pupils were chosen for their musical, not their scholastic, excellence—that the music staff had the final say in whom he taught. Under his tutelage the children won academic honors, including university entrance, to display beside their musical achievements.

At the time of writing, his successor has lately been appointed: Peter Renshaw, a scholarly young man who has preferred to quit specialization in education theory in order to deal with live children. The way his takeover was organized exemplified for me yet again the virtues of British teamwork. For some weeks before Mr. Brackenbury left, he had Peter Renshaw stay at Stoke d'Abernon, teach classes, familiarize himself with students and fellow staff, and generally ease himself into his responsibilities.

After only one year's functioning, the trust formed to administer our finances had not funds to purchase the houses and grounds at Stoke d'Abernon. With money advanced at a privileged rate of interest by the Swiss-Israel Bank, we took a mortgage on the property and began a new round of activities to clear our debts. Much was provided by benefactors, some by charitable trusts, some by ourselves. The proceeds of one concert I gave were split between my school and the Israel Philharmonic Orchestra, and this event brought us much Jewish benevolence, the donors knowing that ours was not a sectarian venture but an international school for children of any creed or color. But indeed all sections of British society helped to stand us on our legs.

At one critical moment Lady Claire Strafford saved the day by organizing an auction of works of art, so that visual art too has played fairy godmother to my school. The forty artists represented included Cecil Beaton, Jacob Epstein, Elizabeth Frink, Oskar Kokoschka, Joan Miró and Henry Moore, as well as Indian and other artists. One early morning the Australian painter Sidney Nolan arrived unannounced at my house in Highgate with his canvas of a Central Australian landscape rolled up under his arm, and did not even wait to be thanked. I think there is no nicer present than an artist's work from his own hands. A work which I bought myself distills India for me, conveying at once the spirit of death and the beauty of decoration: it is the skeleton of a cow, still standing, with ornaments about its neck. Three lithographs were donated by Marc Chagall, whom Diana and I had visited in the South of France. While Mme Chagall and Diana stayed indoors, the painter showed me his garden. To my question whether he had ever painted it, he gave me a touching answer. "My wife came from a wealthy family in Russia," he said. "She has always had a garden, and this one doesn't mean so much to her. But my family was too poor for gardens. Now my garden is such a joy that I daren't paint it for fear it would disappear."

By 1972 the school's enrollment had increased to thirty-eight children and half a dozen resident staff, and the two buildings—the White House and the Music House—were becoming uncomfortably crowded. Grants from three trusts, the Gulbenkian, the Wolfson and the Max Rayne, financed a new building consisting of four connecting pavilions linking the original houses. As well as extra music rooms and bedrooms, this gave us space for a large music library. The same year our Surrey neighbor Sir Ronald Harris restored an old barn and transformed it into a concert hall seating three hundred people. With all this generosity to offer up thanks for, our tenth birthday in September 1973 seemed worth a celebration.

It took the form of a concert given by the school orchestra, in which Rosemary Furniss (by now seventeen and ranking as our oldest inhabitant) played the Bach Double Concerto with me. We had a royal palace, Saint James's in the heart of London, to play in, and royalty to play to. It was a splendid acknowledgment of the affection we had won in British hearts, as well as of our achievements. That same year, further demonstration of these last came with the award of an annual grant from the British Department of Education, which also gave us, along with the Royal Ballet School, a special status as a center of education for the performing arts. Here was acceptance indeed, and an end to living hand to mouth.

Already that ten-year milestone has slipped behind us. We are into our second decade now, confident of our powers, financially secure, managed with wisdom, circumspection and common sense by a board for whom I haven't adequate praise. Under the chairmanship of the Duchess of Hamilton, the board handles human situations as a great conductor handles a score; and I (for all that I am a member of it) find something of an audience's pleasure in witnessing it at work.

And have I myself done in these thirteen years what I envisaged? The answer is: not yet, not quite. I was convinced when I set the school afloat that if I taught the violin as it could be taught, everyone would play beautifully within two or three years. It is my responsibility because I know that, given the caliber of the children who come, great achievement is possible. Already I have much reason to be proud of them.

Their first public appearance was at nearby Croydon in December 1966, within the framework of a series of children's concerts. The works played were one of Handel's Concerti Grossi and the first movement of the Bach Double Concerto. The emphasis was on the orchestra—in contrast, as I have suggested, to the Moscow Central School of Music. In our efforts to produce rounded musicians, we encourage trio playing, quartet playing and all kinds of chamber music, which indeed figures on the timetable as a subject in its own right. Consequently a quartet formed by the pupils performed in 1970 at the festivals at Gstaad an' Windsor and since then groups have twice visited the United States, on one occasion overwhelming faculty and students of the Juilliard School and the Curtis Institute with their performances of Schönberg's *Verklärte Nacht*. Indeed adult musicians could not have played it better; I can say this without conceit, for the credit for their preparation is not mine, but Peter Norris's, who is in charge of chamber music.

At the Queen's request, a third American journey was planned. The children performed brilliantly at the Smithsonian on 8 July 1976, when Her Majesty entertained President Ford in Washington. One other concert will be given, which I hope will inaugurate a reciprocal scholarship, enabling young Americans to come to Surrey and my graduates to study at advanced institutions in the United States. I can think of no better way to celebrate the British-American links that survive two hundred years of separation—unless the United States were to rejoin the Commonwealth and recognize the Queen!

Founded in England, the school has a strong element of France, reflecting my own first European background. Enesco's Gallic presiding spirit apart, Marcel Gazelle was French-Belgian, Robert Masters, who succeeded him as musical director, is half French, Jacqueline Gazelle, who teaches violin, and Maurice Gendron, visiting teacher for cello, are wholly so. In addition, Marcel Ciampi used regularly to visit us and Nadia Boulanger, eighty-nine at the time of writing, still does. Ciampi has now been succeeded by Louis Kentner, while his one-time student Barbara Kerslake is resident teacher of piano. We also have Peter Norris (a Canadian) for chamber music; his wife, Margaret Norris, an invaluable support for me, for violin; and Myra Chahin for cello. All the children learn harmony and composition, solfeggio and singing, as well as their instruments in solo and ensemble playing. For two years the great harpsichordist George Malcolm, with whom I have made many records, was their choirmaster. I am sorry we have lost him, for though the children sing well, they do not sing so well as in his day.

I like to bring distinguished visitors to the school: great pedagogues such as the Andreevskys and Michael Goldstein; great performers such as Itzhak Perlman and Stephane Grappelli and Ravi Shankar; or simply great men like the economist Fritz Schumacher, author of *Small Is Beautiful*. Thus, almost weekly the children benefit from the inspiration of some art, some talent or some wisdom.

One who has come several times to Stoke d'Abernon is Helen Dowling, whose life parallels my own. Although, unlike myself, she studied in Moscow, she too was a pupil of Busch and Enesco. She was a great comfort to Enesco in his last years and now does everything in her power to promote his works and his message. Since I first met her with him in New York in the mid-thirties, I have known her to be a kindred spirit in approach to the violin, to music and to students. Her role in life is to ignite. Her Russian communicative intensity breaks down barriers of reticence to set fire to the commitment concealed within.

Thus, my school is blessed by the influence of many minds and energies. While I am happy to know it is mine, in that I have longed and worked for its existence, I am just as happy to know that it is not mine at all but self-propelled, with a buoyancy and character which don't depend upon my presence. I like to delegate and might very well miss the adventure that every day now brings were my activities narrowed to full-time teaching. As it is, teaching when I can, I find it a tremendous pleasure.

Only four instruments are taught at my school: violin, viola, violoncello and piano. This restriction is deliberate and there is no intention to lift it, for the sad truth of the matter is that the general musical climate of our day disfavors strings. We keep the pianists in a certain proportion to the string players, welcoming them as an adjunct to the strings and because the piano is a great and basic instrument which cannot be left out of the study of Western music; but God knows, without our aid and comfort there are more pianists than the earth can absorb. Our cellists we are happy about, as to both number and quality, but the beautiful, despised viola we have to encourage almost artificially. By the time our violinists are twelve or thirteen and of a size to handle the larger instrument, I persuade some of them to make the transfer; and not a few thus persuaded have proved themselves more apt for their second choice. We try, however, to accept a majority of violinists, and it is with these that I have my great and continuing opportunity to pass on what I have learned; and first and foremost from Enesco.

Enesco accorded my ten-year-old self the serious respect due to an equal, and as he treated me so he treated all human beings—I am sure life did not even have to come to him on two legs to win a courteous reception. In my turn I too respect the individual's way of doing things and would not spoil it by imposing my own. That pedagogy which insists on one conception or one technical means of expressing a conception seems to me constricting. I have my preferences, but I tolerate other visions and believe that someone who plays with conviction should be encouraged in it.

I think, however, that I have something specific to give, deriving from my own experience of the violin. Conscious understanding endures when more mysterious sorts of understanding fail. Some years ago Diana gave me a record of performances made by a number of great violinists in the early days of recording, stars of almost a century ago who were old men when the machine came to capture their evanescent sounds. The extraordinary thing was that the teacher among them, Leopold Auer, played better in old age than the virtuosi, Ysaÿe, Sarasate, Joachim, and the rest. Probably his technique was never a patch on theirs, but what he knew he *knew* and his knowledge survived their brilliance. Similarly, I trust that my knowledge will, other things being equal, keep me playing; and meanwhile that it will render service in my school.

So my teaching occurs on two levels, one specifically violinistic. Only when someone plays adequately do I feel free to speak musically, and then it is that my teaching is most like Enesco's, although it does not have his means. I don't play the piano, or compose, or have his breadth of musical knowledge, but nonetheless I can impart conceptions, and that is perhaps a faint shadow of what he did for me. I am a smaller man than Enesco, possibly more of a born teacher. I talk more than he did, wanting the student not only to do but to understand and be able to defend his position against alternatives. If this reflects a characteristic desire to be right, morally, legally and technically, I hope it may also provide violinistic and even musical security.

As may be imagined, other approaches to violin teaching interest me very keenly: whether the Russian-Jewish, which would produce virtuosi, or Suzuki's group-teaching methods, which, as he told me himself, aim to develop primarily amateurs. Both approaches share a reliance on devoted parents (indeed Suzuki teaches a parent before he takes on a child, so that a musical atmosphere may be maintained at home), but the Japanese is now superseding the Jewish: as Jews find new liberating outlets, the orchestral gaps they leave are being filled by the Japanese. For all his preference for amateurs, this is largely Suzuki's achievement.

I agree with him about many things. His beliefs that music is indeed a mother tongue to be taught from infancy, that it should in fact be part of a child's prenatal experience and thereafter a game, the violin a marvelous toy, are sufficiently justified by the numbers of accomplished violinists he has trained. But there are disadvantages in his teaching. It reaches its effective apex in the years before a child becomes analytical, at about the age of nine or ten; it is not easily transferable to the West, where few parents are at liberty to play the part Suzuki destines for them, few children not already at school or kindergarten. Some years ago the American Paul Rolland produced a book and accompanying series of films adapting Suzuki's methods to the West; anyone interested in class-teaching of the violin could have no better guide. In a specialist school such as mine, however, more specialized instruction is needed. With the help of my students, I have myself made six films, each concentrating on a different stage in violin playing; but I have never structured my teaching into a rigid method. Anything so hard and dry, so suggestive of cement setting in a mold, as "the Menuhin method" or "the Menuhin system" sends me hurrying back to the safety of particular problems and solutions. What above all I try to impart is a sense of fluency, economy and precision in motion.

A major fault in young violinists is the conviction that they and their violins must be riveted together. Their left hands, firmly grasping the instrument, cannot move to play it. Their stiff necks and rigid heads, braced arms and shoulders, are so many fences between them and freedom. I have much sympathy for them because I remember what it was like. My own mistake as a beginner was to tuck away the fourth finger of my left hand, like a guest not wanted at this particular party. To release young muscles from bondage, it is my practice whenever I go to the school to invent a thousand curious exercises. I make a child roll the neck of the violin between thumb and fingers to loosen that desperate clutch; or have him draw circles on the ceiling (not quite the ceiling, but as near as he can reach) to train his hands in effortless carriage; or send his fingers sliding up and down the fingerboard in a certain rhythm; or have him hold his bow in the middle or the wrong way around, to startle him out of conformity and into the sensation of discovery. Or if an up-bow suggests movement to the left, I instruct him to let his head fall to the left too; for the chin clamped uncompromisingly on the violin blocks it from turning freely, restricts the action of hand and wrist and brings all the work to nothing. As a foretaste of the freedom he will someday experience, I take a child's left hand and let his elbow dangle and shake, relaxed and supple.

Commonly beginners used to play their first notes in the first position, the fingers climbing the scale from the open string. Thus, tradition demanded they start in the most difficult posture of all, with the elbow bent at its widest angle, the hand as far as it could be from the body, the violin at its heaviest and the problem of control at its most crucial. I prefer children to start in the third position, their hands operating halfway up the fingerboard. With the hand comfortably close to the body and the violin lightly propped between fingers and thumb, the task of establishing a relationship with their instruments is simpler, and the chance of playing with relaxed security from the beginning incomparably greater.

Coordination of the hands is of basic importance. I invent exercises for this too. For example, to make the children comprehend in their finger bones the minute coordination of right and left hand, I give them a chromatic scale to play with one or two fingers while the right hand does staccato bowing. This is something a child accomplishes instinctively, not knowing how he does it; but I want him to sense exactly where and how the coordination happens—the right hand moving while the left hand holds a note, the left hand changing notes during the right's momentary pause. Other times we coordinate breathing and bowing. The children breathe in on an up-bow, out on a down-bow, or the other way round. The next step is more difficult: they stagger the timing, inhaling or exhaling before or after the bow changes direction. Such exercises are planned to counter bias in favor of one particular coordination, and bring to consciousness the links in the chain of movement. Suppose we needed a new breath each time we put one foot before the other, or a new breath for each bar in a score: each segment of each motion would have its isolated existence and there would be no walking and no symphonies. So we do our athletic exercises at the school, frequently rising to peaks of complexity which integrate turning the violin in one direction, sliding the fingers in another and breathing in syncopated rhythm—developing coordination in all its infinite permutations.

Intuition is born, I think, of many things happening at the same time but not quite simultaneously. Our reason is geared to taking one problem on its own, analyzing it, and reaching a conclusion about how we shall proceed. But when we are faced with ten different factors, all acting upon each other and among them creating some astronomical total of variables, reason is defeated and only intuition can cope. Thus it is in violin playing—too much going on for direction by the conscious mind. In teaching, therefore, one can go only so far: one can prepare the ground, loosen the muscles, strengthen the fingers, point out all the elements to be coordinated so that any combination of movements may be made at any time. Then the player's vision takes over, intuitively selecting from those billions of possibilities the thousands it needs.

When I was a child, the sight of another child carrying a violin case along the street stirred compassion. There he went on his way to his music lesson as though to conviction and sentence, facing the problems I faced but (I reflected) without my parents or teachers or opportunities. Probably he never had a chance to feel inspired or carried away, but, with gritted teeth, got through his obligatory three hours a day, miserably repeating pieces he was utterly sick of. Since then I have grown only the more convinced that such children deserve sympathy, and only the more outraged that an art able to measure man's deepest needs and the heights of his spirit and intellect should be reduced to drudgery for children.

I am determined this shall not happen in my school. As soon as a child can do one thing approximately well—if he can hold the violin without cramp and draw a straight bow—I try to give him a sense of the music so that he will have something to live for. Some teachers would put musical inspiration before correct playing; certainly a child must have an object in his work; but while prepared to be flexible on the subject, I still see technique and interpretation as Siamese twins growing up together.

There is no point in asking for understanding of the music if the child understands little of his instrument. That way lies not enjoyment, but confusion and hopelessness. Equally, until his acquaintance with the violin has won some intimacy, it is pointless simply to tell him he is playing out of tune. The old-fashioned method was to observe, "Your C is sharp," leaving the unfortunate infant to flatten it as best he might. But there may be half a dozen reasons why he hits the C too high, and his particular difficulty must be discovered if it is to be corrected. Is it a basic question of ear training? Or is the path between ear and finger not well-established, so that what the ear winces at the finger has not the skill to alter? Or is it that the second, third or fourth finger is not flexible enough to find the center of the note? If the hand is rigid, or has inhibitions, or is busy clutching the violin, it cannot adjust and will continue playing out of tune for all one's telling.

It is a curious feature of the human mind that that which it cannot correct, it learns to accept. The person who plays out of tune and tries in vain to improve will soon not hear the false notes but only his intention. And yet there can be no two opinions about whether a note is in tune. Therefore, one of a violinist's chief concerns is to hear himself as others hear him, unexonerated by the mental indulgence which makes us blind and deaf to our obstinate imperfections. I hope I have said enough about my approach to the violin to make it clear that for me as a teacher, flexibility has priority over impeccable intonation. We don't at the school expect beginners to have the notes at their fingers' ends, but teach them to find the center of the C by adjustment; an adjustment which soon becomes too rapid for detection and leads ultimately to automatic precision.

Flexibility is all because it leads to all. Without it, there is in handling the violin, no expressing subtlety; and strength in art can be gained only through subtlety. Diligent pummeling of the punchball may improve a prize fighter's performance, though for all I know the trade of slugging one's fellow man has its refinements of feint and cunning. But mastery of artistic expression, fluid, rapid and sensitive, demands an appreciation of minute subtleties, tiny divergences from the norm in the volume and color of sound, infinitesimal rhythmic dislocations from the martial evenness of the metronome. Such an appreciation comes only from listening to, loving and playing music with all one's heart—and with a relaxed body. I think our emphasis on these priorities has produced results.

If the conscious motives which impelled me to found a school—a sense of obligation to past, present and future, the conviction I had something to say, the search for utopia—concealed a subconscious urge, it was surely to prove that I was not a freak in playing the violin well in childhood. Preserved from any feeling of abnormality by my parents' common sense, I grew up to discover with some irritation that the charge of abnormality had constantly to be resisted. As I have suggested, "normality" is a word capable of interpretation, meaning to some people the existing state of affairs while to me it means the potential which the existing state of affairs too often deforms. All children are gifted; nearly all are denied the chance to develop their gifts. The children who come to my school are ordinary, good, musically gifted children who have been given a chance. People never cease to be amazed at them. In front of television cameras children of seven and eight speak, act and play without the least self-consciousness, and I can give a lesson as if no camera were there; children of twelve and fourteen walk onstage to perform with the poise available only to those who find the situation right and natural; as soloists, as members of a trio or quartet, and as orchestral players they combine the enjoyment of the amateur and the dedication of the professional without any overtone of self-regard or any hint of a suggestion that things might be otherwise. To witness the exuberant yet structured, prepared yet spontaneous performance of any of the children moves an audience almost to tears. This, I affirm, is no more than the result of giving children their chance. At my school we have not yet quite caught up with the degree of virtuoso proficiency produced by Russian schools, although we have some likely candidates; but I believe our more flexible approach, even allowing children to play music for which they are not altogether ready, holds greater promise. When I see them finding fulfillment as I did, mastering difficult contemporary music which I had no opportunity to tackle at their age, fifty years ago, remaining for all their achievement glad, clear-eyed, uncynical children, I think my school is a good thing to bequeath and, besides, that it vindicates my life and proves me to have been normal all along.

Epilogue

At this point the reader and I, having reviewed together the better part of the century, may well ask where we are now. What has this span of years accomplished, given its apparent high-mindedness, its efforts to overcome human frailty, to create understanding and bring peace?

Regarding the matter as dispassionately as I can, I must admit that I have accomplished very little. At the most critical moment when, a Jew, I performed in defeated Germany, I did not hasten German-Jewish reconciliation. German reparations would help set up the State of Israel and Israeli tank crews trained in Germany even as I played. In the Middle Eastern crisis of today, my best efforts in the small segment of opinion open to me have done no more than hold the line of international tolerance, if they have done so much.

This sorry balance sheet does not teach me disillusion, however, but only to lower my sights. I have learned that my childish dream of bringing peace to mankind was both too vast—for it failed to take into account that peace and happiness for everybody were not necessarily compatible; and too narrow—for in the manner of the urban Jew I restricted my ambitions to human society. Today I realize that it is to life I owe my allegiance. I am no less an idealist for being more of a realist than I once was. I still look to music to bind and heal; I still think the musician can be a trusted object offering his fellowmen solace but also a reminder of human excellence; I believe as strongly as ever that our finite world turns on finite individual efforts to embody an ideal.

Perhaps more modest stages give me some achievement to claim. Violinistically I can point to an understanding of my instrument which has grown day by day, year by year. I knew the pinnacles of mastery very early, although I could not always sustain my knowledge, nor analyze nor teach it. Today I can do these things. Musically too, the violin repertoire which in childhood I experienced directly I now experience consciously, in every part of my anatomy. Conducting has stretched mind and imagination, balancing the miniature perfection of finger joints upon fingerboard with the large communal interpretation of great scores.

Humbly and gratefully I acknowledge how privileged I am. Apart from the death of a child at birth, I have known tragedy only at second hand. All the immediate protagonists in the foregoing story still live to enrich me with their love. I have been preserved from sudden crisis, from the isolation, scorn and hatred which so many Jews have suffered, from the drabness of existence without purpose. A web of affectionate bonds links me to music lovers up and down the continents, and prepares, even in places where I have not played before, an anticipation of mutual trust. At least I can boast that I have never wanted to be unworthy of this trust, nor looked for freedom in escaping the demands made upon me. The real pleasures are indistinguishable from duties, the real freedom is responsibility, the real safeguard that daily reaching for the ideal which a musician must attempt.

A musician's history is one of special protection, from that first hazard which brings time and circumstance together, planting the seed of talent in the suitable soil. Such a happy accident was my experience. Thereafter, from earliest childhood, I was protected by the need to sublimate. Sublimation implies delay: the immediately satisfied appetite can never wear the form of art. Very few have been my opportunities to choose the immediate, very rarely has compulsion carried all before it. Yet I have spent my life in the direct enjoyment of sensual pleasure, reveling in the sound of the violin. Striving to do my best, I have found fulfillment.

As these lines are written I am nearing my sixtieth birthday, an event which is to usher in twelve months away from the concert hall, promised to Diana three years ago. Already two celebrations have encroached upon my promise—the twentieth Gstaad festival and the two hundredth commemoration of American independence. I trust no other anniversary will stake its claim.

My sixtieth birthday and my sixty-first year (sixty-second, if one counted the prenatal period!) mark a new and refreshing epoch in our lives. Three years ago I promised Diana a sabbatical year: the traveling artist committed three years ahead is, like the indentured immigrant, not his own master. This has now begun. It was ushered in by the thrilling performances, given for the benefit of the Yehudi Menuhin School, Amnesty International, and the Jerusalem Foundation, in which I played in chamber music concerts with Jeremy in New York, London, Paris, Amsterdam, Brussels, and Monte Carlo; in which Slava Rostropovitch (volunteering his services) joined in New York and London, and Ernst Wallfisch in New York. Slava's participation dates back to our unforgettable and passionate reunion in Paris in January 1974 when he came to participate in the twenty-fifth-anniversary concerts of the International Music Council, at which concerts we inaugurated MIMAF, the Musicians' International Mutual Aid Fund. (This fund has grown sizably and promises to become a very important foundation in the service of music and musicians the world over.) Rubbing his eyes in disbelief, Slava realized that he was indeed in our free world. In his exhilaration and exuberance (a permanent state of being with him), he promised me that when I turned sixty he would join me in concerts in the capitals of the world and play for any cause I wished. It is to this happy reunion that I owe the festive occasion in Carnegie Hall when, together with Jeremy, we played the Archduke Trio by Beethoven, and were joined by my old and dear colleague Ernst Wallfisch in the Fauré Piano Quartet. Finally, there was the Brahms Double Concerto in the Royal Albert Hall on May 9, 1976, which was my last official performance. Slava hoisted me bodily to the conductor's podium, ran backstage to fetch my violin, and made me play an encore alone. It was the generous gesture of a loving colleague.

Already two events have encroached upon the sabbatical: the Bicentennial celebration in Washington, D.C., when at Wolf Trap for Kay Jouett Shouse, the nation's indomitable benefactress, and together with André Kostelanetz, I ushered in July 4 at midnight. We played the Concerto in G Minor by Bruch and a work I had commissioned of Alan Hovhaness very specially for the occasion, "American Ode." After the countdown it was thrilling to join in "The Star-Spangled Banner," knowing that the whole nation was looking on and singing along. The other event was my twentieth festival in Gstaad. My school participated on both these occasions: in Washington when the Queen received the President on July 8 at the British embassy; and with orchestral, solo, and chamber music concerts in Gstaad. The town of Gstaad lived up to the occasion with that festive solemnity which is the hallmark of a serious people. We did sixteen concerts ending with Haydn's *Nelson* Mass and including two first performances of Shostakovich's last works: a most moving string quartet which one can only believe he conceived as his own requiem, and a viola and piano sonata.

I am looking forward to the remaining months of my sabbatical, which I am beginning to find ever more delightful as the schedule thins out and empty days are jealously preserved.

I am looking forward to it not because music and/or performance have lost their savor for me, but to explore the unfamiliar delights of idleness and apparent irresponsibility. What will it be like to have no schedule to obey? to find employment for unprecedentedly spacious days? to slow down to walking speed? It is a prospect rich in potential Perhaps I shall acquire a new skill. I could apprentice myself to gardening, or accept an invitation given me by Sidney Nolan to try my hand at painting in his studio. I haven't the least talent, but it would be fun to try. Perhaps, having been a traveler all these years, I may become a tourist, able, at last, to linger in Venice or among the chateaux of the Loire. A thousand suppressed impulses, neglected opportunities and too rarely visited friends await me; the problem will be what to choose. But whatever activity or inactivity lies ahead, one thing is sure. My darling Diana and I will be together, free of pressures for the first time in our life of constant obligation; immensely rewarding though that life has been and, I trust, will be again, I welcome this so different life with a glad and hopeful heart.

Index